Lonely Planet Publications
Melbourne | Oakland | London

Simon Richmond

Cape Town

The Top Five

1 Table Mountain
Ride the cableway to the summit of this splendid mountain (p71)

2 Cape Point
Hike to the tip of the peninsula through a nature reserve (p73)

3 Long Street
Shop and bar-hop on this quintessential Cape Town street (p95)

4 Robben Island
Sail to Cape Town's Alcatraz, a shrine to the Freedom struggle (p100)

5 Kirstenbosch Botanical Gardens
Bring a picnic and enjoy the Sunday afternoon concerts (p105)

Contents

Published by Lonely Planet Publications Pty Ltd
ABN 36 005 607 983

Australia Head Office, Locked Bag 1, Footscray,
Victoria 3011, ☎ 03 8379 8000, fax 03 8379 8111,
talk2us@lonelyplanet.com.au

USA 150 Linden St, Oakland, CA 94607,
☎ 510 893 8555, toll free 800 275 8555,
fax 510 893 8572, info@lonelyplanet.com

UK 72–82 Rosebery Ave, Clerkenwell, London,
EC1R 4RW, ☎ 020 7841 9000, fax 020 7841 9001,
go@lonelyplanet.co.uk

© Lonely Planet 2006
Photographs © Ariadne van Zandbergen and as
listed (p227) 2006

Printed by SNP Security Printing Pte Ltd, Singapore

The Authors

Simon Richmond

Simon first visited Cape Town in 2001 to research both Lonely Planet's *South Africa, Lesotho & Swaziland* and *Cape Town* guides. He has since returned twice more to work on new editions of each book. He's explored practically every corner of the city from Cape Point to Durbanville, and Clifton to Khayelitsha, staying in all kinds of accommodation from shack to penthouse. There are very few restaurants, cafés and bars that have escaped his attention and if there's an activity going, you can bet he's done it, from sand-boarding to paragliding off Lion's Head. His £250 excess-baggage bill at the end of this trip suggests he took the shopping research very seriously.

Simon's Top Cape Town Day

'Remind me again why I'm getting up at 5.30am to climb Lion's Head?' I ask Lucy. 'Because sunrise is when you climb the mountain, and sunset is when you hit the beach', she replies. There's little faulting this logic, especially when I know I can look forward to a delicious breakfast at Manna Epicure (p128) on Kloof St after the dawn hike. With the day just starting, I give the car a work-out on the bendy coastal roads heading over to Hout Bay, taking the long, scenic way to Kalk Bay via spectacular Chapman's Peak Dr. Trust me, there's always something interesting in Kalk Bay's many craft and antique shops, as well as more excellent food at the Olympia Café (p133) or Live Bait (p133) right beside the picturesque harbour.

I head back to the city via Constantia, picking up a bottle of Vin de Constance at Klein Constantia (p45), or maybe going for a stroll through the shady grounds of Groot Constantia (p44). Returning to the City Bowl, I've got time to take in the latest exhibition at the SA National Gallery (p98) before grabbing my beach towel and meeting up with Lucy again for that sunbathing session on Clifton No 3 (p102). The natural place for sundowners is La Med (p140), although Lucy, love her, does favour La Vie (p140). A quick shower and change and it's back into town for a fun-filled dinner at Madame Zingara (p126; what's with that drag belly dancer?), followed by nightcaps and dancing to the disco-fied *Love Boat* theme (lord help us!) at Cruz (p138).

CONTRIBUTING AUTHOR
Al Simmonds

Al Simmonds grew up in Johannesburg and lived in Cape Town before leaving South Africa in 1998 to live in London. There he worked as a travel journalist and, determined to know more about whence he had come, made sure at least one assignment a year covered South Africa.

When the pull of the freelance life became overwhelming, he left the Big Smoke to live in New York and Amsterdam, then hit Europe, the Far East (including the 1998 and 2002 World Cups) and Central America, before returning to his first love, Cape Town, where he now resides. He's been everywhere in South Africa except the northern reaches of the Northern Cape. Next time...

PHOTOGRAPHER
Ariadne van Zandbergen

Belgian-born photographer Ariadne van Zandbergen has been Johannesburg based since overlanding from Europe in 1994. She has trained her lens, often in rudimentary conditions, on remote landscapes and peoples in 25 African countries. Cape Town, with its sophisticated blend of cultures, made for a refreshingly urbane change, although encounters with cantankerous baboons, inquisitive penguins and loony motorists kept her on her toes.

Introducing Cape Town

Good-looking, fun-loving, sporty and sociable. If Cape Town was in the dating game that's how her profile would read. And – for once – it's all true. The Mother City of South Africa occupies one of the world's most stunning locations, with an iconic mountain slap-bang in her centre.

As beautiful as the surrounding beaches and vineyards can be, it's the rugged wilderness of Table Mountain, coated in a unique flora, that grabs everyone's attention.

Long before the Dutch took a fancy to the Cape Peninsula in the 17th century, the land was home to the Khoisan people who valued the spiritual power of the mountains and their life-providing water. While the European immigrants, and the slaves they brought here, have all shaped the physical environment of South Africa's third-largest city, Table Mountain – now protected within a national park (see p66) that covers some 75% of the peninsula – remains at Cape Town's heart. This ever present backdrop to the city's adventure playground, as well as a source of legend and continuing spiritual nourishment. Under the Khoisan name of Hoerikwaggo – meaning 'Mountain in the Sea' – the national park is promoting a new series of trails that will allow visitors, for the first time, to sleep on the mountain top while hiking a world-class trail from Cape Point to the City Bowl.

Complementing the mountain's natural beauty is Cape Town's eye-catching way with design and colour in everything from the brightly painted façades of the Bo-Kaap and the Victorian bathing chalets of Muizenberg, to the contemporary Afro-chic décor of the many excellent guesthouses, restaurants and bars. The city is crammed with galleries (p164) displaying amazing artworks and shops selling wonderfully inventive craftwork. It's also getting a reputation as the fashion nexus of South Africa. This creativity seems to spring naturally from the city's multiethnic population, proof of South Africa's status as the rainbow nation and a visual record of the country's tumultuous recorded history of over 350 years.

For all the city centre's visual harmony and cosmopolitan atmosphere, you don't need to be in Cape Town for long to realise that the scars of modern South Africa's violent birth and apartheid adolescence still run deep. The wealth of Camps Bay and Constantia sits side by side with the ingrained poverty of townships, such as Khayelitsha, and the deprived coloured

LOWDOWN

Population 3.1 million

Time zone GMT plus two hours

3-star room around R800

Glass of wine R10 to R15

Shared taxi ride R3

Essential accessory Craig Native T-shirt

No-no Banging your African drum on Clifton's No 2 beach

suburbs, home to the vast majority of the city's citizens. Friendly as Capetonians can be to visitors, among themselves suspicions and misinterpretations endure, and if you take one of the deservedly popular trips into the townships (p81) you'll be a step ahead of the vast majority of locals.

Seeing life in the townships may shock and upset, but you'll also discover it's not a one-note story of grim survival. There are huge differences in lifestyle and many great examples of civic pride and optimism to balance against the shocking crime and HIV/AIDS statistics. And there's *ubuntu*, true African hospitality and care for fellow human beings. Look across the city and you'll also see people of all skin colours working together to make Cape Town a better place for everyone. Discovering the Mother City's true diversity and spirit is all part of getting the most out of a visit here.

Reality check aside, Cape Town is an old pro at showing visitors a good time. There may not be game parks on Kruger's scale, but there are plenty of great wildlife-spotting opportunities, from the penguins at Boulders to the antelopes, buffaloes and black rhino at Solole Game Reserve. The restaurants and bars compare favourably with those of other cosmopolitan cities. There's a lively cultural scene, particularly when it comes to music, which pervades every corner of the city, and if outdoor activities and adrenaline buzzes are your thing, you've come to the right place. As local troubadour David Krammer's sing-along anthem for the Cricket World Cup has it, 'Welcome to Cape Town/Enjoy the party/Come in and have some fun/Cape Town's number one'.

The capital of Western Cape province and the parliamentary capital of the republic, Cape Town works in a way that so few cities on the African continent do. Historic buildings have been saved, businesses are booming, inner-city crime is coming under control and you'll seldom be stuck for a parking space. Factor back in those stunning mountains, magnificent surf beaches and outstanding vineyards and you'll soon discover – like many before you – that it's easy to lose track of time while exploring all the wonders of this unique Southern African city. Now don't you think it's time you made a date with Cape Town?

City Life

City Life

CAPE TOWN TODAY

It's a feeling that's been growing for several years, but it's now more certain than ever that Cape Town's time as the pre-eminent African city has arrived. From the reimagined, pedestrian-friendly city centre with its lovely Art Deco buildings morphing into ritzy apartments, to cutting-edge energy-efficient housing and the new R104-million shopping mall in Khayelitsha, Cape Town is on a roll, riding the crest of South Africa's steady economic growth and increasing confidence as a nation.

Yes, Capetonian life can be very lush. There are splendid beaches, the magnificence of Table Mountain National Park, the beauty of well-preserved heritage architecture, and centuries-old vineyards and their grand estates. Foreign capital continues to flock here, keeping property prices very healthy. The hippest restaurants, bars and clubs take the latest styles of New York, London and Paris and add a distinctively African twist. The local fashion, design, arts and crafts scenes are all flourishing, adding liberal dashes of colour and creativity to an already tantalisingly cosmopolitan place. You really do feel that this is the rainbow city of the rainbow nation.

For all the great aspects of Cape Town there are the pretty obvious downsides, too. 'A fool's paradise' is what the writer Rian Malan calls it; a place so seductive and attractive that it is easy to ignore the city's harder and more-violent realities. Read the shock-horror headlines of the local newspapers or, worse, make the wrong turn in one of the more-lawless suburbs of the Cape Flats, and you'll quickly discover that these realities are a lot closer to home than you might first realise while sipping cocktails at Camps Bay or shopping on the Waterfront. But then those carefree activities are just as much a part of Cape Town life as crime or AIDS. It's just one of the mildly perplexing, always fascinating contradictions of life in the Mother City.

Life may be tough for much of the city's population, but you only have to spend some time in the townships to realise that it might not be quite so uniformly awful as depicted by the broad brush strokes of the media. Huge strides have been made to get people out of the shacks of the 'informal settlements' into formal housing, with the ANC-led city council of the past few years pouring millions of rands into building programmes in the townships; the Khayelitsha Business District and the N2 Gateway project are two of the most prominent examples.

The Western Cape's current African National Congress (ANC) premier is Ebrahim Rasool, a practising Muslim whose family was moved out of District Six (see p60) when he was 10. His appointment has given a much-needed boost to the self-confidence of Cape Town's majority coloured population. He's providing a role model in a country where there is still much distrust and even hostility between blacks and coloureds, who were pitted against each other under apartheid.

Rasool also epitomises the tolerant, inclusive side of Islam that pervades Cape Town, making it a beacon of hope in a world where religious beliefs are increasingly radicalised.

TOP FIVE QUIRKY HOLIDAYS & EVENTS

- Dance in the streets with lively jazz music and many shiny satin suits at the Cape Town New Year Karnaval (opposite).
- Watch the multicoloured aerial show of the Cape Town International Kite Festival (p11), as good a reason as any to spend a breezy day down in Muizenberg.
- See the dogs come out in honour of Simon's Town's naval mascot at the Just Nuisance Great Dane Parade (p10).
- Fall in love with those cute black-and-white birds down near Simon's Town during the Penguin Festival (p11).
- Get dressed up for Mother City Queer Project (p143), the hottest dance event of the year with compulsory fancy dress.

CITY CALENDAR

Events and celebrations are a regular part of Cape Town life. For a full rundown check with **Cape Town Tourism** (www.tourismcapetown.co.za). See p148 for details of Cape Town's main film festivals and p214 for a list of public holidays. The best time to visit is from December through to the end of February, when the weather is at its best and you have the chance of joining in the city's best festivals: the Cape Town New Year Karnaval and the Mother City Queer Project.

JANUARY & FEBRUARY

CAPE TOWN NEW YEAR KARNAVAL

Cape Minstrel Carnival; ☎ 021-696 9538
If you haven't headed out of town, like most Capetonians do for the New Year holidays, go and see this colourful carnival held on the streets of the City Bowl and Bo-Kaap. See p10 for more information on the minstrel contests that run throughout January and early February.

STANDARD BANK CAPE TOWN JAZZATHON

☎ 021-683 2201; www.jazzathon.co.za
The largest free open-air jazz festival in South Africa runs for four days in early January at the Waterfront, drawing more than a million people to see top acts.

SPIER ARTS SUMMER SEASON

☎ 021-809 1177; www.spier.co.za
From January through to March the Spier wine estate near Stellenbosch runs a series of top-class concerts, operas and plays at its outdoor amphitheatre. Every other even year there is a sculpture exhibition in the surrounding grounds, too.

CAPE TO BAHIA YACHT RACE

☎ 021-421 1351; www.heinekencapetobahia.co.za
For the 12th running of this 3600km yacht race, held every even-numbered year, the destination was changed from Rio to Salvador in Brazil. It starts on the first week in January and draws contestants from around the world.

J&B MET Map pp244-5

☎ 021-700 1600; www.jbmet.co.za
South Africa's richest horse race, with a jackpot of R1.5 million, is a time for big bets and even bigger hats. Head to Kenilworth Race Course to catch the action. It's generally held on the last Saturday in January.

HOT CONVERSATION TOPICS

- Tik – many are concerned about this speed-like drug's impact on the Cape Flats.
- City-centre living – time to sell up in the suburbs and buy a penthouse in the City Bowl?
- Power cuts – another spanner in the works at the Koeberg nuclear power station?
- N2 Gateway project – decent low-cost housing or a way to screen out the informal settlements?
- Firefighting – time to better reward those who fight the annual bush fires that afflict the Cape.

OPENING OF PARLIAMENT

A grand parade with military marching bands halts the traffic down Adderley and Parliament Sts when parliament opens, usually in the first week of February. Come to see the Members of Parliament and dignitaries in their finest outfits, and to glimpse celebrities such as Nelson Mandela.

CAPE TOWN PRIDE FESTIVAL

☎ 083 274 3579; www.capetownpride.co.za
Cape Town's gay and lesbian community flies the rainbow flag with pride during this 10-day festival in February, which includes arts events, as well as the usual dance parties, and culminates in a street parade through Green Point and the Waterkant.

DESIGN INDABA

☎ 021-418 6666; www.designindaba.com
Get ahead of the Cape Town design game at this two-day creative convention, held at the end of February (usually at the Cape Town International Convention Centre), which brings together the varied worlds of fashion, architecture, visual arts, crafts and media. It's where you'll be able to spot emerging design trends and the star designers of tomorrow.

JOIN THE MERRY MINSTRELS

The Mother City's equivalent of Rio's Mardi Gras parade is the **Cape Town New Year Karnaval** (☎ 021-696 9538). It's a noisy, joyous and disorganised affair with practically every colour of satin, sequin and glitter used in the costumes of the marching troupes, which can number over 1000 members.

Although the festival dates back to the early 19th century when slaves enjoyed a day of freedom over the New Year period, the look of today's carnival was inspired by visiting American minstrels in the late 19th century, hence the face make-up, colourful costumes and ribald song-and-dance routines. The vast majority of participants come from the coloured community (although you will notice a few black and even fewer white faces among the troupe participants).

Despite the carnival being a permanent fixture on Cape Town's calendar, in December 2005 it was threatened with cancellation. The Kaapse Karnaval Association, which represents most minstrel groups who take part in the parade, wanted an increase in the R1.3-million funding provided by the provincial government. A day before the New Year's Eve parade, it was all back on again, 'for the love of the culture and people of Cape Town,' as Faggie Carelse, association chairman, said.

Although visitors may have wondered what on earth was going on, most Capetonians weren't fazed by this turn of events. The political sideshow had played out almost the same the previous year. And those with longer memories recalled how the (now politically incorrect) Coon Carnival had always been something of a demonstration of coloured people power: whites who came to watch the parade in apartheid times would risk having their faces blacked up with boot polish.

The main parades are on New Year's Eve and 2 January, kicking off from Darling St in front of Old City Hall and culminating at Green Point Stadium (Map pp252–3). However, the actual Cape Minstrel competition, when troupes are judged on variety of criteria, including costume, singing and dancing, runs throughout January and into early February each Saturday night. If you miss the main parades, there are chances to catch the minstrels in action on these nights at Green Point Stadium, Athlone Stadium (Map pp244–5) and Vygerkraal Stadium (Map pp244–5) – it makes for a really unique Capetonian experience! Note: late-night traffic in the city centre (particularly around Whale and Adderley Sts) on these nights is hectically busy, so we advise you not to drive.

MARCH & APRIL

CAPE ARGUS PICK 'N' PAY CYCLE TOUR

☎ 083 910 6551; www.cycletour.co.za
Held on a Saturday in the middle of March, this is the world's largest timed cycling event, attracting more than 30,000 contestants. The route circles Table Mountain, heading down the Atlantic Coast and along Chapman's Peak Dr. Forget driving around town on the day.

CAPE TOWN FESTIVAL

☎ 021-465 9042; www.capetownfestival.co.za
Held throughout most of March, this arts festival covers the gamut from theatre to film and visual arts, with the aim of bringing Cape Town's communities together.

CAPE TOWN INTERNATIONAL JAZZ FESTIVAL

☎ 021-465 9042; www.capetowninternational jazzfestival.com
Cape Town's biggest jazz event, attracting all the big names from both South Africa and overseas, is usually held at the Cape Town International Convention Centre at the end of March. It includes a free concert in Greenmarket Sq.

JUST NUISANCE GREAT DANE PARADE

☎ 021-786 5798
No, this is not an April Fools' joke. Every 1 April a dog parade is held through Jubilee Sq in Simon's Town to commemorate Able Seaman Just Nuisance, the Great Dane who was a mascot of the Royal Navy during WWII.

OLD MUTUAL TWO OCEANS MARATHON

☎ 021-671 9407; www.twooceansmarathon.org.za
Held in mid-April, this 56km marathon kicks off in Newlands on Main Rd and follows a similar route to the Pick 'n' Pay Cycle Tour around Table Mountain. It generally attracts about 9000 competitors.

MAY

CAPE GOURMET FESTIVAL

☎ 021-797 4500; www.gourmetsa.com
For two weeks from early May, Cape Town goes gourmet with various food-focused events. A highlight is the Table of Unity where a table for 700 diners of varying ethnicities is set up at the top of Table Mountain.

JULY
VODACOM COMEDY FESTIVAL
☎ 021-680 3988; www.computicket.com
Catch some of South Africa's top comedians at this festival held at various venues across town for three weeks in July.

NOKIA CAPE TOWN FASHION WEEK
☎ 021-422 0390; www.capetownfashionweek.co.za
Fashion in Cape Town is sizzling, and this event held in July is the place to catch the hottest designers' work.

AUGUST
CAPE WOW (WOMEN OF THE WORLD) FESTIVAL
☎ 021-448 7984; www.capewow.co.za
South African women get their own day of celebration on 9 August and around this time the Cape WOW arts and culture festival is held. There are lots of free events and the aim is to empower women of all ages.

SEPTEMBER & OCTOBER
FLOWER SHOWS
www.tourismcapetown.co.za
Spring comes to the Cape in September. The wild flowers bloom, and festivals are held in their honour up and down the province; see Cape Town Tourism's website for full details.

CAPE TOWN INTERNATIONAL KITE FESTIVAL
☎ 021-447 9040; www.kitefest.co.za
Held in mid-September, in support of the Cape Mental Health Society, this colourful gathering of kite enthusiasts at Zandvlei, near Muizenberg, is big, entertaining and for a good cause.

PENGUIN FESTIVAL
☎ 021-786 1758
Come celebrate those cute black-and-white birds down at Boulders, near Simon's Town, over a mid-September weekend.

CAPE ARGUS/WOOLWORTHS GUN RUN
☎ 021-511 7130
Starting from Beach Rd in Mouile Point, this popular half-marathon is the only occasion for which the Noon Gun on Signal Hill gets fired on a Sunday – competitors try to finish the race before the gun goes off. It's generally held at the end of September.

STELLENBOSCH FESTIVAL
☎ 021-883 3891; www.stellenboschfestival.co.za
From the end of September to early October, Stellenbosch whoops it up at this celebration of music, art, food, wine, culture and local history.

HERMANUS WHALE FESTIVAL
☎ 028-313 0928; www.whalefestival.co.za
Hermanus gets into its stride as the Cape's premier whale-watching location at the end of September with this family-focused arts festival, which incorporates a range of events around town.

NOVEMBER & DECEMBER
MOTHER CITY QUEER PROJECT
☎ 082 885 0018; www.mcqp.co.za
Massive, must-attend gay dance party held in early December. Run yourself up a fabulous costume – you won't be let in unless you're dressed according to the theme. See p143 for details.

KIRSTENBOSCH SUMMER SUNSET CONCERTS
Map pp244-5
☎ 021-799 8783, Sat & Sun 021-761 4916; www.nbi.ac.za; Kirstenbosch Botanical Gardens, Rhodes Dr, Newlands; adult/child incl entry to gardens R35/10; ☺ from 5.30pm end Nov-Apr
The Sunday-afternoon concerts are a Cape Town institution. Bring a blanket, a bottle of wine and a picnic and join the crowds enjoying anything from arias performed by local divas to a funky jazz combo. There's always a special concert for New Year's Eve, too.

Drummers, Drum Cafe (p145)

CULTURE

One of Cape Town's most attractive features is its multiethnic character. The city's racial mix is different from the rest of the country. Of its population of 3.1 million, more than half are coloured; blacks account for about a third of the total, and whites and others comprise the balance. From its inception, South Africa's Mother City was a melting pot of cultures. The Dutch imported slaves from around Africa and Asia to assist them in building up the colony. Those slaves' descendants, plus what's left of the area's original inhabitants, the San and Khoikhoi (Khoekhoen), make up the city's majority coloured population today.

Cape Town's black population brings its culture to the table, too, with *sangomas* (traditional African healers) and initiation ceremonies, which are a common part of township life (see p16). There's a very prominent Muslim community (see p58) and a small but influential Jewish community (p14). Even within the white community there are distinct differences between those of British and Afrikaans heritage. Add in the gay community – which, with impeccable taste, has adopted Cape Town as its very own Mother City – and you'll begin to realise what a challenge making sense of all this can be.

IDENTITY

In this book we make use of the old apartheid terms: white, black, coloured and Indian. Although there are many people who find these terms distasteful and want to break away from the stereotypes they imply, it's a fact that in South Africa the terms are used by all the population quite often without any rancour or ill feeling. Many South Africans proudly identify themselves with one or other of these groups – for example, you'll meet black South Africans who happily refer to themselves as black rather than South Africans or Africans (which is the ANC's preferred collective expression for all people of African, Indian and mixed-race origin).

Among the millions of human stories of Cape Town, it's only to be expected that the stereotypes often come crashing down – see below and opposite for just two examples of people who have crossed the race and cultural barriers.

Coloureds

Coloureds, sometimes known as Cape coloureds or Cape Malays, are South Africans of long standing. Although many were brought to the early Cape Colony as slaves, others were political prisoners and exiles from the Dutch East Indies. People were brought from countries as far away as India and modern Indonesia, as well as other parts of Africa, but

---

A MAN CALLED AFRICA

'I miss the sense of community,' says Africa Melane. 'It used to take me at least 10 minutes to walk the short distance from the bus stop to my old home in Gugs (Guguletu) because I stopped to say hello to everyone. People are not so friendly here in Tamboerskloof.'

Even so, Africa, a confident, street-smart 28-year-old producer and presenter with the radio station **Cape Talk** (www.567.co.za) says he feels perfectly at ease in this still overwhelmingly white suburb of the city. How does he feel about the racial descriptors of white, black and coloured, then? 'They should be used, reused and abused all the time,' he states firmly, 'until they don't matter any more.'

Because of his trendy media job, his university education and his choice of moving into a well-established rich white suburb of Cape Town, Africa could also be labelled as a 'buppie', the black equivalent of a young urban professional (yuppie). 'I suppose I fall into that category, ' he admits, 'but I hate the label because it implies that the person is superficial.' And this is certainly not something that Africa could be accused of.

While at university (where he studied accountancy) Africa taught himself about HIV and AIDS and designed workshops to train health science and medical students in how best to treat the disease in Cape Town's townships where it is rife. Although he may have left his family home, he has not left behind his Xhosa heritage. At 19 he went through the initiation rites of a young Xhosa man (see p16). He consults a *sangoma* at least once a year for both health and spiritual issues. And although he was brought up nominally as a Methodist, he believes in and pays respect to the spirits of his ancestors.

THE WHITE SANGOMA

With his bare feet, face tattoos, yellow sarong, pink string vest, beaded headbands and telephone wire belts, Chris Reid Ntombemhlophe is about as far from your average white Capetonian as you could get. In his 42 years, this son of a colonial coffee farmer in Zimbabwe has been a horse breeder, a male model and a landscape gardener. But it was when he kicked his addiction to cocaine by moving from Johannesburg (Jo'burg) to the Transkei that he found his true calling in life – as a *sangoma*, a traditional African healer.

It took Chris three and half 'difficult' years living in a village community in the Transkei to fully learn the Xhosa (isiXhosa) language and his traditional healing and divining skills, although like all *sangomas* he believes he has the calling within him. His many *inqwamba* (wrist and ankle bangles of twisted cow and goat skin) signify each of the recent sacrifices he's made during his work; the bangles stay on until they fall off, which is around a year.

Chris has practised as a *sangoma* since 1997; his clients are mostly blacks but increasingly whites and coloureds, too. 'I've even had a government minister,' says Chris who knows that many people 'must think I'm a bit off my head'. It's refreshingly honest comments like these and Chris' openness and level-headedness about what he does that convince you that it is possible for him to have a foot in both the black and white worlds of South Africa. To meet Chris you can book one of his township or botanical gardens tours through Pure Pondo Adventures (p91).

their lingua franca was Malay (at the time an important trading language), which is how they came to be called Cape Malays.

Many coloureds practise Islam, and Cape Muslim culture has survived intact over the centuries, even resisting some of the worst abuses of apartheid. The slaves who moved out with the Dutch to the hinterland, many losing their religion and cultural roots in the process, had a much worse time of it. And yet practically all the coloured population of the Western Cape and Northern Cape provinces today are bound by Afrikaans, the unique language that began to develop from the interaction between the slaves and the Dutch over three centuries ago. One of the oldest documents in Afrikaans is a Quran transcribed using Arabic script.

The most public secular expression of coloured culture today is the riotous Cape Town New Year Karnaval (p10).

Blacks

Although most blacks in Cape Town are Xhosa, hailing from Eastern Cape province, they are not the only group in the city. Cape Town's economy has attracted people from all over Southern Africa, including a fair few immigrants from the rest of the continent – a lot of the car-parking marshals and traders at the city's various craft markets are from other African countries.

Xhosa culture is diverse, with many clan systems and subgroups. Politics makes for another division, with most people supporting the ANC but a sizable minority supporting the more hardline Pan-African Congress (PAC). There are also economic divisions and subgroups based on culture, such as the Rastafarian community in the Marcus Garvey district of the township of Philipi.

Whites

The culture will differ within the white community depending on whether you are a descendant of the Boers or the British. The Boers' history of geographical isolation

THE WRITER'S PERSPECTIVE ON CAPE TOWN

Jonny Steinberg's *The Number* is a hard-hitting account of Cape Town's gangland underworld and the prison system as seen through the eyes of a former gang member. Mike Nichol's *Sea-Mountain, Fire-City* is a good read if you want to get the measure of white paranoia postapartheid and the vicissitudes of building a house on the Cape. In *The Promised Land*, British rave-generation journo Decca Aitkenhead comes to Cape Town in search of the perfect E (ecstasy tablet), but instead finds a city in the grip of vicious gang warfare.

Many travel writers have been drawn to Cape Town as a starting or finishing point on their tours of South Africa, or, as in the case of Peter Moore in *Swahili For the Broken-Hearted* and Paul Theroux in *Dark Star Safari*, an epic journey across the continent itself. The city tends to come off favourably but, along with Dervla Murphy in *South From The Limpopo* and Gavin Bell in *Somewhere Over the Rainbow*, both Theroux and Moore are keen to beat a path to Khayelitsha to observe the grim challenges of township life close-up.

and often deliberate cultural seclusion has created a unique people who are often called 'the white tribe of Africa'. The ethnic composition of Afrikaners is difficult to quantify but it has been estimated at 40% Dutch, 40% German, 7.5% French, 7.5% British and 5% other. Some historians have argued that the '5% other' figure includes a significant proportion of blacks and coloureds.

Afrikaans, the only Germanic language to have evolved outside Europe, is central to the Afrikaner identity, but it has also served to reinforce their isolation from the outside world. The Afrikaners are a religious people and the group's brand of Christian fundamentalism based on 17th-century Calvinism is still a powerful influence. Urbanised middle-class Afrikaners tend to be considerably more moderate, and the further the distance between the horrors of the apartheid era and the 'new South Africa', the more room there is for Afrikaners to be proud of their heritage. You'll find Afrikaans to be a much stronger presence in the northern suburbs of Cape Town and in the country towns of the Cape, including the Winelands around Stellenbosch, which has a prominent Afrikaans university.

Most other white Capetonians are of British extraction. Cape Town, as the seat of British power for so long, is somewhat less Afrikaner in outlook than other parts of the country. White liberal Capetonians were regarded with suspicion by more-conservative whites during the apartheid years.

LIFESTYLE

Pinning down an 'average' Capetonian lifestyle is a tricky if not impossible business. Pious Muslims in the Bo-Kaap head to the mosque for morning prayers while, in the nearby Waterkant, hedonistic partygoers are on their way home. The life of a black live-in maid (average monthly salary R800 to R1000 including board and lodging), her children looked after by her mother or grandmother in the countryside, is radically different from that of the middle-class white family she works for (average monthly salary R15,000 with both husband and wife working).

This is not to say that the 'dream' lifestyle of the Capetonian doesn't exist, only that it's a lot rarer than might be imagined. A fortunate family will live in one of the more salubrious suburbs, say Vredehoek or Newlands, in a multimillion-rand home with a pool. They'll have a holiday home elsewhere in the Western Cape, perhaps up at Paternoster or down around Hermanus. There's a car or two to get the family around, and at least one maid/nanny to take care of the more-tedious bits of housework and childcare. There are school fees to

JEWISH CAPE TOWN

South Africa's oldest Jewish community is in Cape Town. Even though the rules of the Dutch East India Company (Vereenigde Oost-Indische Compagnie; VOC) allowed only for Protestant settlers at the Cape, there are records of Jews converting to Christianity in Cape Town as early as 1669. Jewish immigration picked up speed after the British took charge, with settlers coming mainly from England and Germany. The first congregation was established in 1841 and the first synagogue (now part of the South African Jewish Museum, p98) opened in 1863.

The real boom in Jewish immigration, though, was between 1880 and 1930 when an estimated 15,000 families arrived in South Africa, mainly from Lithuania, Latvia, Poland and Belarus. During this period Jews began to make a large contribution to the city's civic and cultural life. Max Michaelis donated his art collection to the city (see p96) and Hyman Liberman became the first Jewish mayor of Cape Town in 1903, the same year the Great Synagogue was consecrated. Liberman's estate helped fund the building of the SA National Gallery. Other Jewish mayors included Louis Gradner (1933–35) and his son Walter (1965–67).

By 1969 Cape Town had a community of 25,000 Jews, second in number only to the community in Jo'burg, supporting 12 orthodox congregations and 31 Hebrew schools. The tide turned during the apartheid era, however, and today the community stands at around 16,000. Sea Point is now the main Jewish area of Cape Town, although in the past the community had a heavy presence in District Six (see p60) and neighbouring Woodstock. If you have chance, pay a visit to Beinkinstadt (p161), a wonderful emporium of Judaica, on the brink of the old District Six; inside it's as if time has stood still since Moses Beinkinstadt, the current owner's grandfather, first opened the store in 1903.

DEALING WITH RACISM

Although the apartheid regime has been dismantled, cultural apartheid still exists in South Africa. To an extent, discrimination based on wealth is replacing that based on race; most visitors will automatically gain high status. There are though still plenty of people (mainly whites) who sincerely believe that a particular skin colour means a particular mind-set. A few believe it means inferiority.

If you aren't white, many white South Africans will register this. The constant awareness of race, even if it doesn't lead to problems, is an annoying feature of travel in South Africa, whatever your skin colour. Racial discrimination is illegal, but it's unlikely that the overworked and underresourced police force will be interested in most complaints. Tourism authorities are likely to be more sensitive. If you encounter racism in any of the places mentioned in this book, please let us know.

African

If you are of African descent, you may well encounter racism from some white and coloured people. Do not assume a special bond with black South Africans either. The various indigenous peoples of South Africa form distinct and sometimes antagonistic cultural groups. Thus travellers of African descent from France or the USA will not necessarily receive a warmer welcome than anyone else.

White

If you are of European descent, it will be assumed by most white South Africans that you are essentially the same as them. This may mean you'll find yourself having to listen to some obnoxious racist remarks.

Indian

Although Indians were discriminated against by whites during apartheid, blacks saw them as collaborating with the whites. If you are of Indian descent this could mean some low-level antagonism from both blacks and whites.

Asian

East Asians were a problem for apartheid – Japanese were granted 'honorary white' status, and people from other East Asian countries were probably indistinguishable from the Japanese to insular South Africans. Grossly inaccurate stereotyping and cultural ignorance will probably be the main annoyances you will face.

consider, and the cost of keeping a dog – typically a large one – which will act as an extra security device alongside the locked gates, window bars and rapid-response alarm systems that are dotted throughout the home. The fear that someone could take all this away is naggingly constant. Still, it's a good life, with restaurant meals, nights at cinemas and theatres, and frequent visits to the beach.

What this dream family might spend on groceries every month could keep the much more numerous 'average' black families in the Cape Flats going for many months, if not a year. These families might be lucky and live in a concrete-and-brick home, but chances are that they are in a self-built shack that cost about R2700 for all the materials. The furniture is likely to be second-hand; it is highly unlikely that they have a car (if they do it is also likely to be second-hand), just as it is rare to have a fully plumbed bathroom in the house. For water and ablutions there're toilets and a standpipe shared with several other families on the block. The mother will be working in a low-paid job out of which she'll have to find a large chunk of cash for transport and smaller amounts for childcare and the kids' fees at school. A holiday is likely to be a trip once a year on a deathtrap of a bus back to the Eastern Cape to visit relatives in the countryside.

A decent education can make a world of difference to a South African person's chances of prosperity, but even more than a decade after apartheid huge differences remain between schools in the white suburbs of Cape Town and those in the townships in terms of resources, the size of classes and examination pass rates. All parents have to find money to pay part if not all of their kids' school fees, even at the state-run schools, and historical differences mean that the best schools (which are also the most expensive schools to attend) are located in the white areas of the city. Scholarships do exist (see Responsible Luxury, p175), but they obviously can't provide for everyone and many kids, of all colours, miss out.

THE RITES OF INITIATION

Male initiation ceremonies, which can take place from around age 16 to the early 20s, are a consistent part of traditional black African life (and coloured Muslim life where teenage boys are also circumcised, albeit with much less ritual). Initiations typically take place around the end of the year and in June to coincide with school and public holidays.

In the Eastern Cape, young Xhosa men would go into a remote area in the mountains to attend the Vkwaluka, the initiation school where they would be circumcised, live in tents and learn what it is to be a man in tribal society. Some still do return to the Eastern Cape for the ceremony, but others cannot afford to or choose not to do so, thus similar initiation sites are created in makeshift tents erected amid the wastelands around the townships.

Initiations used to take several months, but these days they're likely to last a month or less. Initiates shave off all their hair, shed their clothes and wear just a blanket, and daub their faces in white clay before being circumcised. They receive a stick which symbolises the traditional hunting stick, and which they use instead of their hands for shaking hands during the initiation period. Immediately after the circumcision, for about a week while the wound heals, initiates eat very little and drink nothing. No women are allowed to go near the initiation ground.

Initiations are expensive – around R6000 to R8000, mainly for the cost of the animals (typically sheep or goats) that have to be slaughtered for the various feasts that are part of the ceremony. At the end of the initiation all the items used, including the initiate's old clothes, are burned together with the hut in which he stayed, and the boy emerges as a man. You can spot recent initiates in the townships and Cape Town's city centre by the smart clothes they are wearing, often a sports jacket and a cap.

Traditional

Few blacks in Cape Town maintain a fully traditional lifestyle on a daily basis, but elements of their culture do persist, lending a distinctively African air to the townships. In Site C of Khayelitsha, for example, over half the residents are Xhosa, hailing from the Eastern Cape. They keep very strong ties with the area and its customs.

Herbal medicine shops are regularly used and *sangomas* consulted for all kinds of illnesses. Certain *sangomas* can also help people get in touch with their ancestors, who play a crucial role in the lives of many black Capetonians. Ancestors are believed to watch over their kin and act as intermediaries between this world and that of the spirits. People turn to their ancestors if they have problems or requests. An animal may be slaughtered in their honour and roasted on an open fire as it's believed the ancestors eat the smoke.

Women are far more likely than men to wear some form of traditional clothing, with different subgroups wearing different costumes, colours and arrangements of beads. At important junctions in life, such as birth, coming of age and marriage, various old rites and customs are followed, too.

Gay & Lesbian

Cape Town's credentials as an upstanding gay- and lesbian-friendly destination are not in doubt – the city proudly flies the rainbow flag particularly in the Waterkant. The **Cape Town Pride festival** (www.capetownpride.co.za), held in February, has become a fixture on the city's events calendar, as are the **Out in Africa: SA International Gay & Lesbian Film Festival** (www.oia .co.za), held in February or March, and the Mother City Queer Project dance party (see the boxed text, p143).

It wasn't always this way. In the early days of the Cape Colony, homosexual men were drowned in the harbour. See the movie *Proteus* for the true story of two gay prisoners on Robben Island in the 18th century. The fate of the colony's lesbians isn't recorded (an early example, perhaps, of the lower profile of the lesbian community).

An open gay and lesbian community was also a far-from-prominent feature of the apartheid years, although a few brave souls, such as Pieter-Dirk Uys, used their left-of-centre position to criticise the government (see p146). When political freedom for the country's black majority began to become a reality in the early 1990s, it was taken for granted that gay rights would also be protected under the new constitution. Today South Africa has the only constitution in the world that guarantees freedom of sexual choice. In 2005 the highest court in the land also decreed that same-sex marriages should be allowed; the law permitting them will come into effect in December 2007.

Elements of gay culture have long permeated Cape Town. Take 'moffie', the local derogatory term for a homosexual – it is the Afrikaans word for glove and is also the word used for the leader of a performance troupe in the Cape Town New Year Karnaval (p10). These leaders wear gloves and are often gay, hence moffie's alternative meaning. South African gays have now reclaimed moffie as a word to use among themselves, in much the same way that many gays have appropriated 'queer' in an effort to repudiate its negative connotations.

Gay Capetonians also developed a code language, called Gayle, in which women's names stand in for certain words. For example, a Cilla is a cigarette; Nadia means no; Wendy, white; Priscilla, police; Beaulah, beautiful; Hilda, ugly; and Griselda, gruesome. If you hear someone talking about Dora in a bar, you'll know they're after a drink (they could also be calling someone a drunk!). To learn more about this fascinating underground language read Ken Cage's *Gayle – The Language of Kinks and Queens*, which includes a dictionary of the most popular code words. For more information on gay and lesbian Cape Town, see p214.

FOOD & DRINK

The city's restaurants and cafés offer up a world of eating possibilities, from Turkish and Middle Eastern to Chinese, Japanese and Indian. Some of the Italian restaurants, in particular, are excellent, and there's also a mouthwatering range of delis, often with cafés attached. There are also plenty of fast-food options. Among the local chains are Steers for burgers, Spur for steaks and salad bars, and the internationally known Nandos, which purveys spicy Portuguese-style chicken.

If you're looking for something more unusual, try the home-grown traditional dishes of Cape Malay (see below) and Afrikaner cooking. There's also a strong movement towards modern South African cuisine in Cape Town, which uses local ingredients, such as seafood and some of the *fynbos* plants (the vegetation of the area around Cape Town, composed of proteas, heaths and reeds), in creative ways.

As you'd expect in a city by the water, seafood is plentiful. In many places you'll see 'line fish' advertised – this means the catch of the day. Meaty local fish such as kingklip and snoek are often served; search out the freshest specimens at the Waterfront, Kalk Bay (with its marvellous fish market) and Hout Bay.

Restaurants serving African dishes, not all of which originate in South Africa, are popular. Try a meal at the exceptional Africa Café (p126) or the lively Marco's African Place (p145), both in the City Bowl, or you could head to one of the handful of restaurants in the townships (p134). You'll find that the staple for most blacks here is rice or mealie pap (maize porridge), often served with a fatty stew. It isn't especially appetising, but it's cheap. The same

CAPE MALAY CUISINE

The unique Cape Malay dishes you'll encounter around the Cape are well worth trying. This intriguing mix of Malay and Dutch styles originated in the earliest days of European settlement and marries pungent spices with local produce. It can be stodgy and on the sweet side for some people's tastes.

The Cape Malay dish you'll come across most often is bobotie, a kind of shepherd's pie usually made with lightly curried beef or lamb mince topped with savoury egg custard, and usually served on a bed of turmeric-flavoured rice with a side dab of chutney. Some sophisticated versions of bobotie use other meats and even seafood.

There is a variety of bredies (pot stews of meat or fish, and vegetables); one unusual example is *waterblommetjie bredie*, a mutton dish with faintly peppery water hyacinth flowers and white wine. *Dhaltjies* (chilli bites) are very moreish deep-fried balls of chickpea-flour batter mixed with potato, coriander and spinach. Mild curries are popular and are often served with *rootis*, similar to Indian roti bread. Also taking a cue from Indian cooking are samosas, triangular pockets of crisp fried pastry enclosing a spicy vegetable filling. Meat lovers should try sosaties, which is a Cape Malay–style kebab.

Traditional desserts include *malva* pudding, a delicious sponge traditionally made with apricot jam and vinegar, and the very similar brandy pudding (note that true Cape Malay cuisine – which is strongly associated with the Muslim community – contains no alcohol). You might also want to try koeksisters, a syrup-dipped doughnut.

Among the places to sample this type of food are Biesmiellah (p125) and the Noon Gun Tearoom & Restaurant (p125) in Bo-Kaap, De Volkskombuis (p191) in Stellenbosch, and Topsi & Company (p194) in Franschhoek.

TOP FIVE CAPE COOKBOOKS

- Although he died in 1947, doctor, botanist and man of letters C Louis Leipoldt is still remembered for his early contribution to the understanding of Cape cuisine. The anthology *Leipoldt's Food & Wine* brings together a trio of his books: *Cape Cookery*, *Culinary Treasures* and *Three Hundred Years of Cape Wines*.
- *Cape Flavour – A Gastronomic Meander Through the Winelands*, by Myrna Robins, is a gorgeously photographed collection of the best restaurants, recipes and food sensations of the Cape Winelands, from Stellenbosch to Robertson.
- *The Africa Café Experience*, by Portia de Smidt, is a colourful and tempting book that documents the legend that is the Africa Café (p126). Recipes are gathered from all over the continent, including *ta'amiyya* bean and herb patties from Egypt and chilli chicken wings as done in Mozambique.
- Phillippa Cheifitz' *Cape Town Food* is an award-winning cookery book that focuses on dishes made with local ingredients, such as Cape Town's vast variety of seafood. Learn how to use *waterblommetjies* (indigenous water hyacinths) in a traditional slow-cooked lamb stew.
- Ambitious chefs will want to try re-create dishes from La Colombe (p132) from the recipes in *Feast*, by Franck Dangereaux, a 2004 Gourmand World Cookbook winner.

goes for the *smilies* (sheep's heads) that you'll see boiled up and served on the streets. Other dishes include samp (a mixture of maize and beans), *imifino* (mealie meal and vegetables), and *chakalaka* (a tasty fry-up of onions, tomatoes, peppers, garlic, ginger, sweet chilli sauce and curry powder).

Traditional Afrikaner cuisine shows its Voortrekker heritage in foods such as biltong (the deliciously moreish dried meat) and rusks, perfect for those long journeys into the hinterland. Boerewors (spicy sausage) is the traditional sausage, and must be 90% meat, of which 30% can be fat. Plenty of recipes make use of game; some include venison, which will be some type of buck.

It's OK to drink the tap water. Locally produced fruit juices are excellent. Note that fizzy drink are called cool drinks. Try some of the excellent Cape wines while you're in town; see the Wine chapter (p40) for recommendations.

Draught beers are served in large (500ml) or small (250ml) glasses. Usually you will be sold lager-style beer in cans or *dumpies* (small bottles) for around R8. Black Label and Castle are popular brands, but Amstel and Carlsberg are also good. Look out for Mitchell's and Birkenhead's beers, which come from a couple of small breweries. Windhoek beer, brewed in Namibia, is made with strictly natural ingredients. The alcohol content of beer is around 5%, stronger than UK or US beer. Even Castle Lite has 4% alcohol.

FASHION

Fashion in all its forms – from what you wear to how you decorate your home – is a big deal in Cape Town. The main forum is the annual Design Indaba (p9), which brings together all kinds of creative people. At the 2006 event you could have taken in exhibits by the likes of jewellery designers such as Philippa Green and Ida-Elsje (p165), **Rocketfuel furniture**

(www.rocketfuel.co.za), Elle Decoration Designer of the Year 2004/05 **Haldane Martin** (www
.haldanemartin.co.za), whose Zulu Mama range of furnishings incorporates indigenous
basket-weaving techniques, and 2005/06 Elle Decoration winner Heath Nash (p168).

Many of South Africa's top clothing designers are based in Jo'burg, but they all head
to the Mother City to show off their work in Cape Town's fashion week (p11). Labels to
watch out for include Maya Prass, known for her use of boldly feminine colours, textures
and patterns in her clothes; Amanda Laird Cherry, whose male and female designs can be
found in the Big Blue boutiques (p163); and Stoned Cherrie and Sun Goddess (p166), the
latter picking up on traditional African designs and giving them a modern twist. Craig
Native's T-shirts, printed with new South African slogans and images, have been a big hit –
find them at many of the city's boutiques.

Running for some 25 years longer than the trendy Fashion Week is Cape Town's Spring
Queen and Fashion Parade, an initiative of the Southern African Clothing and Textile Workers
Union (SACTWU). The pageant is usually held in November and features the designs of scores
of women who work in clothing, textile and leather factories across the Western Cape.

For up-and-coming designers head to fashion nexus Young Designers Emporium (p169)
or the boutiques along Long St. Greenmarket Sq is a good place to hunt around for more
African styles of clothing, such as the colourful, highly patterned 'Madiba' shirts popular-
ised by Nelson Mandela. Here you'll also find the cheeky T-shirts of Justin Nurse's Laugh
It Off, which satirise the logos and catch phrases of global brands and multinationals.

SPORT

Capetonians are just as mad about sport as other South Africans. In terms of drawing the
crowds, the biggest game is soccer, and its popularity is set to increase in the run-up to the
2010 World Cup (www.southafrica2101.org). The city's Green Point Stadium (Map pp252–3)
will be rebuilt for the contest as a multipurpose sports facility with a retractable dome to
cope with Cape Town's varied weather. South Africa is also clinging to the hope that their
national squad, known as 'Bafana Bafana' (literally 'Boys Boys', meaning the 'Boys'), can
also be rebuilt – their performance has been something of a joke in recent years, flunking
out of the Africa Cup in the first round in 2006.

Cape Town has two teams in South Africa's national **Premier Soccer League** (www.psl.co.za):
Santos, the national champions in 2001/2002, and **Ajax Cape Town** (www.ajaxct.com). If either
of these teams compete against South Africa's top soccer teams, the Kaizer Chiefs and the
Orlando Pirates, you'll have to fight for tickets. Games are played from August to May.

Rugby (union, not league) is also very popular and traditionally the Afrikaners' sport.
Cross-race support for the game has waned
somewhat in the face of efforts to introduce
greater balance in the ethnic composition
of teams, and things haven't been helped
by scandals involving allegations of racial
intolerance between team members. The
most popular games to watch are during the
Super 14 tournament, in which teams from
South Africa, Australia and New Zealand
compete from late February until the end of
May. If you're in town when one of these is
on it's worth getting a ticket. Games are held
at the Newlands Rugby Stadium (p158).
For more details, check out the website
www.sarugby.net.

Capetonians have a soft spot for cricket –
hardly surprising given the attractiveness
of Newlands Cricket Ground (p158) where
all top national and international games are
played. This is where the city hosted the 2003
Cricket World Cup. The game was the first

JACQUES KALLIS

Cape Town–born Jacques Kallis is the current star of
South African cricket. The 31-year-old batsman's start
in international cricket, though, was not auspicious:
at his test debut in December 1995 against England
he managed only one run. Two years later he made
his mark bringing the Proteas victory over Australia.

South Africa's all-time leading test run scorer,
with a score of 7337, was named International Cricket
Council (ICC) Player of the Year in 2005. He's not the
flashiest of cricketers but is considered one of the
world's best all-rounders for his solid performance
both at the crease and on the field. Celebrating his
first decade in the professional game he launched
the **Jacques Kallis Scholarship Foundation** (www
.jacqueskallis.co.za), which aims to sponsor and in-
vest in the cricketing talent of tomorrow.

of the 'whites only' sports to wholeheartedly adopt a nonracial attitude, and development programmes in the townships are now beginning to pay dividends. The sport took a knocking in South Africa though in 2000 when Hansie Cronje, the youngest captain in the nation's cricketing history and still something of a legend, admitted taking bribes to rig matches. Although many believed he was taking the rap for others, he was banned for life. He died in a plane crash in 2003.

Cape Town's second test ground opened in the township of Langa in 2000. Local cricketers to watch out for include Jacques Kallis (see p19) and Mkya Ntini. Contact **Western Province Cricket Association** (☎ 021-657 2003; www.wpca.org.za) for more information.

The first horse races in Cape Town were held at Green Point in 1795. The sport took hold from then and today Cape Town has two courses, Kenilworth (see p158), which has two tracks, and **Durbanville** (☎ 021-975 2524), northeast of the city. Kenilworth is the location of South Africa's fanciest race meeting, the J&B Met (p9).

MEDIA

Cape Town's two main daily newspapers – the morning *Cape Times* and the afternoon **Cape Argus** (www.capeargus.co.za) – are both tabloids masquerading as broadsheets and they print practically the same news. Hardly surprising since both are in the stable of one of South Africa's largest media organisations, **Independent News and Media** (www.iol.co.za). The headlines of both papers will give you a good idea of what concerns Capetonians – often some lurid tale of crime or government mismanagement or corruption.

Making no pretences at all about the kind of news it pedals is the tabloid *Daily Voice*, available in both English and Afrikaans. Dubbed the Daily Vice by one fulminating preacher, it's been a huge hit with people on the Cape Flats who would never have bought a newspaper in the past. Among its more infamous headlines have been 'Jesus Lives in My Toilet' about thousands of people converging on a tiny flat to view the apparently miraculous Easter vision of an 'angel'; and 'Moffie Hooker Shot in the Gat', referring to the case of a thieving transvestite hooker shot in the backside by a disgruntled client.

Although not nearly so bland as during apartheid when blasphemy was assiduously edited out of imported programmes, South African TV is still nothing to get excited about. The local commercial channel, e-tv, may set pulses racing with its soft-porn movies late on Saturday night, but you could still channel-surf yourself into a coma in a matter of minutes most other days – the breakfast advertorial and shopping shows are particularly awful. The national broadcaster SABC offers up three channels with precious little to choose between them other than their language content.

LANGUAGE

In the Cape Town area three of South Africa's 11 official languages (all equal under the law) are prominent: Afrikaans (spoken by many whites and coloureds), English (spoken by nearly everyone) and Xhosa (isiXhosa; spoken mainly by blacks).

As early as 1685 there were reports of a corrupted version of Dutch being spoken in the Cape in the area where Paarl is today. It was in Paarl, 200 years later, that this new language, taking bits and pieces from German, French, Portuguese, Malay and indigenous African languages, was first codified with consistent spellings and uniform grammar (see the boxed text, p197). In 1905, as the Second Language Movement got into its stride, Afrikaans was stripped of its coloured roots when Dutch words were substituted for those with an African or Asian origin. In the Cape though, where Afrikaans is the predominant language of the coloured community, a version called Cape Taal has persisted and developed along its own unique lines.

The languages of the Cape's indigenous peoples, the San and Khoikhoi, have all but disappeared, like the races that once spoke them. The rock-art gallery of the South African Museum (p99) has some fascinating exhibition materials on these languages. Meanwhile, as ever more Xhosa speakers move to Cape Town, the language is increasingly noticeable and more people (ie whites and coloureds) are learning how to get their tongues around the various clicks that are part of Xhosa pronunciation. For more information on languages, see p222.

ECONOMY & COSTS

Western Cape accounts for about 15% of the country's total GDP, and many of South Africa's petroleum, insurance and retail corporations have their base in Cape Town. Viticulture, clothing, textiles, agriculture and fishing are all important sectors of the local economy, as is tourism. The opening of the Cape Town International Convention Centre has given a significant boost to this sector of the economy, and several high-profile hotel developments are under way, including an ultraluxury hotel complex at the Waterfront by entrepreneur Sol Kerzner of Sun City fame.

Cape Town's economy has been on a roll over the last few years, and is rapidly catching up with similar cities abroad. This in turn means that the city's not quite the bargain that it used to be. There have been accusations that Capetonian businesses have been overcharging, particularly at the high end of tourism where some hotel prices have shot up in excess of international levels. In some respects, Cape Town's prices are just catching up with those of equivalent cities in the world – what still makes the city decent value is the high quality of products and services you get for your cash.

Black Economic Empowerment (BEE) has become the watchword of Cape Town's economy, with many white-owned businesses scrambling to find either black or coloured partners or investors in the wake of the enactment of the BEE Bill in January 2005. Economic charters and codes of good practice to redress the imbalances in South Africa's economy have been drawn up and all businesses now should be implementing BEE strategies. At the same time, the government is also pushing a 'buy South African' policy with the **Proudly SA campaign** (www.proudlysa.co.za) – look out for the colourful logo in the national-flag colours on local products.

Most visitors will find eating and drinking very good value in Cape Town compared to elsewhere in the world; in contrast telephone charges, particularly for mobile phones, are pricey. If you're on a backpacker budget, you'll be looking at spending a minimum of R200 a day, while four-star travellers should reckon on R1000 to R1500 per day.

HOW MUCH?

Copy of the Cape Argus R3.70

Cocktail R20-25

Beer at a backpackers R8

Movie ticket R35

1hr parking in the city centre R6

1hr at an Internet café R10

Ticket to Robben Island R150

1L of unleaded petrol R5.25

Monkeybiz doll R150-500

Entry to nightclub R50

RESPONSIBLE TOURISM

In a country so riven by economic inequality, you may want to make an effort to spend your rands where they'll help most. Here are some ideas:

- Take a township tour (p81) run by township people, not a big company.
- Stay at one of the township B&Bs (p183).
- Buy your souvenirs from the people who make them, not a dealer. For details of shops such as Monkeybiz, Streetwires and Wola Nani – all of which produce goods that help people in the townships – see p160.
- Shop for fruit at roadside stalls rather than at supermarkets.
- Contribute to or volunteer for local charities; see p22 for some suggestions.
- Pay the guys who look after cars around town; in general, they're helping to make the streets safer for everyone.
- Tip waiting and hotel staff and petrol-pump attendants – they rely on this income to supplement their low wages.

South Africa's national parks and reserves are well managed but, in general, environmental laws are weak, and some activities permitted here wouldn't be allowed in other countries. Shark-diving, sand-surfing and 'adventure' 4WD tours, for example, can have a negative effect on the environment, so try to get a feel for operators' commitment to treading lightly on the earth before you make arrangements.

CHARITY BEGINS IN CAPE TOWN

It's hard not to be shocked by the vast disparities in wealth and opportunity encountered in Cape Town. So how can you best help? A good starting point for information is the **Greater Good SA** (www.greatergood.co.za) website, which has details on many local charities and development projects. Also recommended are the website and book **How 2 Help** (www.h2h.info).

The **Tourism Community Development Trust** (www.tcdtrust.org.za) was started in 1999 by several key people in the local backpacker travel industry who wanted to help build a crèche in the Cape Flats townships. Through the hard work of board members from Ashanti Lodge, Day Trippers and Grassroute Tours, this has been achieved. The trust has since grown and become a major organisation taking on other education projects. At either the Backpack (p176) or Ashanti Lodge (p176) you can leave your old clothes so they can be sold to raise money for the trust.

There are several projects that work with Cape Town's street children. **Ons Plek** (☎ 021-465 4829; www.onsplek .org.za/17.0.html) provides a shelter for girls living on the streets, while **One Love** (☎ 021-461 6424; 85 Plein St, City Bowl) feeds homeless children between noon and 1pm Monday to Friday; you can buy food vouchers for between R20 and R100 either here or at several backpacker lodges.

Habitat for Humanity (www.habitat.org.za), which helps build homes in poor communities around the world, has several projects going in Cape Town which you can volunteer for.

The **Chris Hani Community School** (☎ 021-694 9112) in Langa accepts donations of school materials of any kind, while the **Christine Revell Children's Home** (☎ 021-697 1748; crevell@iafrica.com) in Athlone wants volunteers and donations of babies' and children's clothes and toys.

At some Cape Town hotels you'll find details of how you can contribute to the **Hotels Housing Trust** (☎ 021-659 7160; www.hotelshousingtrust.com). Donations to this body are passed on to the Homeless Peoples Federation, which helps those living in shacks with loans to build proper homes.

Also see p175 for details of the **Kay Mason Foundation** (www.kaymasonfoundation.org), which helps talented disadvantaged kids get a better education; p37 for details of the Dance For All and Jikeleza programmes, which encourage children and young adults to lead better lives through dance; and p215 for details of Nazareth House, which takes care of AIDS orphans.

GOVERNMENT & POLITICS

Cape Town is one of the three capitals of South Africa. Pretoria is the administrative capital, Bloemfontein is the judicial capital and Cape Town is the seat of the nation's parliament. There are two houses of parliament: the National Assembly with 400 members and the National Council of Provinces (NCOP) with 100 members.

The head of state is the president, currently Thabo Mbeki, leader of the ANC party. The president is elected by the National Assembly (and thus is always the leader of the majority party) rather than directly by the people. A South African president has more in common with a Westminster-style prime minister than with a US president, although as head of state they do have some executive powers denied most other prime ministers.

Cape Town is also the capital of Western Cape province, which has its own legislature and premier – currently Ebrahim Rasool of the ANC. The ANC also led the Cape Town metropolitan council until March 2006 when they narrowly lost out to the Democratic Alliance (DA). The mayor is the DA's Helen Zille.

ENVIRONMENT
CLIMATE

If you've spent time in the Mediterranean then you've experienced Cape Town's climate. The summers are generally warm and dry, while winters tend to be wet and cool, the rains brought on by fierce northwesterly gales. Neither season experiences extremes of temperature, thanks to prevailing winds.

NEW CONSTITUTION

South Africa's constitution is one of the most enlightened in the world – not surprising when you consider the people's long struggle for freedom. Apart from forbidding discrimination on practically any grounds, among other things, it guarantees freedom of speech and religion, and access to adequate housing, adequate health care and basic adult education.

Be prepared though for 'four seasons in one day'. The peninsula's shape creates micro-climates, so you can be basking in the sun on one side of the mountain and sheltering from chilly rain and winds on the other. It's no accident that Newlands is so lush in comparison to Cape Point – the former receives four times as much rain annually as the latter.

For more on climate see p213.

THE LAND

Cape Town is at the northern end of a peninsula that juts into the Atlantic Ocean on the southwest tip of Southern Africa. The peninsula has a steep, high spine of mountains, beginning at Devil's Peak in Cape Town and running all the way down to Cape Point. Table Mountain, the most prominent feature of these mountains, is more than 1000m high, starting close to sea level. The escarpment running down the Atlantic (west) coast south of Table Mountain forms a striking series of buttresses known as the Twelve Apostles (see p67).

The suburbs and towns on the Atlantic coast, and those on False Bay, west of Muizenberg, cling to a very narrow coastal strip. East of these mountains the land slopes more gently down to the Cape Flats, a sandy plain. Looking east across the Cape Flats you can see more mountain ranges rising up around Stellenbosch and, to the southeast, the Hottentots Holland area. There is no major river in the city area, although there is a system of estuarine lakes northeast of Muizenberg, near the Cape Flats.

Some 600 million years ago, all of what today is Cape Town lay beneath the sea. Volcanic activity pushed the land briefly out of the ocean, but it wasn't until roughly 400 million years later that another series of cataclysmic earth movements forced the land back up again for good. Table Mountain began to be thrown up 250 million years ago, and the plateau around Cape Town gradually eroded to leave behind Table Mountain.

For more on the geology of the Cape see p67.

GREEN CAPE TOWN

So special is the environment of the Cape Peninsula that the whole area has been awarded UN World Heritage status. Yet four centuries on from European settlement it is also an environment that has been radically and often detrimentally changed, with the indigenous flora and fauna now surviving mainly in reserves and on agriculturally unviable land.

Among the environmental challenges facing the Cape Peninsula is dealing with the pollution from a greatly increased population, as well as supplying them with power and water. Typically, Capetonians are applying their energy and creativity to the problems and coming up with solutions ranging from energy-efficient housing to recycling of waste materials into attractive decorative crafts (see p34). To learn more about some of these initiatives you could take one of the specialised tours offered by Cape Capers Tours (p82) or African Soul Tours (p91).

Pocket Nukes

As the ongoing power cuts of 2006 have painfully demonstrated to Capetonians, something needs to be done about the provision of electricity for the city. However, the solution favoured by the government – the development of the experimental Pebble Bed Modular Reactor (PBMR) at the

WHEN THE DOCTOR COMES CALLING

One of the Cape's most characteristic weather phenomena is the South-Easter, a southeasterly wind that howls across the Cape, usually between late November and the end of January, although it can go on for longer. The wind is affectionately known as the Cape doctor as it blasts away the smog of modern life and keeps the air fresh and temperatures cooler than they would be otherwise.

As it crosses False Bay the wind picks up moisture, which it drops over Table Mountain, helping keep the environment lush and green. The doctor also creates Table Mountain's famous 'tablecloth', the layer of cloud that tumbles off the north face of the mountain so spectacularly.

The doctor is not entirely benign, though. It can reach speeds of 130km/h and its persistence and strength can fan forest fires, put the cableway out of action, whip up the ocean and generally drive you mad as it rattles and swirls around the City Bowl, often for days on end.

Jan van Riebeeck's original vegetable garden, Company's Gardens (p93)

current site of the Koeberg nuclear power station – is years behind in its development, due to lack of necessary international financial support and great public antipathy.

South Africa's main energy company, Eskom, is driving the project to build these new small reactors (sometimes referred to as 'pocket nukes'), based on Germany's Thorium High-Temperature Reactor (THTR) from the 1980s. Eskom claims they are the first 'inherently safe' reactors because the fuel cells can withstand the highest foreseeable temperatures and the nuclear core is designed to shut itself down within minutes should a fault that could lead to overheating occur. However, international experts disagree, citing numerous safety concerns.

So far, over R1.5 billion has been invested in developing the technology with at least another R10 billion needed for building the demo at Koeberg and a fuel plant at Pelindaba near Pretoria. It's hoped that the high development costs will be offset by the income generated from the projected international sales of 216 reactors, at an estimated US$225 million per reactor, with a further 24 units earmarked for South Africa. And yet private investors have shunned the project and the national government has had to provide R500 million to keep it going.

Alien Vegetation & Water Shortages

The Cape's dense evergreen forests that were once home to large mammals have long since vanished. Forests of nonindigenous trees, such as oak, pine and eucalyptus, have been planted in their place. In the Cape's kind climate these aliens have thrived, but have also wreaked havoc on the environment. For example, the wind-sculpted pines that coat the lower slopes of Table Mountain are draining the Cape of its precious water supplies; the whole peninsula regularly suffers water shortages. Their presence contributes to the devastating forest fires that regularly sweep across the mountain and have threatened the Cape's unique *fynbos*.

Alien-clearance programmes have been in place since 1997 and are beginning to show very positive results (p69). Also, heavy rainfall and the success of water-conservation programmes helped alleviate the Cape's drought status in 2005 and 2006, and enabled the city authorities to revise their water-restriction policies.

> ### THE CAPE'S TOP FIVE GREEN SPACES
> - Company's Gardens (p93)
> - Kirstenbosch Botanical Gardens (p105)
> - Rondevlei Nature Reserve (p108)
> - Table Mountain National Park (p66)
> - West Coast National Park (p203)

Township Fires & Kuyasa Project

In the townships and informal settlements on the Cape Flats, developing-world economic imperatives result in poor environmental standards. The most obvious sign is the smoke that sometimes drifts around the mountain and over the city, building up into quite heavy pollution after a few windless days. Most of the smoke is from fires used for cooking and heating (people trudging back to the townships carrying loads of wood is a common sight on the roads east of the city), but some is from burning tyres; a few scraps of metal can be gleaned from a tyre and then sold.

Balanced against this is very good environmental news from the townships. In the Kuyasa area of Khayelitsha, a small energy-efficiency housing project has become the first to be registered as a Clean Development Mechanism (CDM) under the Kyoto Protocol and the very first in the world to be awarded Gold Status by meeting 20 sustainable development criteria. The pilot project involved retrofitting 10 low-income houses with solar water heating, thermal insulation and other energy-saving devices. This reduced energy consumption in each home by an average of 40% over 14 months, amounting to a significant financial saving for residents, while improving their standard of living by providing hot water and thermal heating. There are plans now to retrofit a further 2300 houses, creating employment and generating a carbon saving estimated at 137,000 tons over 21 years.

Marine Matters

Overfishing of endangered fish and seafood is a big problem in Cape Town. Illegal fishing of crayfish is particularly rife. For details on how you can assist by avoiding any overfished or illegal species when visiting Cape Town's many seafood restaurants, see p133.

Pollution is also a threat to the marine environment, as demonstrated by an oil spill in Table Bay in June 2000, the worst ever suffered along the notoriously treacherous Cape coast. Over 40% of the African penguin population on Robben and Dassen Islands was threatened, causing conservation bodies such as the **Southern African Foundation for the Conservation of Coastal Birds** (Sanccob; ☎ 021-557 6155; www.sanccob.co.za), the local authorities and even the army to mount the world's biggest rescue operation of its kind to save 21,000 oiled birds.

There is also grave concern about the planned 24-hectare expansion of Cape Town's docks onto reclaimed land. Six million cubic metres of sand will be dredged from the sea bed adjoining Robben Island to construct the extension, causing a massive impact on the marine environment and rapid coastal erosion from the Foreshore north to Melkbosstrand.

LYNEDOCH ECOVILLAGE

A small environmental revolution is in process at the Lynedoch EcoVillage (Map p46), some 15km south of Stellenbosch. It's currently a somewhat scattered collection of small holdings, large wine estates, clusters of farm worker housing and a crossroads with a petrol station, shop and post office, but the aim is to eventually create South Africa's first ecologically designed, intentionally socially mixed community.

To this end a R4-million programme was completed in June 2004, providing an ecologically designed infrastructure (water, roads, sanitation, electricity and telecommunications) for 34 housing sites in the EcoVillage's first development phase. Fifteen of these houses, ranging from semidetached to terraces, were subsidised and earmarked for farm workers, while the remaining 19 were purchased by private buyers. It's compulsory for every property owner to join the home-owners association, entitling them to have a say on all community issues as well as future planning and growth.

The village uses a range of water-saving and alternative-energy strategies. Houses will have water-saving taps and showerheads, and the waste water will be recycled organically and reused for toilet flushing and irrigation. The sanitised waste left over will be used as a high-grade fertiliser. Each house will also be thermally insulated and fitted with solar panels and solar water heaters, supplemented by electricity from the grid. This mixed system is estimated to reduce each household's electricity consumption by 60%.

What used to be a huge corrugated-iron shed built for student raves has been renovated to accommodate the Lynedoch Primary School (up to Grade 9) for 475 children from farm worker families, a large all-purpose hall, and the offices and classrooms of the **Sustainability Institute** (www.sustainabilityinstitute.net) who are guiding the EcoVillage project.

URBAN PLANNING & DEVELOPMENT

Cape Town is still shackled with the legacy of apartheid's notion of 'urban planning' – designated areas for blacks, whites and coloureds. These, of course, no longer exist, but the infrastructure – or lack of it – that goes with them cannot be changed overnight, as the millions who live in the destitute Cape Flats know only too well. A major share of the city council's resources goes into improving the lot of townships with new homes and community facilities, such as the N2 Gateway and Khayelitsha Business District projects.

The council is also aware, however, that it cannot neglect the money-generating city centre and Atlantic coast area. To this end the **Cape Town Partnership** (www.capetowncid.co.za), an initiative between business and local government, was formed in 1999. It has since had huge success in improving security and cleanliness in the City Bowl, Gardens and Green Point areas through its programme of City Improvement Districts (CIDs). The body is now focusing on the bigger picture, aiming to make the City Bowl more pedestrian-friendly, to get more people living in the city centre (hence all those loft-apartment developments in old city buildings and warehouses), and to introduce social programmes that deal with the problem of street kids and provide affordable housing for low-income groups.

Already, Church Sq has been cleared of parking spaces and reconstructed as a public space; similar proposals are being considered for the Grand Pde. There's a plan to pedestrianise all of Parliament St from the end of Roeland St down to Darling St, and traffic lanes along part of Wale St will be reduced from four to two to create Cathedral Sq in front of St George's Cathedral.

Next up will be an upgrading of the city's main railway station, which dates from the early 1960s. Every day, some 120,000 people pass through the station, which still bears the marks of the apartheid past in the separate entrances for blacks and whites and confusing layers of public-transport interconnections. The plan is to rationalise and upgrade the space and facilities including new retail units and possibly even a hotel. An improved railway station will lend impetus to the shifting of the city's business district down towards the Foreshore, where the port facilities are also being expanded.

A spur to all this development is the coming of the 2010 World Cup; soccer games will be played at a rebuilt Green Point Stadium, and the city is already working on upgrading the airport and public transport routes.

For more about modern Capetonian architecture, see p30.

Arts & Architecture ∎

Arts & Architecture

Perhaps it's the blend of cultures and alternative perspectives on life, nurtured by inspiring surroundings, that has made Cape Town such a fruitful location for art and architecture. As one of the richest places in a rich country, the funds are there to support and encourage the arts. And in the townships, an abundance of energy, inventiveness and creativity makes up for a lack of cash.

From the 17th-century Castle of Good Hope to the 21st-century towers rising on the Foreshore, Cape Town's stock of arresting architecture is one of its most attractive features. Much that might have been destroyed in other places has been preserved, and a walking tour of Cape Town's City Bowl (p114) is a great way to get a feel for the built history of the city. At the same time you'll gain an insight into the city's vibrant visual-arts scene, from kaleidoscopic and inventive crafts to arty photography and sculpture.

Music is part of the lifeblood of the Mother City, which has a particularly strong reputation for jazz. The performing-arts scene is also healthy, with comedy and small fringe productions offering up the best dividends. If none of that appeals, then there's no shortage of books by local and international writers that shed light into the dark, hidden corners of the city's soul.

ARCHITECTURE

DUTCH COLONIAL

When the Dutch colonists arrived in 1652, they brought their European ideas of architecture with them, but had to adapt to the local conditions and materials. There was plenty of stone on hand from Table Mountain to build the Castle of Good Hope (p93) between 1666 and 1679.

Although the castle is frequently cited as South Africa's oldest surviving colonial structure, Jan van Riebeeck's vegetable garden, forerunner of the Company's Gardens (p93), predates it by 14 years. And, the first incarnation of the Slave Lodge (p96), at the gardens' northern end, was built in 1660 as a single-storey building to house up to 1000 wretched souls. (It was substantially changed under later British administrations.)

To begin with, houses were utilitarian structures, such as the thatched and whitewashed **Posthuys** (Map p257; ☎ 021-788 7972; Main Rd, Muizenberg; admission by donation; ☉ 10am-2pm), dating from 1673. This simple rustic style of building is one that you'll still find today along the Western Cape coast, particularly in fishing villages such as Paternoster (p205).

Thanks to Britain's wars with France, the British turned to the Cape for wine, the Dutch colonists prospered and, during the 18th and 19th centuries, the colonists were able to build many of the impressive estates that survive today. Governor Simon van der Stel's quintessential manor house, Groot Constantia (p44), went up in 1692, establishing the prototype for other glorious estates to follow in the Winelands further inland, such as Vergelegen (p47) and Boschendal (p48).

Bordering the Company's Gardens is the lovely Tuynhuis (Map pp248–9) dating from 1700, but altered during the British administration of the 19th century. From the front gate you'll just about be able to make out the monogram of the Dutch East India Company (Vereenigde Oost-Indische Compagnie; VOC) on the building's pediment – as close as you'll get since Tuynhuis is now the official residence of South Africa's president, and off limits to tourists.

ARCHITECTURE BOOKS

- *Cape Dutch Houses & Other Old Favourites*, by Phillida Brooke Simons, contains good photographs and lively text that make this a fine review of the Cape's most elegant old homes.
- All the inventive design and vibrant colours of township architecture are displayed in the coffee-table book *Shack Chic*, photographed by Craig Fraser.

On Strand St, the fancy façade of the late-18th-century Koopmans-de Wet House (p95) is attributed to Louis Thibault, who, as the VOC's lieutenant of engineers, was responsible for the design of most of Cape Town's public buildings in this period. Thibault also had a hand in the handsome Rust en Vreugd (p98), which dates from 1777 to 1778 and is notable for its delicately carved rococo fanlight above the main door and its double balconies and portico.

Of course, not everyone lived in such a grand manner. In the city centre, the best place to get an idea of what Cape Town looked like during the 18th century to ordinary folk is to take a stroll through the Bo-Kaap (p92). You'll notice flat roofs instead of gables, and a lack of shutters on the windows. These features are the result of building regulations instituted by the VOC in the wake of fires that swept the city.

BRITISH COLONIAL

When the British took over from the Dutch in the early 19th century, they had their own ways of doing things, and this extended to the architectural look of the city. British governor Lord Charles Somerset made the biggest impact during his 1814-to-1826 tenure. It was he who ordered the restyling of Tuynhuis to bring it into line with Regency tastes for verandas and front gardens.

Built in about 1840, the two-storey brick Bertram House (p97), at the southern end of Government Ave, is an example of late-Georgian style.

As the British Empire reached its zenith in the late 19th century, Cape Town boomed and a slew of monumental buildings were erected. Walk down Adderley St and through the Company's Gardens and you'll pass the 1880 Standard Bank with its pediment, dome and soaring columns; the 1885 Houses of Parliament (p95), outside which stands a statue (1890) of Queen Victoria; and the Byzantine-influenced Old Synagogue (p98) dating from 1862. The neighbouring and neo-Egyptian-styled Great Synagogue with its twin towers is from 1905.

Long St is where you can see Victorian Cape Town at its most appealing, with the wrought-iron balconies and varying façades of shops and buildings, such as the Long St Baths (p152). In the adjacent suburbs of Tamboerskloof and Oranjezicht, many mansions of that era still survive.

Cecil John Rhodes, prime minister of the Cape Colony from 1890 to 1896, commissioned young English architect Herbert Baker (p32) to redesign his home, Groote Schuur (p104), in Rondebosch, thus kicking off the style known as Cape Dutch Revival. Another famous Baker building, also commissioned by Rhodes, is Rust-en-Vrede (p108) by the sea at Muizenberg, completed in 1902 just after the statesman died at the neighbouring cottage.

As the Victorian era came to a close, Cape Town's grandest public building, the Old Town Hall (Map pp248–9), rose on the southwest side of Grand Pde in 1905; it was from the building's balcony that Nelson Mandela made his first public address as a free man in 1990.

EARLY TWENTIETH CENTURY

Edwardian Cape Town is best represented by the Centre for the Book (Map pp248–9), which opened in 1913 as the headquarters of the now-defunct University of Good Hope. More recently it has become an annexe of the National Library of South Africa, and gained some notoriety as the venue for the inquiry into cricket match fixing in 2000.

A second building boom in the 1920s and '30s led to the construction of many fine Art Deco buildings in the city centre. Prime examples include the blocks around Greenmarket Sq and the handsome 1939 Mutual Heights (p97), the continent's first skyscraper, decorated with friezes and frescoes, all with South African themes. To get acquainted with Cape Town's Art Deco architecture, follow the walk on p114.

Meanwhile, the economic boom that provided funds for the new city-centre buildings also stoked demand for cheap coloured and black labour. These people needed somewhere to live and the solution was found out on the empty, sandy Cape Flats. Langa, meaning 'Sun', was established in 1927 and is South Africa's oldest planned township. As in many townships, the roads are wide and in excellent condition, thus allowing for quick access by the authorities should there be trouble. Although it's shacks that are most widely associated with the townships, a walk around Langa or other townships today reveals that this is far from the only architecture in these areas (see p30).

THE EVOLUTION OF TOWNSHIP ARCHITECTURE

Contrary to popular belief, the townships are not uniformly comprised of slum dwellings. Everyone from the poor to the reasonably well-off live in these suburbs, and the buildings you'll find can be broken into five main categories:

- Shacks – it's estimated that there are around one million people living in squatter camps or 'informal settlements' of self-built shacks. Cobbled together from a variety of materials, including old packing crates, and decorated with, among other things, magazine pages and old food-tin labels, the design and structure of a shack depends on the financial situation of the owner and how long they have lived there. Vicky's B&B (p184) in Khayelitsha is a good example of a long-established shack.

- Hostels – built originally for migrant labourers before WWII, these two-level brick dormitories were broken up into basic units, each accommodating 16 men, who shared one shower, one toilet and one small kitchen. Tiny bedrooms housed up to three men each. After the pass laws (which stated that those who didn't have a job outside the Homelands were not allowed to leave) were abolished, most men brought their families to live with them. Each unit became home to up to 16 families, each room sleeping up to three families. Although some families still live in such conditions, other hostels have been modernised to provide less-cramped and much more habitable apartments.

- Terrace housing – in the older townships of Langa and Guguletu you'll come across one-storey terrace housing, built between the 1920s and 1940s. Like the hostels, conditions in these 30-sq-metre 'railway carriage' houses were very basic and crowded. Since the end of apartheid these houses have been owned by the former tenants, who are now responsible for their maintenance. Residents have sometimes expanded them, when they can, into the front and back yards.

- Reconstruction and Development Programme (RDP) houses – in the last 10 years, tens of thousands of these low-cost houses have been built in the townships. Averaging around 28 sq metres in size, these 'matchbox' houses are little more than four concrete-block walls topped with a corrugated-iron roof. Even so, for many people they are a great improvement on the fire-prone shacks they lived in previously. Also see p112 for information on a group of township women who successfully designed and built their own homes.

- Township villas – there are areas of Langa and Khayelitsha that are very middle class and where you'll find spacious bungalow-style houses and villas of a high standard. The area where Minah Radebe's very convivial B&B (p184) is located in Langa is known locally as 'Beverly Hills'.

MODERN

The economic recession brought on by international sanctions meant there was little good architectural development in Cape Town during the apartheid era. Examples of rationalist architecture include the hideous Artscape arts centre (p145) and the adjoining Civic Centre (see opposite) on the Foreshore, which demonstrate the obsession with concrete that was typical of international modernism.

The best building to come out of this era is the Baxter Theatre (p146) in Rondebosch. Designed by Jack Barnett, its flat roof is famously dimpled with orange fibreglass downlights that glow fabulously at night. Also notable is the striking Taal Monument (p196) in Paarl, with a 57m concrete tower designed by Jan van Wijk.

The less said about the total lack of planning or official architectural concern for the townships the better, although it is worth mentioning the tremendous ingenuity and resilience that residents show in creating livable homes from scrap. A visit to the townships today reveals colourfully painted shacks and murals, homes and churches made from shipping crates, and more recent imaginative structures, such as the Guga S'Thebe Arts & Cultural Centre (p111) in Langa.

For the vast majority of visitors, contemporary Capetonian architecture is summed up in the redevelopment of the Victoria & Alfred Waterfront (p99). Recent architectural additions to the Waterfront include the Nelson Mandela Gateway (p100) and Clock Tower Precinct, built in 2001 as the new departure point for Robben Island, and the ritzy millionaire's playground of the **V&A Marina** (www.waterfrontmarina.co.za), with some 600 apartments and 200 boat moorings. After a slow start, foundations are now being dug for casino and luxury-hotel magnate Sol Kerzner's One and Only, a R450-million resort project next to the Marina.

The Cape Town International Convention Centre (p146), with its shiplike prow and sleek glass-and-steel hotel, is another new building drawing favourable nods and helping push the City Bowl back towards the waterfront, from which it has been cut off for decades. Next up will be the R390-million residential, commercial and retail centre Icon, Cape Town's first major black-empowerment development designed by DHK architects.

The Cape Town property boom is also creating an environment for some interesting new residential buildings and conversions of old office blocks into apartments, such as Mutual Heights (p97) and the three old buildings that are part of **Rhodes Mandela Place** (www.euro capeinvest.com/mrp/index.html). Winning prizes for its work is architectural practice **Van der Merwe Miszewski** (Map pp248–9; www.vandermerwemiszewski.com; 163 Bree St); its **Tree House** (Map p254; 30 Glen Cres, Higgovale) was voted best building in South Africa in an opinion poll organised by the South African Institute for Architects. The practice's offices are based in one of the more unusual and beautiful of the City Bowl's listed buildings.

ARCHITECTURAL HITS & MISSES

The Best

- Baxter Theatre (p146) – a rare architectural achievement of the 1970s.
- Groote Schuur (p104) – the Cape Dutch revival started here with the work of Sir Herbert Baker.
- Guga S'Thebe Arts & Cultural Centre (p111) – this colourful and creative building is a star of township architecture.
- Mutual Heights (p97) – now luxury apartments, this old insurance-company building is an Art Deco treasure.
- Rust en Vreugd (p98) – the finest surviving example of an 18th-century Cape Dutch townhouse.
- Nelson Mandela Gateway (p100) – this contemporary architectural standout is the museum and departure point for ferries to Robben Island.

The Rest

- Athlone Power Station (Map pp244–5) – are the giant 'salt and pepper shaker' towers a benefit or blight on the Cape Town skyline? You decide as you pass them en route to the city from the airport.
- Civic Centre (Map pp248–9) – *Death Star* of apartheid-era Cape Town, this ugly building is so badly located that the road running under it has been known to turn into a savage wind tunnel capable of flipping cars over.
- Unfinished Hwy (Map pp248–9) – beloved by action-movie directors as a ready-made set, there is at least one less highway to cut off downtown Cape Town from the sea.
- Disa Park (Map pp246–7) – known as the Tampon Towers, these three cylindrical towers clutter up the view to Devil's Peak from the city.
- Good Hope Centre (Map pp248–9) – isn't it time this hideous concrete tentlike structure was pensioned off now that Cape Town has a modern convention centre?
- Tree House (above) – the public and fellow architects may love it, but having been inside this design icon we think its layout clumsy and ill-conceived. Maybe that's why it was for sale.

Baxter Theatre (p146), Rondebosch

ARTS

VISUAL ARTS

A wander around any of Cape Town's major public and private galleries demonstrates that the contemporary art scene is tremendously exciting and imaginative. Visual art's history on the Cape, however, stretches back to the original San inhabitants – they left their mark on the landscape in the form of rock paintings and subtle rock engravings. Despite having been faded by aeons of exposure, these works of art are remarkable; a fantastic example is the Linton Panel in the South African Museum (p99). Today San motifs are commonly employed on tourist art such as decorative mats and carved ostrich eggs.

The city has many examples of public art, including the bright murals and mosaics of the townships and Brett Murray's amusing, iconoclastic *Africa* sculpture (p114). In St George's Mall, it still turns heads today, as do his distinctive 'Boogie Lights' series of wall lamps, which can be bought at various shops around the city including African Image (p161). Murray's most significant work, *Baobabs, Stormclouds, Animals and People,* hangs at the Cape Town International Convention Centre (p146). This collaboration with the late San artist Tuoi Steffaans Samcuia, of the !Xun and Khwe San Art and Cultural Project, is astonishing in its scale and design – huge steel figures, animals and trees standing out against the maple wall panels. Also check out the new sculptures of South Africa's Nobel prize winners at the Waterfront's Nobel Sq (p101).

Other local artists to look out for include Conrad Botes (see opposite), Sanell Aggenbach, winner of the ABSA Atelier Award in 2003, Willie Bester, whose mixed-media creations of township life are very powerful, and the more conventional John Krammer, who captures the ordinary, serene quality of the South African landscape. At the SA National Gallery (p98), you'll be able to find the paintings of the republic's leading artist William Kentridge, as well as those of Gerard Sekoto, a black artist whose works capture the vibrancy of District Six.

At the Irma Stern Museum (p104) you can view the vivid works of the leading South African female painter of her time. Stern's art was influenced by German expressionism and incorporated elements of traditional African art.

Some people come to Cape Town in search of works by the famous Russian-born artist Vladimir Tretchikoff, who still lives (in ill health) in the leafy suburb of Bishopscourt. His signature images – mesmerising portraits of blue-faced Eurasian and African beauties – have become icons of the kitsch lounge-music generation. You won't find any of the originals in the main Cape Town galleries, but in the bar of Head South Lodge (p178) you'll find a fantastic collection of his prints, which are increasingly rare.

For a preview of the Capetonian art scene check out the website www.artthrob.co.za, which showcases the best in South African contemporary art and has plenty of up-to-the-minute news. Also look into what's going on at **Greatmore Studios** (Map pp246–7; ☎ 021-447 9699; www.greatmoreart.org; 47-49 Greatmore St, Woodstock), where South African and international artists work together, exchanging ideas and techniques.

Traditional Artworks

For decades, African art was dismissed by European colonisers as 'mere craft', as distinct from 'art'. Be prepared to surrender this artificial Western distinction as you root around the craft shops and markets of Cape Town.

The art of the Bantu-speaking peoples is similar to that of the San as a result of their long history of cultural interaction. Their traditional nomadic lifestyle led to their artefacts being portable and generally utilitarian. Headrests, spoons and beadwork are not created as mere commodities: they are individual statements of self and have always entailed long hours of careful labour.

POTTERY

The master potters of the Venda people, who live in the northeastern corner of Northern Province, are all women. Their hand-fashioned pots come in 10 different sizes and designs. Each one has a different function: cooking, serving food or liquids, or storage. The pots feature brightly coloured geometric designs and are more ornamental than functional.

Traditional African designs have influenced the creations of Capetonian potters such as Clementina van der Walt (p170), Carrol Boyes (p166) and Barbara Jackson, whose vases can be bought at Africa Nova (p163). There are also many talented young coloured and black ceramicists crafting pots for the Potter's Shop & Studio (p170) in Kalk Bay and Muizenberg.

BEADWORK

The traditional African craft of beadwork has really taken off in Cape Town, spearheaded by the success of Monkeybiz (p162). There is some very significant new art being created in beads. Qalo, a studio of 16 Xhosa beaders based in Cape Town, has worked with leading local artists, such as Conrad Botes, Julia Clark and Doreen Southwood, on a project commissioned by the **Hollard Contemporary Bead Collection** (www.coeo.co.za) and exhibited recently at the Michaelis Collection (p96).

Apart from the modern interpretations, you'll still come across traditional Zulu beadwork used for decoration and traditional ceremonies. It takes many forms, from the small, square *umgexo* (necklace), which is widely available and makes a good gift, to the more elaborate *umbelenja*, a short skirt or tasselled belt worn by girls from puberty until they are married. *Amadavathi* (bead anklets) are worn by men and women.

Beads are also traditionally used as a means of communication, especially as love letters. Messages are 'spelt out' by the colour and arrangement of the beads. For example, red symbolises passion or anger; black, difficulties or night; blue, yearning; white or pale blue, pure love; brown, disgust or despondency; and green, peace or bliss. To find out more, head to the Bead Centre of Africa (p161), which has a small display area devoted to traditional African beadwork.

BASKETWORK

Zulu hand-woven baskets, although created in a variety of styles and colours, almost always have a function. The raw materials vary depending on their seasonal availability – a basket could be woven from various grasses, palm fronds, bark, or even telephone wire.

Two decorative basket patterns predominate: the triangle, which denotes the male, and the diamond, which denotes the female. A design on the basket of two triangular shapes above one another in an hourglass form indicates that the male owner of the basket is married; similarly, two diamonds so arranged means the female owner of the basket is married.

CONRAD BOTES

Winner of the ABSA Atelier Award 2004, Conrad Botes made his mark on the South African art scene with his strange, weird cult comic *Bitterkomix*, founded along with Anton Kannemeyer. He also collaborated with Brett Murray on designing the 'Boogie Lights' series of wall lamps. His colourful graphic images, both beautiful and horrific, have been shown in exhibitions in New York, the UK and Italy, as well as at the Havana Biennale in 2006. In Cape Town you can view his work – which, apart from comics, takes the form of silkscreen prints, lithographs and paintings on glass – at the Photographers Gallery (p164). Also read his biography and see examples of his work at www.artthrob.co.za (navigate to the Artbio section).

Crafts, Monkeybiz (p162), Bo-Kaap

TOWNSHIP CRAFTS

New and imaginative crafts have sprung up in the townships, borrowing from old traditions but using materials that are readily available. For example, old soft-drink cans and food tins are used to make hats, picture frames, toy cars and planes, while wire and metal bottle tops are used for bags and vases. Complex wirework sculptures and mixed-media paintings and collages are common. Printing and rug-making are also taking off.

One of the most successful projects has been Kommetjie Environmental Awareness Group (KEAG), based at Imhoff Farm (p109). Using waste plastic, tin cans and glass they have created many inventive decorative objects; you'll see their multicoloured tassel curtains and plastic animal heads in shops such as African Image (p161). Other notable craft projects include Streetwires (p163), Miele (p169) at the Montebello centre, Wola Nani (p163) and the Philani Nutrition Centre (p111).

WOODWORK

Venda woodcarvings are also commonly sold in Cape Town's African antique and curio shops. Traditionally, woodcarving was a men-only occupation, but these days expert female woodcarvers can be found. A number of local woods are used, including *mudzwin*, *mutango* and *musimbiri*. Carved items include bowls, spoons, trays, pots, walking sticks, chains attached to calabashes, and knobkerries (sticks with a round knob at one end, used as clubs or missiles).

MUSIC

Jazz

Cape Town is one of the world's jazz capitals and is home to some internationally known musicians, including the singer-songwriter **Jonathan Butler** (www.jonathanbutler.com), and the saxophonists Robbie Jansen (known as the Cape Doctor) and **Winston 'Ngozi' Mankunku** (www.sheer.co.za/winston.html).

The elder statesman of the scene is pianist **Abdullah Ibrahim** (www.abdullahibrahim.com /indexf.html). Born Adolph Johannes Brand in the District Six area of Cape Town in 1934, he began performing at 15 under the name Dollar Brand, and formed the Jazz Epistles with the legendary Hugh Masekela. In 1962, after moving to Zurich, he was spotted by Duke Ellington, who arranged recording sessions for him at Reprise Records and sponsored his appearance at the Newport Jazz Festival in 1965. Brand converted to Islam in 1968 and took the name Abdullah Ibrahim. He returned briefly to South Africa in the mid-1970s and in 1974 recorded the seminal album *Manenberg* with saxophonist Basil Coetzee.

Other respected local artists to watch out for include guitarist **Jimmy Dludlu** (www.music.org .za), pianist **Paul Hamner** (www.sheer.co.za/paul.html) and singer **Judith Sephuma** (www.music .org.za). All these musicians occasionally play in town – your best chance of catching them will be at a jazz festival, such as the Cape Town International Jazz Festival (p10) in March.

Dance, Rock & Pop

Bridging the divide between jazz and electronic dance music are **Goldfish** (www.goldfishlive .com). David Poole and Dominic Peters combine samplers, a groove box, keyboards, vo-coder, upright bass, flute and saxophone in their live performances; catch them in regular gigs at Planet (p139) and Baraza (p140), as well as other venues around town.

Techno, trance and jungle all found their way into Cape Town's dance clubs. Here you can also tune in to *kwaito*, the local dance-music sensation that's a mix of *mbaqanga* jive, hip-hop, house and ragga. The music of local singing superstar Brenda Fassie has a strong *kwaito* flavour. Dubbed 'Madonna of the Townships' by *Time* maga-zine, Langa-born Fassie led a troubled life and died in 2004 at the age of 39.

Hip-hop is also big, with bands includ-ing **Godessa** (www.godessa.com), the very cool trio of township girls. Moodphase 5ive is one of the better groups around that mixes hip-hop with soul; check out their 2003 re-lease *Super Deluxe Mode*. Few Afro-fusion groups have been as big recently as **Freshly Ground** (www.freshlyground.com). This multi-racial seven-piece band, based in Cape Town, went double platinum with their lat-est album *Nomvula* and draw huge crowds whenever they play in town.

> ### TOP FIVE CAPE TOWN SOUNDTRACKS
>
> - *Nomvula,* by Freshly Ground – the multiracial Afro-fusion combo's follow-up to their equally foot-tapping debut *Jika Jika.*
> - *Healing Destination,* by the Goema Captains of Cape Town – jazz composer laureate Mac McKenzie leads an all-star orchestra, including pianist Hilton Schilder and saxophonist Robbie Jansen.
> - *Diamond of Day,* by Robin Auld – catchy acoustic guitar tunes by the Kommetjie surfer rock legend.
> - *Caught in the Loop,* by Goldfish – electronic jazz and break beats by a talented Capetonian duo.
> - *The Hello Goodbye Boys,* by Arno Carstens – the pretty-boy rocker proves he's more than South Africa's Bryan Adams.

On the rock and pop scene, Cape Town has also produced some notable acts – look out for concerts by Skallabrak and Kobus! and Kallitz (a play on 'coloureds') who hail from the Cape Flats and perform gangsta rap in Afrikaans.

Singer-songwriters include the acoustic roots rocker **Robin Auld** (www.robinauld.co.za /home.asp), whose latest release is *Jungle of One*, and **Arno Carstens** (www.arnocarstens.com), lead singer of the defunct Springbok Nude Girls who's having even more success now he's gone solo. Before he hit the international big time with his musical *Kat and the Kings*, **David Kramer** (www.davidkramer.co.za) was already hugely popular as the journeyman guitarist who sang in Afrikaans; hear his songs on the album *Bukgat*.

LITERATURE

Apart from fellow Capetonian JM Coetzee (see p37), the contemporary fiction writer most associated with the Mother City is André Brink. Professor of English at the University of Cape Town, Brink has been writing since the 1960s and has published over 40 novels, including: *A Dry White Season* (1979), about the search for justice during the apartheid era, and made into a movie staring Donald Sutherland and Marlon Brandon; *A Chain of Voices* (1982), about slavery in the 18th-century Cape; *The Other Side of Silence* (2002), a story set in colonial Africa in the early 20th century; and *An Instant in the Wind* (1976)

TOP TEN NOVELS

- *'Buckingham Palace', District Six* (1986), by Richard Rive, contains eloquent stories about the inhabitants of five houses in the heart of District Six.
- Set in Stellenbosch, the dual narrative of *Coldsleep Lullaby* (2005), by Andrew Brown, skilfully entwines a modern-day police thriller with a tale of a 17th-century wine maker lusting after a slave girl.
- The Booker Prize–winning *Disgrace* (1999), by JM Coetzee, is a powerful tale of a Capetonian professor's disastrous move to a rural farm following an ill-judged affair with a student.
- *Mother to Mother* (1998), by Sindiwe Magona, is a fictionalised account of the murder of white American Amy Biehl, sensitively told through the eyes of her mother and the mother of the killer.
- *The Reluctant Passenger* (2003), by Michael Heyns, is a lively satire about a mad plan to develop Cape Point and the efforts of the protagonist to save the baboons.
- *Rights of Desire* (2001), by André Brink, is a lurid tale of incest, murder and rape set in modern-day Cape Town.
- *Sachs Street* (2001), by Rayda Jacobs, is the tale of a young girl growing up in Cape Town's Bo-Kaap in the 1950s, listening to stories from her grandmother.
- There's magical realism in the tender and witty *A Time of Angels* (2003), by Patricia Schonstein, a tale about a Jewish clairvoyant who reads people's futures on Long St.
- Set in Hermanus, *The Whale Caller* (2005) is the fifth novel of acclaimed black writer Zakes Mda, and is an imaginative tale about that eternal triangle: man, woman and whale!
- *You Can't Get Lost In Cape Town* (2000), by Zoë Wicomb, is a coming-of-age tale that paints a complex and evocative picture about the experience of the coloured community in Cape Town during the apartheid era.

and *Rumours of Rain* (1978), both short-listed for the Booker Prize. His latest novel, *Preying Mantis* (2005), mixes comedy and tragedy in the story of Cupido Cockroach, the first Khoi missionary ordained on the Cape.

Out of the coloured experience in District Six came two notable writers, Alex La Guma and Richard Rive. La Guma's books include *A Walk in the Night*, a collection of short stories set in District Six, and *And a Threefold Cord*, which examines the poverty, misery and loneliness of slum life. He died in exile in Havana, Cuba in 1985. Rive's most notable book is *Buckingham Palace*, a thought-provoking and sensitive set of stories from District Six that serves as a memory of life there before the forced removals. Rive was murdered at his Cape Town home in 1989, aged 59.

Acclaimed writer Bessie Head (1937–86) was born in South Africa but spent most of her life in Botswana. *The Cardinals*, believed to be the first long piece of fiction she produced, is the only one set in South Africa. It draws on her experiences as a young journalist and coloured woman in Cape Town in the early 1960s.

Sindiwe Magona was born in a village in the Transkei but grew up in the Cape Town township of Guguletu. *To My Children's Children* (1990) and *Forced to Grow* (1992) are both autobiographical, while *Mother to Mother* (1998) is a fictionalised account of the correspondence between the mother of Amy Biehl, a white American woman murdered in the Cape Flats in 1993, and the mother of her killer.

PERFORMING ARTS

Theatre

There's an understandable lack of interest from most economically challenged Capetonians in theatre, matched by an equal paucity of government subsidy for the performing arts. So it's surprising how lively and diverse the local theatre scene is, offering everything from big-scale musicals and one-man shows to edgy dramas reflecting modern South Africa.

Enfant terrible Brett Bailey's theatre company **Third World Bunfight** (www.thirdworldbunfight .co.za) is certainly one troupe to watch. Bailey specialises in using black actors to tell uniquely African stories in productions such as *Mumbo Jumbo*, which explores the interaction between the realms of theatre and ritual. The production, which has also been performed at London's Barbican Theatre, hit the front pages of the South African newspapers when the cast sacrificed a real chicken at its season finale in Cape Town. Third World Bunfight is the resident performing company at the Spier wine estate (p47), and in 2006 scored a critical hit with *Orfeus*, Bailey's reimagining of Orpheus' journey into the Underworld.

Another innovative company is Theatre for Africa, run by the Capetonian theatrical family of father Nicholas and sons Matthew and Luke Ellenbogen. Their award-winning productions often combine music, mime (usually of African wildlife) and acting with traditional African stories. In recent years they've mounted productions in the Old Zoo (p147) on the eastern slopes of Table Mountain, an atmospheric venue that is worth attending in its own right.

Songwriter and director David Kramer and musician Taliep Peterson teamed up to work on two musicals, *District Six* and *Poison,* before hitting the big time with their jazz homage *Kat and the Kings*, which swept up awards in London in 1999 and received standing ovations on Broadway. Their latest collaboration *Goema*, celebrating the tradition of Afrikaans folks songs, was a huge success when it premiered in Cape Town in 2005; even though it's largely in Afrikaans, the structure of the musical, which also traces the history of Cape Town and the contribution made by the slaves and their descendants, is easy to follow and enormous fun to watch.

Traditional Shakespearean theatre gets a run in the open air every summer at Maynardville (p147); the festival celebrated its 50th anniversary in 2006. It's also well worth checking out the productions held at the Spier estate during the Spier Arts Summer Season festival (p9).

Dance

Alongside Capetonians' love of music is their love of dance. The city supports several dance companies, including the **Cape Town City Ballet** (www.capetowncityballet.org.za), **Jazzart Dance Theatre** (www.jazzart.co.za), South Africa's oldest modern dance company, and **Cape Dance Company** (www.capedancecompany.bizland.com), made up of talented youths from 13 to 23.

Former professional dancer Phillip Boyd's **Dance For All** (☎ 021-633 4363; www.danceforall .co.za) trains young dancers from the townships and poverty-stricken suburbs of the Cape. Programme graduate Theo Ndindwa has gone on to study at London's Rambert Ballet School and perform at Sadlers Wells. Contact the company to find out about tours of its teaching venues run from 2.45pm Monday to Thursday.

A similar project operating with street kids in Green Point and children in the township at Hout Bay is **Jikeleza** (☎ 021-712 1255; www.jikeleza.co.za), which means 'Turn Around' and teaches life skills as well as contemporary dance. Both Jikeleza and Dance For All stage end-of-year concerts that are well worth attending.

CAPE TOWN'S MAN OF LETTERS

Born in Cape Town in 1940, JM Coetzee (pronounced 'kut-*say*-uh') is the first writer to have won the coveted Booker Prize twice. He was also awarded the Nobel prize for literature in 2003, the Swedish Academy hailing him for being a 'scrupulous doubter, ruthless in his criticism of the cruel rationalism and cosmetic morality of Western Civilisation'.

For some clues into what informed this world view, start by reading his childhood memoir *Boyhood* (1997). Coetzee (the J and M stand for John Maxwell) studied English and mathematics at Cape Town University. His first novel *Dusklands* was published in 1974, while he was teaching in the US, but it was his third, *Waiting For The Barbarians* (1980), that made readers and critics aware of his singular talent.

The Life and Times of Michael K (1983), which imagined a South Africa embroiled in civil war, won him his first Booker Prize. Thankfully life didn't imitate Coetzee's art, although in his second Booker winner *Disgrace* (1999), the supposedly peaceful postapartheid landscape is cruelly exposed. *Age of Iron* (1990) is another novel set in South Africa about the lives of the homeless. In *Foe* (1986) he rewrites Robinson Crusoe from a female castaway's perspective, while the St Petersburg of Dostoevsky is the setting for *Master of Petersburg* (1994).

Youth (2002) is a fictionalised account based on the time Coetzee spent as a computer programmer in England during the 1960s. The line between fact and fiction in his books became even more blurred with *Elizabeth Costello* (2003), in which the title character, a novelist in her sixties, gives a series of lectures, which in turn are based on similar lectures Coetzee himself delivered at Princeton in 1999. Ms Costello turns up again in his latest novel *Slow Man* (2005), about a man coming to terms with the amputation of his leg. It's set in Adelaide, Australia, where Coetzee immigrated in 2002, and where he became a citizen in 2006.

CINEMA

South African cinema appears to be on a roll. *Yesterday*, winner of Best African Film in 2004, became the nation's first film to be nominated for an Oscar in the Best Foreign Language category in 2005. The following year the Oscar was in the bag for Gavin Hood's stylish and hard-hitting township gangster drama *Tsotsi*.

Cape Town is a major centre for South African cinema and movie-making. The city acts as a magnet for many talented people in the industry and you'll frequently see production crews shooting on location around town. Many of the crews make commercials for overseas clients who love Cape Town's bright weather, its picturesque locations and its generally low-cost, high-quality labour.

All this said, you'll search in vain at Cape Town's multiplexes for locally made movies. The Labia's African Screen (p148) is the only Cape Town cinema that regularly screens South African movies. Your best chance of catching home-grown product is at the city's several film festivals or on the shelves of DVD shops.

Releases to look out for include the American documentary *Long Night's Journey into Day*, nominated for Best Documentary at the 2001 Oscars. This very moving Sundance Film Festival winner follows four cases from the Truth & Reconciliation Commission hearings, including that of Amy Biehl, the white American murdered in the Cape Flats in 1993.

Scooping up prizes at the Sundance Film Festival in 2002 was the documentary feature *Amandla*, a South African–US coproduction about the role of protest songs in the country's struggle to rid itself of apartheid. Among the many star South African performers testifying in the film is Cape Town's world-famous jazz pianist Abdullah Ibrahim, who coins the immortal phrase that South Africa is the only country in the world to have undergone 'a revolution in four-part harmony'.

John Boorman has directed *In My Country*, the movie version of Antjie Krog's *Country of My Skull*, starring Samuel L Jackson and Juliette Binoche to generally respectful reviews. Another recent movie dealing with the horrors of the apartheid era is *Red Dust*, starring Hilary Swank.

Proteus, by John Greyson and Jack Lewis, based on a true 18th-century story, is an imaginatively filmed gay love story set among the colonial-era prisoners of Robben Island. *U-Carmen e Khayelitsha*, Golden Bear winner at the 2005 Berlin International Film Festival, is based on Bizet's opera *Carmen* and was shot entirely on location in Khayelitsha. It's the first movie for local drama group **Dimpho Di Kopane** (www.ddk.org.za). Their follow-up *Son of Man*, a controversial reworking of the Gospels in modern Africa, is also gathering prizes and glowing reviews on the festival circuit.

Wine

Wine

A visit to Cape Town without tasting the local wines would be like going to Scotland and avoiding whisky. This is where South Africa's wine industry – now the ninth largest in the world – began back in the 17th century. Today, within a day's drive of the city, there are over 200 wineries; there're even plans for a new one inside Rhodes Mandela Place in the city centre, making wine from grapes grown in a tiny vineyard in Vredehoek.

Scores of new wine producers join the industry each year, and while many are content to remain as micro-wineries, honing their wines to perfection, others are seeking to capitalise on the industry's popularity by adding museums, restaurants, accommodation and other attractions. We've reviewed some of the more notable of these in this chapter, along with vineyards that are renowned for their fine wines – all are within easy reach of the city. For those without their own wheels, there are plenty of tours of the Winelands (p43).

If you're looking to broaden your knowledge of the local wines further, you can take one of the wine-appreciation courses run by the **Cape Wine Academy** (Map p46; ☎ 021-889 8844; www .capewineacademy.co.za). Although the headquarters are in Stellenbosch, there are courses held in Cape Town in two locations: the **Cellar Cuvee Classique** (Map pp246–7; Palms Décor & Lifestyle Centre, 145 Sir Lowry Rd, Foreshore) and **Manuka Café & Fine Wines** (Map pp244–5; Steenberg Lifestyle Village, Tokai). You'll need about six weeks to complete a course. The Nose Wine Bar (p138), in Cape Town, also offers a six-week course for R300. A hands-on wine-making course (R50 per person) is run by **Fynbos Estate** (Map p186; ☎ 022-487 1153; www.fynbosestate.co.za) in the Paardeberg mountains, 15km outside Malmesbury, an hour's drive from Cape Town.

The annual guide **John Platter South African Wines** (www.platteronline.com) is *the* book to consult if you want full tasting notes on the thousands of different local wines. Also worth searching out is Jean-Pierre Roussow's *Mixed Case – A Unique Guide to the Cape Winelands*. You can also read Roussow's quirky reviews on his website www.handtomouth.co.za.

If you don't have time to get out to the wineries, there are several wine shops in Cape Town with excellent selections, including Vaughan Johnson's Wine & Cigar Shop (p167) and Wine Concepts (p165).

TOP FIVE TIPPLES *Al Simmonds*

The following are South Africa's most popular red and white wines by retail price, according to Vaughan Johnson's Wine & Cigar Shop (p167).

Reds

- Chateau Libertas (R25) – perhaps the most reliable table wine in the country. Depending on which bottle you get, this velvety blend can have you disbelieving the price tag.
- Beyerskloof Pinotage (R40) – a fruity choice, and a great introduction to this uniquely South African cultivar.
- Rupert & Rothschild Classique (R85) – an elegant cabernet sauvignon-merlot with blackcurrant overtones. Hugely popular.
- Meerlust Rubicon (R195) – this South African standard-bearer is a simply exquisite wine that every moneyed wine-lover in the country buys for their wedding anniversary and then can't bring themselves to open.
- Rustenberg Peter Barlow (R360) – an intensely concentrated blackberry-aroma cabernet-merlot that's a good seller despite the hefty price tag.

Whites

- Du Toitskloof Sauvignon Blanc (R25) – a lively white perfect for a seafood braai.
- Haute Cabrière (R49) – consistently delicious medium-bodied chardonnay-pinot noir from the Franschhoek winery.
- Steenberg Sauvignon Blanc (R70) – a fresh, fragrant perennial favourite with hints of gooseberry and lemon.
- Thelema Chardonnay (R90) – a long-standing robust dry wine with citrus and hazelnut on the nose.
- Hamilton Russell Chardonnay (R176) – a classic chardonnay with biscuit aromas and a mineral flavour.

HISTORY

'Today, praise be the Lord, wine was pressed for the first time from Cape grapes.'

Jan van Riebeeck, 2 February 1659

Although the founder of the Cape Colony, Jan van Riebeeck, planted vines and made wine himself, it was not until the arrival of Governor Simon van der Stel in 1679 that wine-making began in earnest. Van der Stel created Groot Constantia, the superb estate on the flanks of Table Mountain, and passed on his wine-making skills to the burghers who settled around Stellenbosch.

Between 1688 and 1690, some 200 Huguenots arrived in the country. They were granted land in the region, particularly around Franschhoek (which translates as 'French Corner'), and, although only a few had wine-making experience, they gave the infant industry fresh impetus.

For a long time, Cape wines other than those produced at Groot Constantia were not in great demand and most grapes ended up in brandy. The industry received a boost in the early 19th century as war between Britain and France meant more South African wine was imported to the UK.

Apartheid-era sanctions and the power of the Kooperatieve Wijnbouwers Vereeniging (KWV; the cooperative formed in 1918 to control minimum prices, production areas and quota limits) didn't exactly encourage innovation and instead hampered the industry. Since 1992 the KWV, now a private company, has lost much of its former influence.

Many new and progressive wine makers are leading South Africa's reemergence onto the world market. New wine-producing areas are being established away from the hotter inland areas, in particular in the cooler coastal areas east of Cape Town around Mossel Bay, Walker Bay and Elgin, and to the north around Durbanville and Darling.

WORKERS' WINES

The black and coloured workforce on the vineyards numbers some 350,000 toiling in vine-yards owned by around 4500 whites. Workers often receive the minimum monthly wage in the industry of R650, or less if they are women. The infamous 'tot' system, whereby the wages of labourers are paid partly in wine still happens, and the consequences, socially and physiologically, have been disastrous.

Labour legislation protects workers, but it's not always complied with. Many workers are unaware of their rights and few farm workers are organised. However, after years of slow progress, a step in the right direction was made in November 2002 with the establishment of the nonprofit **Wine Industry and Ethical Trade Association** (WIETA; www.wieta.org.za), whose aim it is to lobby for a better deal for those working in the wine industry. UK wine retailers Tesco, Co-op, Marks & Spencer and ASDA have signed up as members and other UK retailers have shown their support for the scheme, which has already accredited 12 vineyards for following its ethical code; check its website for details.

Various individual wineries are leading the way, too. Out at Solms-Delta (p50), owner Mark Solms has set up the Wijn de Caab Trust to represent the estate's resident employees and their families. Profits from the wine estate are shared on a 40/60 basis with the wine company and the trust beneficiaries. In the Robertson region, 150km east of Cape Town, the Retief family of **Van Loveren Private Cellar** (☎ 023-615 1505; www.vanloveren.co.za) is trans-ferring one of its farms to a trust to be comanaged by the workers.

The number of wineries that are fully or partly owned by coloured and black workers is growing. **Thabani** (☎ 021-412 9302; www.thabani.co.za; ☒ not open to the public), in Stellenbosch, is South Africa's first wholly black-owned wine company. It hit the big time in the US when Oprah Winfrey served its lively sauvignon blanc at a party for poet Maya

TOP FIVE WINERIES

The following are our five favourite wineries to visit:

- Boschendal (p48) – this classic estate has a fairy-tale location and fine wine, food and architecture.
- Buitenverwachting (p44) – enjoy a lovely picnic on an immaculate lawn, and wash it down with the quaffable chardonnay or Rhine riesling.
- Cabrière Estate (p48) – attend the Saturday-morning cellar tour to witness the owner slice off the top of a sparkling bottle of wine with his sabre.
- Fairview (p51) – sample from a selection of some 23 wines, including the workers' empowerment wine, Fair Valley, as well as many goat's- and cow's-milk cheeses.
- Vergelegen (p47) – the Winelands' most elegant estate produces some equally stylish wines, the flagship being its very fruity Vergelegen red.

Angelou. Students of Thabani wine maker Jabulani Ntshangase are now being snapped up by big vineyards, including KWV.

Going from strength to strength is **Thandi** (☎ 021-881 3870; www.thandi.co.za; ⏰ 9am-5pm Mon-Sat), located in the Elgin area. Thandi (Xhosa for 'Love' or 'Cherish') is the first winery in the world to be Fairtrade certified and its wines, which are available at Tesco in the UK, are beginning to win awards.

Hoping to emulate both of these operations' success is Tseliso Rangaka, a former Johannesburg (Jo'burg) copywriter turned Stellenbosch wine maker. His brand M'hudi is being helped along by Villiera (p47).

The **Fair Valley Workers Association** (Map p49; ☎ 021-863 2450) is a 17-hectare workers' farm next to Fairview. It's still developing its own vineyards, but has already produced several seasons of chenin blanc (sold through the UK wine chain Oddbins) made with grapes bought in from Fairview, as well as a sauvignon blanc and a pinotage. Tastings and sales are available at Fairview (p51).

At **Nelson's Creek** (Map p49; ☎ 021-869 8453; www.nelsoncreek.co.za; Rte 44, tastings free; ⏰ 9am-5pm Mon-Fri, 9am-2pm Sat), north of Paarl, the owner has donated part of the estate to his workers to produce their own wines. Under the label New Beginnings, these wines – a classic dry red, a rosé and a dry white – are being sold in the UK, the Netherlands and Japan.

Tukulu (☎ 021-809 7000; www.tukulu.co.za; ⏰ not open to the public), from the Darling area, is the flagship Black Economic Empowerment (BEE) brand in the stable of industry giant Distell. This highly successful operation has won awards for its pinotage and is receiving rave reviews for its chenin blanc.

VARIETIES OF WINE

The big news in South African wine circles is the use of new and rarer grape varieties. Keep an eye out for wines aiming to be the white pinotage, made with either tempranillo or the South African–developed nouvelle grape (a crossing of semillon and crouchen blanc, better known as Cape riesling).

Regular pinotage, a cross between pinot noir and *cinsault* (shiraz), which produces a very bold wine, is the Cape's signature grape. Together with other robust red varieties such as shiraz (Syrah) and cabernet sauvignon, it's being challenged by lighter blends of cabernet sauvignon, merlot, shiraz and cabernet franc, making a style closer to Bordeaux styles. The reds attracting the highest prices are cabernet sauvignon and the Bordeaux-style blends. A Cape blend must contain at least 30% pinotage.

The most common variety of white wine is *steen* (chenin blanc). In the last decade or so, more fashionable varieties such as chardonnay and sauvignon blanc have been planted on a wide scale. Other widely planted whites include colombard, semillon, Cape riesling and sweet muscats. Table whites, especially chardonnay, once tended to be heavily oaked and high in alcohol, but lighter, more fruity whites are now in the ascendancy. For good sauvignon blancs, look to wineries in the cooler regions of Constantia, Elgin and Hermanus.

Cap Classique is the name that South Africa's wine industry has come up with for its Champenoise-style wines – many are as good as the real thing, with recommendations being the sparklers of Graham Beck (p48), Cabrière Estate (p48) and Villiera (p47). The very first bottle-fermented sparkling wine produced at the Cape by the Huguenots was called Kaapse Vonkel (Cape Sparkle).

The Worcester region is the country's leading producer of fortified wines, including port, brandy and South Africa's own hanepoot. This dessert wine is made from the Mediterranean grape variety known as muscat of Alexandria to produce a sweet, high-alcohol tipple for the domestic market. In Worcester you'll also find the KWV Brandy Cellar, the largest in the world and the final stop on the Brandy Route, which runs from Van Ryn Brandy Cellar (p47). For more information contact the **South African Brandy Foundation** (☎ 021-887 3157; www.sabrandy.co.za).

WINERY TOURS

With so many nice wines to sample, it's understandable that you may feel anxious about driving yourself around and staying sober. To the rescue come several tour companies that run from Cape Town, Stellenbosch and Franschhoek.

You'll need to make an advance booking for tours. Most tour companies will pick you up from you accommodation and will, depending on the size of the group, tailor the tour to your individual wishes.

CAPE WINE TOURS

☎ 021-462 1121, 083 659 8434; capewinetours@telkomsa.net; day tour R365
A tour of the Winelands kicks off at Villiera in the Stellenbosch region where you'll go on a cellar tour and learn about sparkling wine-making. Other wineries visited include Spier (to see the cheetah project), Fairview and Tokara on the way to Franschhoek.

CHEESE & WINE TOURS

☎ 086 124 3373; www.cheeseandwine.co.za; tour R675
Meet cheese and wine makers at niche farms and vineyards on this tour, departing from Cape Town Tourism in City Bowl (Map pp248–9) and Waterfront (Map pp252–3).

EASY RIDER WINE TOURS Map p189

☎ 021-886 4651; www.jump.to/stumble; tour R250
Backpackers and travellers have been enjoying Easy Rider's fun wine tours out of Stellenbosch for years. They kick off with a cellar tour and include visits to at least four or five wineries in the region, usually covering Boschendal and Fairview.

FERDINAND'S TOURS & ADVENTURES

☎ 021-913 8800, 072 132 2482; ferdinand@telkomsa.net; tour R350
The boozy backpackers' wine tour. You'll get to visit Durbanville Hills, Simonsig in Stellenbosch, Seidelberg in Paarl, a cheese farm and a brandy distillery.

FRANSCHHOEK TRAILS

☎ 021-876 2983; erica@hautespoir.co.za; tour R350
This company specialises in a range of vineyard walks, with tastings, snacks and nature trails thrown in.

GOURMET WINE TOURS

☎ 021-705 4317, 083 229 3581; www.gourmet winetours.co.za
Stephen Flesch, a former chairman of the Wine Taster Guild of South Africa, has over 35 years of wine-tasting experience and runs tours to the wineries of your choice. Rates for a full/half day are R1100/750 for one person and R450/300 for each additional person.

VINEYARD VENTURES

☎ 021-434 8888; www.vineyardventures.co.za; tour R500
This long-running specialist wine-tour company can customise a wine tour to your needs or suggest places to visit off the beaten track.

WINE DESK AT THE WATERFRONT

Map pp252-3
☎ 021-405 4550; www.winedeskwaterfront.co.za; Clocktower, Waterfront; tour R490
Drop by the desk at the Waterfront to find out about the daily wine tours, which take in a different selection of wineries each day. The company's Saturday-morning wine club visits two or three different wineries, ending with a meal on one of the farms.

WINE WALKS

☎ 083 631 5944; info@winewalks.co.za; tour R395
Local expert Anne Lee Steyn takes visitors on an 8km walking tour of wineries in the Simonsberg area. The walk includes a picnic lunch and tastings; ask Anne about group discounts.

WINE REGIONS
CONSTANTIA

On the eastern slopes of Table Mountain, Constantia is the oldest of South Africa's wine-growing regions. Groot Constantia, the original estate established by Simon van der Stel in 1685, was divided up after his death in 1712, so today you can also visit Buitenverwachtig and Klein Constantia, both originally part of the Van der Stel estates. Steenberg Vineyards, which also makes wine for the nearby Constantia Uitsig estate, completes the Constantia wine route.

If you're short of time, head for Groot Constantia, which is among the grandest vineyards and homesteads in the Cape. A delightful way to spend a day, though, is to take a cycling tour of this lush area with Downhill Adventures (p150).

BUITENVERWACHTING Map pp244-5
☎ 021-794 5190; www.buitenverwachting.co.za; Klein Constantia Rd; tastings free; ☉ 9am-5pm Mon-Fri, 9am-1pm Sat

Buitenverwachting means 'Beyond Expectations', which is certainly the feeling one gets on visiting this 100-hectare estate that's known for offering good working and living conditions for its employees. For R90 per person you can enjoy a picnic lunch in front of the 1786 manor house (book on ☎ 083 257 6083 or 082 974 8543). The internationally renowned Christine claret usually sells out on the day of its release each year (around November) and the chardonnay and Rhine riesling are among its standout whites.

CONSTANTIA UITSIG Map pp244-5
☎ 021-794 1810; www.uitsig.co.za; Spaanschemat River Rd; tastings free; ☉ 9am-4.30pm Mon-Fri, 10am-3.30pm Sat & Sun

The wine on sale here is actually made at the nearby Steenberg Vineyards. You can also taste wines from some 60 other estates. It's one for foodies since it boasts three excellent restaurants – Constantia Uitsig, La Colombe (p132) and the River Café (p132) – and a luxury hotel (p181).

GROOT CONSTANTIA Map pp244-5
☎ 021-794 5128; www.grootconstantia.co.za; Groot Constantia Rd, High Constantia; tastings incl glass R25; ☉ 9am-6pm Dec-Apr, 9am-5pm May-Nov

A superb example of Cape Dutch architecture, Groot Constantia is set in beautiful grounds. Not surprisingly, it can become busy with tour groups, but the estate is big enough for you to escape the crowds, if needs be. In the 18th century, Constantia wines were exported around the world and were highly acclaimed; today you should try its sauvignon blanc, riesling and pinotage.

The beautifully restored homestead is a museum (☎ 021-795 5140; www.museums .org.za/grootcon; adult/child R8/2; ☉ 10am-5pm) and is appropriately furnished; take a look at the tiny slave quarters beneath the main building. The Cloete Cellar, the estate's original wine cellar, now houses old carriages and a display of storage vessels. Book for tours of the modern cellar, which run every hour in summer. It's a lovely spot to bring a picnic, although there are also a couple of restaurants on the estate, including Jonkerhuis (p132).

Manor house, Groot Constantia (above)

KLEIN CONSTANTIA Map pp244-5

☎ 021-794 5188; www.kleinconstantia.com; Klein Constantia Rd; tastings free; ☺ 9am-5pm Mon-Fri, 9am-1pm Sat

This winery, part of the original Constantia estate, is famous for its Vin de Constance, a deliciously sweet muscat wine (R245). It was Napoleon's solace on St Helena, and Jane Austen had one of her heroines recommend it for having the power to heal 'a disappointed heart'. We can't guarantee that, but we can say that while Klein Constantia doesn't offer the frills and bonuses of other wineries, it's still worth visiting for its excellent tasting room and informative displays. Also try the riesling, sauvignon blanc and Marlbrook, a classic Bordeaux-style blend. At the estate's entrance, pause to look at the *karamat* (saint's tomb) of Sheik Abdurachman Matebe Shah; he was buried in 1661.

STEENBERG VINEYARDS Map pp244-5

☎ 021-713 2211; www.steenberg-vineyards.com; Steenberg Rd; tastings free; ☺ 9am-4.30pm Mon-Fri, 9.30am-1.30pm Sat

The oldest Cape wine estate after Constantia, Steenberg began life under the name Swaane-weide (Feeding Place of the Swans) in 1682. Its great merlot, sauvignon blanc reserve and semillon are the wines to sample. The estate also encompasses **Steenberg Hotel**, a five-star country hotel in the original restored manor house, and an 18-hole golf course. Cellar tours are by appointment and run at 10am and 3pm Monday to Friday (R15).

DURBANVILLE

The other major wine-growing area within Cape Town's metropolitan borders is **Durbanville** (Map p186; www.durbanvillewine .co.za), around 20 minutes' drive north of the city centre. Vines have been grown here since 1698 and the area's signature grape is sauvignon blanc, which benefits from the cooler winds the hills receive off the coast. Spend a pleasant day with time to spare exploring the eight wineries in the area.

DURBANVILLE HILLS

☎ 021-558 1300; www.durbanvillehills.co.za; M13, Durbanville; tastings R10, tour & tastings R20; ☺ 9am-4.30pm Mon-Fri, 9.30am-2.30pm Sat, 11am-3pm Sun

Tired of the Cape Dutch–style wine cellars? Then visit this winery in an ultramodern building commanding a hilltop above the Durbanville vineyards. There's a splendid view of Table Bay and Table Mountain from its stone-clad bastion. Best known for its merlot and its sauvignon blanc, the winery also has a good restaurant, **@The Hills** (meals around R70; ☺ noon-3pm Tue-Sun, 7-10pm Wed-Sat Oct-Mar, call for dinner opening times in other months).

MEERENDAL

☎ 021-975 1655; www.meerendal.co.za; M48 Visserhok, Durbanville; tastings R10; ☺ 8am-5pm

With some of the oldest pinotage and shiraz vineyards in South Africa, Meerendal certainly has a pedigree for its wines. Its fortunes have really taken off since 2004 when new owners took over the historic farm. Locals rave about the quality of its formal restaurant Wheatfields, the more casual Barn & Lawn bistro, and its deli food, which can be enjoyed with a drop of its sauvignon blanc on the wooden deck. Book for the Sunday buffet (adult/child R120/45).

STELLENBOSCH

It was Stellenbosch in the 1970s that first promoted a 'wine route', an idea that has since been enthusiastically taken up by every wine-growing region in South Africa. For details of wineries in this area not listed here, contact the **Stellenbosch Wine Routes** (☎ 021-886 4310; www.wine route.co.za), or the **Stellenbosch Publicity Association** (Map p189; ☎ 021-883 3584; www .tourismstellenbosch.co.za; 36 Market St; ☺ 8am-6pm Mon-Fri, 9am-5pm Sat, 9am-4pm Sun). For information on other sights in the area, and for sleeping and eating options, see p188.

BLAAUWKLIPPEN Map p46

☎ 021-880 0133; www.blaauwklippen.com; Rte 44; tastings R25; ☺ 9am-5pm Mon-Sat, 9am-4pm Sun

This rustic, 300-year-old estate with several fine Cape Dutch buildings is known for its excellent red wines, particularly its cabernet sauvignon and zinfandel. Cellar tours are by appointment and lunch is available (call for times, as they change according to the season). It's a good one for kids on weekends when it has horse-and-carriage rides around the estate (R10).

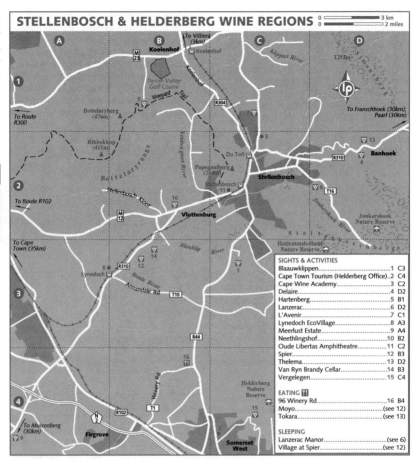

STELLENBOSCH & HELDERBERG WINE REGIONS

SIGHTS & ACTIVITIES

Blaauwklippen	1 C3
Cape Town Tourism (Helderberg Office)	2 C4
Cape Wine Academy	3 C2
Delaire	4 D2
Hartenberg	5 B1
Lanzerac	6 D2
L'Avenir	7 C1
Lynedoch EcoVillage	8 A3
Meerlust Estate	9 A4
Neethlingshof	10 B2
Oude Libertas Amphitheatre	11 C2
Spier	12 B3
Thelema	13 D2
Van Ryn Brandy Cellar	14 B3
Vergelegen	15 C4

EATING

96 Winery Rd	16 B4
Moyo	(see 12)
Tokara	(see 13)

SLEEPING

Lanzerac Manor	(see 6)
Village at Spier	(see 12)

DELAIRE Map p46

☎ 021-885 1756; www.delairewinery.co.za; Rte 310; tastings R10; ☾ 10am-5pm

Known as the 'vineyard in the sky' because of its location at the top of the Helshoogte Pass on Rte 310, the views are, naturally, stunning. Delaire is a friendly place, and has wheelchair access to the restaurant, picnics available October to April (bookings essential), and log cabin accommodation. Try the cabernet sauvignon and merlot.

HARTENBERG Map p46

☎ 021-882 2541; www.hartenbergestate.com; off M23; tastings free; ☾ 9am-5pm Mon-Fri, 9am-3pm Sat

Thanks to a favourable microclimate, this estate, founded in 1692, produces many award-winning wines, notably its cabernet sauvignon, merlot and shiraz. Lunch is available at Hartenberg from noon to 2pm (bookings are essential). The estate is located off Bottelary Rd, 10km northwest of Stellenbosch.

LANZERAC Map p46

☎ 021-886 5641; www.lanzeracwines.co.za; off Jonkershoek Rd, Jonkershoek Valley; tastings R16; ☾ 9am-4.30pm Mon-Thu, 9am-4pm Fri, 10am-2pm Sat, 11am-3pm Sun

Lanzerac produces a very good merlot and quaffable cabernet sauvignon and chardonnay. The tastings include a free glass and biscuits. Here you'll also find Stellenbosch's most luxurious hotel, **Lanzerac Manor** (p192).

L'AVENIR Map p46

☎ 021-889 5001; www.lavenir.co.za; Rte 44; tastings R10-20; ⏰ 10am-5pm Mon-Fri, 10am-4pm Sat
Its name means 'the Future', but it's this estate's track record that earns it repeat visitors, who come not for the facilities (there's no restaurant) but for the simply splendid wines: the chenin blanc is divine and the pinotage has won more awards for this cultivar than any other in the country. Ask about staying overnight in the cottages. The estate is 5km out of Stellenbosch on the way to Paarl.

MEERLUST ESTATE Map p46

☎ 021-843 3587; www.meerlust.co.za; Rte 310; tastings R20; ⏰ 9am-4pm Mon-Fri, 10am-2pm Sat
One of South Africa's most celebrated wine estates (in operation since 1693), Meerlust turns out Rubicon, a wine that John Platter's guide calls the 'preeminent Cape claret'. Its new tasting room, decorated with the owner's collection of posters and a fine history of the winery, is worth a look.

NEETHLINGSHOF Map p46

☎ 021-883 8898; www.neethlingshof.co.za; M12; tastings R20; ⏰ 9am-5pm Mon-Fri, 10am-6pm Sat-Sun
A stunning tree-lined approach leads to a charming 300-year-old estate with a rose garden and tearoom. There are cellar and vineyard tours, and the pinotage and cabernet sauvignon, from this, one of the most popular estates in the Winelands, have won several awards.

SPIER Map p46

☎ 021-809 1100; www.spier.co.za; Rte 310; tastings R12; ⏰ 9am-5pm
There's something for everyone at this mega-estate, which offers steam-train trips (☎ 021-419 5222; www.vintagetrains.co.za) from Cape Town, horse riding, a cheetah-conservation project, a performing-arts centre, beautifully restored Cape Dutch buildings and several restaurants, including the spectacular if somewhat cheesy African-themed Moyo (p191). Its wines are nothing to shout about, but during the tasting you can try lots of other vineyards' wines. Check out the annual arts festival (p9) that runs from January to March – it's as good a reason as any for coming here. If you want to stay over there's a good Cape Malay–style hotel, the Village at Spier (p192).

THELEMA Map p46

☎ 021-885 1924; www.thelema.co.za; Rte 310; tastings free; ⏰ 9am-5pm Mon-Fri, 9am-1pm Sat
At the head of the Helshoogte Pass, opposite Delaire, this relatively young winery overlooking the Drakenstein Mountains has already earned a sterling reputation thanks to its fine cabernet sauvignon, merlot and chardonnay wines.

VAN RYN BRANDY CELLAR Map p46

☎ 021-881 3875; www.distell.co.za; Van Ryn Rd, off Rte 310, Vlottenburg; tastings R15; ⏰ 8am-5pm Mon-Fri, 9am-1.30pm Sat
Van Ryn is at the start of the Western Cape Brandy Route. They generally run three tours daily here and include a tasting. In the boardroom you can view fine South African artworks, including works by Irma Stern and the incredibly lifelike sculptures of Anton van Wouw. It's 8km southwest of Stellenbosch.

VILLIERA

☎ 021-865 2002; www.villiera.com; Koelenhof; tastings free; ⏰ 8.30am-5pm Mon-Fri, 8.30am-1pm Sat
Apart from supplying wines to Woolworths in South Africa and Marks & Spencer in the UK (its Crows Fountain range), this winery also produces several excellent méthode cap classique wines, which include a brut natural made from naturally fermented chardonnay with no added sulphur. It also works with M'hudi wines, a black-owned neighbouring wine farm, producing a chenin blanc, sauvignon blanc and pinotage.

HELDERBERG

This area around Somerset West, which is 20km south of Stellenbosch, has some 20 wineries, including Vergelegen, arguably the most beautiful estate in the Cape. For more information on the area contact the Helderberg office of Cape Town Tourism (Map p46; ☎ 021-840 1400; www.tourismcapetown .co.za; 186 Main Rd, Somerset West).

VERGELEGEN Map p46

☎ 021-847 1334; www.vergelegen.co.za; Lourensford Rd, Somerset West; admission R10, tastings R2.50-10; ⏰ 9.30am-4pm
Simon van der Stel's son Willem first planted vines here in 1700. The buildings and elegant grounds have ravishing mountain views and a 'stately home' feel to

them. On the dining front you can choose from the casual Rose Terrace overlooking the Rose Garden, the upmarket Lady Phillips Restaurant, or a picnic hamper (R110 per person) – bookings are essential for the last two options; neither is available between April and September.

FRANSCHHOEK

Many of Franschhoek's wineries are within walking distance of the town centre, but to get to others (indeed, to reach the town), you're best off with your own transport. To find out about more wineries in the area see www.franschhoekwines.co.za.

BACKSBERG Map p49

☎ 021-875 5141; www.backsberg.co.za; Rte 310; tastings R15; ⏰ 8.30am-5pm Mon-Fri, 9am-2pm Sat, 11am-3pm Sun Sep-Jun

An immensely popular estate thanks to its reliable label and lavish outdoor lunches, Backsberg is more or less equidistant between Franschhoek and Stellenbosch. Its white wines have won awards, but, along with L'Avenir (p47), this is one of the country's best examples of the home-grown pinotage cultivar.

BOSCHENDAL Map p49

☎ 021-870 4210; www.boschendal.com; Rte 310; ⏰ 8.30am-4.30pm Nov-Apr, 8.30am-4.30pm Mon-Sat May-Oct

Tucked beneath some awesome mountains, this is the classic Winelands estate, with lovely architecture, food and wine. Note the Taphuis wine-tasting area (where tastings cost R15, or R22 for a formal tasting with a guide) is at the opposite end of the estate from the Groote Drakenstein manor house (admission R10) and restaurants. Its reds, including cabernet sauvignon and merlot, get top marks. The blowout buffet lunch (R195) in the main restaurant is mainly a group affair. Far nicer, especially in fine weather, is Le Café where you can have a snack or something more substantial. Also very popular are 'Le Pique Nique' hampers (R95 per person, minimum two people) served under parasols on the lawn from mid-October to the end of April (for bookings call ☎ 021-870 4274). Boschendal is on Rte 310 towards Stellenbosch.

CABRIÈRE ESTATE Map p193

☎ 021-876 8500; www.cabriere.co.za; Berg St; tastings with/without cellar tour R25/20; ⏰ 9.30am-4.30pm Mon-Fri, 10.30am-3.30pm Sat, tours 11am & 3pm Mon-Fri, 11am Sat

The tastings at this estate include a couple of sparkling wines and one of the vineyard's excellent range of white, red and dessert wines and brandies. No wonder it's so popular. At the Saturday session, stand by for the proprietor's party trick of slicing open a bottle of bubbly with a sabre. Try the wines in paired combinations with food at the Haute Cabrière Cellar (p194).

CHAMONIX Map p49

☎ 021-876 2494; www.chamonix.co.za; Uitkyk St; tastings R15; ⏰ 9.30am-4.30pm, cellar tours 11am & 3pm by appointment

The tasting room at this winery is in a converted blacksmith's workshop; there's also a range of schnapps and mineral water to sample. The pretty restaurant La Maison de Chamonix (mains R70-90; ⏰ lunch Mon-Sun, dinner Fri & Sat) has a reasonably priced lunch menu. You can also stay in self-catered cottages (R200 per person) amid the vineyards.

GRAHAM BECK Map p49

☎ 021-874 1258; www.grahambeckwines.co.za; Rte 45; tastings free; ⏰ 9am-5pm Mon-Fri, 9am-2pm Sat

As at the main estate out at Robertson, the buildings here are all determinedly modern with some striking contemporary sculptures to match. Its eminently drinkable products include fizzers that give French champagnes a run for their money, and the Rhona Muscadel that's heaven in a glass.

GRANDE PROVENCE Map p193

☎ 021-876 8600; www.grandeprovence.co.za; Main Rd, Franschhoek; tastings R12; ⏰ 10am-6pm Nov-Apr, 9am-5pm May-Oct

A beautifully revamped 18th-century manor house is home to a stylish restaurant and a splendid gallery showcasing the best local artists. In the tasting room you can try the very easy-drinking Angel Tears blends or the more upmarket Grande Provence wines. The Jonkershuis lounge (used for meetings and conferences) is worth a look and if you really want to push the boat out, the luxurious Owner's Cottage is available to sleep in.

FRANSCHHOEK & PAARL WINE REGIONS

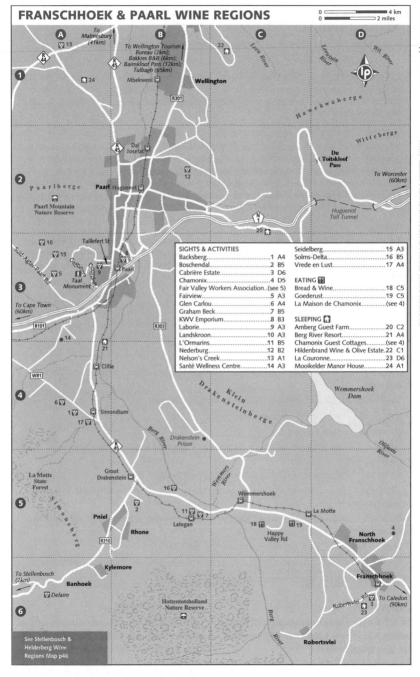

0 —————— 4 km
0 —————— 2 miles

To Malmesbury (41km)

To Wellington Tourism Bureau (2km); Bakkies B&B (6km); Bainskloof Pass (12km); Tulbagh (65km)

Wellington

Mbekweni

R301

Leeu River

Leeustein River

Wit River

Hawekwaberge

Wittenberge

Dal Josefat

Paarlberge

Paarl   Huguenot

Paarl Mountain Nature Reserve

Du Toitskloof Pass

To Worcester (60km)

Huguenot Toll Tunnel

Taillefert St

Suid-Agter-Paarl Rd

Paarl

Taal Monument

To Cape Town (60km)

R101

R303

Cillie

WR1

Simondium

Berg River

Drakenstein Prison

Klein Drakensteinberge

Wemmershoek Dam

Olifants River

La Motte State Forest

Groot Drakenstein

Wemmers River

Wemmershoek

La Motte

Simonsberg

Pniel

Rhone

R310

Lategan

Happy Valley Rd

North Franschhoek

Kylemore

Banhoek

Delaire

Hottentotsholland Nature Reserve

Franschhoek

Robertsvlei Rd

To Caledon (90km)

Berg River

Robertsvlei

To Stellenbosch (2km)

See Stellenbosch & Helderberg Wine Regions Map p46

SIGHTS & ACTIVITIES

Backsberg	1 A4
Boschendal	2 B5
Cabrière Estate	3 D6
Chamonix	4 D5
Fair Valley Workers Association	(see 5)
Fairview	5 A3
Glen Carlou	6 A4
Graham Beck	7 B5
KWV Emporium	8 B3
Laborie	9 A3
Landskroon	10 A3
L'Ormarins	11 B5
Nederburg	12 B2
Nelson's Creek	13 A1
Santé Wellness Centre	14 A3
Seidelberg	15 A3
Solms-Delta	16 B5
Vrede en Lust	17 A4

EATING 🍴

Bread & Wine	18 C5
Goederust	19 C5
La Maison de Chamonix	(see 4)

SLEEPING 🏠

Amberg Guest Farm	20 C2
Berg River Resort	21 A4
Chamonix Guest Cottages	(see 4)
Hildenbrand Wine & Olive Estate	22 C1
La Couronne	23 D6
Mooikelder Manor House	24 A1

WINE FOR BEGINNERS *by Al Simmonds*

Just starting out? Use this handy guide and you'll never be caught confusing your vin rouge with your vanity.

Starting Off

It's a good idea to decide on a cellar before you head off, and to call ahead to make sure they're open and that they have space for tasting (many can get very busy from December to March). Allow around an hour for every estate you visit (not including stopping for food). It's worth joining at least one cellar tour; these can be fascinating. Appoint a designated driver.

Tasting

Most cellars will ask you to buy a tasting glass, or include one in the tasting price. These are generally marked with the estate logo, so double as souvenirs. Don't ask for too much wine; estates tend to put a cap on how much they'll let you drink. When tasting, try to ask for wines by cultivar (see below) – this makes it seem like you're choosing a wine by type and taste rather than if it's drinkable (or cheap). Try to start with dry white wines, then move on to red, and sweet/dessert wines last. Smell the wine and pour some into your mouth. Do not swallow, and spit it out after a few swirls into a spittoon. Clear your palate with some water and continue. Note that smoking is not allowed in tasting rooms.

Ageing

The age of a wine can determine when it should be drunk. Usually the wine maker decides how long a wine will age in the bottle before it is released. Most wines are made to be drunk soon after being bought; finer wines, usually reds, benefit from additional 'ageing' by the consumer. Ask the estate when its wines will be ready for drinking, and match this with your needs.

Buying

You can buy wines by the bottle or case to take with you, but most estates have home-delivery services and will allow you to buy mixed cases (bottles of different labels). Wines start at about R30 per bottle, with a very good wine usually costing around R60 per bottle. Fork out R100 and up, and you'll get a smashing bottle of vino.

Quick Glossary

aroma – the smell of a wine; some people use the term aroma for younger wines and bouquet for those that have been aged

blend – a mix of two or more cultivars in one wine, eg colombard-chardonnay

body – the tactile impression of wine in your mouth

cru – a particular vineyard of merit

cultivar – also known as 'varietal', this refers to the type of grape grown and used in cultivation, eg zinfandel, pinotage, riesling

dry – a wine that is not sweet, one that can feel rough or dry in the mouth

estate wine – wine made from grapes grown only on the estate in question, as opposed to that made with grapes bought from another estate

finish – the impression a wine leaves in the mouth after it is drunk, particularly in terms of length and persistence of flavour

plonk – a corruption of 'blanc', used to refer to cheap or poor-tasting wine

vintage – the year in which the grapes used in making a particular wine were harvested, often applied to an excellent label

---

L'ORMARINS Map p49

☎ 021-874 1026; www.lormarins.co.za; off Rte 45; tastings R20; ☽ 9am-4.30pm Mon-Fri, 10am-3pm Sat, tours by appointment

A pleasant enough estate, but it's the wines that have punters coming back for more. Try its excellent selection of dry white blends.

SOLMS-DELTA Map p49

☎ 021-874 3937; www.solms-delta.com; Delta Rd, off R45, Franschhoek; tastings free; ☽ 9am-5pm

Only a couple of wines have been produced so far by the current owners of this 300-year-old wine farm, but a visit here is highly recommended to view the **Museum**

Van de Caab, in the original wine cellar. This remarkable museum tells the story of the Delta wine farm from the perspective of the people who worked and still work on it – the presentation of extensive research is excellent. Outside you can see the archaeological site of the farm's first homesteads. Sixty percent of the vineyard's profits goes back to the employees.

VREDE EN LUST Map p49
☎ 021-874 1611; www.vnl.co.za; cnr Rte 45 & Klapmuts Rd, Simondium; tastings R15; ☼ 10am-5pm
The first vintage for this replanted vineyard was released in 2002, although the estate dates back to 1688 when original owner Jacques de Savoye named it 'Peace and Eagerness'. It specialises in blends. The location and buildings are very attractive and there's a deli and restaurant where you can try locally made cheeses and bread.

PAARL
For information about wineries in the area other than those listed here, contact Paarl Vintners (☎ 021-872 3841). For information on other sights in the area, and for sleeping and eating options, see p195.

FAIRVIEW Map p49
☎ 021-863 2450; www.fairview.co.za; Suid-Agter-Paarl Rd, off Rte 101; tastings R10; ☼ 8.30am-5pm Mon-Fri, 8.30am-1pm Sat
This is a wonderful winery, though perhaps not the place to come for a calm wine tasting. Peacocks and goats in a tower (apparently goats love to climb) greet you on arrival, and tastings are great value since they cover two dozen wines *and* a wide range of goat's- and cow's-milk cheeses. You can sample and buy the pinotage and chenin blanc of the Fair Valley Workers Association (p42) here too.

GLEN CARLOU Map p49
☎ 021-875 5528; www.glencarlou.co.za; Simondium Rd, Klapmuts; tastings free; ☼ 9am-4.45pm Mon-Fri, 9am-1pm Sun
A quaint estate, with a new gallery and tasting room with panoramic views of Tortoise Hill. Its shiraz is made with a small percentage of viognier and mourvèdre grapes.

KWV EMPORIUM Map p49
☎ 021-807 3007; www.kwv-international.com; Kohler St; tastings R20; ☼ 9am-4pm Mon-Sat
This is one of the country's best-known wineries because its products are mostly sold overseas. Some KWV port and sherry is available inside South Africa, and its fortified wines, in particular, are among the world's best. Cellar tours are at its complex near the railway line. Call for times of cellar tours (R20), which are worth taking if only to see the enormous Cathedral Cellar that was built in 1930.

LABORIE Map p49
☎ 021-807 3390; www.kwv-international.com; Taillefert St; tastings R9; ☼ 9am-5pm Oct-Apr, 9am-5pm Mon-Sat May-Sep
Laborie is KWV's attractive showcase vineyard, located just off Main Rd. It's known for its shiraz and Alambic Brandy. The restaurant (☎ 021-807 3095; mains R45-70) is in an old Cape Dutch building and serves dishes such as springbok shanks and kingklip.

LANDSKROON Map p49
☎ 021-863 1039; Suid-Agter-Paarl Rd, off Rte 101; tastings R10; ☼ 8.30am-5pm Mon-Fri, 9am-1pm Sat
Five generations of the De Villiers family have been perfecting their wine-making skills on this pleasant estate. Overlooking the vines, there's a nice terrace on which you can quaff the cabernet sauvignon and celebrated port.

NEDERBURG Map p49
☎ 021-862 3104; www.nederburg.co.za; off Meaker Rd; tastings R10; ☼ 8.30am-5pm Mon-Fri, 10am-2pm Sat year-round, 10am-4pm Sat, 11am-4pm Sun Dec-Mar
This is one of South Africa's most well known labels. It's a big but professional and welcoming operation featuring a vast range of wines. It offers an informative food and wine tasting (R20) that teaches you which types of flavour the wines will work best with. The picnic lunches cost R90 per person (December to March only, bookings essential) and are very popular. Nederburg is off the N1 exit 62, 7km east of Paarl.

SEIDELBERG Map p49

☎ 021-863 3495; www.seidelberg.co.za;
Suid-Agter-Paarl Rd, off Rte 101; tastings
with/without cellar tour R18/12; ⏱ 9am-6pm
Mon-Fri, 10am-6pm Sat & Sun

Tucked in between Fairview and Lands-
kroon, serene Seidelberg offers an escape
from the bacchanalian hordes. Uniquely
it features tours and demonstrations of
on-site bronze casting and glass-blowing,
with a corresponding gallery. There's a
restaurant offering light meals and terrific
views, perfectly complemented by a strong
selection of reds.

OTHER WINE REGIONS

If you have more time, a trip further afield to the
wine-growing regions of Robertson (Map p186),
Tulbagh (Map p186) and Darling (Map p186) should
prove rewarding. Named, respectively, the **Robertson Wine Valley** (☎ 023-626 3167; www.robert
sonwinevalley.com), the **Tulbagh Wine Route**
(☎ 023-230 1348; www.tulbaghwineroute.com)
and the **Darling Wine Experience** (☎ 022-492
3361), these areas are not as tourist-heavy as the
Cape Winelands yet still boast beautiful estates and
excellent wines.

History ■

History

THE RECENT PAST

Bush fires may be a natural part of Table Mountain's life cycle, but that doesn't make them any more welcome. In January 2006 a cigarette butt allegedly tossed by an English tourist set off a fire on the northern flank of Table Mountain that eventually engulfed a 700-hectare area from Devil's Peak to Lion's Head. A 65-year-old British tourist died from smoke inhalation but, although hundreds of people were evacuated, no homes were damaged.

In contrast, regular blazes throughout the year lay waste to hundreds of shacks in the townships, leaving thousands with nothing other than the clothes they stand in. The clearly overstretched fire brigade complains of underpay and poor working conditions – some members hadn't even received a new uniform since the time of apartheid.

Fires of quite another type were also snuffed out on Clifton Beach No 2 in late January 2006. Audiences of around 1000 were attending the Monday-night drumming circle on the beach, accompanied by the pyrotechnics of a group of fire dancers. The well-heeled residents of Clifton complained, prompting a squadron of police to raid the beach, snuffing out spectators' candles, searching bags for alcohol (illegal on the beach) and other substances, and generally being spoilsports.

Also messing up Cape Town's life was the troubled Koeberg nuclear power station, which at full capacity provides just under half of the Western Cape's peak electricity demand. On Christmas Day 2005, one of Koeberg's two generation units was shut down due to damage caused by a loose bolt left behind during routine maintenance. Intermittent power cuts followed and became more frequent when Koeberg's second power unit failed a couple of months later. There was chaos as the robots (traffic lights) failed and cash registers and computers seized up. Sales of generators soared.

The power cuts, combined with charges of corruption and cronyism levelled at the city's African National Congress (ANC)–controlled council, led to the party narrowly losing out to the Democratic Alliance (DA) in the municipal elections of March 2006. Although the third-placed Independent Party refused to work with the DA, negotiations with other smaller parties secured the DA's Helen Zille as Cape Town's new major. That same day the country's last white president, FW de Klerk, celebrated his 70th birthday at a party in the Mount Nelson Hotel where Nelson Mandela was the surprise guest of honour on a list that read like a who's who of modern South Africa.

FROM THE BEGINNING
THE SAN & KHOIKHOI PEOPLES

South Africa lays strong claim to being the cradle of mankind. At Langebaan Lagoon (north of Cape Town), the discovery of 117,000-year-old fossilised footprints prompted one researcher to speculate that 'Eve' (the very first human, the common ancestor of us all) lived here.

Little is known about these first humans, but there are signs that they conducted funerals, an indication of at least basic culture. Academics don't know whether the earliest-recorded inhabitants of South Africa – the San people – are direct descendants or if they returned to the area after aeons of travel anything between 40,000 and 25,000 years ago.

The term Khoisan is used to describe both the San who were nomadic hunters and gatherers, and the Khoikhoi (also known as Khoekhoen, possibly meaning 'Men of Men') who were seminomadic hunters and pastoralists. It is believed the Khoikhoi developed from San

c 100,000 BC	AD 1488
San people settle Southern Africa	Bartholomeu Dias sails around the Cape of Good Hope

groups in present-day Botswana. For centuries, perhaps even millennia, the San and the Khoikhoi intermarried and coexisted, so the distinction was by no means clear.

Culturally and physically, the Khoisan developed differently from the Negroid peoples of Africa, although it's possible that they came into contact with pastoralist Bantu-speaking tribes as, in addition to hunting and gathering food, they became pastoralists, with cattle and sheep. The Khoisan migrated south, reaching the Cape of Good Hope about 2000 years ago. It was not uncommon for impoverished Khoikhoi to revert to a hunter-gatherer existence, or for the San to acquire domestic animals.

FIRST EUROPEAN VISITORS

The first recorded Europeans to sight the Cape were the Portuguese, who passed by on their search for a sea route to India and for the most precious of medieval commodities: spices. Bartholomeu Dias rounded the Cape in 1488, naming it Cabo da Boa Esperança (Cape of Good Hope), but didn't linger long, as his sights were fixed on the trade riches of the east coast of Africa and the Indies.

The Portuguese had no interest in a permanent settlement. The Cape offered them little more than fresh water, since their attempts to trade with the Khoisan often ended in violence, and the coast and its fierce weather posed a terrible threat to their tiny caravels.

By the end of the 16th century, English and Dutch traders were beginning to challenge the Portuguese, and the Cape became a regular stopover for their scurvy-ridden crews. In 1647 a Dutch vessel was wrecked in Table Bay; its crew built a fort and stayed for a year before they were rescued.

This crystallised the value of a permanent settlement in the minds of the directors of the Dutch East India Company (Vereenigde Oost-Indische Compagnie; VOC). They had no intention of colonising the country, but simply wanted to establish a secure base where ships could shelter and stock up on fresh supplies of meat, fruit and vegetables.

THE DUTCH ARRIVE

Jan van Riebeeck was chosen by the VOC to lead an expedition of 80 company employees – mainly poorly educated soldiers and sailors – charged with building a fort, bartering with the Khoisan for meat, and planting a garden. He reached Table Bay on 6 April 1652, built a mud-walled fort not far from the site of the stone Castle of Good Hope (p93) that survives today, and planted the gardens now known as the Company's Gardens (p93).

1652	c 1690
The Dutch establish a settlement in Table Bay (Cape Town)	Boers move into the hinterland around present-day Cape Town

Kirstenbosch Botanical Gardens (p105)

The Dutch were not greeted with open arms by either the San (later to be called Bushmen by the European settlers) or the Khoikhoi (likewise called Hottentots); intermittent hostilities broke out. In 1660, in a gesture that took on an awful symbolism, Van Riebeeck planted a wild almond hedge to protect his European settlement from the Khoisan. The hedge ran around the western foot of Table Mountain down to Table Bay, and a section of it can still be seen in the Kirstenbosch Botanical Gardens (p105). The irony was that contact between the Europeans and the Khoisan would prove far more dangerous for the locals, who were mortally vulnerable to the guns and diseases of the colonists.

The Khoisan proving uncooperative, the Cape settlement was soon suffering a chronic labour shortage. From 1657 Van Riebeeck started releasing VOC employees, allowing them to farm land independently, thus beginning the colonisation process of Southern Africa and giving birth to the Boers (see opposite). The following year he began to import slaves from West Africa, Madagascar, India, Ceylon, Malaya and Indonesia, among other places. By the time the slave trade was ended in 1807, some 60,000 slaves had been brought to the Cape, laying the foundations for the unique mix of cultures and races found here today.

THE SETTLEMENT GROWS

The process of colonisation kicked off a series of wars between the Khoikhoi and the Dutch in which the locals were obviously no match for the well-armed and organised Europeans. The Dutch, who were keen to bolster their numbers, allowed some 200 Huguenots, French Calvinists fleeing persecution by King Louis XIV, to settle on the Cape in 1688.

There was a shortage of women in the colony, so female slaves and Khoisan women were exploited both for labour and for sex. In time, the slaves intermixed with the Khoisan, too. The offspring of these unions form the basis of sections of today's coloured population.

Under the VOC's almost complete control, Kaapstad (the Dutch name for Cape Town) provided a comfortable European lifestyle for a growing number of artisans and entrepreneurs servicing ships and crews. By the middle of the 18th century there were around 3000 people living in the riotous port, known as the 'Tavern of the Seas' by every navigator, privateer and merchant travelling between Europe and the East (including Australia).

1795	1808
British capture Cape Town	Slave trade abolished

THE BRITISH TAKE OVER

As the 18th century progressed, the global power of the Dutch was waning and under challenge by the British. The fourth Anglo-Dutch War was fought between 1780 and 1783. French regiments were sent to Cape Town to help the Dutch defend the city, but the British eventually prevailed at the Battle of Muizenberg in 1795 and took control of the Cape from the VOC, which by then was bankrupt.

The Treaty of Amiens (1803) had the British cede the Cape back to the Dutch, but this proved just a lull in the Napoleonic Wars. In 1806 at Bloubergstrand, 25km north of Cape Town, the British again defeated the Dutch. The colony was ceded to the British on 13 August 1814.

The British abolished the slave trade in 1808 and the remaining Khoisan were finally given the explicit protection of the law (including the right to own land) in 1828. These moves contributed to Afrikaners' dissatisfaction and their mass migration, which came to be known as the Great Trek, inland from the Cape Colony.

Despite outlawing slavery, the British introduced new laws that laid the basis for an exploitive labour system little different from slavery. Thousands of dispossessed blacks sought work in the colony, but it was made a crime to be in the colony without a pass – and without work. It was also a crime to leave a job.

CAPE ECONOMY BOOMS

The British introduced free trade, which greatly benefited Cape Town's economy. Cape wines, in particular, were a huge hit, accounting for some 10% of British wine consumption by 1822. During the first half of the 19th century, before the Suez Canal opened, British officers serving in India would holiday at the Cape.

Capetonians successfully managed to stop the British government's attempt to turn the colony into another Australia when their governor, Sir Harry Smith, forbade 282 British prisoners from leaving the ship *Neptune* when it docked in Cape Town in 1849. The *Neptune* continued to Tasmania and the Capetonians, who had challenged the might of the empire, became bolder in their demands for self-government.

In 1854 a representative parliament was formed in Cape Town, but much to the dismay of Dutch and English farmers to the north and east, the British government and Cape liberals insisted on a multiracial constituency (albeit with financial requirements that excluded the vast majority of blacks and coloureds).

In 1860 construction of the Alfred Basin in the docks commenced, which finally provided Cape Town with a stormproof port. The opening of the Suez Canal in 1869 dramatically decreased the amount of shipping that sailed via the Cape, but the discovery of diamonds and gold in the centre of South Africa in the 1870s and '80s helped Cape Town maintain its position as the country's premier port.

Immigrants flooded into the city and the population trebled from 33,000 in 1875 to over 100,000 people at the turn of the 20th century.

WHO ARE THE BOERS?

The Afrikaner population of South Africa today has its roots in the Dutch and early European settlers of the Cape. The more independent of these settlers soon began drifting away from the strict regime of the VOC into the countryside. These were the first of the Trekboers (literally 'Trekking Farmers'), who were later known just as Boers.

Fiercely independent, with livelihoods based on rearing cattle, the Boers were not so different from the Khoisan they came into conflict with as they colonised the interior. Many Boers were illiterate and most had no source of information other than the Bible. Isolated from other Europeans, they developed their own separate culture and eventually their own language, Afrikaans, derived from the argot of their slaves.

1814	1834
Cape Colony ceded to British	Slaves emancipated

ISLAMIC CAPE TOWN

Islam first came to the Cape with the slaves brought by the Dutch from the Indian subcontinent and Indonesia. Although the religion could not be practised openly in the colony until 1804, the presence of influential and charismatic political and religious figures among the slaves helped a cohesive Cape Muslim community to develop. One such political dissident was the exiled Islamic leader Tuan Guru from Tidore, who arrived in 1780. During his 13 years on Robben Island Tuan Guru accurately copied the Quran from memory. In 1798 he helped establish the Owal Mosque, the city's first mosque, in the Bo-Kaap, thus making this area the heart of the Islamic community in Cape Town, as it still is today.

Tuan Guru is buried in the Bo-Kaap's Tana Baru cemetery, one of the oldest in South Africa, at the western end of Longmarket St. His grave is one of the 20 or so *karamats* (tombs of Muslim saints) encircling Cape Town and visited by the faithful on mini pilgrimages. Other *karamats* are found on Robben Island (that of Sayed Abdurahman Matura), at the gate to the Klein Constantia wine estate (that of Sheik Abdurachman Matebe Shah), and by the Eerste River in Macassar (that of Sheik Yussof, the most significant Muslim leader of his time).

Despite fears during the 1990s that Cape Town could become embroiled in violent Islamic fundamentalism (see p63), religious divisions and suspicion are not something that mark the city today. You'll encounter many friendly faces while wandering around the Bo-Kaap, where you can drop by the local museum (p93) to find out more about the community. A sizable Muslim community also lived in Simon's Town before the Group Areas Act evictions of the late 1960s. Its history can be traced at the Heritage Museum (p108) in Simon's Town.

One of the most important events in Islamic Cape Town's calendar is Eid, the last night of Ramadan, falling at the end of October or early November. Some 6000 Muslims bring a picnic to break the fast and gather along Sea Point's promenade to watch the moon rise.

BOER WAR & AFTER

After the Great Trek, the Boers established several independent republics, the largest being the Orange Free State (today's Free State province) and the Transvaal (today's Northern Province, Gauteng and Mpumalanga).

When the world's richest gold reef was found in the Transvaal (a village called Johannesburg sprang up beside it), the British were miffed that the Boers should control such wealth and precipitated war in 1899. The Boers were vastly outnumbered but their tenacity and knowledge of the country resulted in a long and bitter conflict. The British finally defeated them in 1902.

Cape Town was not directly involved in any of the fighting but it did play a key role in landing and supplying the half a million imperial and colonial troops who fought on the British side. The Mount Nelson Hotel was used as headquarters by Lords Roberts and Kitchener.

Bubonic plague in 1901 gave the government an excuse to introduce racial segregation, even though the disease had actually arrived in the Cape on a ship from Argentina. Blacks were moved to two locations, one near the docks and the other at Ndabeni on the western flank of Table Mountain. This was the start of what later would develop into the townships of the Cape Flats.

After the war, the British made some efforts towards reconciliation, and instituted moves towards the union of the separate South African provinces. In the Cape, blacks and coloureds retained a limited franchise (although only whites could become members of the national parliament, and eligible blacks and coloureds constituted only around 7% of the electorate), but did not have the vote in other provinces.

The issue of which city should become the capital was solved by the unwieldy compromise of making Cape Town the seat of the legislature, Pretoria the administrative capital, and Bloemfontein the judicial capital. The Union of South Africa came into being in the year of 1910.

1881	1899
Boers defeat British, and Transvaal becomes South African Republic	Anglo-Boer War starts; finishes in 1902

APARTHEID RULES

Afrikaners were economically and socially disadvantaged when compared with the English-speaking minority, which controlled most of the capital and industry in the new country. This, plus lingering bitterness over the war and Afrikaners' distaste at having to compete with blacks and coloureds for low-paying jobs, led to strident Afrikaner nationalism and the formation of the National Party (NP).

In 1948 the National Party came to power on a platform of apartheid (literally, 'the state of being apart'). In a series of bitter court and constitutional battles, the right of coloureds to vote in the Cape was removed (blacks had been denied the vote since 1910) and the insane apparatus of apartheid was erected.

Mixed marriages were prohibited, interracial sex was made illegal and every person was classified by race. The Group Areas Act defined where people of each 'race' could live and the Separate Amenities Act created separate public facilities: separate beaches, separate buses, separate toilets, separate schools and separate park benches. Blacks were compelled to carry passes at all times and were prohibited from living in or even visiting towns without specific permission.

The Dutch Reformed Church justified apartheid on religious grounds, claiming the separateness of the races was divinely ordained. The *volk* (literally, the 'people', but it really meant just Afrikaners) had a holy mission to preserve the purity of the white race in its promised land.

FICTIONAL HOMELANDS

A system of Homelands was set up in 1951, whereby the proportion of land available for black ownership in South Africa increased very slightly to 13%. Blacks then made up about 75% of the population. The Homelands idea was that each black group had a traditional area where it belonged – and must now stay. The government defined 10 such groups, which were based largely on dubious 19th-century scholarship. The area around Cape Town was declared a 'coloured preference area', which meant that no black person could be employed unless it could be proved that there was no coloured person suitable for the job.

Apart from the inequity of the land allocation, not to mention the injustice of making decisions for and about people who were not allowed to vote, this plan ignored the huge numbers of blacks who had never lived in their 'Homeland'. Millions of people who had lived in other areas for generations were forcibly removed and dumped in bleak, unproductive areas with no infrastructure.

The Homelands were regarded as self-governing states and it was planned that they would become independent countries. Four of the 10 Homelands were nominally independent by the time apartheid was demolished (they were not recognised as independent countries by the UN), and their dictators held power with the help of the South African military.

Of course, the white population depended on cheap black labour to keep the economy booming, so many black 'guest workers' were admitted to South Africa. But, unless a black had a job and a pass, they were liable to be jailed and sent back to their Homeland. This caused massive disruption to black communities and families. Not surprisingly, people without jobs gravitated to cities such as Cape Town to be near their husbands, wives and parents.

No new black housing was built, and as a result, illegal squatter camps mushroomed on the sandy plains to the east of Cape Town. In response, government bulldozers flattened the shanties, and their occupants were dragged away and dumped in the Homelands. Within weeks, inevitably, the shanties would rise again.

1910	1923
Union of South Africa created, federating the British colonies and the old Boer republics; blacks denied the vote	Black Urban Areas Act passed, a main element in the development of segregation and discrimination

MANDELA JAILED

In 1960 the ANC and the Pan-African Congress (PAC) organised marches against the hated pass laws, which required blacks and coloureds to carry passbooks authorising them to be in a particular area. At Langa and Nyanga on the Cape Flats, police killed five protesters. The Sharpeville massacres in Gauteng were concurrent and resulted in the banning of the ANC and PAC.

In response to the crisis, a warrant for the arrest of Nelson Mandela (see the boxed text, opposite) and other ANC leaders was issued. In mid-1963 Mandela was captured and sentenced to life imprisonment. Like many black leaders before him, Mandela was imprisoned on Robben Island (p100), in the middle of Table Bay. He remained here until 1982 when he was moved to Pollsmoor Prison south of Constantia on the Cape. His final place of incarceration was Victor Vester Prison near Paarl.

The government tried for decades to eradicate squatter towns, such as Crossroads, which were focal points for black resistance to the apartheid regime. In its last attempt between May and June 1986, an estimated 70,000 people were driven from their homes and hundreds were killed. Even this brutal attack was unsuccessful in eradicating the towns, and the government accepted the inevitable and began to upgrade conditions. Since then vast townships have sprung up across the Cape Flats. No-one knows exactly how many people call them home, but it could be more than 1.5 million. For more about the history of the townships see p110.

THE COLOURED EXPERIENCE

Apartheid's divide-and-rule tactics – favouring coloureds above blacks – stoked the animosity that lingers between the Cape's coloured and black communities today (see p12). Even so, coloureds did suffer under apartheid, and none more so than those living in the poor inner-city area known as District Six.

In its time District Six, immediately east of the city centre, was the suburb that, more than any other, gave Cape Town its cosmopolitan atmosphere and life. Every race lived there and the streets were alive with people, from children to traders, buskers to petty criminals. Jazz was its life blood and the district was home to many musicians, including the internationally renowned pianist Dollar Brand (now called Abdullah Ibrahim, see p34).

In 1966 District Six was classified as a white area. Its 50,000 people, some of whose families had been there for five generations, were gradually evicted and dumped in bleak and soulless townships like Athlone, Mitchell's Plain and Atlantis. Friends, neighbours, and even relations were separated. Bulldozers moved in and the multiracial heart was ripped out of the city, while in the townships, depressed and dispirited youths increasingly joined gangs and turned to crime.

The coloured Cape Muslim community of the Bo-Kaap, on the northeastern edge of Signal Hill, was more fortunate. Home to Cape Town's first mosque (the Owal Mosque on Dorp St dates back to 1798), the district was once known as the Malay Quarter because it was where many of the imported slaves from the start of the Cape Colony lived with their masters.

In 1952 the entire Bo-Kaap region was declared to be a coloured area under the terms of the Group Areas Act. There were forced removals, but the residents of the community, which was more homogeneous than that of District Six, banded together in order to successfully fight for and retain ownership of their homes, many of which were declared National Monuments in the 1960s (so, fortunately, at least they were saved from the bulldozers).

1948	1960
National Party wins government and retains control until 1994; apartheid laws begin to be passed	Sharpeville massacres; ANC and PAC banned

NELSON MANDELA

His Xhosa name Rolihlahla translates as 'Trouble Maker' although today Nelson Mandela is more often called Madiba, an honorary title adopted by elders of his clan – a mark of respect for a man without whom the country would most likely not be the peaceful and successful place it is today. A Nobel-peace-prize winner (together with FW de Klerk in 1993), he's been awarded honorary doctorates by countless universities around the world, and even had a nuclear particle named after him.

On 2 May 1994, after 27 years in prison and even more fighting the apartheid system, he said, 'This is the time to heal the old wounds and build a new South Africa'. It's a testament to his force of personality, transparent decency and integrity that Mandela, a man once vilified by the ruling whites, helped unite all South Africans at the most crucial of times.

The son of the third wife of a Xhosa chief, Mandela was born on 18 July 1918 in the small village of Mveso on the Mbashe River. A bright and determined child, he eventually overcame prejudice and his own poverty to qualify as a lawyer, setting up a practice with Oliver Tambo in Johannesburg (Jo'burg). In 1944 he helped form the Youth League of the African National Congress (ANC) with Walter Sisulu and Oliver Tambo. Its aim was to end the racist policies of the white South African government.

Mandela's stature as a future leader of the country grew during the 1950s when he and 156 other ANC and Communist Party members were charged with and later cleared of treason. Such was Mandela's threat to the government that he was forced to go underground to continue the struggle. He was captured and sentenced to life imprisonment in 1963.

It wouldn't be until 1990 that he would be freed. A year later he was elected president of the ANC and continued the long negotiations (which had started secretly while he was in prison) to end minority rule. In the first free elections in 1994, he was elected president of South Africa.

The prison years inevitably took their toll not only on his health but also on his marriage to the increasingly renegade Winnie; in 1992, the couple separated, and were divorced in 1996.

In 1998, a year after he retired as ANC president, he married Graca Machel, the widow of a former president of Mozambique, on his 80th birthday. Despite announcing his official retirement from the international stage in 2004, this charismatic man remains pretty active. Some of his time is taken up with the **Nelson Mandela Foundation** (www.nelsonmandela.org), which tackles the problems faced by people with HIV/AIDS and children in rural schools in South Africa.

For more information read Mandela's autobiography, *Long Walk to Freedom*, the first draft of which was written while he was still on Robben Island, and Anthony Sampson's exhaustive *Mandela: The Authorized Biography*. Also check out www.pbs.org/wgbh/pages/frontline/shows/mandela, the informative website of a documentary series on Mandela, and the Mandela page of the ANC's website (www.anc.org.za/people/mandela/).

1963	1985
Nelson Mandela, Walter Sisulu and others jailed for life	State of emergency declared in South Africa; official murder and torture become rife, black resistance strengthens

NOOR EBRAHIM'S STORY

'I used to live at 247 Caledon St,' begins Noor Ebrahim, pointing at the street map covering the floor of the District Six Museum. Noor is one of the 60,000-plus people forcibly removed from the inner-city district during the 1960s and '70s. His story is one of the many you can discover on a visit to the District Six Museum (p94).

Noor's grandfather came to Cape Town in 1890 from Surat in India. An energetic man who had four wives and 30 children, he built up a good business making ginger beer. Noor's father was one of the old man's sons to his first wife, a Scot called Fanny Grainger, and Noor grew up in the heart of District Six. 'It was a very cosmopolitan area. Many whites lived there – they owned the shops. There were blacks, Portuguese, Chinese and Hindus all living as one big happy family.'

'We didn't know it was going to happen,' remembers Noor of the 1966 order declaring District Six a white area under the Group Areas Act. 'We saw the headlines in the paper and people were angry and sad but for a while little happened.' Then in 1970 the demolitions started and gradually the residents moved out.

Noor's family hung on until 1976, when they were given two weeks to vacate the house that his grandfather had bought some 70 years previously. By that time they'd seen families, neighbours and friends split up and sent to separate townships determined by their race. They'd prepared by buying a new home in the coloured township of Athlone – otherwise they'd have been forced to go to Mitchell's Plain, today one of the most violent suburbs on the Cape Flats.

Noor will never forget the day he left District Six. 'I got in the car with my wife and two children and drove off, but only got as far as the corner before I had to stop. I got out of the car and started to cry as I saw the bulldozers move in immediately. Many people died of broken hearts – that's what apartheid was. It was really sick.'

As a way of reclaiming his destroyed past, Noor, like several other former District Six residents, wrote a book and, since 1994, has worked as a guide at the museum. He was naturally delighted when the land was officially handed back to former residents in 2000, although he is yet to return.

'My life was in District Six.' he says. 'My heart and home was there. I'm really looking forward to going back.'

PATH TO DEMOCRACY

In the 1980s the apartheid regime began to crumble amid deepening economic gloom caused by international sanctions and the increasing militancy of black opposition groups (which began with the Soweto student uprising in 1976).

In 1982 Nelson Mandela and other ANC leaders were moved from Robben Island to Pollsmoor Prison in Cape Town. (In 1986 senior politicians began secretly talking with them.) In 1983 the United Democratic Front (UDF) was formed when 15,000 antiapartheid activists gathered at Mitchell's Plain in the Cape Flats. At the same time the state's military crackdowns in the townships became even more brutal.

In early 1990 President FW de Klerk began to repeal discriminatory laws, and the ANC, PAC and Communist Party were legalised. On 11 February Nelson Mandela was released. His first public speech since he had been incarcerated 27 years earlier was delivered from the balcony of City Hall to a massive crowd filling the Grand Pde.

From this time onwards virtually all the old apartheid regulations were repealed and, in late 1991, the Convention for a Democratic South Africa (Codesa) began negotiations on the formation of a multiracial transitional government and a new constitution extending political rights to all groups.

Months of negotiations and brinkmanship finally produced a compromise and an election date, although at considerable human cost. Political violence exploded across the country during this time, some of it sparked by the police and the army. Despite this, the 1994 election was amazingly peaceful.

The ANC won 62.7% of the vote, less than the 66.7% that would have enabled it to rewrite the constitution. In Western Cape, though, the majority coloured population voted in the NP as the provincial government, seemingly happier to live with the devil they knew than with the ANC.

1990	1991
ANC, PAC and Communist Party bans lifted; Nelson Mandela freed	Talks on a new constitution begin, political violence escalates

RISE & FALL OF PAGAD

During the 1990s drugs and the associated crime became such a problem in the Cape that communities, and in particular the coloured community, began to take matters into their own hands. People against Gangsterism and Drugs (Pagad) was formed in 1995, as an offshoot of the Islamic organisation Qibla. The group saw itself as defending the coloured community from the crooked cops and drug lords who allowed gangs to control the coloured townships.

At first the police tolerated Pagad, but their vigilante tactics turned sour in 1996 with the horrific (and televised) death of gangster Rashaad Staggie. A lynch mob burned then repeatedly shot the dying gangster. Other gang leaders were killed but Cape Town really began to worry when bombs, believed to have been planted by the more radical of Pagad's members, began to go off around the city. One of the worst was in 1998 at Planet Hollywood at the Waterfront, although by 2000 many other explosions had happened at police stations, synagogues and a gay nightclub. In September 2000 a magistrate presiding in a case involving Pagad members was murdered in a drive-by shooting.

Although Pagad leader Abdus Salaam Ebrahim was imprisoned in 2002 for seven years for public violence, no-one has been convicted, let alone charged for the Cape Town bombings, which thankfully seem to have stopped. Pagad, now designated a terrorist organisation by the government, keeps a much lower and quieter profile.

SHIFTING ALLIANCES

In December 1997 Mandela stepped down as ANC president and was succeeded by his deputy, Thabo Mbeki. Two years later South Africa held its second free elections. There had been speculation that the ANC vote might drop, but in fact it increased, putting the party within one seat of the two-thirds majority that would allow it to alter the constitution.

In the Western Cape elections in 2000, however, the ANC fared worse. The pact between the old NP, restyled as the New National Party (NNP), and the Democratic Party (DP) to create the Democratic Alliance (DA), brought them victory not only in the provincial elections but also in the metropolitan elections. Two years later, in a previously unthinkable alliance, the NNP ditched the DP to join forces with the ANC, putting the ANC in control of Cape Town for the first time and bringing the city its very first black female mayor, Nomaindia Mfeketo.

TRUTH & RECONCILIATION COMMISSION

One of the first acts of the new ANC government was to set up the Truth & Reconciliation Commission (TRC) to expose the crimes of the apartheid era. This admirable institution carried out Archbishop Desmond Tutu's dictum: 'Without forgiveness there is no future, but without confession there can be no forgiveness'. Many stories of horrific brutality and injustice were heard by the commission during its five-year life, offering some catharsis to individuals and communities shattered by their past.

The TRC operated by allowing victims to tell their stories and perpetrators to confess their guilt, with amnesty offered to those who made a clean breast of it. Those who chose not to appear before the commission face criminal prosecution if their guilt can be proven, and that's the problem. Although some soldiers, police and 'ordinary' citizens have confessed their crimes, it seems unlikely that those who gave the orders and dictated the policies will ever come forward (former president PW Botha was one famous no-show), and gathering evidence against them has proven difficult.

For more about the TRC read the award-winning account *Country of My Skull* by journalist and poet Antjie Krog, or Desmond Tutu's balanced and honest *No Future Without Forgiveness*.

1993	1994
New constitution enacted, signalling end of apartheid and birth of new South Africa	Democratic elections held; Nelson Mandela succeeds FW de Klerk as South African president

Conscious of their core vote in the Cape Flats the ANC-led city council vowed to improve the lot of township folk by upgrading the infrastructure in the informal settlements and investing more in decent low-cost housing, such as the N2 Gateway Project along the motor corridor linking the city with the airport. Urban renewal projects were also announced for Mitchells Plain, one of the most populous coloured areas of the city. Meanwhile, the City Bowl and surrounding areas continued to benefit from increased security and the development of ritzy, loft-style apartments in grand, old structures such as Mutual Heights (p97).

Full integration of the city's mixed population, though, is a long way off, if it's achievable at all. The vast majority of Capetonians continue to live in the bleak, impoverished communities of the Cape Flats, split along racial lines and suffering horrendous economic, social and health problems.

1997

Mandela retires as ANC president, succeeded by Thabo Mbeki

2004

First of the returnees to District Six are handed keys to their rebuilt homes

Table Mountain National Park

Table Mountain National Park

To the Khoisan (Khoesaan) who lived on the peninsula long before Europeans arrived, it was Hoerikwaggo (Mountain in the Sea) a place of legend and life-giving fresh water. To Nelson Mandela and his fellow prisoners on Robben Island it was a beacon of hope. To the millions of people who have climbed or been transported in the cableway to its 1088m peak, it is the ultimate viewpoint over the city. We're talking about Table Mountain, Cape Town's icon, and star attraction of **Table Mountain National Park** (Map p68; ☎ 021-701 8692; www.tmnp.co.za).

The park covers 24,500 hectares, about 73% of the entire Cape Peninsula, and stretches from Signal Hill to Cape Point, encompassing both Devil's Peak and Lion's Head, which abut Table Mountain, as well as the Silvermine Nature Reserve, Tokai, Boulders Beach and the Cape of Good Hope Nature Reserve. All these areas are covered in this chapter, as are details of the ground-breaking series of overnight hikes through the park (see p75) launched in 2005.

HISTORY

At over 100 sites in the national park, such as Peers Cave (see p72) in Silvermine and a cave in Smitswinkel Bay near the entrance to Cape Point, evidence has been found of the indigenous people who lived on the Cape long before the first recorded arrival of Europeans in 1503. This is when Portuguese navigator Admiral Antonio de Saldanha bagged the title of the first white guy to climb Table Mountain; he named it Taboa do Cabo (Table of the Cape). The Dutch thought this name appropriate, too, and so it stuck. It was the Dutch who coined the term Lion's Head (Leeuwen Kop).

At the Cape Point end of the national park, the name game also got underway with the Portuguese. Bartholomeu Dias coined the name Cabo da Boa Esperança (Cape of Good Hope), which by a smidgen qualifies as the southwesternmost point of the African continent; a recently discovered cross carved into the rock near here could indicate the spot where Dias stepped onto the Cape in 1488. In comparison to the port that grew rapidly at the foot of Table Mountain, Europeans were slow to come to live in rugged, windswept Cape Point, the first farms being granted here in the 1780s. The areas really didn't become fully accessible until 1915 when the coastal road from Simon's Town was completed.

The campaign to designate the Cape Point area a nature reserve first got underway in the 1920s when there was a chance that the land could have been turned over to developers. At the same time the future prime minister General Jan Smuts – a keen hiker – started a public appeal to secure formal protection for Table Mountain; there's a track on the mountain named after him. The Cape of Good Hope Nature Reserve was eventually secured in 1939. This was the first formal conservation on the Cape, although Cecil Rhodes (see p105) had used

SUNPATHS OF TABLE MOUNTAIN

Dean Liprini, an archaeoastronomer, has been researching what he believes to be the sacred sites of the Khoisan and perhaps even older people on the Cape for the last 15 years. His astonishing theory is that the Cape is crisscrossed by a grid of sight lines and carefully selected points comprising caves, sound chambers, geometrical marker stones and sun and moon shrines, some in the uncanny shape of giant human faces. Sunrise and sunset is exactly aligned with these points at the summer and winter solstices and the spring and autumn equinoxes, thus indicating they formed a way for the ancient people to measure the passing of the year and record auspicious dates.

As whacky as it may sound, there is certainly something in Liprini's theory, as you'll discover if you take a tour with him or one of his colleagues (p75). Observed from certain angles, unmistakable profiles of faces appear in the rocks, some with 'eye' holes that catch the light – one such rock is a granite boulder on Lion's Head, while another is the 'Pyramid All Seeing Eye' just off the M6 between Glencairn and Sunnydale. Liprini's hikes will also take you to the Cave of Ascension, above the ancient burial site of Peers Cave (p72), and to Llandudno on the coast where the setting sun casts an eerie trail of light though the giant granite boulders. To find out more about the sunpaths, check the website www.sunpath.co.za or buy Liprini's recently published book *Pathways of the Sun*.

a small part of this vast fortune to buy up much of the eastern slopes of Table Mountain; he gifted this land, which includes Kirstenbosch and the Cecilia Estate stretching to Constantia Nek, to the public in his will.

Although the Van Zyl Commission in the 1950s baulked at creating a single controlling authority for the park, in 1958 all land on Table Mountain above the 152m contour line was declared a National Monument. The city of Cape Town proclaimed the Table Mountain Nature Reserve in 1963 and the Silvermine Nature Reserve in 1965. By the 1970s 14 different bodies were in control of the publicly owned natural areas of the Cape – a situation that was obviously unsatisfactory. It would take until the end of apartheid before all the various bodies could be brought to the table, and it wasn't until 1998 that a single Cape Peninsula National Park became a reality. In 2004 the park was renamed Table Mountain National Park.

THE LAND

Table Mountain's flat-top shape as we know it today probably first came about 60 million years ago, although the mountain as a whole started to be thrown up about 250 million years, making it the elder statesman of world mountains. In comparison, the Alps are only 32 million years old and the Himalayas 40 million years old.

The types of rock that make up the mountain and the Cape Peninsula are broken into three major geological types. The oldest, dating back 540 million years, is Malmesbury shale – this forms the base of most of the City Bowl and can be seen along the Sea Point shoreline, on Signal Hill and on the lower slopes of Devil's Peak. It's fairly soft and weathers easily. The second oldest is the tough Cape granite, which forms the foundation for Table Mountain and can also be seen on Lion's Head and the boulders at Clifton and Boulders Beaches. The third type of rock is called Table Mountain Sandstone, a combination of sandstone and quartzite.

It's thought that originally the summit of Table Mountain was a couple of kilometres higher that it is today. Over time this rock has weathered to create the distinctive hollows and oddly shaped rocks found on the mountain's summit and at Cape Point. The sandy soil on top of these rocks is very poor in nutrients. The plants that grow in this soil – the *fynbos* (see p68) – don't make for very good eating, hence the lack of large herbivores grazing in the region.

THE TWELVE APOSTLES

One of the most dramatic features of Table Mountain is the series of buttresses that runs down its western flank behind Camps Bay. They're known as the Twelve Apostles even though there are well over 12 of them and none is individually named after an apostle! The Dutch called them De Gevelbergen, which means Gable Mountains; the current name is said to have been coined by British governor Sir Rufane Donkin in 1820.

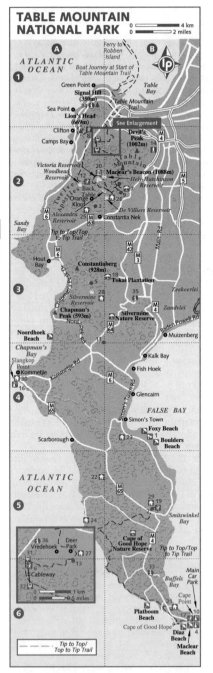

TABLE MOUNTAIN NATIONAL PARK

FLORA

In June 2004 the Cape Floristic Region (CFR) was awarded World Heritage status. The CFR, which covers the entire Cape Peninsula, is the richest and smallest of the world's six floral kingdoms and home to some 8200 plant species – more than three times as many per square kilometre as in the whole of South America! Table Mountain and the peninsula alone contain 2285 plant species, more than in all of Britain.

The most common type of vegetation is *fynbos* (from the Dutch meaning 'fine bush'; pronounced fain-bos). *Fynbos* somehow thrives in the area's nitrogen-poor soil – it's supposed that the plants' fine, leathery leaves improve their odds of survival by discouraging predators. *Fynbos* is composed of three main elements: proteas (including the king protea, South Africa's national emblem), ericas (heaths and mosses) and restios (reeds). Walking through the park you'll see many common examples of *fynbos* flowers, such as gladiolus, freesias and daisies, all of which have been exported to other parts of the world.

On Signal Hill and the lower slopes of Devil's Peak you'll find the second main type of vegetation in the park, *renosterbos* (literally 'rhinoceros bush'), composed predominantly of a grey ericoid shrub, and peppered with grasses and geophytes (plants that grow from underground bulbs). In the cool, well-watered ravines on the eastern slopes of Table Mountain you'll also find small pockets of Afro-montane forest, such as at Orange Kloof where only 12 entry permits are issued daily.

While the biodiversity of the Cape Peninsula is incredible, it is also threatened. More than 1400 *fynbos* plants are endangered or vulnerable to extinction; some have minute natural ranges. Most *fynbos* plants need fire to germinate and flower, but unseasonal and accidental fires – such as the one that swept across the northern flank of Table Mountain in January 2006 – can cause great harm. The fires burn far longer and more fiercely, too, because of the presence of alien plants (see the boxed text, below), such as the various pines and wattles that also pose a threat because of the vast amounts of water they suck up.

FAUNA

The animal most closely associated with Table Mountain is the dassie (rock hyrax). Despite the resemblance to a plump hamster, these small furry animals are – incredibly – related to the elephant. You'll most likely see dassies sunning themselves on rocks around the upper cableway station.

Other than dassies, the national park is home to well over 100 invertebrates and two vertebrates (including the incredibly rare Table Mountain ghost frog) not found anywhere else on earth. Among the feral population of introduced fallow deer that roam the lower slopes of Table Mountain around the Rhodes Memorial, you may spot an animal long regarded as extinct: the quagga. This partially striped zebra was formerly thought to be a distinct species, but DNA obtained from a stuffed quagga in Cape Town's South African Museum showed it to be a subspecies of the widespread Burchell's zebra. A breeding programme, started in 1987, has proved successful in 'resurrecting' the quagga.

Mammals in the Cape of Good Hope Nature Reserve include eight antelope species, Cape mountain zebras and a troupe of Chacma baboons. Many signs warn you not to feed the baboons (and you shouldn't – they're potentially dangerous; see p73).

BATTLING THE ALIEN INVASION

As well as guns and diseases, the European colonists also brought their plants to the Cape, some of which have proved to be aggressively invasive and damaging to the environment. Pines, oaks, poplars, wattles and three species of hakea were planted.

The park has recognised the need to bring these thirsty alien invaders under control. A public-private partnership campaign **Ukuvuka** (www.ukuvuka.org.za) was started in the wake of the devastating forest fires that swept across the Cape in 2000. Ukuvuka is Xhosa (isiXhosa) for 'Wake Up'. The campaign aims to rid the peninsula of invasive alien plants, rehabilitate fire-damaged areas and educate vulnerable communities, such as the townships, about fires. This programme and others have been successful so far, clearing around a third of the park's management area of invasive aliens. They have also helped employ nearly 300 people from the townships adjacent to the park.

It's not just alien plants that have been destructive to the Cape environment, but also imported animals, such as fallow deer and the Himalayan tahr. In 1936 a pair of tahrs escaped from Groote Schuur Zoo on the slopes of Devil's Peak; by the 1970s that couple had multiplied into a herd of 600, wreaking much damage throughout the park. A culling programme has since brought the tahr population under control.

Across the park there's an abundance of bird and insect life. The most famous birds are the jackass penguins, so called because of their donkeylike squawk. You'll find some 3000 of the friendly penguins at Boulders Beach (p72).

The national park's area of responsibility also extends out to sea, with a single 975-sq-km Marine Protected Area being proclaimed in 2003. On the False Bay side you'll be able to spot southern right and humpback whales (p109). Dolphins, Cape fur seals at Duiker Island (reached from Hout Bay; see p103) and loggerhead and leatherback turtles are among the other marine animals you could hope to see.

SAFETY

Just because Table Mountain National Park is on the doorstep of the city doesn't make this wilderness area, extending above 1000m, any less dangerous and unpredictable. Hardly a week goes by without some accident or fatality on the mountain, often due to a climbing expedition gone wrong. More people have died on Table Mountain than on Mt Everest. The mountain fires of recent years have also claimed their victims, and there have been reports of muggings on the slopes of Table Mountain and Lion's Head.

To ensure visitor safety there are around 60 staff and an equal number of volunteers on hand in the park; you'll find park visitor information centres (Map p68) on Signal Hill, the Tafelberg Rd, Platteklip Gorge, Lion's Head and Deer Park. At the Table Mountain National Park Head Office visitors can find out more about various areas of the park, pick up leaflets, buy books, and register and pay for various hikes and accommodation in the park. Visitors themselves should also be well prepared before setting off into the park. Even if taking the cableway to the summit, be aware that the weather up top can change very rapidly.

However hot it is, it's always a good idea to hike with long trousers. The *fynbos* may look soft and feathery but much of it is tough and scratchy. There's also the seriously nasty blister bush (its leaves look like those of continental parsley); if you brush against this plant it can leave blisters on your skin that refuse to heal for years.

If you do run into problems or believe that others are in trouble call **Metro Wilderness Search & Rescue** (☎ 10177, from a mobile phone 112).

MAPS, BOOKS & WEBSITES

The national park endorses the pictorial *Mountains in the Sea: Table Mountain to Cape Point*, by John Yeld, as the best single guidebook. It is indeed an impressive store of information, covering practically everything you'd care to know about the park, including guides to flora and fauna and the most popular walks. The maps in the guide are produced by Peter Slingsby, whose series of handy, detailed maps covering different sections of the park also get the thumbs up from the park authorities and the Mountain Club of South Africa. Slingsby's website, www.themaps.co.za, includes some free downloads of maps.

One good map that covers the entire peninsula is the handsome *National Geographic AdventureMAP*, produced in conjunction with Map Studio. As its title suggests the map covers all kinds of adventures you could have on the Cape, apart from hiking or climbing in the national park.

Mike Lundy's regularly updated *Best Walks in the Cape Peninsula* remains a popular choice for casual hikers; each month

TABLE MOUNTAIN DOS & DON'TS

The following are a few basic dos and don'ts for tackling the national park.

Do

- Tell someone the route you're planning to climb and take a map (or, better still, a guide).
- Take plenty of water and some food.
- Take weatherproof clothing – the weather can change for the worse with lightning speed.
- Wear proper hiking boots or shoes and a sun hat.
- Take a mobile phone, if you have one.

Don't

- Climb alone.
- Leave litter on the mountain.
- Make a fire on the mountain – they're banned.

you'll find details of one of his walks posted on the www.hikecapetown.co.za website. You could also search out Shirley Brossy's *A Walking Guide for Table Mountain*, which details 34 walks in the park, or *Table Mountain Classics*, by Tony Lourens, which will be of interest to more-serious mountain climbers as it covers routes where ropes are necessary. Walks and a hell of a lot of other activities are covered in Fiona McIntosh's useful *Table Mountain Activity Guide*.

Other helpful books are *Wild About Cape Town*, by Duncan Butchart, a pocket-sized photo guide to the common animals and plants on the peninsula. For those interested in geology, John Compton's *The Rocks and Mountains of Cape Town* and Map Studio's fold-out map and chart *How The Cape Got Its Shape* are worth searching out.

SIGHTS

The following section covers the main sights within the park, starting with the cableway and moving down the peninsula to Cape Point. For details of Signal Hill, which is part of the park, see p96, and for hikes within the park, see p73.

CABLEWAY Map p68

☎ 021-424 8181; www.tablemountain.net; one way/return adult R60/110, child R30/60; ☼ 8.30am-7pm Feb-Nov, 8am-10pm Dec-Jan

Riding the cableway up Table Mountain is a no-brainer; the views from the revolving car and the summit are phenomenal. Once you are at the top there are souvenir shops, a café and some easy walks to follow. Departures are every 10 minutes in high season (December to February) and every 20 minutes in low season (May to September), but the cableway doesn't operate when it's dangerously windy, and there's obviously not much point going up if you are simply going to be wrapped in the cloud known as the 'tablecloth'. Call in advance to see if it's operating. The best visibility and conditions are likely to be first thing in the morning or in the evening.

If you don't have your own transport, Rikkis (☎ 021-418 6713; www.rikkis.co.za; ☼ 7am-7pm Mon-Fri, 8am-4pm Sat) will come up here for R16; a non-shared taxi will cost around R50.

RESERVOIRS Map p68

On the area of Table Mountain known as the Back Table, you'll find five dams and reservoirs created in the late 19th and early 20th centuries to provide a secure water supply for the booming population of Cape Town. Work commenced on the first dam in 1890 and the 995-megalitre reservoir, Woodhead Reservoir, was named after the mayor of the time Sir John Woodhead when it was eventually completed in 1897. At the same time the independent municipality of Wynberg began working on a series of dams: Victoria Reservoir was completed in 1896, Alexandra Reservoir was finished in 1903 and the De Villiers Reservoir in 1907. The city of Cape Town also added the 924-megalitre Hely-Hutchinson Reservoir (named after Governor Sir Walter Hely-Hutchinson) in 1904.

In hikes around the Back Table you can admire the construction skill and detail of these dams and learn something of their history at the Waterworks Museum (☎ 021-686 3408). This small building at the northern corner of the Hely-Hutchinson Reservoir is often closed, but is usually opened if you're on one of the Hoerikwaggo Trails hikes (p75). Inside, various bits of machinery used to build the dams are displayed, including the Barclay locomotive made in Scotland in 1898, dismantled and reconstructed on top of the mountain.

TOKAI PLANTATION Map p68

This wooded area, south of Constantia, is a favourite spot for picnics and walks, the most challenging of which is the 6km hike to Elephant's Eye Cave within the Silvermine Nature Reserve. The zigzag path is fairly steep and offers little shade as you climb higher up Constantiaberg (928m), so bring a hat and water. At the walk's base you'll find the Tokai Arboretum, a historic planting of 1555 different trees representing 274 species, begun in 1885 by Joseph Storr Lister, the conservator of forests for the Cape Colony. There's a pleasant café here where you can pick up a map of walks in the area.

To reach the forest from the city centre, follow the M3 towards Muizenberg and take the Retreat and Tokai exit.

SILVERMINE NATURE RESERVE Map p68

☎ 021-715 0011; www.tmnp.co.za; Ou Kaapse Weg; adult/child R10/5; ☉ 7am-6pm Oct-Mar, 8am-5pm Apr-Sep

This reserve is named after the fruitless attempts by the Dutch to prospect for silver in this area from 1675 to 1685. Today the reserve's focal point is the **Silvermine Reservoir**, constructed in 1898. It's a beautiful spot for a picnic or leisurely walk around the reservoir on a boardwalk that is wheelchair accessible. The reservoir waters are tannin stained and although there are signs forbidding swimming, you'll often find locals taking a dip here.

On the southeastern edge of the reserve is **Peers Cave**: a trail leads here from a marked parking spot on the Ou Kaapse Weg. The cave, which is actually an overhang, is named after Victor Peers, who with his son Bertie, started excavating the site in 1927, collecting evidence of the Khoisan's habitation of the area dating as far back as 10,000 years. The most dramatic find was of an 11,000-year-old-skull; it's thought this was an ancient burial site. Declared a National Monument in 1941, the cave provides a dramatic viewpoint out across Noordhoek towards the sea and is well worth visiting.

BOULDERS BEACH PENGUIN COLONY Map p68

☎ 021-701 8692; www.tmnp.co.za; adult/child R20/5; ☉ 7am-7.30pm Dec-Jan, 8am-6.30pm Feb-May & Sep-Nov, 8am-5pm Jun-Aug

Some 3km south of Simon's Town is Boulders, a picturesque area with a number of large boulders and small sandy coves, within which you'll find Boulders Beach, home to a colony of 3000 jackass (African) penguins. Delightful as they are, the penguins are also pretty stinky, which may put you off from getting too close.

There are two entrances to the penguins' protected area. The first, as you come along Queens Rd (the continuation of St George's St) from Simon's Town, is at the end of Seaforth Rd; the second is at Bellevue Rd, where you'll also find accommodation and places to eat. You can observe the penguins from the boardwalk at Foxy Beach and at Boulders Beach. The sea is calm and shallow in the coves, so Boulders is popular with families and can get extremely crowded, especially on holidays and weekends.

Rikkis (☎ 021-418 6713; www.rikkis.co.za; ☉ 7am-7pm Mon-Fri, 8am-4pm Sat) meet all trains to Simon's Town and also go to Boulders.

Penguins, Boulders Beach (above)

BABOON MATTERS

The signs at Cape Point warning you not to feed the baboons are there for a reason. After years of interacting with tourists, the baboons will quite happily grab food from your hands or climb in the open doors and windows of your car to get at it. *Never* challenge them as they will turn aggressive. The damage inflicted might end up being far more serious than baboon crap over your car seats, so keep an eye out and your food carefully hidden away.

Showing a much gentler side to baboon life is the project **Baboon Matters** (☎ 021-783 3882; www.baboon matters.org.za; adult/child R200/100). On a two-to-three-hour guided hike you'll get to spend time observing a baboon troop at very close quarters – it's an amazing experience. The tours usually depart from the **Southern Right Hotel** (Map pp244–5; 14 Glen Rd, Glencairn), but the guides can pick you up from anywhere in Simon's Town. The project was started to help preserve the Chacma baboon population, estimated at 247 and dangerously close to extinction on the Cape. Monitors have been employed to keep the baboons out of the villages where they come into conflict with humans; 25% of the tour fee goes towards the project.

CAPE OF GOOD HOPE NATURE RESERVE Map p68

☎ 021-780 9204; www.tmnp.co.za; adult/child R45/15; ⏱ 6am-6pm Oct-Mar, 7am-5pm Apr-Sep
With truly awesome scenery, some fantastic walks and deserted beaches, plus the chance to spot wildlife (including bonteboks, elands and zebras), a visit to this nature reserve (known locally as Cape Point) can easily swallow up a day. You'll not have seen the half of it if you go on one of the many tours, which whip into the reserve, pause at the **Buffelsfontein Visitor Centre** (Map p68; ☎ 021-780 9204; www.tmnp.co.za), then allow you just enough time to walk to Cape Point, grab lunch, and get your picture snapped at the Cape of Good Hope (Africa's most southwesterly point) on the way back.

The best way to explore the reserve is on foot or by bike. It's particularly beautiful in spring, when the wild flowers are in bloom. Get a map at the entrance gate if you plan to go walking, but bear in mind that there is minimal shade in the park and the weather can change quickly. Also see p74 for details of the reserve's popular two-day hike.

It's not a hard walk, but if you're feeling lazy a **funicular railway** (one way/return adult R32/24, child R16/12; ⏱ 10am-5pm) runs up from beside the restaurant to the souvenir kiosk next to the **old lighthouse** (1860). The old lighthouse was too often obscured by mist and fog, so a new lighthouse was built at Dias Point in 1919 – take the thrilling walkway along the rocks here to avoid the crowds.

There are some excellent beaches, usually deserted. This can make them dangerous if you get into difficulties in the water, so take care. One of the best beaches for swimming or walking is **Platboom Beach**, and the pretty one at **Buffels Bay** is also safe for swimming. **Maclear Beach**, near the main car park, is good for walks or diving but is too rocky for enjoyable swimming. Further down towards Cape Point is beautiful **Diaz Beach**. Access is on foot from the car park.

If you forget to bring your own picnic, sandwiches and snacks can be bought at the Buffelsfontein Visitor Centre and a shop next to the funicular, where you'll also find the Two Oceans restaurant, which is generally packed with tour-bus crowds.

Numerous tour companies include Cape Point on their itineraries; both **Day Trippers** (p91) and **Downhill Adventures** (p150) are recommended because they offer the chance to cycle within the park. The only public transport to the Cape is with **Rikkis** (☎ 021-418 6713; www.rikkis.co.za; ⏱ 7am-7pm Mon-Fri, 8am-4pm Sat), which run from Simon's Town train station. The best option is to hire a car for the day, so you can explore the rest of the peninsula.

HIKING

There are hundreds of routes on Table Mountain alone, covering everything from easy strolls to extreme rock climbing. Signage on the routes is improving (see the boxed text, p75), but it's far from comprehensive and even with a map it's easy to get lost; read our safety tips (p70) before setting off. Below we cover details of the most popular routes.

Apart from hiking, the park provides an ideal venue for many other activities, such as abseiling, mountain biking, rock climbing and paragliding – details of these can be found in the Activities chapter (p150).

CLIMBING TABLE MOUNTAIN

None of the routes up Table Mountain are easy, but the **Platteklip Gorge** (Map p68) walk on the City Bowl side is at least straightforward. Unless you're fit, try walking down before you attempt the walk up. It takes about 2½ hours from the upper cableway station to the lower, taking it fairly easy. Be warned that the route is exposed to the sun and, for much of the way, a vertical slog.

Another far-trickier possibility recommended for experienced climbers only is the **India Fenster** (Map p68) route that starts from directly behind the lower cableway station and heads straight up. The hikers you see from the cableway, perched like mountain goats on apparently sheer cliffs, are taking this route.

Relaxing on a deck overlooking Table Mountain

The **Pipe Track** (Map p68) is a less-steep route that runs along the west side of the mountain towards the Twelve Apostles; it's best walked in the early morning before the sun hits this side of the mountain.

There are also two popular routes up the mountain from Kirstenbosch Botanical Gardens along either **Skeleton Gorge** (Map p68; which involves negotiating some sections with chains) or **Nursery Ravine** (Map p68). These can be covered in three hours by someone of moderate fitness. The trails are well marked, and steep in places, but the way to the gardens from the cableway and vice versa is not signposted.

CLIMBING LION'S HEAD

The 45-minute, 2.2km hike from Kloof Nek to the peak of Lion's Head (Map p68) is deservedly popular. A lot of people do it as an early-morning constitutional and it's a ritual to go up on and watch the sun go down a full-moon night. The moonlight aids the walk back down, although you should always bring a torch (flashlight) and go with company. The track is easy to follow and its start is clearly marked at the top of Kloof Nek Rd, where you'll also find a national park information hut; it involves a little climbing but there are chains on the rocks to help.

CAPE OF GOOD HOPE TRAIL

You'll need to book to walk the two-day/one-night Cape of Good Hope Trail, which traces a spectacular 33.8km circular route through the reserve. The cost is R88 (not including the reserve entry fee) with accommodation at the basic Protea and Restio huts at the southern end of the reserve. Contact the reserve's **Buffelsfontein Visitor Centre** (Map p68; ☎ 021-780 9204; www.tmnp.co.za) for further details.

There are plenty of other great walks in the reserve if you don't have time for the two-day trail. On the False Bay side, try the straightforward 3.5km walk from **Buffels Bay** to the spectacular Paulsberg peak, whose sheer cliff plunges 369m into the sea.

GUIDED HIKES

Check **Cumhike** (www.cumhike.org.au) and the **Trails Club of South Africa** (www.trailsclub.co.za) for details of guided hikes held each weekend, many in the national park. Also contact the **Buffelsfontein Visitor Centre** (Map p68; ☎ 021-780 9204; www.tmnp.co.za) about volunteer guided walks each weekend in the Cape of Good Hope Nature Reserve, and about the two-day Cape of Good Hope circular trail throughout the reserve, for which you need to make a reservation.

HOERIKWAGGO TRAILS

In 2005 Table Mountain National Park launched the first of its planned trio of **Hoerikwaggo Trails** (www.hoerikwaggotrails.co.za), designed to allow visitors, for the first time, to sleep on the mountain, and eventually to hike 80km or so from the City Bowl to Cape Point.

The three-day **Table Mountain Trail** is a fully guided hike starting at the Waterfront with a boat ride out into Table Bay and proceeding through the City Bowl to spend the night at the historic Plattenklip Wash Houses (p76) in Vredehoek, on the lower northern slopes of the mountain. On day two the hike continues up to the cableway and then to the summit and across to the Overseer's Cottage (p76), beside the De Villiers Reservoir on Table Mountain's Back Table. On the final day you explore the Back Table, including the reservoirs and Waterworks Museum (see p71), and descend via the eastern slopes of the Mountain to Kirstenbosch Botanical Gardens (p105).

The trail costs R1900 per person (based on double occupancy of a room), which includes all meals, portering of luggage and accommodation of a very high standard. There's a maximum of 16 people on a hike.

By the start of 2007 the less-pampered **Tip to Top Trail** should be up and running. This six-day, five-night guided hike beginning at Cape Point will involve carrying your own food, gear and sleeping bag and camping at fixed spots in or close to the park. The proposed route will have hikers camping the first night at Smitswinkel Bay on False Bay and continuing up this coast to spend the second night at an old navy signal station above Simon's Town. On day three the route crosses the peninsula to the Atlantic coast, with the night spent in the wireless station next to the lighthouse at Slangkop Point. On day four the hike continues along the beach to Chapman's Peak and on to the Silvermine Nature Reserve where you'll stay in the Silvermine camp site. Day five takes you through the reserve to Orange Kloof. On the final day you'll head for Plattenklip Gorge for the climb down into the City Bowl.

By the end of 2007 a luxury version **Top to Tip**, running in the opposite direction, and sleeping in comfortable huts, should be available.

KABBO AFRICAN ADVENTURES
☎ 021-701 0867, 072 024 6537;
www.kabboadventures.com
Using accredited mountain guides, this operation has put together its own version of the Hoerikwaggo Trail, using the Mountain Club's hut on the Back Table as well as backpackers and camping sites close to the City Bowl to Cape Point route. An overnight trip to the mountain costs R725, while a summit hike or sunrise/sunset walk is R320.

SUNPATH
☎ 072 417 6800; www.sunpath.co.za;
tours R100-325
Dean Liprini and his fellow guides will take you on a series of fascinating hikes into the national park and around the peninsula to discover the ancient sunpaths thought to have been used by the indigenous people of the Cape (see p67).

VENTURE FORTH
☎ 021-556 4150; www.ventureforth.co.za
Excellent guided hikes and rock climbs with enthusiastic, savvy guides. Outings (start-ing from R400 per person) are tailored to individual requirements and aim to get you off the beaten track.

THE PEOPLE'S PARK

Though Table Mountain National Park records about 4.5 million visitors a year, relatively few of these visits are from Cape Town's coloured and black communities. There are historical reasons for this: during the apartheid era the entire mountain area was declared a whites-only area. Even today many coloured and black Capetonians still see the park as somewhere only for the rich, the whites and the tourists.

To achieve its aim of 'a park for all, forever' the park authorities have thought about ways to encouraged disadvantaged groups onto the mountain. Upgrading of the park's paths and signs, and training of guides for the trail has provided employment for over 300 people from townships. Also, the first Hoerikwaggo Trail to be launched in June 2005 was the two-day, one-night People's Trail aimed at school groups. The trail runs from Constantia Nek up the Back Table through Orange Kloof to stay the night at the basic People's Cottage.

SLEEPING

If you're not on one of the Hoerikwaggo Trail hikes (p75), the only accommodation you'll be able to book in the national park is Olifantsbos and Eland & Duiker Cottages at Cape Point.

TABLE MOUNTAIN

Until the national park launched its Hoerikwaggo Trails the only hut for sleeping on the mountain was that belonging to the Mountain Club of South Africa (p155). Now hikers on the Table Mountain Trail (p75) can stay at the revamped Overseer's Cottage (Map p68) beside De Villiers Reservoir on the Back Table. Actually consisting of two cottages, the Overseer's Cottage

is decorated in a smart, contemporary style, with a comfortable lounge heated by an open fire – very welcome when night falls or the weather changes for the worse. The rooms have either bunk beds or single beds.

In Vredehoek, on the edge of Deer Park, one of the Platteklip Wash Houses (Map p68) has been converted into very stylish accommodation for the first night of the Table Mountain Trail. The decoration here includes pieces by top Capetonian craftspeople and there's also Internet access. In good weather meals are eaten outside beside the *bomah* (sunken campfire circle) and there are hammocks to relax in.

CAPE OF GOOD HOPE RESERVE

For bookings for all the following contact the Buffelsfontein Visitor Centre (Map p68; ☎ 021-780 9204; www.tmnp.co.za).

The pretty whitewashed cottage Olifantsbos (Map p68; 1-6 people R1750, annexe per person R185) is an excellent self-catering option in an isolated position just steps from the beach and the pounding waves of the Atlantic. Together with its annexe it sleeps a maximum of 12 people.

The Eland & Duiker Cottages (Map p68; 1-6 people R590) also sleep a maximum of six people each and are located at the northern section of the reserve. Currently the simple but pleasantly decorated cottages share a compound with the reserve's offices, but there are plans to move these out and turn the area over entirely to tourists. One nice feature are the cottages' outdoor showers.

On the two-day Cape of Good Hope Trail, accommodation is in Erica in one of the stone cottages on the north side of De Gama Peak that were once part of a WWII radar station; their elevated position allows you to see both sunset and sunrise. The dormitory sleeps six in bunk beds and you need to bring your own sleeping bag and cater for yourself. There's a hot shower.

Sights ■

Sights

Cape Town's mountainous geography means that to see the pick of the city's sights you'll travel the length and breadth of the peninsula. The area we define as the City Centre – including the Bo-Kaap, Waterkant and Gardens areas – will be where you'll most likely spend the bulk of your time. Commonly known as the City Bowl, Cape Town's compact commercial heart is squeezed between the northern flank of Table Mountain, Signal Hill and Table Bay.

The rest of the city naturally falls into four other districts. The section called Beaches & Suburbs under the Atlantic Coast heading covers all the coastal communities between Blou-bergstrand in the northeast down to Hout Bay. The mountainous nature of the peninsula means that the smaller, more southerly Atlantic coast communities of Noordhoek, Kommetjie and Scarborough are more easily visited as part of a trip around False Bay. Hence you'll find details of these places, along with coverage of Muizenberg, Kalk Bay, and the naval port of Simon's Town in the False Bay & Southern Peninsula section.

Heading west around Table Mountain and Devil's Peak will bring you to the Southern Suburbs, beginning with the bohemian, edgy areas of Woodstock and Observatory, and moving through to the increasingly salubrious Rondebosch, Newlands and Constantia. In stark contrast are the vast black townships and poor coloured suburbs southeast of Table Mountain known collectively as the Cape Flats. Here you'll find Langa, Athlone, Guguletu, Crossroads and, the biggest community of all, Khayelitsha.

For information on Table Mountain National Park, which covers around 75% of the peninsula, see p66. And see each section in this chapter and the Directory (p208) for transport details.

ITINERARIES

One Day

Ride the cableway up **Table Mountain** (p71). After admiring the view and stretching your legs, return to the city and wander through the leafy **Company's Gardens** (p93), nipping into the **SA National Gallery** (p98) to sample the best of the country's art. Get a taste of African cuisine at **Café African Image** (p124) or join the style set at **Birds Café** (p124), then head over to the **District Six Museum** (p94). If you've managed to get a ticket, take an afternoon tour of **Robben Island** (p100); otherwise the colourful **Bo-Kaap, Long St** (p161) and **Greenmarket Square** (p162) beckon for souvenir shopping. If you've been to Robben Island, it's convenient to hang out at the Waterfront, say having cocktails at **Alba Lounge** (p139), dinner at **One.Waterfront** (p130), then maybe taking in a jazz performance at the **Green Dolphin** (p144) or **Mannenburg's Jazz Café** (p144). If you've stayed in the City Bowl, then dine at **Ginja** (p126) or **Madame Zingara** (p126), and grab a nightcap at **Marvel** (p137) or **Gallery Bar** (p137) on Long St.

Three Days

Kick off day two by exploring the southern end of the Cape Peninsula and the False Bay coast. The obvious destination is magnificent **Cape of Good Hope Nature Reserve** (Cape Point; p73), where you could easily spend the whole day. However, it would be

---

IT'S FREE

You don't need to spend a huge amount to have a good time in Cape Town and there are quite a few places where you don't need to spend anything at all! Although there is no shortage of ways to lighten the pocket at the **Waterfront** (p101), the buskers and musical performances are free, as is watching the comings and goings around the harbour.

There's no charge for hiking in **Table Mountain National Park** (p66) or lazing on any of the Cape's plentiful range of beaches. Entry to the **Company's Gardens** (p93) is free and, if you can get yourself out to the wineries of **Constantia** (p44) most wine tastings are gratis. Entry to the both the **SA National Gallery** (p98) and **South African Museum** (p99) is by donation only on Saturday, as it is every day at the **Michaelis Collection** (p96) in Greenmarket Sq.

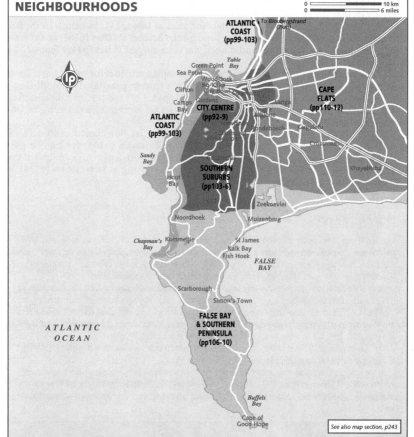

a shame to miss out on charming **Simon's Town** (p107), the cute penguin colony at **Boulders** (p72), and the antique shops and picturesque fishing harbour at **Kalk Bay** (p106). A good option for lunch is Kalk Bay's **Olympia Café** (p133). Fine bars such as the **Brass Bell** (p141) and **Polana** (p141) mean there's every reason to hang around in the evening, too.

On day three explore the southern suburbs, starting with a visit to the lovely **Irma Stern Museum** (p104) and then a spot of wine tasting in **Constantia** (p44); lunch at **La Colombe** (p132) is recommended but make sure you book. Work off the calories with an afternoon stroll around **Kirstenbosch Botanical Gardens** (p105). On the way back into town, drop by the **Rhodes Memorial** (p105), with its sweeping view across the Cape Flats. Put on your dancing shoes in the evening and head over to the Waterkant, dining at the **Nose Wine Bar** (p138) or **Anatoli** (p127), and bopping the night away with the gorgeous guys and girls at **Cruz** (p138) or **Bronx** (p138).

One Week

Head out of town on day four. Beautiful scenery and a fantastic choice of wine and cuisine make the Winelands around **Stellenbosch** (p188), **Franschhoek** (p193) and **Paarl** (p195) the obvious choice. The best place to stop over is Franschhoek, the epicurean capital of the Cape with exceptional restaurants such as **Ici** (p195) and **Reuben's** (p194). On the way there or back, drop by **Vergelegen** (p47), one of the most impressive old wine estates.

Day five might see you taking a half-day tour of the Cape Flats **townships** (opposite). These generally include the District Six Museum, thus freeing up more time to relax on day one. Consider having lunch at a township restaurant, such as **Eziko** (p134) in Langa. In the late afternoon, pack your sun cream and towel and hit the beaches at **Clifton** (p102) or **Camps Bay** (p102); hang out here for drinks and dinner, too – we suggest **La Med** (p140) followed by **Paranga** (p131).

It's time for some of those outdoor, adrenaline-pumping activities for which Cape Town is famous on day six. If the wind is playing ball, do a tandem paraglide (p156) off Lion's Head. Otherwise climb Table Mountain and abseil (p153) off the top, or take a surfing lesson (p157) at Muizenberg. Join the boho student set for an evening's carousing in Observatory at **Café Ganesh** (p131) and **Café Carte Blanche** (p140).

Souvenir shopping at the Waterfront or back in the City Bowl could easily take up your last day in town; drop by **Monkeybiz** (p162) and **Streetwires** (p163) for unique gifts that also help disadvantaged communities. Wrap it all up with a pan-African feast at the **Africa Café** (p126), or the best of modern South African cooking at **Savoy Cabbage** (p126) or **Aubergine** (p129).

FOR CHILDREN

Cape Town, with its fun family attractions such as the **Two Oceans Aquarium** (p101), **Solole Game Reserve** (p110) and **Ratanga Junction amusement park** (p148), is a great place to bring the kids. South Africans tend to be family oriented, so most places cope with children's needs. 'Family' restaurants, such as **Spur** (www.spur.co.za), which has branches all over Cape Town, offer children's portions, as do some of the more upmarket places.

Many of the sights and attractions of interest to parents are also entertaining to kids. The Table Mountain **cableway** (p71), the attractions at the **Waterfront** (p101), especially the seals, which can usually be seen at Bertie's Landing, and **Cape Point** (p73), with its baboons and other animals, delight kids. And while we're on about wildlife, there're always those sure-fire crowd pleasers, the penguins at **Boulders** (p72), and thousands of birds and monkeys to see at **World of Birds** (p103). For a ride on a donkey or camel head to **Imhoff Farm** (p109).

The **Planetarium** (p97) screens a kids' star show daily, and there are plenty of other displays to grab the attention of inquisitive children at the attached **South African Museum** (p99).

At the beach parents should watch out for rough surf (not to mention hypothermia-inducing water temperatures!); the rock pool at **St James** (p119) on the False Bay coast is recommended, as is **Muizenberg beach** (p108) on a warm, calm day. And the **Sea Point Pavilion** (p153) has a great family swimming pool that is significantly warmer than the surrounding ocean.

ORGANISED TOURS

Do not fear: if you're short of time, have a specific interest, or would just like some expert help in seeing Cape Town, there will be an organised tour for you. For details of winery tours see p43.

Harbour Cruises

If only to take in the panoramic view of Table Mountain from the water, a cruise into Table Bay should not be missed. There is a host of operators at the Waterfront waiting to assist you; see www.waterfront .co.za/play/leisure for full details. Other boat cruise options include ones from Hout Bay (see p103) and Simon's Town.

LADY J Map pp252-3

☎ 021-425 0200; victoriacharters@webmail.co.za; Quay 5, Waterfront; adult/child R30/15

Spot the seals and learn about the maritime history of Cape Town on a fascinating 30-minute tour of the Waterfront harbour. This is a good option if the sea is choppy and you don't fancy a longer tour out into Table Bay.

SOUTHERN RIGHT Map p258

☎ 083 257 7760, 021-786 2136; dhurwitz@iafrica .com; Simon's Town harbour jetty, Simon's Town; harbour cruise R30

This company runs the popular 40-minute Spirit of Just Nuisance cruise around Simon's Town harbour. It also offers speedboat trips to Cape Point (adult/child R200/100) and Seal Island (R250/125), where you can see not only hundreds of seals but the sharks who famously breach the water to eat them! During the whale-spotting season (see the boxed text, p109) it also offers cruises to get up close to these magnificent animals.

WATERFRONT BOAT COMPANY

Map pp252-3

☎ 021-418 5806; www.waterfrontboats.co.za; Shop 7, Quay 5, Waterfront

The largest of the Waterfront's boating operations offers a variety of cruises, including short harbour cruises and the highly recommended, 1½-hour sunset cruise (R180) on its handsome wood and brass-fitted schooners *Spirit of Victoria* or *Esperance*. A jet-boat ride is R250 for an hour.

City & Bus Tours

General city and bus tours can be arranged through major tour companies such as Hylton Ross (☎ 021-511 1784; www.hyltonross .co.za) and Springbok Atlas (☎ 021-460 4700; www.springbokatlas.co.za).

CAPE TOWN ON FOOT

☎ 021-487 6800

Contact Cape Town Tourism (p219) for details of these daily walking tours of the city centre (R100; ☺ 11am-1.30pm) or the Bo-Kaap (R75; ☺ 9.15-10.30am Mon-Fri) led by experienced guide Ursula Stevens. A combined city highlights and Bo-Kaap tour (R100; ☺ 10am-12.15pm) runs every Saturday.

CITY SIGHTSEEING CAPE TOWN

☎ 021-511 1784; www.hyltonross.co.za; adult/child R90/40

There are now two routes for this open-top, double-decker bus tour run by Hylton Ross. The Red Route is the original circular tour (taking just over two hours), starting at the Ferryman's Tavern at the Waterfront, heading into the city centre, up to the cable car and down to Camps Bay and back along Sea Point promenade. The new Blue Route also runs in a circle from the Waterfront but goes via Kirstenbosch and Hout Bay. They're hop-on, hop-off services and run at roughly half-hour intervals between 9.30am and 3.30pm with extra services in peak season (December to February).

FOOTSTEPS TO FREEDOM

☎ 021-426 4260, 083 452 1112; www.footstepstofreedom.co.za

This professional group has a trio of daily walks, departing from Cape Town Tourism (Map pp248-9; Burg St), all around the city centre. One of these focuses on Art Deco architecture and Sir Herbert Baker, and there are also trips to the townships and around the Bo-Kaap. Rates range from R100 for city walks, to R350 for the walk plus township tour. Private tours can be arranged.

Township & Cultural Tours

Township tours have become an essential part of a visit to Cape Town. Many visitors quite rightly wonder about the ethics of visiting desperately poor places under the guise of tourism. Our advice is to put your fears aside and sign up. The best tours help give you a far more accurate understanding of the split nature of the city and the challenges faced by the vast majority of Capetonians in their daily lives. They also reveal that life in the townships, while undoubtedly deprived for many, is not uniformly miserable and that there are many wonderful things to see and people to meet.

For a preview of a township tour, see the boxed text on p112. A half-day tour is sufficient – the full-day tours usually tack on a trip to Robben Island that is best done separately and for which you don't need a guide. Trips out to Langa and Khayelitsha usually involve getting on some form of transport, usually a small coach, but there are other options, including walking tours in the smaller townships of Masiphumelele and Imizamo Yethu. Also ask the tour operator how much of what you spend actually goes to help people in the townships, since few tours are actually run by Cape Flats residents. Bookings can be made directly with the operators or through **Cape Town Tourism** (p219).

When booking tours with the following operators, check whether they can pick you up from your accommodation, or whether you have to meet them at a specific place.

ADVENTURE KALK BAY
☎ 021-788 5113, 073 211 4508; arcadia@49er.co.za
Contact Judy Herbert to find out about this community-based tourism project, which offers guided walks around Kalk Bay and harbour and explains the fishing culture of the village (R30, plus lunch R100). For the half-day fishing trip (R120) you'll need to be up before dawn and will have to get yourself down to Kalk Bay, so consider arranging a homestay with one of the local families (R220 full board; arrange this through Judy).

ANDULELA
☎ 021-790 2592; www.andulela.com
Apart from offering interesting cookery tours of both the Bo-Kaap and the township of Kayamandi in Stellenbosch (see p151), this innovative company can arrange a range of other offbeat adventures. It teams up with **Coffee Beans Routes** (right) for the jazz safari and has plans to introduce a tour giving an insight into the Cape Minstrel Carnival.

CAPE CAPERS TOURS
☎ 083 358 0193; www.tourcapers.co.za
Award-winning guide Faizal Gangat is a garrulous fellow of Indian heritage who grew up among the Xhosa of the Eastern Cape. He leads a band of informative guides to the townships, with tours concentrating on Langa (R280 per person; see p112) or the Cape Care Route (R460) and highlighting community and environmental projects. Cape Capers also has a half-day tour of the Bo-Kaap and former District Six area.

CHARLOTTE'S WALKING TOURS
☎ 083 982 5692; nomthunzie@webmail.co.za
The ebullient Charlotte Swatbooi will introduce you to spaza (convenience) shops, shebeens, schools, development programmes and local artists on her walking tour of the township of Masiphumelele, on the way to Kommetjie. You'll have to make your own way to Masiphumelele, but it's a good alternative to the standard bus tour around the Cape Flats townships.

COFFEE BEANS ROUTES
☎ 021-448 8080, 084 762 4944;
www.coffeebeans.co.za
This self-styled 'urban regeneration agency' offers really unique tours at around R390 per person. Head up to Kalkfontein, a township north of the city, in the company of local poet Jethro Louw. Or take the great Cape Town Jazz Safari (from 7pm Monday) where you'll meet jazz musicians and catch a jam session at **Swingers** (p144). On Friday the agency runs a trip to Marcus Garvey, a Rastafarian settlement in Philippi for a fun night of Jamaican food and reggae at a dancehall after midnight. There are also full-moon and Winelands tours.

DINNER@MANDELAS
☎ 021-790 5817, 082 855 0931; Imizamo Yethu, Hout Bay; tour R225
A highly recommended alternative or addition to the daytime township tour is this evening tour and dinner combination at the Imizamo Yethu township in Hout Bay, which runs every Monday and Thursday at 7pm from the **Long St Café** (Map pp248–9; 259 Long St, City Bowl). The meal, which covers all the African traditional dishes and is veggie friendly, is held at Tamfanfa's Tavern and is preceded by lively African dancing and a choir singing in Xhosa (isiXhosa) and English.

(Continued on page 91)

1 Hair salon, Khayelitsha township, Cape Flats (p110) 2 Flower seller, Trafalgar Place (p92), City Bowl 3 Wire sculptor, Streetwires (p163), Bo-Kaap 4 School children

1 *Street graffiti* 2 *Buildings, Long Street (p95), City Bowl* 3 *Chiappini Street, Bo-Kaap (p92)* 4 *Africa Café (p126), City Bowl* 5 *Clementina Ceramics & A.R.T. Gallery (p170), Kalk Bay* 6 *Voting mural, Parliament Street, near Houses of Parliament (p95), City Bowl* 7 *Sculpture, Streetwires (p163), Bo-Kaap*

1 *Kirstenbosch Botanical Gardens (p105), Newlands* 2 *Poster of Nelson Mandela (p61) at Robben Island prison* 3 *Waterfront (p101)* 4 *Table Mountain (p66)*

1 *Wine cellar, Groot Constantia (p44)* **2** *Shacks in Imizamo Yethu township (p82), Hout Bay* **3** *Vine-pruning, with Table Mountain (p66) as a backdrop*

1 *Papier-mâché bowls, Wole Nani (p163), City Bowl* **2** *Ba Kensington Place hotel (p17* **3** *Late-night street food vendor, Long Street (p123), City Bowl*

1 Surfing, Noordhoek beach (p109)
2 Protea fynbos (p68) 3 Beach
huts 4 African penguins, Boulders
Beach (p72)

1 Overhead of Clifton (p102
with the Twelve Apostles in
background **2** Homes on
Chiappini Street, Bo-Kaap (p
3 Cape Town cityscape

(Continued from page 82)

GRASSROUTE TOURS

☎ 021-706 1006; www.grassroutetours.co.za
This is one of the most experienced operators of townships tours (half/full day R290/450). Daytime tours usually drop by **Vicky's B&B** (p184) for a chat with this Khayelitsha legend, while evening tours (R340 including dinner) include a visit to a shebeen and a ride on a donkey cart. The company also offers a walking tour of the Bo-Kaap (R260), a full day in the Winelands (R450), and a trip to Hermanus (R480).

ONE CITY TOURS

☎ 021-555 1468, 082 970 0564
The successful guide Sam Ntimba has now set up his own tour company. His half-day trip (R250) includes visits to a dormitory and shebeen in Langa and a crèche project in Khayelitsha. His Sunday tours to see a gospel choir in a Baptist church in Langa are very popular.

PURE PONDO ADVENTURES

☎ 072 302 9489; www.purepondo.co.za
/cape_town_tours.htm
Chris Reid Ntombemhlophe (see the boxed text, p13) leads tours into the townships using local transport and taking you to traditional herbalist shops and to meet other *sangomas* (traditional African healers). He also conducts a fascinating medicinal-plant tour through Kirstenbosch.

TOWNSHIP TOURS SA

☎ 083 719 4870; www.suedafrika.net
/imizamoyethu
Afrika Moni guides you on a two-hour walking tour (R85) of the Hout Bay township of Imizamo Yethu, which includes a visit to a *sangoma*, a drink of home-brew at a shebeen, and viewing of art projects. Tours run daily at 10.30am, 1pm and 4pm: bookings essential.

TSOGA TOURS Map pp244-5

☎ 021-694 9106; tsogatours@hotmail.com; Tsoga Environmental Resource Centre, Washington St, Langa
For a good walking tour of Langa, hook up with the young guides at the environmental resource centre. A tour lasting around 40 minutes costs R30.

Other Tours

AFRICAN SOUL TOURS

☎ 082 396 7806; www.africansoultours.co.za
If you're interested in environmental matters then join this group's half-day Earth Warrior Tour (R250). During the tour you'll learn all about the reality of waste in Cape Town, and visit a successful recycling project and permaculture gardening project. It also offers a traditional-medicine tour of Kirstenbosch and various township and city tours.

BIRDWATCH CAPE

☎ 021-762 5059; www.birdwatch.co.za
Bird expert Richard Grant runs these informative tours, pointing out the many unique species of the Cape floral kingdom; a half-day trip costs R270. He also offers trips further afield in the Karoo, the Kalahari and along the Garden Route.

BLUE BUYOU

☎ 021-617 1763, 083 293 6555;
www.bluebuyou.co.za
If shopping is your thing, then join Sandra Fairfax on her tailor-made shopping tours of the Mother City – there's not much this woman doesn't know about the best things for sale.

DAY TRIPPERS

☎ 021-511 4766; www.daytrippers.co.za
Long-running and very reliable tour company about which we continue to receive excellent feedback. Mountain bikes are taken along on most trips, which cost R385 and include Cape Point, the Winelands and, in season, whale-watching.

GATEWAY TO NEWLANDS

☎ 021-686 2151, 021-686 2150;
www.newlandstours.co.za
Sports fans may be interested in taking these tours of Cape Town's main cricket and rugby stadiums, and the **Sports Science Institute of South Africa** (p151). Whistle-stop tours kick off at adult/child R35/22, while longer tours, which include the Rugby Museum, cost adult/child R60/36.

IMVUBU NATURE TOURS

☎ 021-706 0842; www.imvubu.co.za
Imvubu, meaning 'hippopotamus' in both Xhosa and Zulu, is the name given by Graham and Joy to their nature-tour company

based at the **Rondevlei Nature Reserve** (p108). Take one of their tours (adult/child R30/15) around the reserve and you might be lucky enough to see the elusive hippos. Increase your chances by arranging to stay at the island bush camp. Boat trips, for a minimum of four people, are held between August and February and cost R30 per person.

CITY CENTRE

Eating p123; Shopping p161; Sleeping p172; Walking Tours p114; Entertainment p136

The City Bowl is the Mother City's commercial and historical heart, home to the castle and garden set out by the original Dutch settlers, as well as the nation's parliament and newest skyscrapers. During the day it bustles with colourful street life, from the art and souvenir stalls lining the length of St George's Mall to the flower sellers of Trafalgar Pl off Adderley St.

For all its daytime activity, come nightfall most parts of the City Bowl turn deathly quiet. This is likely to change, though, as more and more old office blocks and commercial buildings are transformed into swanky apartments, such as the Rhodes Mandela complex. New buildings are also planned for the Foreshore, the bleak swathe of reclaimed land that is squashed between the City Bowl and Table Bay, including several big hotels and the proposed **Desmond Tutu Museum of Peace** (www.tutufoundation-usa.org/center.html).

CAPE TOWN PASS

If you want to pack in a lot of sightseeing in Cape Town (and we do mean a lot!), consider investing in the **Cape Town Pass** (☎ 021-886 7080; www .thecapetownpass.co.za). The pass, which is valid for one, two, three or six consecutive days (adult R275/425/495/750, child R180/285/350/550), covers entry to some 70-odd Cape Peninsula and Winelands attractions; the only main exceptions are the Table Mountain cable car and Robben Island.

You'll have to work pretty hard to get the full value from the one- or two-day cards, but the three- and six-day ones can work out to be a good deal. The pass also offers discounts at many places, as well as free mobile phone rental and a local SIM card from Vodashop-Cellucity. It's available at Cape Town Tourism's main City Bowl (Map pp248–9) and Waterfront (Map pp252–3) offices, or you can buy it online and have it delivered to where you'll be staying.

TRANSPORT

The City Bowl is so compact that it's easy to walk pretty much everywhere. An alternative is to hop in a Rikki (tiny open van) or one of the shared taxis that cover the city in an informal network of routes. At night the safe option is to take a regular taxi.

West of the City Bowl is the Bo-Kaap, a tightknit Muslim area of brightly painted houses where time is measured by the regular calls to prayer from the suburb's many mosques. Attractive as the Bo-Kaap is in the daytime, this is not an area in which to wander alone late at night. You'll be safe enough, though, in the neighbouring Waterkant, where gentrification is in full flood. Here the renovated workers' cottages house chic inns, boutiques and the play areas of Cape Town's gay village, all focused around the Italianate shopping plaza of the Cape Quarter.

The largely desolate tract of land east of the City Bowl is officially called Zonnebloem (meaning 'Sunflower' in Afrikaans), but is better known as District Six. A poor but multiracial community flourished here until the late 1960s when, in the madness of apartheid, it was razed to the ground and redesignated a whites-only area. Despite some recent development it's a forbidding area and you'll be asking for trouble wandering around alone, especially after dark.

The Company's Gardens, around which are some of the city's top museums, is the verdant conduit linking the City Bowl with the high-class residential areas of Gardens, Tamboerskloof, Oranjezicht, Vredehoek and Higgovale. Here you'll find some of Cape Town's most appealing and individual accommodation options. Need we mention that the area is dominated by the massive bulk of Table Mountain and the adjacent rocky hump of Lion's Head? You'll hardly be able to keep your eyes off it, especially when the famous tablecloth of cloud is tumbling off the flat summit.

Orientation

The City Bowl is bordered by Buitenkant St to the southeast, Buitengracht St to the northwest, and Orange St and Annandale Rd to the south. Its main thoroughfare is Adderley St, which continues through the Company's Gardens as Government Ave. Further to the west, up the slopes of Signal

Hill, is the Bo-Kaap, the focus of which is Wale St. Waterkant is a tiny area bounded to the east by Buitengracht St and to the west by Highfield Rd, with Somerset Rd and Strand St completing the box. Zonnebloem (District Six) stretches east from Canterbury St to Searl St.

Kloof St is the backbone of Gardens. West and up Signal Hill is Tamboerskloof, while Oranjezicht lies to the east behind De Waal Park. Vredehoek is further to the east up the side to Table Mountain, while Higgovale is to the west.

CITY BOWL & BO-KAAP

BO-KAAP MUSEUM Map pp248-9
☎ 021-481 3939; www.museums.org.za/bokaap/index.html; 71 Wale St, Bo-Kaap; adult/child R5/2; ◷ 9.30am-4.30pm Mon-Sat

Giving a measure of focus to the Bo-Kaap is this small museum, which provides some insight into the lifestyle of a prosperous 19th-century Cape Muslim family, and a somewhat idealised view of Islamic practice in Cape Town. The most interesting exhibit, although it lacks decent captions, is the selection of black-and-white photos of local life displayed in the upstairs room, across the courtyard. The house itself, built in 1763, is the oldest in the area.

CASTLE OF GOOD HOPE Map pp248-9
☎ 021-787 1249; www.castleofgoodhope.co.za; entrance on Buitenkant St, City Bowl; adult/child Mon-Sat R20/10, Sun R10/5; ◷ 9am-4pm, tours 11am, noon & 2pm Mon-Sat; Ⓟ

Many visitors are quite surprised to find a castle in Cape Town. Built between 1666 and 1679 by the Dutch, the stone-walled pentag-

Castle of Good Hope (above)

onal structure has never seen action in all its 350 years, unless you count the more-recent stormings by hordes of school kids and tourists. It's worth timing your visit for one of the tours (the noon tour on weekdays coincides with the changing of the guard, since the castle is still the headquarters for the Western Cape military command), although you can quite easily find your own way around. An ancient key ceremony at the castle's main gate is also held at 10am weekdays.

Inside are extensive displays of militaria and some interesting information about the castle's archaeology and the reconstruction of the so-called Dolphin Pool. The highlight is the bulk of the **William Fehr Collection** (◷ 9.30am-4pm), including some fabulous bits of Cape Dutch furniture, such as a table seating 100 and paintings by John Thomas Baines.

COMPANY'S GARDENS Map pp248-9
Government Ave, City Bowl; ◷ 7am-7pm

What started as the vegetable patch for the Dutch East India Company (Vereenigde Oost-Indische Compagnie; VOC) is now a shady green escape in the heart of the city, and a lovely place to relax during the heat of the day. The surviving 6 hectares of Jan van Riebeeck's original 18-hectare garden are found around Government Ave, with gates next to the National Library of South African and off both Museum and Queen Victoria Sts. As the VOC's sources of supply diversified, the grounds became a superb pleasure garden, planted with a fine collection of botanical specimens from South Africa and the rest of the world, including frangipanis, African flame trees, aloes and roses.

The squirrels that scamper here were imported to Cape Town from North America by Cecil Rhodes, whose statue stands in the centre of the gardens (see the boxed text, p94). Just outside the southern end of the Gardens on Museum St is the Sir Herbert Baker–designed **Delville Wood Memorial**,

Sights

CITY CENTRE

honouring South African soldiers who fell during a five-day WWI battle. A craft market is held next to the café in the centre of the garden once or twice a month; inquire at the garden's information centre for details

DISTRICT SIX MUSEUM Map pp248-9

☎ 021-466 7200; www.districtsix.co.za; 25A Buitenkant St, City Bowl; adult/child R15/10; ☺ 9am-3pm Mon, 9am-4pm Tue-Sat

Your one essential museum visit in Cape Town should be to this museum. As much *for* the people of the now-vanished District Six as it is *about* them, this is a hugely moving and informative exhibition that is worth repeat visits. Note that almost all township

tours stop here first to explain the history of the pass laws. The floor of the main hall is covered with a large-scale map of District Six, on which former residents have labelled where their demolished homes and features of their neighbourhood were.

Reconstructions of home interiors, photographs, recordings and written testimonials build up an evocative picture of a shattered but not entirely broken community. The staff, practically all displaced residents, each have a heartbreaking story to tell (see the boxed text, p62). At the back of the museum is a pleasant café. Speak to staff about arranging a **walking tour** (☎ 021-466 7208; tour R50) of the old District Six, for a minimum of 10 people.

GOLD OF AFRICA MUSEUM Map pp248-9

☎ 021-405 1540; www.goldofafrica.com; 96 Strand St, City Bowl; adult/child R20/10; ☺ 9.30am-5pm Mon-Sat

A third of the world's gold is produced in South Africa. In this glitzy museum, based in historic Martin Melck House (dating from 1783) and established by Anglogold, the biggest gold-mining company in the world, gorgeous gold jewellery from across the continent is displayed. There are some

THE SLOW REBIRTH OF DISTRICT SIX

In October 2005 Capetonians heard news that many hoped they would never hear again: people had been evicted from District Six. This time it was the local authorities moving on squatters from an informal settlement, but the headlines still brought back painful memories of the 1960s and '70s when families who had lived in the area for generations were forcibly evicted as the apartheid government tried to enforce District Six as a whites-only area (see p60).

Since democracy, the rebuilding of District Six has been a priority, but it is slow going. In November 2000 President Thabo Mbeki signed a document handing back the confiscated land to the former residents, and in 2004 the first set of keys to the new homes built here were handed over to 87-year-old Ebrahiem Murat and 82-year-old Dan Mdzabela. The **District Six Beneficiary Trust** (www.d6bentrust.org.za) plans to build 2000 homes in the next few years, but partly due to lack of funds the area remains largely empty. There are some 1800 people on the waiting list for homes, but it will be impossible for everyone to return to exactly where they lived since new constructions, such as the Cape Technikon college, now occupy part of the area.

stunning pieces, mostly from West Africa, with lots of background information. The shop is worth a browse for interesting gold souvenirs, including copies of some of the pieces in the museum, and you can sign up for jewellery-design (R650) and gold-leaf (R450) courses in the on-site workshop.

GROOTE KERK Map pp248-9
☎ 021-461 7044; Church Sq, City Bowl; admission free; ⏰ 10am-2pm Mon-Fri, services 10am & 7pm Sun

The highlights of the mother church of the Dutch Reformed Church (Nederduitse Gereformeerde Kerk; NG Kerk) are its mammoth organ and ornate Burmese teak pulpit, carved by master sculptors Anton Anreith and Jan Graaff. The building's otherwise an architectural mishmash with only parts dating from the 1704 original and other bits from 1841. While here ponder the fact that for the first 100 years or so of the church's life, slaves were sold immediately outside.

HOUSES OF PARLIAMENT Map pp248-9
☎ 021-403 2266; www.parliament.gov.za; Parliament St, City Bowl; admission free; ⏰ tours by appointment Mon-Fri

Although it sounds unlikely, visiting South Africa's parliament can make for a diverting tour, especially if you're interested in the country's modern history. Opened in 1885, the hallowed halls have seen some pretty momentous events; this is where British prime minister Harold Macmillan made his 'Wind of Change' speech in 1960, and where President Hendrik Verwoerd, architect of apartheid, was stabbed to death in 1966. Enthusiastic tour guides will fill you in on the mechanisms and political make-up of their new democracy. If parliament is sit-

ting, fix your tour for the afternoon so you can see the politicians in action. You must present your passport to gain entry.

KOOPMANS-DE WET HOUSE Map pp248-9
☎ 021-481 3935; www.museums.org.za/koopmans; 35 Strand St, City Bowl; adult/child R5/2; ⏰ 9.30am-4pm Tue-Thu

Step back two centuries from 21st-century Cape Town when you enter this classic example of a Cape Dutch townhouse, furnished with 18th- and early-19th-century antiques. It's an atmospheric place with ancient vines growing in the courtyard and floorboards that squeak just as they probably did during the times of Marie Koopmans-de Wet, the socialite owner after whom the house is named.

LONG STREET Map pp248-9
Although it's being upgraded as savvy commercial operators move in, the essentially bohemian, alcohol-fuelled nature of Long St remains. The most attractive section, lined with Victorian-era buildings featuring lovely wrought-iron balconies, runs from the junction with Buitensingle St north to around Strand St; below here the street gets very seedy with many strip clubs and louche bars. Whether you come to browse the antique shops, second-hand bookstores, or the street wear boutiques, or party at the host of bars and clubs that crank up at night, a stroll along Long St is an essential element of a Cape Town visit.

The thoroughfare once formed the border of the Muslim Bo-Kaap, so you'll find several old mosques along the street, including the **Palm Tree Mosque** at 185 Long St, dating from 1780 and one of the city's oldest. For information about the **Long St Baths** see p152.

Sights

CITY CENTRE

THE EGG MAN

While visiting the cobblestoned **Greenmarket Sq** (p162), or wandering along nearby St Georges Mall, chances are you'll see one of Cape Town's most striking street performance artists: the Egg Man. Despite the 15kg weight of his amazing head-dress, which is created from eggs of all sizes, and his shamanistic-style costumes dangling with broken bits of mirror, beads and shells, Gregory de Silva remains cheerful and unflustered, happily posing for photos (please drop a few rand into his hat for his troubles). Chat to him and you'll discover that this creative 26-year-old from Benin is aiming to build the largest hat in Africa.

LUTHERAN CHURCH Map pp248-9
☎ 021-421 5854; 98 Strand St, City Bowl; admission free; ☽ 10am-2pm Mon-Fri
Converted from a barn in 1780, the first Lutheran church in the Cape has a striking pulpit, perhaps the best created by the master German sculptor Anton Anreith, whose work can also be seen in **Groote Kerk** (p95) and at **Groot Constantia** (p44). Go to the room behind the pulpit to see the collection of old Bibles.

MICHAELIS COLLECTION Map pp248-9
☎ 021-481 3933; www.museums.org.za/michaelis; Greenmarket Sq, City Bowl; admission by donation; ☽ 10am-5pm Mon-Fri, 10am-4pm Sat
The beautifully restored Old Townhouse, a Cape rococo building dating from 1755, now houses the impressive art collection of Sir Max Michaelis, donated to the city in 1914. Dutch and Flemish paintings and etchings from the 16th and 17th centuries (including works by Rembrandt, Frans Hals and Anthony van Dyck) hang side by side with contemporary works – the contrasts between old and new are fascinating. The cool interior is a relief from buzzing Greenmarket Sq outside, while the relaxed Ivy Garden Restaurant in the courtyard behind is worth considering for a drink or light lunch.

SIGNAL HILL & NOON GUN Map pp248-9
Separating Sea Point from the City Bowl, Signal Hill provides magnificent views from its 350m-high summit, especially at night. Once also known as Lion's Rump, as it is attached to Lion's Head by a 'spine' of

hills, it is officially part of Table Mountain National Park. To reach the summit head up Kloof Nek Rd from the city and take the first turn-off to the right at the top of the hill.

Signal Hill was the early settlement's lookout point, and it was from here that flags were hoisted when a ship was spotted, giving the citizens below time to prepare their goods for sale and dust off their tankards.

At noon, Monday to Saturday, a cannon known as the Noon Gun is fired from the lower slopes of Signal Hill. You can hear it all over town. Traditionally this allowed the burghers in the town below to check their watches. It's a stiff walk up here through the Bo-Kaap – take Longmarket St and keep going until it ends. The **Noon Gun Tearoom & Restaurant** (p125) is a good place to catch your breath.

SLAVE LODGE Map pp248-9
☎ 021-460 8240; www.museums.org.za /slavelodge; 49 Adderley St, City Bowl; adult/child R10/5; ☽ 10am-4.30pm Mon-Sat
The process of changing the former Cultural History Museum into a museum devoted to the history and experience of slaves and their descendants in the Cape moves along slowly. Some of the museum's collection of artefacts from ancient Egypt, Greece, Rome and the Far East remain on the 1st floor, while the ground floor is now devoted to the slave history, and kicks off with an informative video.

TOP FIVE VIEWPOINTS

- **Bloubergstrand** (p101) – this windswept beach north of the city affords a postcard-perfect view of Table Mountain.
- **Cape Point** (p73) – walk to just above the Cape's original lighthouse for breathtaking views of the peninsula.
- **Chapman's Peak Dr** (p102) – pause along this thrilling cliffside road to take in the elegant sweep of horseshoe-shaped Hout Bay.
- **Lion's Head** (p74) – take a 45-minute hike to the summit for a wonderful view of the coast and magnificent mountain crags known as the Twelve Apostles.
- **Table Mountain** (p66) – you've done the rest, now do the best. Head to the top for sweeping vistas across the city from the sea to the Cape Flats.

REINVENTING THE OLD MUTUAL

In 2001 the Old Mutual Building (Map pp248–9), on the corner of Parliament and Darling Sts, was going slowly but steadily to ruin, a sad end for what was in its day not only the tallest structure in Africa bar the Pyramids, but also the most expensive. Commissioned by the Old Mutual financial company, the building was the pinnacle of Cape Town's lust for Art Deco architecture. It was clad in rose- and gold-veined black marble and decorated with one of the longest continuous stone friezes in the world (designed by Ivan Mitford-Barberton and chiselled by master stonemasons the Lorenzi brothers).

Unfortunately the building's completion in 1939 was eclipsed by the start of WWII. Additionally its prime position on the Foreshore was immediately quashed when the city decided to extend the land 2km further into the bay. Old Mutual starting moving its business out of the building to the suburbs in the 1950s. If it hadn't been awarded protected heritage status, it's likely the building would have been demolished. Thankfully the Old Mutual's fortunes changed when a young architect Robert Silke, working for Louis Karol, saw its potential for being converted into apartments. The building was renamed Mutual Heights and when the 178 apartments went on sale in 2002, they sold out in a matter of weeks, thus kicking off a frenzy among developers to convert similarly long-neglected and empty city-centre office blocks.

Much of the building's original detail and decoration has been left intact, including the elevators, original door handles (now used on all the apartment doors) and Art Deco light fittings, rehung in the hallways. The impressive central banking hall – a space fit for a grand MGM musical – is in the process of being converted into a retail showcase for the **Cape Craft and Design Institute** (www.capecraftanddesign.org.za). If you want a taste of the high life it's possible to rent out the building's stunning four-bedroom penthouse (see p174).

Sights

CITY CENTRE

One of the oldest buildings in South Africa, dating back to 1660, the Slave Lodge has a fascinating history in itself. Until 1811 the building was home, if you could call it that, to as many as 1000 slaves, who lived in damp, insanitary, crowded conditions. Up to 20% died each year. The slaves were bought and sold just around the corner on Spin St.

From the late 18th century the lodge was used as a brothel, a jail for petty criminals and political exiles from Indonesia, and a mental asylum. In 1811 it became Cape Town's first post office. Later it became a library, and it was the Cape Supreme Court until 1914. The walls of the original Slave Lodge flank the interior courtyard, where you can find the tombstones of Cape Town's founder, Jan van Riebeeck, and his wife, Maria de la Queillerie. The tombstones were moved here from Jakarta where Van Riebeeck is buried.

GARDENS & SURROUNDS

For details of the cableway and hikes up Table Mountain and Lion's Head see p71 and p74.

BERTRAM HOUSE Map p254

☎ 021-481 3940; www.museums.org.za/bertram; cnr Orange St & Government Ave, Gardens; adult/child R5/2; ☿ 10am-4pm Tue-Thu

A minor diversion if you're at this end of the Company's Gardens is to drop by the only surviving Georgian-style brick house in Cape Town, dating from the 1840s. Inside

it's decorated appropriately to its era with Regency-style furnishings and 19th-century English porcelain.

CAPE TOWN HOLOCAUST CENTRE

Map p254

☎ 021-462 5553; www.ctholocaust.co.za; 88 Hatfield St, Gardens; admission free; ☿ 10am-5pm Sun-Thu, 10am-1pm Fri

This small museum, in the same complex of buildings as the **South African Jewish Museum** (p98), packs a lot in with a considerable emotional punch. The history of anti-Semitism is set in a South African context with parallels drawn to the local struggle for freedom. Videos of Holocaust survivors telling their harrowing tales are worth watching at the end.

PLANETARIUM Map p254

☎ 021-481 3900; www.museums.org.za /planetarium; 25 Queen Victoria St, Gardens; adult/child R20/6; ☿ 10am-5pm

Attached to the South African Museum, the displays and star shows here unravel the mysteries of the southern hemisphere's night sky. Shows using images caught by the Southern African Large Telescope in the Karoo (which has the largest aperture of any telescope in the world) are held at 2pm, Monday to Friday, 2.30pm Saturday and Sunday, and 8pm Tuesday including a lecture. Children's shows are at noon and 1pm Saturday and Sunday.

PLACES OF WORSHIP

Many of the following key places of worship are worth visiting for their historical relevance and interesting architecture, as much as for their religious significance.

Great Synagogue (Map p254; ☎ 021-465 1405; 88 Hatfield St, Gardens) Jewish; see opposite.

Groote Kerk (Map pp248–9; ☎ 021-461 7044, Church Sq, City Bowl) Dutch Reformed; see p95.

Lutheran Church (Map pp248–9; ☎ 021-421 5854; 98 Strand St, City Bowl) Lutheran; see p96.

Metropolitan Methodist Church (Map pp248–9; ☎ 021-422 2744; Greenmarket Sq, City Bowl) Methodist.

Owal Mosque (Map pp248–9; Dorp St, Bo-Kaap) Muslim.

St George's Cathedral (Map pp248–9; ☎ 021-424 7360; www.stgeorgescathedral.com; 1 Wale St, City Bowl) Anglican.

St Mary's Cathedral (Map pp248–9; ☎ 021-461 1167; Roeland St, City Bowl) Roman Catholic.

RUST EN VREUGD Map p254

☎ 021-464 3280; www.museums.org.za /rustvreugd; 78 Buitenkant St, Gardens; admission by donation; ☼ 8.30am-4.30pm Mon-Fri
This delightful mansion, dating from 1777 to 1778, and fronted by a period-style garden recreated in 1986 from the original layout, was once the home of the state prosecutor. It now houses part of the William Fehr collection of paintings and furniture (the major part is in the Castle of Good Hope). Paintings by John Thomas Baines show early scenes from colonial Cape Town, while the sketches of Cape Dutch architecture by Alys Fane Trotter are some of the best you'll see.

SA NATIONAL GALLERY Map p254

☎ 021-467 4660; www.museums.org.za/sang; Government Ave, Gardens; adult/child R10/5, Sat by donation; ☼ 10am-5pm Tue-Sun
South Africa's premier art space scored a coup in 2006 by hosting the *Picasso in Africa* exhibition. Even without the drawing power of a world-famous painter, there's still a lot of awfully good art here to warrant a visit. The permanent collection harks back to Dutch times and includes some extraordinary pieces. It's often contempor-

ary works, however, such as the *Butcher Boys* sculpture by Jane Alexander, looking like a trio of *Lord of the Rings* orcs who have stumbled into the gallery, that stand out the most. Also check out the remarkable teak door in the courtyard, carved by Herbert Vladimir Meyerowitz with scenes representing the global wanderings of the Jews. His carvings also adorn the tops of the door frames throughout the gallery. There's a pleasant café and a good shop with some interesting books and gifts.

SOUTH AFRICAN JEWISH MUSEUM
Map p254

☎ 021-465 1546; www.sajewishmuseum.co.za; 88 Hatfield St, Gardens; adult/child R35/15; ☼ 10am-5pm Sun-Thu, 10am-2pm Fri
The fascinating history of Jews in South Africa (see p14) is recorded in this imaginatively designed museum, incorporating the beautifully restored **Old Synagogue** (1863). Downstairs you'll find a partial re-creation of a Lithuanian *shtetl* (village); many of South Africa's Jews fled this part of Eastern Europe during the pogroms and persecution of the late 19th and early 20th centuries. There's also a computerised system where you can trace Jewish relations in South Africa, and excellent temporary exhibitions.

Across the courtyard from the museum's exit is a good gift shop and the kosher **Café Riteve**. In the auditorium beneath the Cape Town Holocaust Centre, make sure you see the 20-minute documentary film *A Righteous Man* about Nelson Mandela's connection with the South African Jewish community.

Delville Wood Memorial (p93) and the South African Museum (opposite)

Within the complex it's also possible to visit the beautifully decorated **Great Synagogue** (guided tours free; ☉ 10am-4pm Sun-Thu), dating from 1905 and one of a handful of buildings in Cape Town built in the neo-Egyptian style.

SOUTH AFRICAN MUSEUM Map p254

☎ 021-481 3800; www.museums.org.za/sam; 25 Queen Victoria St, Gardens; adult/child R10/5, Sat by donation; ☉ 10am-5pm

Although there has been some reorganisation in recent years, and a few new exhibits, in general South Africa's oldest museum is showing its age. Despite not being a must-see, it does contain a wide and often intriguing series of exhibitions, many on the country's natural history.

The best galleries are the newest, showcasing the art and culture of the area's first peoples, the Khoikhoi and San, and including the famous **Linton Panel**, an amazing example of San rock art. There's an extraordinary delicacy to the paintings, particularly the ones of graceful elands.

Also worth looking out for are the startlingly lifelike displays in the **African Cultures Gallery** of African people (cast from living subjects); the terracotta **Lydenburg Heads**, the earliest-known examples of African sculpture (AD 500–700); a 2m-wide nest of the sociable weaver bird, a veritable avian apartment block, in the **Wonders of Nature Gallery**; and the atmospheric **Whale Well**, hung with giant whale skeletons and models and resounding with taped recordings of their calls.

ATLANTIC COAST

Eating p129; Shopping p165; Sleeping p178, Entertainment p140

For spectacular scenery look no further than the Atlantic coast of the Cape Peninsula. It's mainly beach territory with the emphasis on sunbathing. Although it's possible to shelter from the summer southeasterlies (see p157), the water comes straight from the Antarctic and swimming is exhilarating (ie freezing).

The bland suburban neighbourhoods of Bloubergstrand and Milnerton to the north of the city will not be top of anyone's sightseeing wish list, but they still have their attractions, namely a beach with a view and a gigantic shopping centre, respectively. In contrast, the Victoria & Alfred Waterfront (always just called the Waterfront) is likely

TRANSPORT

Shared taxis run regularly along Main Rd through Green Point to the end of Regent Rd in Sea Point. **Golden Arrow** (☎ 0800 656 463; www.gabs.co.za) buses follow the same route, then continue to Victoria Rd and down to Hout Bay. An alternative is the City Sightseeing Cape Town tour buses (p81) that run on a fixed-loop route from the Waterfront to both Camps Bay and Hout Bay. From Hout Bay, though, it's private transport only along Chapman's Peak Dr to all points further south on the peninsula. Be warned that parking at Clifton and Camps Bay in summer can be a nightmare, especially on the weekend.

to be one of the first places you head to. It's a great example of how to best redevelop a declining dock area into a tourist hot spot. The atmosphere is always buzzing and there's plenty to do, including making a trip out to Robben Island, the infamous prison island that is now a fascinating museum.

The outcrop of largely open land west of the Waterfront is Green Point, where you'll find one of Cape Town's major stadiums, a golf course and a large Sunday market. As well as being the name of the actual point, Green Point is also the name of the surrounding suburb, which includes rocky Mouille Point, right on the Atlantic coast and an atmospheric place for a seaside stroll. There's a lot of upmarket development going on in Green Point, particularly along Main Rd, although this is also where you'll find Cape Town's prostitutes plying their trade.

The next seaside suburb heading south is Three Anchor Bay, which blends seamlessly into Sea Point and Fresnaye. This less-fancy residential area has long been popular with Cape Town's Jewish and gay communities. The numerous pastel-shaded Art Deco apartment blocks fringing the coast have an almost Miami Beach elegance, while Main Rd and Regent St are lined with good, cheap restaurants, cafés and shops, including the new hub of the area, the Piazza St John shopping centre on Main Rd.

Moving south, the exclusive and wealthy residential neighbourhoods of Bantry Bay, Clifton and Camps Bay follow hard and fast on each other in a tumble of mansions with to-die-for sea views. Camps Bay, in particular, is a popular spot with visitors and locals; it has excellent, largely upmarket accommodation, restaurants and bars for those all-important drinks at sunset.

There's a stretch of protected parkland at Ouderkraal before the even more exclusive shop-free village of Llandudno, clinging to steep slopes above a sheltered beach. The remains of the tanker *Romelia*, which was wrecked in 1977, lie off Sunset Rocks here and down a coastal path, the nude-bathing beach, Sandy Bay.

Over the pass beside Little Lion's Head (436m), Victoria Rd drops to the fishing community of Hout Bay nestling behind the almost vertical Sentinel and the steep slopes of Chapman's Peak. Inland from the 1km stretch of white sand, there's a fast-growing satellite town that still manages to retain something of its village atmosphere. There's also the township of Imizamo Yethu, also known as Mandela Park, in which it's possible to do a walking tour (p91).

Orientation

Bloubergstrand lies 25km north of the city on Table Bay; take the R27 off the N1 to get there. The N1 also goes right past Canal Walk in Milnerton.

The increased development at the Waterfront and along the Foreshore makes it safe to walk here during the day from City Bowl: it's best to stick to Dock Rd. Otherwise, shuttle buses run frequently from Adderley St in front of the main train station up Strand St to the centre of the Waterfront. They also leave from near the Sea Point Pavilion in Sea Point. If you're driving, there are lots of free parking spaces around the Waterfront and, if they're full, there's plenty of paid parking at fairly inexpensive rates.

ROBBEN ISLAND
ROBBEN ISLAND & NELSON MANDELA GATEWAY Map pp252-3
☎ 021-413 4220; www.robben-island.org.za; adult/child R150/75; ☉ hourly ferries 9am-3pm, sunset tour 5pm Dec-Jan

Cape Town's most infamous island lies some 12km out from the shore in Table Bay. On approach the flat island, just 2km by 4km, may look like a pleasant place with its neat village of stone buildings and white church steeple, but to the prisoners who were incarcerated here from the early days of the VOC right up until 1996, it was nothing short of hell. Now a museum and UN World Heritage site, Robben Island's most famous involuntary resident was Nelson Mandela and for

this reason alone it is one of the most popular pilgrimage spots in all of Cape Town.

Success comes at a price, and while we heartily recommend going to Robben Island, a visit here is not without its drawbacks. Most likely you will have to endure crowds and being hustled around on a guided tour that, at a maximum of two hours on the island (plus a 30-minute boat ride in both directions), is woefully short. You will learn much of what happened to Mandela and others like him, since one of the former inmates will lead you around the prison. It seems a perverse form of torture to have these guys recount their harrowing time as prisoners here, but the best of the guides rise above this to embody the true spirit of reconciliation.

The standard tours, which have set departure and return times when you buy your ticket, include a walk through the old prison (with the obligatory peek into Mandela's cell), as well as a 45-minute bus ride around the island with commentary on the various places of note, such as the prison house of Pan-African Congress (PAC) leader Robert Sobuke, the lime quarry in which Mandela and many others slaved, and the church used during the island's stint as a leper colony. If you're lucky, you'll have 10 to 15 minutes to wander around on your own.

The guides will suggest checking out the jackass penguin colony near the landing jetty, but we recommend heading straight to the prison's A section to view the remarkable exhibition Cell Stories. In each of 40 isolation cells is an artefact and story from a former political prisoner: chess pieces drawn on scraps of paper; a soccer trophy; a Christmas card from an abandoned wife. It's all unbelievably moving. This is not part of the regular tour, but there's nothing to stop you slipping away to see it should you find the guide's commentary or the crowds not to your liking.

ATLANTIC COAST TOP FIVE

- Confront South Africa's troubled past on Robben Island (left).
- Dive with sharks at Two Oceans Aquarium (opposite and p154).
- Strip off on beautiful Sandy Bay Beach (p102).
- Motor along spectacular Chapman's Peak Dr (p102).
- Swim at Sea Point Pavilion (p153).

Tours depart from the **Nelson Mandela Gateway** (admission free; ☺ 9am-8.30pm) beside the Clock Tower at the Waterfront. Even if you don't plan a visit to the island, it's worth dropping by the museum here, which focuses on the struggle for freedom. Start by watching the video message from former political prisoners and detainees screened on the ground floor; the exhibition continues both upstairs and downstairs. For island tours an advance booking is recommended; at holiday times all tours can be booked up for days. Make the bookings at the Nelson Mandela Gateway departure point or at **Cape Town Tourism** (p219) in the city.

GREEN POINT & WATERFRONT

Much of the success of the **Waterfront** (www .waterfront.co.za) is due to the fact that it remains a working harbour. The Alfred and Victoria Basins date from 1860 and are named after Queen Victoria and her son Alfred. Although these wharves are too small for modern container vessels and tankers, the Victoria Basin is still used by tugs, harbour vessels of various kinds, and fishing boats. In the Alfred Basin you'll see ships under repair, and seals splashing around and lazing on the giant tyres that line the docks.

The Waterfront has tons of strict security and, although it is safe to walk around at all hours, there are plenty of merry men, so lone women should be a little cautious. See the Eating (p129), Entertainment (p139) and Shopping (p165) chapters for our pick of the numerous restaurants, bars and shops here.

CAPE MEDICAL MUSEUM Map pp252-3
☎ 021-418 5663; Portswood Rd, Green Point; admission by donation; ☺ 9am-4pm Tue-Fri
The new Disease and History exhibit at this quirky museum is perhaps worth a few moments of your time: it details in lengthy descriptions and some gruesome photographs the history of major diseases at the Cape, from scurvy to HIV/AIDS. Also here are a re-created Victorian doctor's room and pharmacy.

NOBEL SQUARE Map pp252-3
Dock Rd, Waterfront
Here's your chance to have your photo taken with Desmond Tutu and Nelson Mandela. Larger-than-life statues of both men, designed by Claudette Schreuders, stand be-

side those of South Africa's two other Nobel prize winners – Nkosi Albert Luthuli and FW de Klerk – in Nobel Sq, unveiled in December 2005. At the opposite end of the small square is the *Peace and Democracy* sculpture, by Noria Mahasa, which symbolises the contribution of women and children to the struggle. It's etched with pertinent quotes, translated into all the major languages of the country, by each of the great men.

SA MARITIME MUSEUM Map pp252-3
☎ 021-405 2880; www.museums.org.za /maritime; Dock Rd, Waterfront; adult/child R10/5; ☺ 10am-5pm
This specialist museum, which is stocked to the gunwales with model ships plus some full-sized ones, is set to move to another area of the Waterfront, although at the time of writing the exact location hadn't been confirmed. Admission will continue to include entry to **SAS Somerset**, a wartime vessel now permanently docked beside the museum.

TWO OCEANS AQUARIUM Map pp252-3
☎ 021-418 3823; www.aquarium.co.za; Dock Rd, Waterfront; adult/child R65/30; ☺ 9.30am-6pm
Always a hit with the kids, this excellent aquarium features denizens of the deep from the cold and the warm oceans that border the Cape Peninsula, including ragged-tooth sharks. There are seals, penguins, turtles, an astounding kelp forest open to the sky, and pools in which kids can touch sea creatures. Qualified divers can get in the water for a closer look (see p154). Get your hand stamped on entry and you can return any time during the same day for free.

BEACHES & SUBURBS

Bloubergstrand
BLOUBERGSTRAND BEACH
The British won their 1806 battle for the Cape on this beach. The panoramic view it provides of Table Mountain is its most famous feature, although the seemingly eternal wind makes it popular with windsurfers. There are also opportunities for some surfing (best with a moderate northeasterly wind, a small swell and an incoming tide). The village of Bloubergstrand itself is attractive enough, with picnic areas, some long, uncrowded, windy stretches of sand, and a good pub, the **Blue Peter** (p140).

Sea Point

SEA POINT Map p255

Sea Point's coast is rocky and swimming is dangerous, although there are a couple of rock pools. At the north end, **Graaff's Pool** is for men only and is generally favoured by nudists. Just south of here is **Milton's Pool**, which also has a stretch of beach. If you're too thin-skinned for the frigid sea, there's always Sea Point's lovely Art Deco public pool (see p153). The promenade running the length of the seafront around to Green Point is also a great place to jog or go for a stroll.

Clifton

CLIFTON BEACHES Map pp246-7

Giant granite boulders split the four linked beaches at Clifton, accessible by steps from Victoria Rd. Almost always sheltered from the wind, they are top sunbathing spots, despite the lack of local facilities. On Monday night African drummers and fire dancers have been known to gather here, although in January 2006 the crowds had grown so large that police waded in to break up the fun (see p54). Local lore has it that **No 1** and **No 2** beaches are for models and confirmed narcissists, **No 3** is the gay beach, and **No 4** is for families. If you haven't brought your own supplies, vendors hawk drinks and ice creams along the beach, and you can hire a sun lounge and umbrella for around R50.

Beach, Clifton (above)

CAPE TOWN'S TOP FIVE BEACHES

- Muizenberg (p108) – colourful Victorian chalets, warm(ish) water and fun surfing.
- Clifton No 3 (left) – where the gay community leads, the rest follow.
- Buffels Bay (p73) – sweeping views across False Bay from this quiet Cape Point beach.
- Long Beach (p109) – hard-core surfers adore this idyllic and aptly named swathe of sand.
- Foxy Beach (p72) – paddle with the Boulders penguins here.

Camps Bay

CAMPS BAY BEACH Map p256

With the spectacular Twelve Apostles of Table Mountain as a backdrop, and soft white sand, Camps Bay is one of the city's most popular beaches. It's within 15 minutes' drive of the city centre so can get crowded, particularly on weekends. The beach is often windy, and the water is decidedly on the cool side. There are no lifeguards and the surf is strong, so take care if you do swim.

Sandy Bay

LLANDUDNO & SANDY BAY BEACHES Map pp244-5

At Llandudno there's surfing on the beach breaks (mostly rights), best at high tide with a small swell and a southeasterly wind. You'll also need to head here if you want to get to Sandy Bay, Cape Town's nudist beach and gay stamping ground. It's a particularly beautiful stretch of sand and there's no pressure to take your clothes off if you don't want to. Like many such beaches, Sandy Bay has no direct access roads. From the M6, turn towards Llandudno, keep to the left at the fork, and head towards the sea until you reach the Sunset Rocks parking area. The beach is roughly a 15-minute walk to the south. Waves here are best at low tide with a southeasterly wind.

Hout Bay

CHAPMAN'S PEAK DRIVE Map pp244-5

☎ 021-790 9163; cars R22, motorcycles R15

Get ready for a thrilling drive along this 5km toll road (R22) linking Hout Bay with Noordhoek. It's one of the most spectacular stretches of coastal road in the world.

Despite recent safety work done to protect against dangerous rock slides, the road still gets closed during bad weather. There are a few places to stop to admire the view and it's certainly worth taking the road at least one way en-route to Cape Point. Perched on a rock near the Hout Bay end of the drive is a bronze **leopard statue** (Map p258). It has been sitting there since 1963 and is a reminder of the wildlife that once roamed the area's forests (which have also largely vanished).

DUIKER ISLAND CRUISES Map p258

Although increasingly given over to tourism, Hout Bay's harbour still functions and the southern arm of the bay is an important fishing port and processing centre. From here you can catch a boat to Duiker Island (also known as Seal Island because of its colony of Cape fur seals, but not to be confused with the official Seal Island in False Bay). Three companies run these cruises daily, usually with guaranteed sailings in the mornings. The cheapest, with a none-too-spectacular glass-bottomed boat, is **Circe Launches** (☎ 021-790 1040; www .circelaunches.co.za; adult/child R35/10); the others are **Drumbeat Charters** (☎ 021-791 4441; adult/child R50/20) and **Nauticat Charters** (☎ 021-790 7278; www.nauticatcharters .co.za; adult/child R50/20).

HOUT BAY MUSEUM Map p258

☎ 021-790 3270; 4 Andrews Rd, Hout Bay; adult/child R5/2; ⏱ 8am-4.30pm Mon-Thu, 8am-4pm Fri; Ⓟ

There's little to detain you at this one-room museum next to the tourist office, with minor-league displays on local history. Contact the museum about the guided walks (R10 donation) that are sometimes run on the weekends.

WORLD OF BIRDS Map pp244-5

☎ 021-790 2730; www.worldofbirds.org.za; Valley Rd, Hout Bay; adult/child R50/32; ⏱ 9am-5pm; Ⓟ

Everything, from barbets to weavers via flamingos and ostriches, is found here among the 3000 different birds and small mammals covering some 400 different species. A real effort has been made to make the aviaries, which are South Africa's largest, as natural looking as possible with the use of lots of tropical landscaping. In the monkey jungle you can interact with the cheeky squirrel monkeys.

SOUTHERN SUBURBS

Eating p131; Shopping p168; Sleeping p181; Entertainment p136

If you want to see how the other half in Cape Town lives – the rich half – take a trip into the Southern Suburbs, the residential areas clinging to the eastern slopes of Table Mountain. Heading south out of the City Bowl and around Devil's Peak you'll first pass through Woodstock, Observatory ('Obs' for short), Mowbray and Rondebosch. All have a laid-back, bohemian air, and a mixed racial profile. This is the territory of the University of Cape Town (UCT), whose buildings can be seen up on the side of Table Mountain.

Leafy Newlands and Bishopscourt are clearly affluent, mainly white suburbs. This said, the area around Claremont station is a fascinating study in contrasts, with black and coloured traders crowding the streets around the ritzy Cavendish Square mall; Mandela has a home in Bishopscourt; and white beggars are now a common sight on Newlands' streets. Times are certainly changing.

Wynberg, the next major suburb south, is another place where the haves rub shoulders with the have-nots. The most likely reason you'll head here is to attend a performance at the **Maynardville Open-Air Theatre** (p147) and to explore the quaint enclave known as Chelsea Village. Immediately to the west is Constantia, home to South Africa's oldest wineries (p44) where the superwealthy live in huge mansions that are well protected behind high walls. It's a verdant area that culminates in **Tokai** (p71), with its shady forest reserve.

Orientation

Drivers should take the N2 from the city centre or the M3 from Orange St in Gardens. These freeways merge near the Groote Schuur Hospital in Observatory, then run around Devil's Peak. The M3 sheers off to the right soon after (take care manoeuvring

Sights

SOUTHERN SUBURBS

> ### TRANSPORT
>
> The Southern Suburbs sights are all fairly spread out, so having access to a car is ideal if you plan to tour here. The best public-transport option is the Simon's Town railway line, with stops at Observatory, Rondebosch, Newlands and Claremont. The City Sightseeing Cape Town Blue Route bus (see p81) will also get you to and from Kirstenbosch.

into the right lanes!) and then runs parallel to the east side of the mountain with clearly indicated turn-offs for UCT, the Rhodes Memorial, Newlands and the Kirstenbosch Botanical Gardens. Stick on the M3 to get to Constantia and Tokai.

Main Rd, beginning in Observatory and running parallel to the M3, goes through Rondebosch, and past the Irma Stern Museum and the Baxter Theatre on its way to Newlands and Claremont where it becomes Newlands Rd. If you're heading to the cricket ground, Newlands train station is next to the east exit. For the rugby stadium and South African Breweries you'll need to exit on the west side of the station and walk north for about five minutes along Sport Pienaar Rd to Boundary Rd.

OBSERVATORY
TRANSPLANT MUSEUM Map p256
☎ 021-404 5232; www.capegateway.gov.za /eng/your_gov/5972/facilities/131/100419; Groote Schuur Hospital, Observatory; adult/child R10/5; 9am-2pm Mon-Fri; P

Capetonians are very proud that their city was the first place in the world where a successful heart transplant operation was carried out (never mind that the recipient died a few days later). This museum allows you to see the very theatre in Groote Schuur Hospital where history was made in 1967. The displays have a fascinating Dr Kildare quality to them, especially given the heart-throb status of Dr Christiaan Barnard at the time. To reach the hospital from Observatory Train Station, walk west along Station Rd for about 10 minutes. If you're driving from the city, take the Eastern Blvd (N2) turn-off at Browning Rd, and then turn right on Main Rd.

RONDEBOSCH & PINELANDS
GROOTE SCHUUR Map pp246-7
☎ 021-686 9100; Groote Schuur Estate, Klipper Rd; admission R60; tours by appointment only; P

Once belonging to Cecil Rhodes (see opposite), this is one of the nation's seminal buildings – a symbol of the country's past and its future. Since Rhodes bequeathed it to the nation, it has been home to a succession of prime ministers, culminating with FW de Klerk. The beautifully restored interior, all teak panels and heavy colonial furniture, antiques and tapestries of the finest calibre, is suitably imposing.

The best feature is the colonnaded veranda overlooking the formal gardens, sloping uphill towards an avenue of pine trees and sweeping views of Devil's Peak. The tour includes tea on the veranda. You must bring your passport to gain entry to this high-security area; the entrance is unmarked but easily spotted on the left as you take the Princess Anne Ave exit off the M3.

IRMA STERN MUSEUM Map pp246-7
☎ 021-685 5686; www.irmastern.co.za; Cecil Rd, Rosebank; adult/child R10/5; 10am-5pm Tue-Sat

Pioneering 20th-century artist Irma Stern (1894–1966) lived in this house for 38 years and her studio has been left intact, as if she'd just stepped out into the verdant garden for some fresh air. Her ethnographic art-and-craft collection from around the world is as fascinating as her own expressionist art, which has been compared to Gauguin's.

To reach the museum from Rosebank station, walk a few minutes west to Main Rd, cross over and walk up Chapel St.

OUDE MOLEN ECO VILLAGE Map p256
☎ 021-448 6419; Alexandra Rd, Pinelands; P

The only organic farm within Cape Town's city limits can be found at the Oude Molen Eco Village. This is only one of the several grass-roots-style operations occupying this once-abandoned section of the buildings and grounds of the Valkenberg mental hospital. You can volunteer to work at the farm through the Workers on Organic Farms scheme (www.wwoof.org), as well as stay at a backpackers lodge called Lighthouse Farm Lodge (p181), or go horse riding (p155). A large government grant is enabling the folks who run the site to turn it into a showcase for sustainable development.

RHODES MEMORIAL Map pp246-7
Groote Schuur Estate, above University of Cape Town

Modelled after the arch at London's Hyde Park Corner, the impressive granite memorial to the mining magnate and former prime minister (see below) stands on the eastern slopes of Table Mountain. Rhodes bought all this land in 1895 for £9000 as part of a plan to preserve a relatively untouched section of the mountain for future generations. Despite there being a sweeping view from the memorial to the Cape Flats and the mountain ranges beyond – and, by implication, right into the heart of Africa – the statue of Rhodes himself has the man looking rather grumpy. Behind the memorial there's a pleasant tearoom, the Rhodes Memorial Restaurant, in an old stone cottage. The exit for the memorial is at the Princess Anne Interchange on the M3.

UNIVERSITY OF CAPE TOWN
Map pp246-7
UCT; www.uct.ac.za

For the nonacademic there's no real reason to visit the University of Cape Town, but it's nonetheless an impressive place to walk around. Unlike most universities, UCT presents a fairly cohesive architectural front, with ivy-covered neoclassical façades, and a fine set of stone steps leading to the temple-like Jameson building. Visitors can usually get parking permits at the university – call in at the information office on the entry road, near the bottom of the steps.

As you're following the M3 from the city, just after the open paddocks on Devil's Peak, you'll pass the old **Mostert's Mill**, a real Dutch windmill dating from 1796, on the left. Just past the old windmill, also on the left, is the exit for the university. To get here, turn right at the T-intersection after you've taken the exit.

Alternatively, if you approach UCT from Woolsack Dr, you'll pass the **Woolsack**, a cottage designed in 1900 by Sir Herbert Baker for Cecil Rhodes, who once owned the entire area. The cottage was the winter residence of Rudyard Kipling from 1900 to 1907 and it's said he wrote the poem *If* here.

NEWLANDS
KIRSTENBOSCH BOTANICAL GARDENS Map pp244-5
☎ 021-799 8783, Sat & Sun 021-761 4916; www.sanbi.org; Rhodes Dr, Newlands; adult/child R25/5; ☷ 8am-7pm Sep-Mar, 8am-6pm Apr-Aug; Ⓟ

Covering over 500 hectares of Table Mountain, this is one of the most beautiful gardens in the world. The landscaped section merges almost imperceptibly with the *fynbos* (fine bush) vegetation cloaking the mountain and overlooking False Bay and the Cape Flats.

The gardens were established by Jan van Riebeeck, who appointed a forester in 1657. A group of shipwrecked French refugees on their way to Madagascar was employed during 1660 to plant the famous wild almond hedge as the boundary of the Dutch outpost (it's still here). Van Riebeeck called his private farm Boschheuwel, and most likely it wasn't until the 1700s, when the gardens were managed by JF Kirsten, that they got the name Kirstenbosch.

Sights

SOUTHERN SUBURBS

CECIL RHODES: EMPIRE BUILDER

The epitome of a self-made man, Cecil John Rhodes (1853–1902) was a legend in his own lifetime. When he arrived in South Africa in 1870, he was a sickly, impoverished son of an English vicar. The climate obviously agreed with Rhodes, as he not only recovered his health but went on to found the De Beers mining company (which in 1891 owned 90% of the world's diamond mines) and become prime minister of the Cape in 1890 at the age of 37.

As part of his dream of building a railway from the Cape to Cairo (running through British territory all the way), Rhodes pushed north to establish mines and develop trade. He established British control in Bechuanaland (later Botswana) and the area that was to become Rhodesia (later Zimbabwe). His grand ideas of Empire went too far, though, when he became involved in a failed uprising in the Boer-run Transvaal Republic in 1895. An embarrassed British government forced Rhodes to resign as prime minister in 1896, but Rhodesia and Bechuanaland remained his personal fiefdoms.

His personal life was troubled. Rhodes never married, although he became entangled in the schemes of the glamorous and ruthless Princess Randziwill, who was later jailed for her swindles. It's rumoured that he may have been gay. His health again in decline, Rhodes returned to Cape Town in 1902, only to die from his ailments at the age of 49 at his home in Muizenberg. Rhodes' reputation was largely rehabilitated by his will. He devoted most of his fortune to the Rhodes scholarship, which sends recipients to Oxford University, and his land and many properties in Cape Town now belong to the nation.

Apart from the almond hedge, some magnificent oaks, and the Moreton Bay fig and camphor trees planted by Cecil Rhodes, the gardens are devoted almost exclusively to indigenous plants. About 9000 of Southern Africa's 22,000 plant species are grown here. You'll find a kopje (hill) that has been planted with pelargoniums; a sculpture garden; a section for plants used for *muti* (medicine) by *sangomas* (traditional African healers); and a fragrance garden with raised beds and plants that can be smelt and felt, which were developed so that sight-impaired people could enjoy the garden – the plant labels here are also in Braille.

The main entrance at the Newlands end of the gardens is where you'll find plenty of parking, the information centre, an excellent souvenir shop and the atmosphere-controlled **conservatory** (🕙 9am-6pm). The conservatory displays plant communities from a variety of terrains, the most interesting of which is the Namaqualand and Kalahari section, with baobabs and quiver trees. Further along Rhodes Dr is the Ryecroft Gate entrance, the first you'll come to if you approach the gardens from Constantia.

Call to find out about free guided walks, or hire the My Guide electronic gizmo (R35) to receive recorded information about the various plants you'll pass on the three sign-posted circular walks. There is always something flowering, but the gardens are at their best between mid-August and mid-October.

The **Sunday afternoon concerts** (adult/child incl entry to the gardens R35/10; 🕙 from 5.30pm end Nov-Apr) are a Cape Town institution, attracting some of the biggest names in South African music. When the biggest groups, such as Freshly Ground, play it's advisable to get here well before the gates to the concert area open at 3pm; see p11 for more.

If you're driving from the city centre, the turn-off to the gardens is on the right at the intersection of Union Ave (the M3) and Rhodes Ave (the M63). Alternatively, walk down from the top of Table Mountain; see p74 for details.

SOUTH AFRICAN BREWERIES

Map pp246-7

☎ 021-658 7386; 3 Main Rd, Newlands; admission free; 🕙 tours by appointment only; Ⓟ
If wine tasting isn't your thing, then consider a visit to this Newlands-based operation, now owned by SABMiller, the world's second-biggest brewery. Free guided tours (minimum eight people), lasting around two hours, will take you through parts of the brewery dating back to the mid-1800s that have been granted National Monument status. Your reward at the end is a tasting session in the Letterstedt underground pub.

FALSE BAY & SOUTHERN PENINSULA

Eating p133; Shopping p169; Sleeping p182; Walking Tours p119; Entertainment p136

The southern end of the Cape Peninsula is practically a world unto itself, far divorced from the big-city bustle of the northern end of town. You'll be amply rewarded for taking a few days to explore the deep south's sights, the principal of which is magnificent **Cape Point** (p73). The beaches on the eastern False Bay side of the coast are not quite as scenically spectacular as those on the Atlantic side, but the water is often 5ºC or more warmer, and can reach 20ºC in summer. This makes swimming far more pleasant. For a good roundup of what's currently going on down this end of the peninsula check out www.capepointroute.co.za.

The first major False Bay community you hit after taking the M3 from the city is Muizenberg, one of the Cape's oldest settlements, established by the Dutch as a staging post for horse-drawn traffic in 1743. Muizenberg's heyday was the early 20th century when it was a prestigious seaside resort favoured by Cape Town's wealthy elite. By the turn of the millennium, it had fallen on hard times and had become an area synonymous with poor whites, black immigrants from neighbouring countries, and crime. Now its fortunes are on the up again with many derelict buildings being renovated or totally rebuilt along the waterfront and trendy new cafés and shops opening up.

East of Muizenberg is the low-lying marshy area known as Zeekovlei where you'll find a large lake and the Rondevlei Nature Reserve.

Heading west of Muizenberg along the bay the genteel suburb of St James shades into the charming fishing village of Kalk Bay. Named after the kilns that produced lime from seashells, used for painting buildings in the 17th century, this is a delightful destination offering many antique and craft shops, good café's and a lively daily fish market. During apartheid Kalk Bay was neglected by government and business as it was mainly a coloured area. All that is now changing with a huge property development, the **Majestic Kalk Bay** (www.the majesticinkalkbay.com), underway along Main Rd. This is likely to change the serene nature of the village, but the extra commerce is especially welcome as the local fishing community is suffering hard times in the wake of the government's decision to slash the number of fishing licences issued.

The next suburbs along, Fish Hoek and Clovelly, have wide, safe beaches but are less attractive than their neighbours. Best to press on to Simon's Town, the nation's third-oldest European settlement. Named after governor Simon van der Stel, this was the VOC's winter anchorage from 1741 and became a naval base for the British in 1814. It has remained one ever since, the frigates now joined by pleasure boats that depart for thrilling cruises to Cape Point; for details see p81. St George's St, the main thoroughfare, is lined with preserved Victorian buildings. At the southern end of town is **Boulders** (p72) – the reason for the name becomes evident once you hit the beach, which is dotted with massive boulders. It's here that you'll also see the area's famous colony of penguins.

Heading across the peninsula, from Simon's Town through the mountaintop **Silvermine Nature Reserve** (p72), will bring you back to the Atlantic coast. Here you find Noordhoek, famous principally for its wide sandy beach and for being the southern start of the spectacular Chapman's Peak Dr. Further south is the surfing mecca of Kommetjie (pronounced komickey, but also known as just 'Kom'), an equally small, quiet and isolated crayfishing village, marked by the cast-iron Slangkop Lighthouse. Scarborough is the last coastal community before you round the peninsula to the entry to the **Cape of Good Hope Nature Reserve** (p73).

Orientation

By car, False Bay is reached most quickly along the M3. Main Rd is the coastal thoroughfare linking Muizenberg, St James, Kalk Bay and Fish Hoek, although a prettier (and often less congested) alternative route between Muizenberg and Kalk Bay is mountainside Boyes Rd, which provides fantastic views down the peninsula. From Fish Hoek, you can either head west across the peninsula to Kommetjie or continue down coastal Simonstown Rd to Simon's Town. In the centre of Simon's Town this road becomes St George's St and then later the M4 as it heads inexorably towards the entrance to Cape Point. Noordhoek and Kommetjie can also be approached by either Chapman's Peak Dr from Hout Bay, or via the scenic Ou Kaapse Rd running from Westlake just south of Constantia.

MUIZENBERG

JOAN ST LEGER LINDBERGH ARTS CENTRE Map p257

☎ 021-788 2795; www.muizenberg.info /jsllaf.asp; 18 Beach Rd, Muizenberg; ☯ 8.30am-4.30pm Mon-Fri

The great granddaughter of the founder of the *Cape Times*, Joan St Leger was an artist and poet. She bequeathed her Sir Herbert Baker–designed home plus the adjoining properties to make this excellent arts and cultural centre. It comprises four houses – **Sandhills**, where Baker lived for a short while and which is now a guesthouse (p182), **Swanbourne**, **Rokeby** and **Crawford-Lea**. Apart from the guesthouse, there're changing art displays, a wonderful reference library, a gallery of evocative photos of how

FALSE BAY & SOUTHERN PENINSULA TOP FIVE

- Cruise the antique shops, cafés and fishing harbour at Kalk Bay (opposite).
- Take a tractor-pulled safari tour through the Solole Game Reserve (p110).
- Explore the wild tip of the peninsula in the Cape of Good Hope Nature Reserve (p73).
- Meet the penguins at Boulders (p72).
- Kayak along the coast from Simon's Town (p156).

Muizenberg once looked, and a good café. Concerts are held on the first Thursday morning of the month (R40) and the last Wednesday evening of the month (R90 to R110) in the conservatory.

MUIZENBERG BEACH Map p257

This surf beach, popular with families, is famous for its row of primary-colour-painted Victorian bathing chalets. Surf boards can be hired and lessons booked at either **Roxy Surf Club** (p157) or **Gary's Surf School** (p157), and lockers are available in the pavilions on the promenade. The beach shelves gently and the sea is generally safer (not to mention warmer) than elsewhere along the peninsula. There's a fun **water slide** (30min/1hr/day pass R15/20/35; ☼ 9am-6pm) and plenty of parking, too.

NATALE LABIA MUSEUM Map p257

☎ 021-788 4106; www.museums.org.za/natale; 192 Main Rd, Muizenberg; admission R3; ☼ by appointment only Mon
Call ahead to see whether anything is showing at this charming Venetian-style mansion, a satellite of the South African National Gallery. The house still belongs to the family of the Italian count Natale Labia who had it built in 1930 when it served as the Italian legation. The interiors are exquisite and even if it's closed the pretty exterior is worth a brief look.

ZEEKOEVLEI

RONDEVLEI NATURE RESERVE

Map pp244-5
☎ 021-706 2404; www.rondevlei.co.za; Fisherman's Walk Rd, Zeekoevlei; adult/child R5/2.50; ☼ 7.30am-5pm year-round, 7.30am-7pm Sat & Sun Dec-Feb; Ⓟ
Hippos hadn't lived in the marshes here for 300 years until they were reintroduced in 1981 to this small, picturesque nature reserve northeast of Muizenberg. There are now eight hippos, but they're shy creatures and it's unlikely that you'll spot them unless you stay overnight – for details of how to do this, contact **Imvubu Nature Tours** (p91), based at the reserve. Guided walks are available, and you can spot some 231 species of birds from the waterside trail, as well as from two viewing towers and hides.

ST JAMES

RHODES COTTAGE MUSEUM Map p257

☎ 021-788 1816; 246 Main Rd, St James; admission by donation; ☼ 10am-4pm
Yet another of Sir Herbert Baker's designs, **Rust-en-Vrede**, Cecil Rhodes' pretty cottage is now an engaging museum where you can find out all about Rhodes (see p105), who died in a neighbouring cottage in 1902. The cottage has pleasant gardens, which are a lovely spot to rest and spot whales from during the season.

KALK BAY

KALK BAY HARBOUR Map p257

Kalk Bay's attractive fishing harbour is at its most picturesque in the late morning when the community's few remaining fishing boats pitch up with their daily catch and a lively quayside market ensues. This is an excellent place to buy fresh fish for a braai (barbecue).

FISH HOEK

JAGER'S WALK Map pp244-5

At the southern end of the beach at Fish Hoek, this paved walk provides a pleasant stroll of around 1km to Sunny Cove (which is on the train line). If you're feeling energetic, you could walk the remaining 5km from here along an unpaved road to Simon's Town.

SIMON'S TOWN

HERITAGE MUSEUM Map p258

☎ 021-786 2302; www.simonstown.com/museum /sthm.htm; Almay House, King George Way, Simon's Town; adult/child R5/2; ☼ 11am-4pm Tue-Fri, 11am-1pm Sat, by appointment only Sun
Simon's Town's community of Cape Muslims was 7000 strong before apartheid forcibly removed most of them, mainly to the suburb of Ocean's View across on the Atlantic side of the peninsula. This interesting small museum, dedicated to the evictees and based in Almay House dating from 1858, is enthusiastically curated by Zainab Davidson, whose family was kicked out in 1975. Nearby Alfred Lane leads to the handsome mosque and attached school built in 1926.

SIMON'S TOWN MUSEUM Map p258
☎ 021-786 3046; www.simonstown.com
/museum/stm_main.htm; Court Rd, Simon's Town;
adult/child R5/2; 9am-4pm Mon-Fri,
10am-1pm Sat, 11am-3pm Sun
Housed in the old governor's residence
(1777), the exhibits in this rambling
museum trace Simon's Town's history.
Included is a display on Just Nuisance, the
Great Dane that was adopted as a navy
mascot in WWII, and whose grave, off
Redhill Dr above the town, makes for a
healthy walk from the harbour. There's also
a statue of Just Nuisance in Jubilee Sq, by
the harbour.

SOUTH AFRICAN NAVAL MUSEUM
Map p258
☎ 021-787 4635; www.simonstown.com
/navalmuseum; St George's St, Simon's Town;
admission free; 10am-4pm
Definitely one for naval enthusiasts, this
museum nonetheless has plenty of interesting exhibits, including a mock submarine,
that let you play out boyish adventure
fantasies.

Statue of Just Nuisance (above), Simon's Town

From late May to early December, False Bay is a favourite haunt of whales and their calves, with the
peak viewing season being October and November.
Southern right whales, humpback whales and bryde
(pronounced bree-dah) whales are the most commonly sighted, and they often come close to the
shore. Good viewing spots include the coastal walk
from Muizenberg to St James (p119); the Brass Bell
(p141) at Kalk Bay; and Jager's Walk (opposite) at
Fish Hoek. You can also take whale-watching cruises
(p81) from Simon's Town's harbour.

NOORDHOEK
NOORDHOEK BEACH Map pp244-5
This magnificent 5km stretch of beach is favoured by surfers and horse riders. It tends
to be windy, and dangerous for swimmers.
The Hoek, as it is known to surfers, is an
excellent right beach break at the northern
end that can hold large waves (only at low
tide); it's best with a southeasterly wind.

KOMMETJIE
IMHOFF FARM Map pp244-5
☎ 021-783 4545; www.imhofffarm.co.za;
Kommetjie Rd; admission free; 10am-5pm
Tue-Sun; P
There's a great deal to see and do at this
historic and very attractive farmstead, just
outside Kommetjie. Among the attractions are craft shops and studios, a café,
the Kommetjie Environmental Awareness
Group (KEAG; whose creative decorative
products, made with waste plastic, tin cans
and glass, you'll see increasingly around
the Cape), a snake and reptile park, a farm-
yard stocked with animals, and camel and
donkey rides.

KOMMETJIE BEACHES Map pp244-5
A focal point for surfing on the Cape, Kommetjie offers an assortment of reefs that
hold a very big swell. Outer Kommetjie is a
left point out from Slangkop Lighthouse at
the southern end of the village. Inner Kommetjie is a more-protected, smaller left with
lots of kelp (only at high tide). They both
work best with a southeasterly or southwesterly wind. For breezy beach walks, it
doesn't get much better than the aptly
named Long Beach, accessed off Benning Dr.

Sights

FALSE BAY & SOUTHERN PENINSULA

SOLOLE GAME RESERVE Map pp244-5

☎ 021-785 3248; www.solole.co.za; 6 Wood Rd, Sunnydale; ⏲ 9.30am-5.30pm Mon-Fri, 9am-5pm Sat & Sun; Ⓟ

It's hardly Kruger National Park, but there's much to recommend in this game reserve, which covers 350 hectares on the way to Kommetjie, not least the cheeky irreverence. For example, a 45-minute game drive costs R30 unless you're an 'ill-disciplined brat' and then its R5000! Kids both big and small will enjoy riding up the mountainside in an open cart tugged by a giant tractor. You'll view nine different species of buck, buffalo and the lone black rhino, Mokwena, the first to be returned to the Cape in several centuries. Guided walks (R90) are also available, or you can game spot for free at the hide by the excellent restaurant Mnandis (p134). The package of game tour, lunch and township tour (across the road at Masiphumelele) is good value at R200.

CAPE POINT

For information on the Cape of Good Hope Nature Reserve, see p73.

CAPE POINT OSTRICH FARM

Map pp244-5

☎ 021-780 9294; www.capepointostrichfarm.com; Sun Valley; guided tour adult/child R25/10; ⏲ 9.30am-5.30pm; Ⓟ

Ostriches are aplenty at this family-run farm and tourist complex just 600m from Cape Point's main gate. Tours are conducted at regular intervals around the breeding facilities. The well-stocked shop is notable, if for nothing else than the myriad artistic ways that ostrich eggs can be turned into decorative objects.

CAPE FLATS

Eating p134; Sleeping p183

The Cape Flats suburbs, sprawling across the flat and dusty plains east of Table Mountain, seldom get good press, stricken as they are with violent crime, crippling poverty and astronomic rates of HIV/AIDS infection. The down-at-heel coloured communities and informal settlements of the largely black townships would seem unlikely candidates as tourist destinations, let alone be among the places that might

end up providing your fondest memories of Cape Town. Yet a township tour (see p81 and p112), and an evening soaking up the carnival atmosphere of the Cape Minstrel competition (see p10) in Athlone are among our highlights of the Mother City.

A township tour is one of the most illuminating and life-affirming things you can do while in Cape Town. You'll see how the vast majority of Capetonians really live and learn a hell of a lot about South African history and the cultures of black South Africans. Better still is to stay overnight at one of several B&Bs (p183) in Langa (meaning 'Sun' in Xhosa), founded in 1927 and the oldest planned township in South Africa, or in Khayelitsha, one of the nation's largest townships with an estimated population of more than 1.8 million.

It's not all one-note misery. The infrastructure in the townships has certainly improved since 1994 (it could hardly have got any worse), with the rows of concrete Reconstruction and Development Programme (RDP) houses being the most visible examples. There's even a website Etownship (www .etownship.co.za) which highlights a bunch of great developments and activities. However, vast squatter camps, with communal standpipes for water and toilets shared among scores of people, still remain and are expanding all the time.

Orientation

Many township tours follow similar itineraries. After starting in the Bo-Kaap for a brief discussion of Cape Town's colonial history, you'll move on to the District Six Museum (p94). You'll then be driven to the Cape Flats to visit some or all of the following townships: Langa, Guguletu, Crossroads and Khayelitsha. Tour guides are generally flexible in where they go, and respond to the wishes of the group. The listings below detail possible stops.

TRANSPORT

As long as you have a specific destination, say one of the township B&Bs, its safe enough to drive yourself into the townships, but as always with poor areas, be cautious if you do this and try not to throw temptation in front of the less fortunate. Otherwise the best ways to see the townships are on organised half-day tours. See p81 for more details.

KHAYELITSHA

GOLDEN'S FLOWERS Map pp244-5

One of the major success stories of the township-tour circuit is Golden Sonwabo Nonquase who together with his family makes beautiful flowers from scrap tins at his Khayelitsha home. The idea came to him in a recurring dream and is now widely copied and adapted by other Cape Flats crafters.

KHAYELITSHA CRAFT MARKET

Map pp244-5

☎ 021-361 2904; www.stmichaels.org.za; St Michael's Church, Ncumo Rd, Harare, Khayelitsha; ◷ 9am-5pm Mon-Fri, 9am-1pm Sat

This church-run empowerment project is a great place to look for interesting souvenirs, and you can be sure that your money goes directly to the people who need it most. A Marimba band usually plays and you can buy its CDs.

PHILANI NUTRITION CENTRE

Map pp244-5

☎ 021-387 5124; www.philani.org.za

This long-running community-based health-and-nutrition organisation has six projects running in the townships, including a weaving factory and shop in Khayelitsha's Site C and a printing project. Women are taught how to feed their families adequately on a low budget, and the crèche and various projects enable them to earn an income through weaving rugs and wall hangings, making paper, printing and other crafts. Philani goods are available from many shops around the Cape.

ROSIE'S SOUP KITCHEN Map pp244-5

☎ 021-362 6131

From Monday to Saturday the saintly Rosie serves some 600 meals a day to the poor at 60¢ a plate. A wooden shed outside her home has been built as a canteen.

TYGERBERG TOURISM FACILITY

Map pp244-5

Many Khayelitsha residents view this often-empty cultural and tourism centre as a huge white elephant. Its principal benefit comes from the impressive wooden staircase leading to the top of a sand hill, the highest point in the townships, for a sweeping view of the surroundings.

GUGULETU

SIVUYILE TOURISM CENTRE

Map pp244-5

☎ 021-637 8449; cnr NY1 & NY4, College of Cape Town, Guguletu; ◷ 8am-5pm Mon-Fri, 8am-2pm Sat

Inside a local technical college, this tourism centre has an interesting photographic display on the townships, artists at work, an Internet café and a good gift shop. You'll also find the creative Uncedo Pottery Project (☎ 021-633 5461) here.

LANGA

GUGA S'THEBE ARTS & CULTURAL CENTRE Map pp244-5

☎ 021-695 3493, 082 746 0246; cnr Washington & Church Sts, Langa; ◷ 9am-5pm Mon-Fri, 9am-1pm Sat

Brilliantly decorated with gorgeous ceramic murals, this is one of the most impressive buildings in the townships if not in all of Cape Town. A host of community classes are held here, including beadwork and the making of traditional garments and pottery. Performances by local groups are often held in the outdoor amphitheatre.

While here also check out the wonderful mosaic-decorated plinths along the street outside. Each side of the four plinths has a different theme, one of which is the only memorial to the SS *Mendi*, a troop ship that sank in the English Channel in 1917 drowning 600 members of the South African Native Labour Corps. The huge mural painted on the building opposite the cultural centre was done by Philip Kgosana, the man held aloft in the composition – it commemorates the defiance campaign of 1960.

TSOGA ENVIRONMENTAL RESOURCE CENTRE Map pp244-5

☎ 021-694 0004; Washington St, Langa; ◷ 8am-5pm Mon-Fri

Prince Charles planted a tree in 1997 at this centre built on a patch of once-barren wasteland in the heart of Langa. It's doing well, as is the centre, where respect for the environment is encouraged through recycling and the cultivation of a market garden. The latest venture is providing walking tours (p91). The restaurant Eziko (p134) is across the road.

A TOUR THROUGH LANGA Simon Richmond

Langa, nestling behind the twin towers of Athlone Power Station and the newly built N2 Gateway complex of council hous-ing, is Cape Town's oldest area of forced black resettlement dating back to 1927. Today it's home to 250,000 people – the same number who live in the city centre but squashed into a suburb some 48 times smaller.

Faizal Gangat of **Cape Capers Tours** (p82) tells me he chooses to focus on Langa for his township tour because the suburb's history mirrors the long march to freedom experienced by the rest of South Africa. On the drive to Langa from the Waterfront, Faizal provides a running commentary on that troubled history and explains the various unusual things I might see. For example, on a patch of waste ground in front of the power station, what looks like the start of a squatter settlement is actually the initiation ground for Langa's young men.

In front of the St Andrews Mission Centre, Faizal details its success with the Fatherhood Project of workshops to get errant fathers to accept their family obligations. He points out how the roads and pavements have recently been improved, how trees are being planted, and how the locals are now better dressed, better groomed, and have far more of a spring in their step. At the **Guga S'Thebe Arts & Cultural Centre** (p111), where a pottery class or musical recital may be happening, there's an even stronger impression of the vitality of Langa.

At the **Tsoga Environmental Resource Centre** (p111), Faizal hands over to Khanyiso, a young guide who walks me through a shebeen, a butcher's and past Langa High School, alma mater of the late pop star Brenda Fassie and Cape Town's former mayor Nomaindia Mfeketo. In his company I'm welcomed into the cramped living quarters of the dilapidated workers' hostels from the 1930s where two or three families still share one room (rent R20 per month) and barefoot children play in the rubbish-strewn courtyards. At least these people have brick walls and a solid roof over their heads; at the end of the road the 'informal settlement' of shacks houses thousands more.

Over a simple, tasty lunch at **Eziko** (p134) I take it all in, digesting the contrasts of a place where those in crippling poverty live next to the middle class of Langa's 'Beverly Hills' district of big brick villas. It's not my first time in the township and it's unlikely to be my last. Despite the obvious problems, every visit impresses on me how life is generally improving and how creative and resilient people can be in the face of hardship.

VICTORIA MXENGE
VICTORIA MXENGE WOMEN'S
GROUP Map pp244-5
☎ 072 235 5854, 072 236 4340;
www.africandream.org
On a small plot of land just south of the junction of Lansdowne and Ottery Rds is the small community of Victoria Mxenge, named after one of the heroes of the struggle. At the community's centre you can hear from the local women how, sick of living in shacks, they started a joint savings scheme and

taught themselves every aspect of building to design and constructed their own homes. For little more than the cost of the very basic and tiny RDP home (see the boxed text, p30), the women can build three-bedroom homes of around 85 sq metres.

So successful has their self-help project been that they now advise other women's groups around the world how to build homes. For more details about the project, check out the website: navigate to the Cape Care Route section and click on the link for Victoria Mxenge and Peace Lily Project.

Walking Tours

Walking Tours

Central Cape Town is an ambler's delight. A wander down Long St and across Greenmarket Square to St George's Mall will provide enough colour and interest for most casual strollers, but if you want a more-focused point to your perambulations try out the first couple of walks detailed here. If it's the sea breeze you hanker for, journey down to False Bay and enjoy the sweeping coastal views around Muizenberg. If you're interested in organised tours, see p81.

ART & ARCHITECTURE WALK

A building boom in Cape Town during the 1930s resulted in the city centre having a remarkable number of grand Art Deco buildings, many of which are now being turned from office blocks into residential units. This walk takes you past some of the key buildings, which stand side by side with contrasting architectural styles from earlier and later periods. You'll also see a couple of pieces of contemporary public art. There are plenty of opportunities to shop, eat, drink and rest along the way.

Starting from **Cape Town Train Station** 1, a squat building dating from the 1960s, look across to the corner of Adderley and Riebeeck Sts to view the **Colosseum Building** 2. Designed by WH Grant, one of Cape Town's foremost Art Deco architects, this pale green-and-cream-painted building has striking 'Aztec style' mouldings. Turn left onto the pedestrianised St George's Mall; here, opposite Waterkant St, is Brett Murray's quirky statue **Africa** 3. This African-curio bronze statue, sprouting bright-yellow Bart Simpson heads, is typical of Murray's satirical style and caused much public debate on its unveiling in 2000.

Continue to the junction with Strand St, turn right then turn left onto Burg St. At No 24 is **New Zealand House** 4, designed by WH Grant in a style known as Cape Mediterranean. Next door at No 26, the elegant symmetry of **Hardware House** 5 leads you on to the more-elaborate pink, grey and cream **Namaqua House** 6, on the corner of Shortmarket St.

You're now in cobbled **Greenmarket Square** 7 (p162), created as a farmers market in the early 18th century and filled from Monday to Saturday with one of the city's best crafts and souvenir markets (p162). Three quarters of the buildings surrounding the square hail from the 1930s, the main exception being the **Old Townhouse** 8, completed in 1761 and now home to the Michaelis Collection (p96) of Dutch and Flemish masterpieces.

Market, Greenmarket Square (p162)

Walking in a clockwise direction around the square, check out **Kimberley House 9** at 34 Shortmarket St, which is built of sandstone and decorated with an attractive diamond-theme design. **Market House 10**, fronting onto the square, is the most elaborately decorated building of all and has majestic stone-carved eagles and flowers on its façade.

Next to Market House, the dazzling-white **Protea Insurance Building 11** was built in 1928 and renovated in 1990. Opposite is **Shell House 12**, once the South African headquarters of Shell, now housing a hotel and restaurant. Exit the square on Burg St and take the next right onto the pedestrianised portion of **Church St 13**. There's a flea market here from Monday to Saturday and you'll also find a fine collection of galleries and craft shops.

On the corner of Burg and Wale Sts is the **Waalburg Building 14**. Take a moment to admire the bronze and Table Mountain–stone panels decorating the building's façade and depicting scenes of South African life. On the other corner of Burg St, the **Rhodes Mandela complex 15** is taking shape: this promises to be one of the more interesting of the City Bowl's new regeneration projects.

WALK FACTS

Start Cape Town Train Station
End Church Sq
Distance 2km
Duration Two hours minimum
Fuel stops Crush (p123) and Speakers Corner (p124)

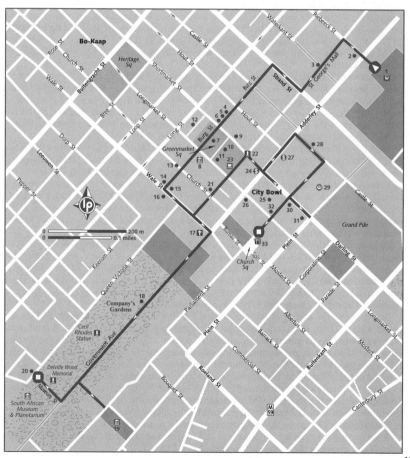

Handicrafts, stall in St George's Mall (p161)

Across Wale St is the **Western Cape Legislature 16**, its grey bulk enlivened by the fun stone-carved detail of animal heads. Just past **St George's Cathedral 17**, also on Wale St, is the entrance to **Company's Gardens 18** (p93). It's a lovely place to rest and, if you have time, you can also explore the country's best collection of contemporary art at the **SA National Gallery 19** (p98). Before leaving, nip out to the Queen Victoria St side of the gardens to view one of the city's favourite Art Deco buildings: **Holyrood 20**, an apartment block reminiscent of a vacuum cleaner.

Retrace your steps to Wale St, turn into St George's Mall and continue to Longmarket St, passing **Newspaper House 21** at No 122, another Cape Mediterranean–style building by Grant. Set into the pavement at the junction of Shortmarket St and St George's Mall is a piece of modern art that is easily overlooked: **Come to Pass 22** is by Fritha Langerman and Katherine Bull, winners of the Cape Town Public Sculpture Competition in 2002. If you're feeling peckish, a good option is the nearby **Crush 23** (p123) on St George's Mall.

Turn down Shortmarket St, walk to the junction with Adderley St and pause to witness the evolution of contrasting architectural styles along what was once the city's premier shopping street. Immediately to your right is the **First National Bank 24**, completed in 1913, and one of the final projects of Sir Herbert Baker (see p32): pop inside to see some of the bank's original fittings. Opposite is the brutal concrete-slab tower **Cartwright's Corner 25**, named after a department store that once stood here. The 1970s office block has been converted into some of the city's swankiest apartment buildings. A similar fate has occurred to the far more ornate **Adderley Terrace 26**, on the corner of Adderley and Longmarket Sts.

Head up Adderley St, past the grand Edwardian edifice of the **Standard Bank 27** and turn right into **Trafalgar Place 28**: this broad alleyway is where scores of flower sellers gather day and night to offer bunches of roses, lilies and other blooms. At the end of the alleyway is the **General Post Office 29**. There is still a post office here, although much of the ground floor has been taken over by smaller market stalls. Look above them to discover colourful painted panels of Cape Town scenes by GW Pilkington and Sydney Carter.

Emerge onto the corner of Parliament and Darling Sts to face **Mutual Heights 30** (see the boxed text, p97), the most impressive Art Deco building in all of Cape Town. A craft complex is planned for its ground floor, but even if it hasn't opened yet, duck into the soaring entrance hall to admire the beautiful gold-veined black marble and chrome decoration. Also take some time to inspect the incredibly detailed stone friezes around the building's façade; the side of the building on Parliament St is adorned with noble carvings of African races.

Next to Mutual Heights, on the corner of Darling and Plein Sts, is the grey-and-blue **Scotts Building 31**, displaying yet again Grant's elegant designs. Return to Parliament St and walk to the intersection with Longmarket St marked by the glossy black chrome-and-glass façade of **Mullers Opticians 32**, one of the best preserved Art Deco shop fronts in the city.

A few steps further along Parliament St will bring you to Church Square, where you can refresh and revive in the lovely café **Speakers Corner 33** (p124).

HISTORY WALK

Cape Town's turbulent history is revealed in the many buildings, statues and street names that grace the City Bowl and Bo-Kaap. This walk will give you an insight into the forces and personalities that have shaped the city you see today.

South Africa's oldest European fortification, the star-shaped **Castle of Good Hope** 1 (p93) is an appropriate place to start. Immediately west is **Grand Parade** 2, the former military-parade and public-execution ground, which is now home to a lively market every Wednesday and Saturday. Jan van Riebeeck's original mud-walled fort was here, too, and you can see its position outlined in red at the Plein St end of the parade. The balcony of the impressive **Old Town Hall** 3, on the southwest side of the parade, is where Nelson Mandela gave his first public speech in 27 years following his release from prison in February 1990.

Walk up Buitenkant St to the **District Six Museum** 4 (p94) to learn about the history of this demolished inner-city area, a victim of apartheid's laws. From the museum

WALK FACTS

Start Castle of Good Hope
End Heritage Sq
Distance 3km
Duration Two hours minimum
Fuel stops Caveau (p137) and Birds Café (p124)

www.lonelyplanet.com

Walking Tours **HISTORY WALK**

Market, Grand Parade (p117)

turn right onto Albertus St, then turn right again at Corporation St to reach Mostert St and its continuation, Spin St. On the traffic island beside Church Sq, look down to see a circular plaque marking the location of the old **slave tree 5** under which slaves were sold until emancipation in 1834. In front of you is the **Groote Kerk 6** (p95), mother church for the Dutch Reformed Church. Across the road is the old **Slave Lodge 7** (p96), now a museum; at the back of the lodge on Parliament St look up at the sculpted relief on the pediment of an exhausted-looking lion and unicorn, a satirical comment by the stone mason on the Empire following the Napoleonic Wars.

Bureau St leads into Adderley St, named after the politician Charles Adderley who barracked successfully in London for Cape Town not to be turned into a penal colony. Prior to the mid-19th century, Adderley St was called the Heerengracht (Gentleman's Canal) after the waterway that once ran from the **Company's Gardens 8** (p93) down here to the sea. Explore the gardens by all means, but if you're pushed for time continue northwest up Wale St, past **St George's Cathedral 9**, for several blocks until you cross Buitengracht St (another canal filled over and made into a road) and the start of the area known as the Bo-Kaap.

To discover something on the history of this strongly Muslim area of the city, drop by the **Bo-Kaap Museum 10** (p93), on Wale St. The Bo-Kaap's steep streets, some of which are still cobbled, are lined with 18th-century flat-roofed houses and mosques; you'll hear the call to prayer from the **Owal Mosque 11**, on Dorp St, the oldest such place of worship in Cape Town. Chiappini and Rose Sts contain the prettiest houses, many of which sport bright paint jobs.

Along Rose St you'll find **Monkeybiz 12** (p162), while around the corner on Shortmarket St is **Streetwires 13** (p163), two businesses doing their bit to empower the disadvantaged and alleviate some of the city's social problems. Continue down Shortmarket St to the junction with Buitengracht St, across which you'll see a large car park covering **Van Riebeeck Square 14**. On the Bree St side is **St Stephen's Church 15**, built in 1799, originally the African Theatre and later a school for freed slaves, before it became a church in 1839.

Adjacent to Van Riebeeck Sq is **Heritage Square 16**, a beautiful collection of Cape Georgian and Victorian buildings saved from the wrecking ball in 1996. It's since been transformed into one of the city's trendiest dining and drinking enclaves, and includes the Cape Heritage Hotel (p174). There are plenty of places to grab something to eat and drink in Heritage Sq, including the wine bar **Caveau 17** (p137). Alternatively take a right turn along Bree St and head to the junction with Church St, where you'll find **Birds Café 18** (p124) one of the city's most delightful cafés.

MUIZENBERG–ST JAMES ROUND WALK

Muizenberg is currently undergoing something of a renaissance. This invigorating coastal walk allows you to discover the cafés and shops that are opening up in the area, as well as the wealth of notable architecture and spectacular views of False Bay that these grand properties command.

Starting at **Muizenberg Station** 1, exit onto Main Rd heading north past Muizenberg Park. Turn left on the corner of this small park up Camp Rd, passing the old red-and-white **synagogue** 2; Muizenberg had a large Jewish population in the 1920s and '30s. A flight of concrete steps leads up to Boyes Dr. From here the road gently climbs the slope until you have a commanding view across Muizenberg and its broad, flat beach. You'll pass a wrought-iron gate leading down to the **grave** 3 of the mining magnate Sir Abe Bailey (1864–1940) whose house **Rust-en-Vrede** 4 (p108), with its red tiles and high gables, can be glimpsed on Main Rd below. Rust-en-Vrede was commissioned by Cecil Rhodes, but he never lived in it; Rhodes died in a nearby cottage before the house could be completed.

As you round the corner, panoramic views open up across False Bay towards Simon's Town and Cape Point. This is also a prime location for whale-watching from October to November. On the right is the Silvermine Nature Reserve (p72); there are several marked tracks up the mountain here should you wish to gain a higher vantage point. If not, keep walking until you see the primary-colour-painted Victorian-style **bathing huts** 5 at St James. The Jacob's ladder steps lead steeply down from Boyes Dr to Main Rd and the underpass at St James Station, which leads through to the coastal walking path. Take a dip in the tidal pool to cool down and then continue along the coastal path back towards Muizenberg.

WALK FACTS

Start Train, Muizenberg Station
End Muizenberg Station
Distance 3km
Duration One hour
Fuel stops Olive Station (p133) and Empire Café (p133)

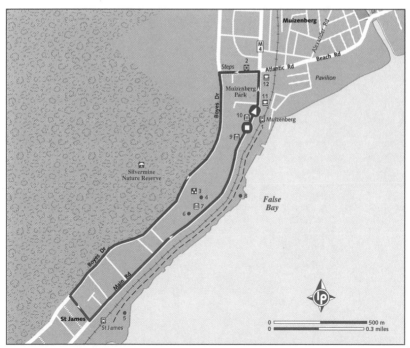

As you approach the grand Spanish-style **mansion** 6 with green-glazed roof tiles (called Gracelands after Elvis' pad), you'll see another underpass that will allow you to nip across to busy Main Rd and visit **Rhodes' Cottage** 7. Back on the coastal path, on the right-hand side is the thatched **Bailey's Cottage** 8, once Sir Abe Bailey's guest cottage and now reserved for use by members of parliament. Closer to Muizenberg, on Main Rd, you'll also pass the Italianate **Natale Labia Museum** 9 (p108) and the white-washed **Posthuys** 10. Dating from around 1740 and one of Cape Town's oldest European-style buildings, the Posthuys is now a small museum of limited appeal. It's only a minute's walk from here back to Muizenberg Station. Recommended places for refreshments are either the **Olive Station** 11 (p133) or the **Empire Café** 12 (p133).

Eating

Eating

Dining in the Mother City is a pleasure. There are places to suit practically everyone's tastes and budgets, with a particularly strong selection of cafés and delis. With both the sea and fruitful farmlands on hand, you can be pretty much assured of fresh, top-quality ingredients wherever you eat.

If we have a gripe, it's that accomplished cooking tends to run in third place to the inventive décors and lively atmospheres of many restaurants. That old South African predilection for incinerated meat, stodge and viscous sauces seems ingrained. But we have been pleased to see that the influx of capital and demands of overseas visitors in recent years has begun to raise the standard and selection of what qualifies as a great meal.

Most restaurants are licensed but some allow you to bring your own wine for little or no corkage. Call ahead to check the restaurant's policy. For more information on wine, see p40. Many bars serve excellent food; see p136 for some recommendations. And for details of cookery courses where you can learn how to prepare traditional Cape Malay and African dishes, see p151.

The magazine **Eat Out** (www.eatout.co.za), an annual restaurant guide to South Africa, is the place to look for the latest dining news; the website has a searchable database of reviewed Cape Town eateries.

Opening Hours

Cafés and restaurants generally open seven days a week, the former serving food from 7.30am to about 5pm. A few places (commonly in the City Bowl) are closed on Sunday or occasionally Monday. If a restaurant opens for lunch it will generally be from 11.30am to 3pm; dinner usually kicks off around 7pm with last orders at 10pm.

How Much?

Dining here is good value compared to what you'd pay for a similar standard of food elsewhere in the developed world. For breakfast or a quick alcohol-free lunch you'll be looking at around R50 to R70. The cost of dinner, including a couple of glasses of wine, is more typically in the range of R150 to R200, although you can easily pay R300 or more. The reviews in this chapter are broken down by neighbourhood, and under each neighbourhood heading, the reviews are listed in budget order, with the cheapest first.

Watch out for the sign 'Sq' on the menu where the price should be. This usually applies to premium seafood items, such as crayfish and Mozambique prawns, and means that you'll pay whatever the establishment considers the market price that day. Check what the price is for the dish (not just per kilogram) before you finally order if you want to avoid a nasty shock in the bill.

Booking Tables

Most restaurants take reservations for lunch and dinner, so call ahead if you want to ensure a seat. We've included reservation recommendations for especially popular restaurants.

Tipping

Waiters in Cape Town earn a pittance and rely heavily on tips. The standard tip for good service is 10% to 15%, but leave more if you think the staff have earned it. A few places include a service charge on the bill.

PRICE GUIDE

$$$	over R100 a meal
$$	R70-100 a meal
$	under R70 a meal

TOP FIVE PICNIC SPOTS

Cape Town's many green spaces and beaches are crying out for a well-stocked picnic hamper. Our favourite locations for an alfresco feast:

- Clifton (p102) – sunset supper on the beach. Bring candles for the ultimate romantic experience, but keep the alcohol hidden – it's actually illegal to imbibe on the beach.
- Cape of Good Hope Nature Reserve (known locally as Cape Point; p73) – take your pick from several beautiful and largely deserted beaches in the nature reserve, and keep an eye out for hungry baboons.
- Kirstenbosch Botanical Gardens (p105) – a Sunday-afternoon institution, particularly from December to March when you can enjoy a concert on these verdant, rolling lawns.
- Constantia – at Buitenverwachting (p44) picnics come prepacked (R90); book on ☎ 083 257 6083 or 082 974 8543. Or take your own to enjoy in the lovely grounds of Groot Constantia (p44).
- Silvermine (p72) – spread your picnic blanket beside the tannin-stained waters of the reserve's central reservoir.

Self-Catering

Cape Town has some fantastic delis, such as **Melissa's** (p129), **Gionvanni's Deli World** (p129), **Newport Market & Deli** (p130), **New York Bagels** (p130) and **Carlucci's** (Map p254; ☎ 021-465 0795; 22 Upper Orange St, Oranjezicht), which are ideal places to stock up for a picnic.

The main supermarkets – Pick 'n' Pay, Checkers and the more upscale Woolworths (modelled on Marks & Spencer in the UK) – are also well stocked and reasonably priced. You'll find branches of the three operations at **Victoria Wharf** (Map pp252–3; Waterfront), **Gardens Centre** (Map p254: Mill St, Gardens) and **Cavendish Square** (Map pp246–7; Cavendish St, Claremont) shopping malls. In the City Bowl there is a **Pick 'n' Pay** (Map pp248–9; Picbal Arcade, 58 Strand St) as well as **Checkers** (Map pp248–9; Golden Acre Centre, Adderley St).

Meal Times

Capetonians start the day early, particularly in the summer months; join them for breakfast between 7am and 9am. Lunch runs anywhere from noon to 3pm, while dinner starts around 7pm and finishes at 10pm. Note that at weekends dining later in the evening is more common, so if you're finding it difficult to get a reservation, ask for an early dinner and promise you'll be done by 9pm.

CITY CENTRE

Dining options are spread liberally across the city centre, with particular concentrations in the hip Waterkant district, Heritage Sq (which has no fewer than five restaurants and cafés), and that eternal favourite, Long St. Cafés are plentiful around Greenmarket Sq and St George's Mall, too. The Bo-Kaap, a good location for Cape Malay food, is best visited during the day; in the evenings it's dead.

CITY BOWL & BO-KAAP

CHARLY'S BAKERY

Map pp248-9   Bakery & Café $

☎ 021-461 5181; www.charlysbakery.co.za;
20 Roeland St, City Bowl; cupcakes R10;
⏰ 7.30am-4pm Mon-Fri
Don't leave Cape Town without having eaten one of Charly's chocolate cupcakes,

famously decorated with blindingly bright icing designs by his wife Jacqui. There's also a fantastic range of baked goods, including pies.

CRUSH Map pp248-9   Café $

☎ 021-422 5533; 100 St George's Mall, City Bowl;
mains R20-30; ⏰ 7am-7pm
One on the most pleasant and interesting places to eat on St George's Mall, Crush offers freshly squeezed juices, smoothies and tasty wraps, proving healthy eating need not be boring. There's also a branch on the **Foreshore** (Map pp248–9; Lower Loop St).

BLOWING SMOKE

Restaurants that allow smoking will have a separate section for smokers.

LOLA'S Map pp248-9   Café/Vegetarian $

☎ 021-423 0885; 228 Long St, City Bowl; mains R20-30; ☻ 8am-midnight

Whether you come for breakfast or a late-night coffee or beer, a visit to pastel-painted Lola's is a right of passage on Long St. Grab a street table and watch the passing parade.

PORTOBELLO Map pp248-9   Café/Vegetarian $

☎ 021-426 1418; 111 Long St, City Bowl; mains R20-30; ☻ 8am-5pm Mon-Fri, 9am-3pm Sat

This rustic and peaceful veggie café serves a great range of all-day breakfasts, toasties and freshly made sandwiches. If none of that appeals, go for the lunch buffet: R30 for three hot or cold servings, R40 for four serves.

FRIEDA'S Map pp248-9   Café $

☎ 021-421 2404; 15 Bree St, City Bowl; mains R30-40; ☻ 8am-4pm Mon-Fri

Hung with giant paper lanterns and plastered with technicolour Indian posters, jumble-sale chic is the look at this cavernous and highly convivial café. It's in the louche but up-and-coming area at the base of Bree St. It does a fine line in sandwiches, wraps, salads and comfort food, including lasagne.

MR PICKWICK'S Map pp248-9   Café $

☎ 021-423 3710; 158 Long St, City Bowl; mains R30-40; ☻ 8am-1.45am Mon, Tue & Thu, 8am-2.45am Wed, 8am-3.45am Fri & Sat, 7am-12.45am Sun

Few places in Cape Town keep hours as long as raucous Mr Pick's, which explains its long-running appeal to the clubbing set. At all times, though, this licensed, deli-style café is worth dropping by for the good snacks and meals.

R CAFFÉ Map pp248-9   Café $

☎ 021-424 1124; 138 Long St, City Bowl; mains R30-40; ☻ 6.30am-5pm Mon-Fri, 8.30am-4pm Sat

An appealing addition to Long St's collection of cafés. Minimalist décor and lots of space allow you to enjoy an awesome berry smoothie or the homemade quiches and sandwiches.

SPEAKERS CORNER Map pp248-9   Café $

☎ 021-461 8872; 3 Church Sq, Parliament St, City Bowl; mains R30-40; ☻ 6.30am-7pm Mon-Fri, 8.30am-2pm Sat

The spirited debate of politicos from nearby parliament rings through this smart café. The menu is delicious: the cakes and desserts are especially yummy. Here's hoping it survives the redevelopment of the building – if not, try the sister operation **Bread, Milk & Honey** (Map pp248–9; ☎ 084 585 8085; 10 Spin St, City Bowl) across the square.

SUNDANCE Map pp248-9   Café $

☎ 021-465 9990; www.sundancecoffeeco.com; 21 Adderley St, City Bowl; sandwiches R30-40; ☻ 6.30am-9.30pm

Leading the way with daily opening hours in the city, this mini-chain café is stealing some of Vida e Caffé's thunder on the coffee scene. It does good set-menu coffee and sandwich menus for breakfast and lunch. There's another branch in **City Bowl** (Map pp248–9; 59 Buitengracht St), on the corner of Heritage Sq.

BIRDS CAFÉ Map pp248-9   Café $

☎ 021-426 2534; 127 Bree St, City Bowl; mains R40; ☻ 8am-5pm Mon-Fri, 9am-2pm Sat

This delightful café, run by a Namibian family, takes birds as its theme. The sophisticated yet rustic style – think milk-bottle-crate seats in a grand old Dutch building, and handmade crockery – matches the artisanal food, which includes delicious homemade pies, strudels and chunky scones.

CAFÉ AFRICAN IMAGE

Map pp248-9   African/Café $

☎ 021-426 1857; 48 Church St, City Bowl; mains R30-45; ☻ 8am-6pm Mon-Fri, 8am-3pm Sat

Easily Cape Town's most colourful café, sporting groovy African-print cushions and tablecloths, a fabulous chandelier made of recycled plastic and a wall painting of a voluptuous African mermaid. Sample Tanzanian fish curry, African village stew or a range of healthy salads.

CAPE TOWN'S TOP FIVE RESTAURANTS

- Aubergine (p129)
- Madam Zingara (p126)
- Ginja (p126)
- Savoy Cabbage (p126)
- La Colombe (p132)

TOP FIVE EAT STREETS

- Kloof St, Gardens (p128) – this road up Table Mountain is paved with dining treasures.
- Lower Main Rd, Observatory (p131) – join the bohos and student set at Cape Town's best range of cheap and colourful ethnic eateries.
- Main Rd, Kalk Bay (p133) – fuel up on the culinary goodies available along the False Bay coast.
- Church St, City Bowl (p123) – between Haiku and Birds Café on the corner of Bree St, you'll find a smattering of the city centre's top casual dining spots.
- Main Rd, Green Point (p129) – the Portside complex has added to the appeal of this long-established dining strip.

CASTLE HOTEL Map pp248-9   Portuguese $$

☎ 021-461 4946; cnr Canterbury & Constitution Sts, City Bowl; mains R40-80; ☽ noon-3pm, 7-10pm Mon-Fri, 7-10pm Sat

Amazing what a lick of paint, some arty photos and sexy young waiters can do to the room above a very untrendy pub (see p136). A well-executed menu of generously portioned Portuguese staples, such as *trinchado* (beef stew; R64) and peri peri chicken (R37), make dining here a pleasure.

BIESMIELLAH Map pp248-9   Cape Malay $$

☎ 021-423 0850; Wale St, Bo-Kaap; mains R50; ☽ noon-10pm Mon-Sat

Many swear by the authenticity of the Cape Malay and Indian food at this Bo-Kaap institution, decorated with tapestries of the Taj. There's certainly no doubting its spiciness! It's all halal and no alcohol is served.

COL' CACCHIO Map pp248-9   Italian $$

☎ 021-419 4848; Seeff House, 42 Hans Strijdom Ave, Foreshore; mains R50; ☽ noon-11pm Mon-Fri, 6.30-11pm Sat & Sun

One of the best reasons for venturing towards the Foreshore to eat is this long-running pizzeria. The 29 varieties of topping are inventive, the bases light and crispy, and there are even options for those avoiding wheat and dairy.

GRANDE CAFÉ Map pp248-9   Brasserie $$

☎ 021-424 1748; 114 Hout Lane, Bo-Kaap; mains R30-70; ☽ 8am-10pm

Despite the name, this unpretentious place has a relaxed vibe, pleasant décor and decent food – big salads, sandwiches, pastas and the like – which you can enjoy on an raised outdoor deck.

NOON GUN TEAROOM & RESTAURANT Map pp248-9   Cape Malay $$

☎ 021-424 0529; 273 Longmarket St, Bo-Kaap; mains R50-70; ☽ 10am-10pm Mon-Sat

There's a fantastic view of Table Mountain and the bay from this simple, family-run restaurant high on Signal Hill. Cape Malay dishes such as bobotie (delicate curried mince with a topping of savoury egg custard, usually served on a bed of turmeric-flavoured rice), bredies (pot stews of meat or fish, and vegetables) and *dhaltjies* (deep-fried balls of chickpea-flour batter mixed with potato, coriander and spinach), are excellent.

ROYALE EATERY

Map pp248-9   Gourmet Burgers $$

☎ 021-422 4536; 273 Long St, City Bowl; mains R60; ☽ noon-midnight Mon-Sat

Our favourite gourmet burger bar keeps growing, taking over the upstairs area of its original venue and opening a cute satellite branch in a former brothel around the corner on Vredenburg Lane. For something different try the Big Bird ostrich burger.

BUKHARA Map pp248-9   Indian $$

☎ 021-424 0000; www.bukhara.com; 33 Church St, City Bowl; mains R70; ☽ noon-3pm Mon-Sat, 6.30-11pm

Bukhara's been serving highly palatable traditional North Indian and Tandoori-style cuisine in a dark and stylish setting for over a decade. The vegetarian options are plentiful.

FIVE FLIES

Map pp248-9   Modern South African $$$

☎ 021-424 4442; 14-16 Keerom St, City Bowl; 2/3/4 courses R100/135/155; ☽ noon-3pm & 7-11pm Mon-Fri

There are few more atmospheric places to dine in Cape Town than in the wood-panelled Dutch Club building (1752), which also has tables set up in a central cobbled courtyard. Unfortunately, however, the contemporary cooking is sometimes poorly executed.

CAPE TOWN'S TOP FIVE CAFÉS

- Birds Café (p124)
- Manna Epicure (p128)
- Olympia Café & Deli (p133)
- Frieda's (p124)
- Café Neo (p129)

HAIKU
Map pp248-9   Asian $$$

☎ 021-424 7000; 33 Church St, City Bowl; mains R35-70; ⏱ noon-2.30pm & 6-10.30pm Mon-Fri, 6-10.30pm Sat

This is the guys from Bukhara's take on a modern, sophisticated Asian brasserie, with a sushi counter thrown in for good Oriental measure. The 'Asian tapas' menu promiscuously plunders dishes from Japan, China and Southeast Asia, and the quality is good. Booking for dinner, when the minimum spend is R132, is recommended. The entrance is on Burg St.

VERANDA
Map pp248-9   Modern South African $$$

☎ 021-424 7247; Metropole Hotel, 38 Long St, City Bowl; mains R55-70; ⏱ 6.30-11pm

This starched-white, smart restaurant on the 1st floor of a boutique hotel serves delicious and beautifully presented food. It's worth booking to sit in Veranda's enclosed veranda overlooking Long St.

MADAME ZINGARA & CARA LAZULI
Map pp248-9   Modern South African $$$

☎ 021-426 2458; 192 Loop St, City Bowl; mains R70; ⏱ 7-11pm Mon-Sat

Silly hats to wear, candlelight and courtyards, belly dancers, snake charmers, magicians and super-friendly waitresses – we defy you not to have a wildly fun night at the bohemian Madame Zingara and its sister establishment Cara Lazuli. The same hearty menu of big-flavour dishes, such as beef in chilli-chocolate sauce, is served in both interlinked spaces, and portions are huge.

SAVOY CABBAGE
Map pp248-9   Modern South African $$$

☎ 021-424 2626; 101 Hout Lane, City Bowl; mains R70-90; ⏱ noon-2.30pm Mon-Fri, 7-10.30pm Sat

The standard-bearer of the city's contemporary dining scene remains a great place

for inventive cooking, and gives diners the chance to try local game meats, such as zebra and wildebeest. The tomato tart is legendary, as are the stuffed cabbage rolls.

MINATO
Map pp248-9   Japanese $$$

☎ 021-423 4712; 4 Buiten St, City Bowl; mains R70; ⏱ 7-9pm Mon-Fri

Make a booking or come early as the Japanese chef and proprietor, Muraoka-san, only serves 35 people per night and closes up when he feels like it. The sushi and authentic Japanese food far surpass those at trendier sushi joints around town. Cash only.

95 KEEROM
Map pp248-9   Italian $$$

☎ 021-422 0765; 95 Keerom St, City Bowl; mains R50-100; ⏱ 12.30-2pm Mon-Fri, 7pm-11pm Mon-Sat

Bookings are essential for this superstylish Italian restaurant round the back of the Rhodes House nightclub, especially if you want to sit near the famed olive tree, the centrepiece of the 1st floor. Given the quality of food, the prices are very reasonable, particularly for the handmade pastas.

AFRICA CAFÉ
Map pp248-9   African $$$

☎ 021-422 0221; www.africacafe.co.za; 108 Shortmarket St, City Bowl; set banquet R160; ⏱ 6.30-11pm

Age hasn't withered the Africa Café's appeal as the best place to sample African food. Come with a hearty appetite as the set feast comprises some 15 dishes from across the continent, of which you can eat as much as you like. The décor and friendly staff who dance and sing around the restaurant are equally fantastic. If only all tourist-oriented restaurants were as good as this. Booking advised.

GINJA
Map pp248-9   Modern South African/Asian $$$

☎ 021-426 2368; 121 Castle St, Bo-Kaap; 1/2/3 courses R95/175/195; ⏱ 7-10pm Mon-Sat

You must book well ahead for this dining gem, based in a renovated warehouse. Chef Mike Basset conjures up inventive fusion dishes, such as the amazing skewers of salt-and-pepper prawns dipped in coriander foam and sprayed with coriander perfume. Upstairs is the more-casual bar and brasserie Shoga (p138).

WATERKANT

The Cape Quarter continues to be the nexus around which this trendy, compact neighbourhood revolves, although new residential developments nearby are bound to offer up alternative options.

DUTCH Map pp248-9 — Café $

☎ 021-425 0157; 34 Napier St, Waterkant; mains R30; ⏰ 8am-5pm Mon-Fri, 8am-3pm Sat
A Euro vibe lingers over this popular orange-coloured Waterkant café. People-watch from the terrace while sipping a cappuccino or tucking into a toasted ciabatta.

LA PETITE TARTE Map pp248-9 — Café $

☎ 021-425 9077; Shop A11, Cape Quarter, 72 Waterkant St, Waterkant; mains R30-40; ⏰ 8am-3pm Mon-Fri, 8am-2pm Sat
Fancy teas and delicious homemade, sweet and savoury French-style tarts are served at this adorable café on the Dixon St side of the Cape Quarter – it's a great spot for a pick-me-up or light meal.

ANATOLI Map pp248-9 — Turkish $$

☎ 021-419 2501; 24 Napier St, Waterkant; meals R70-100; ⏰ 6.30-11.30pm Mon-Sat
This little piece of Istanbul in Cape Town has been serving its tasty meze (R15 to R28 per dish), both hot and cold, for around 20 years. It remains a very popular party spot and at the weekends you might even be treated to a belly dance.

ANDIAMO Map pp248-9 — Italian $$$

☎ 021-421 3687; Shop C2, Cape Quarter, 72 Waterkant St, Waterkant; mains R60; ⏰ 8am-11pm
Andiamo's tables had colonised a large chunk of the Cape Quarter since our last visit, confirming its popularity as one of the best casual eateries in the area. The well-stocked deli also serves as a chichi food store for Waterkant's well-heeled residents.

PIGALLE Map pp248-9 — Seafood $$$

☎ 021-421 4343; 57A Somerset Rd, Waterkant; mains R80-100; ⏰ noon-3pm Mon-Sat, 7pm-midnight Mon-Sun
Enter off Highfield Rd into a dramatic interior that's hung with huge silver chandeliers, and features multiple Elvis prints on the wallpaper. The menu offers retro favourites, such as shrimp cocktail; the seafood platter (R250) is good value. There's live music most nights, too.

TANK Map pp248-9 — Seafood $$$

☎ 021-419 0007; Shop B15, Cape Quarter, 72 Waterkant St, Waterkant; mains R80-100; ⏰ noon-3pm & 6-11pm Tue-Sun
A luminous bar, giant fish tank and obligatory sushi bar create the ideal environment for the chic set. If you don't fancy the sushi, which isn't too bad, there are some appealing Pacific-rim-style dishes, including seared tuna.

Eating

CITY CENTRE

Dutch (above)

GARDENS & SURROUNDS

Fashionable Kloof St is the focus of dining in this part of the city, but you'll also uncover a few other gems around Dunkley Sq, east of the Company's Gardens, and further up the hill in Vredehoek.

VIDA E CAFFÉ Map p254 · Café $

☎ 021-426 0627; www.caffe.co.za; 34 Kloof St, Gardens; mains R20; ⏰ 7.30am-5pm Mon-Fri
Capetonians have taken this home-grown chain's freshly brewed coffee, orange juice, Portuguese-style pastries and filled rolls to their hearts. It's ideal for breakfast or a fast lunch. There are also branches at **Victoria Wharf** (Map pp252–3; Waterfront), **Thibault Square** (Map pp248–9) in the City Bowl, **Cavendish Square** (Map pp246–7), and at the **Portside complex** (Map pp252–3; Somerset Rd) in Green Point.

HMMM Map p254 · Bakery & Café $

☎ 021-462 1950; 6 Clare St, Gardens; mains R20-30; ⏰ 8.30am-5pm Mon-Fri, 8.30am-noon Sat
Come discover this charming café and bakery set in an up-and-coming former industrial area. It bakes delicious cakes, biscuits (try the chocolate-and-chilli flavour) and makes its own ice cream. Sandwiches and soups round out the menu.

WILD THINGS Map p254 · Café $

☎ 021-424 3445; 96 Kloof St, Tamboerskloof; mains R30; ⏰ 7am-7pm Mon-Fri, 7.30am-7pm Sat, 8am-5pm Sun
Specialising in game meats such as kudu, springbok, gemsbok and eland, this deli-café prepares its own biltong, bakes its own pies and offers a range of tempting preserves, as well as fresh oysters. Try the traditional venison bobotie with rice (R28) or the venison sandwich (R24.50).

DEER PARK CAFÉ Map p254 · Café $

☎ 021-462 6311; 2 Deer Park Dr West, Vredehoek; mains R30-40; ⏰ 8am-4pm Mon & Tue, 8am-10pm Wed-Sat, 8am-6pm Sun
Families love this relaxed café, fronting onto a playground. The chunky wooden furniture gives it the feel of a big nursery, but the tasty food is anything but child's play. There're some great vegetarian options and a kids' menu. Yum (☎ 021-461 7607), next door, is also worth checking out.

LAZARI Map p254 · Café $

☎ 021-461 9895; cnr Upper Maynard St & Vredehoek Ave, Vredehoek; mains R30-40; ⏰ 7.30am-6pm Mon-Fri, 8am-3pm Sat, 9am-3pm Sun
Few patrons work as hard as Chris Lazari to be friendly to their customers who, understandably, are a loyal bunch. A metrosexual air hangs over the buzzy joint – great for brunch or an indulgent moment over coffee and cake.

CAFÉ GAINSBOURG Map p254 · Café $

☎ 021-422 1780; 64 Kloof St, Gardens; mains R40-50; ⏰ 7.30am-10.30pm Mon-Fri, 8.30am-10.30pm Sat & Sun
Success has allowed this minimalist-decorated café to expand its dining area and menu. It's a great spot for any of the day's three meals, with its lamb shanks, burgers and salads being especially recommended.

GREENS Map p254 · Brasserie $$$

☎ 021-422 4415; 5 Park Rd, Gardens; mains R35-60; ⏰ 8am-5pm Mon, 8am-11pm Tue-Sun
Keeping handily long hours (and open on Sundays), this relaxed brasserie with a spacious outdoor seating area specialises in wood-fired pizza, which comes with classic, Californian (topped with fresh greens) or gourmet toppings. It also has a good selection of wines by the glass.

KITAMA Map p254 · Asian $$$

☎ 021-422 1633; Rheede Street Mall, Rheede St, Gardens; mains R60; ⏰ 6am-11pm Mon-Sat
The menu at this hip, self-styled 'eastern eatery' rambles around the Orient, but the food on the whole is tasty, beautifully presented and comes in giant portions. The décor, including a table that doubles as a fish tank and candy-floss-style lampshades, is striking.

MANNA EPICURE

Map p254 · Modern South African $$$
☎ 021-426 2413; 151 Kloof St, Tamboerskloof; mains R40-80; ⏰ 8am-7pm Tue-Sat, 8am-3pm Sun
Join the style set for a deliciously simple breakfast or lunch at this trendy white-box café, or come for late-afternoon cocktails and tapas on the veranda. The freshly baked breads – coconut, or pecan and raisin – alone are worth dragging yourself up the hill for. Check out the toilets where the designers had a lot of fun with a calking gun.

Eating · CITY CENTRE

CAPE COLONY

Map p254   Modern South African $$$

☎ 021-483 1850; Mount Nelson Hotel, 76 Orange St, Gardens; mains R80-120; ☽ 6.30-10.30pm

Although it's far from Cape Town's liveliest dining scene, the imaginative and beautifully presented food complements the sumptuousness of the Mount Nelson's premier restaurant. We enjoyed the luxurious take on a Cape Malay curry. Jazz and a dinner dance take place on Saturday night. Booking is essential. Also consider dropping by the Nellie for a delicious afternoon tea (R120) from 2.30pm to 5.30pm, served in the lovely lounge or under the trees in the garden.

AUBERGINE Map p254   Modern South African $$$

☎ 021-465 4909; www.aubergine.co.za; 39 Barnet St, Gardens; mains R65-125; ☽ noon-3pm Thu, 7-10pm Mon-Sat

At some Cape Town restaurants it's all about the wild party atmosphere. Here it's all about the food, which is world class. Harald Bresselschmidt's innovative dishes, such as warthog *confit*, fried crocodile fillet or salmon-trout ice cream are on the à la carte menu, but we recommend indulging in the degustation menu (three/four/five courses R220/260/295). This includes old favourites, such as prawn and fish satay on vegetable spaghetti or a sweet-pumpkin soufflé. A sommelier is on hand to advise on wine and service is uniformly excellent.

Afternoon tea, Cape Colony (above)

ATLANTIC COAST
GREEN POINT & WATERFRONT

It's natural that you'll want to dine with an ocean view while in Cape Town. The Waterfront's plethora of restaurants and cafés fit the bill nicely, although it's essentially a giant tourist trap. Better value and a less-touristy dining experience are on offer a short walk away in Green Point and Mouille Point.

GIONVANNI'S DELI WORLD

Map pp252-3   Deli/Café $

☎ 021-434 6983; 103 Main Rd, Green Point; mains R20-30; ☽ 8.30am-9pm

Bursting with flavoursome products, Gionvanni's can make any sandwich you fancy – ideal for a picnic if you're on your way to the beach. The pavement café is a popular hang-out; try the Red Espresso, a shot of rooibos tea prepared like a regular espresso.

MELISSA'S Map pp252-3   Deli/Café $

www.melissas.co.za; 1 Portside, cnr Upper Portswood & Main Rds, Green Point; mains R30; ☽ 7.30am-8pm Mon-Fri, 8am-8pm Sat & Sun

We love the latest in Melissa's chain of distinguished deli and café emporiums on the corner of Green Point's trendy Portside complex. Pay by the kilogram for the delicious buffets, then browse the shelves for goodies – such as handmade fudge, nougat, potato chips and muesli rusks – for a picnic or gourmet gifts. Other branches are in **Newlands** (Map pp246–7; cnr Kildare & Main Rds) and in **Tamboerskloof** (Map p254; 94 Kloof St).

CAFÉ NEO Map pp252-3   Greek/Café $

☎ 021-433 0849; 129 Beach Rd, South Seas, Mouille Point; mains R30-40; ☽ 7am-7pm

Our favourite seaside café has a relaxed vibe and pleasingly contemporary design. Check out the big blackboard menu and order your food and drinks at the counter before taking a seat on the deck overlooking the red-and-white lighthouse.

MARIO'S Map pp252-3   Italian $$$

☎ 021-439 6644; 89 Main Rd, Green Point; mains R40-70; ☽ noon-2.30pm Tue-Fri & Sun, 6.45-10.30pm Tue-Sun

Homely and unpretentious is the best way to describe this eternally favourite Italian restaurant. It serves a wide range of dishes, including perfectly *al dente* pasta. Customer praise is scribbled all over the walls and ceiling.

WILLOUGHBY & CO

Map pp252-3 Seafood $$$

☎ 021-418 6115; Shop 6132, Victoria Wharf, Waterfront; mains R60-70; ☒ deli 9am-8.30pm, restaurant 11.30am-10.45pm

We'll let its dodgy location in the middle of a shopping mall pass and throw our weight behind the frequent recommendations from Capetonians. This seafood operation serves bumper plates of sushi, calamari prepared in a variety of ways, and hearty pan-fried fish dishes.

MANO'S

Map pp252-3 Mediterranean/Portuguese $$$

☎ 021-434 1090; 39 Main Rd, Green Point; mains R40-80; ☒ noon-3pm Mon-Fri, 7-11pm Mon-Sat

A simple menu of Greek salad, fillet steak, chicken schnitzel, and egg and chips might not set your mouth drooling, but the crowds that regularly dine here would beg to differ, proving you don't need to be fancy to be successful. It also runs the similarly pared-back **Castle Hotel** (p125).

WAKAME Map pp252-3 Seafood $$$

☎ 021-433 2377; www.wakame.co.za; cnr of Beach Rd & Surrey Pl, Mouille Point; mains R70; ☒ noon-10pm

Tucking into Wakame's salt-and-pepper squid or sushi platter while gazing at the glorious coastal view is a wonderful way to pass an afternoon. Book for a balcony spot for sunset drinks, away from the crowds at Camp's Bay. Downstairs is the **Newport Market & Deli** (☒ 7.30am-8pm Mon-Fri, 8am-8pm Sat & Sun), another of Cape Town's cool deli-cafés.

EMILY'S Map pp252-3 Modern South African $$$

☎ 021-421 1133; Shop 202, Clock Tower Centre, Waterfront; mains R80; ☒ noon-3pm Mon-Sat, 7-11pm Mon-Sun

Flamboyant is a word that could have been coined for Emily's, both for its décor and its approach to cooking, which can seem wildly reckless in its mixture of ingredients. Everything is beautifully presented and there's an epic wine list. It also runs the café in the historic Clock Tower outside – a nice spot for a sundowner or snack.

ONE.WATERFRONT

Map pp252-3 Modern South African $$$

☎ 021-418 0520; Cape Grace, West Quay, Waterfront; mains R70-100; ☒ noon-3pm & 7-10.30pm

Bruce Robertson is an accomplished chef and, although it's the daring combinations of ingredients that catch the eye on the menu, the best dishes are those that keep it simple (such as the lovely fish cakes). The inventive vegetarian options are welcome, too.

BEACHES & SUBURBS

Along Sea Point's Main Rd and Regent St, you can cruise a range of budget dining spots, such as **Ari's Souvlaki** (Map p255; ☎ 021-439 6683; 83A Regent St; ☒ 10am-midnight), a Greek joint, or the 24-hour **Saul's** (Map p255; ☎ 021-434 5404; 152 Main Rd), famed for its gut-busting burgers. In Camps Bay, a playground of the rich and beautiful, making a booking is essential if you wish to get a prime spot for sunset drinks and nibbles. Further south in Hout Bay there are several good places to dine, too.

Sea Point

KAUAI Map p255 Hawaiian $

☎ 021-434 7645; cnr Regent St & Clarens Rd, Sea Point; mains R20-40; ☒ 8am-10pm Mon-Sat, 9am-10pm Sun

If only all fast food was as healthy as that from this slick Hawaiian-franchise operation. It offers a tempting range of smoothies, juices and wraps. There are other branches around the city, including one at **Lifestyles on Kloof** (Map p254; 50 Kloof St, Gardens) and one in the **City Bowl** (Map pp248–9; Mostert St).

NEW YORK BAGELS Map p255 Deli/Café $

☎ 021-439 7523; 51 Regent Rd, Sea Point; mains R30-40; ☒ 7am-11pm

At this Sea Point institution you can browse the well-stocked deli or tempting food court. Put together a mix 'n' match meal of, say, a hot-beef-on-rye sandwich followed by freshly made waffles and fruit salad.

CEDAR Map p255 Lebanese $

☎ 021-433 2546; 100 Main Rd, Sea Point; mains R40; ☒ 11.30am-9.30pm

Nothing fancy but this family-run operation rates highly for its tasty range of meze and

Middle Eastern dishes. There are also many flavoured tobaccos for its hookah pipes.

LA PERLA Map p255   Italian $$
☎ 021-439 9538; cnr Church & Beach Rds, Sea Point; mains R70; ☺ noon-11.30pm

Retro-stylish La Perla has been a permanent fixture on the Sea Point promenade for decades. Enjoy something from its long menu of pasta, fish and meat dishes on the terrace shaded by stout palms, or retreat to its intimate bar.

SEA POINT GARDENS

Map p255   European $$$
☎ 021-439 2820; 78 Regent St, Sea Point; 2/3 courses R99/129; ☺ noon-10.30pm

Dine on dishes such as tuna carpaccio and sole with Béarnaise sauce, in the romantic courtyard garden with its Italianate fountain. This 1919 villa was once the official residence of Cape Town's mayor. Afterwards, head upstairs to the slinky cocktail lounge Asylum (☺ 5pm-2am).

Camps Bay

SINNFULL Map p256   Café $
☎ 021-438 3541; Shop 5, Promenade Centre, Victoria Rd, Camps Bay; ice cream R10; ☺ 10am-11pm

In need of a sugar rush or something to cool the tongue? Head to this haven of delicious ice creams and cakes tucked away upstairs in the Promenade Centre. It also has an Internet café.

SANDBAR Map p256   Café $
☎ 021-438 8336; 31 Victoria Rd, Camps Bay; mains R30-40; ☺ 9.30am-10pm

This good-value, relaxed café proves you don't need to have a glitzy venue or big prices to succeed in Camps Bay. Sit at street tables and enjoy good sandwiches and light meals.

PARANGA Map p256   Modern South African $$$
☎ 021-438 0404; Shop 1, Promenade Centre, Victoria Rd, Camps Bay; mains R90

Paranga's success means it now sells its own chill-out CDs and branded range of clothing alongside its seafood, salads, burgers and sushi. The soft, cream-coloured furnishings and terrace make it one of the most pleasant places to dine on a very competitive strip.

Hout Bay

FISH ON THE ROCKS Map p258   Seafood $
☎ 021-790 0001; Harbour Rd, Hout Bay; mains R25; ☺ 10.30am-8.15pm

While the tourist coaches all stop at the kitsch and pricey Mariner's Wharf (Map p258; ☺ 021-790 1100; Harbour Rd; mains R70-100; ☺ 9am-9pm), locals know it's better to continue to the end of Hout Bay Harbour Rd to find some of Cape Town's best fish and chips. Watch out for the dive-bombing seagulls if you eat on the rocks, though.

SUIKERBOSSIE Map pp244-5   European $$$
☎ 021-790 1450; 1 Victoria Ave, Hout Bay; mains R70; ☺ 9am-4.30pm Tue-Sun

The garden at this large 1930s house, perched at the top of the hill before you descend to Hout Bay, is a lovely spot for breakfast or afternoon tea. It's often used for functions, so call ahead. The Sunday carvery (R120) is very popular.

SOUTHERN SUBURBS

Around Lower Main Rd in Observatory the menus are slanted towards the tastes and budgets of the resident student population. More-upmarket restaurants can be found in and around Constantia's wineries. Kirstenbosch also has decent cafés in case you forget your picnic basket.

OBSERVATORY

MIMI Map p256   Café $
☎ 021-447 3316; 107 Lower Main Rd, Observatory; mains R20-30; ☺ 8.30am-6pm Mon-Sat

This pleasant café is a good place for a snack or lunch. You'll find plenty of magazines to browse through and there is a wide range of sandwiches and wraps available, including a decent selection of vegetarian ones.

CAFÉ GANESH Map p256   Indian/African $
☎ 021-448 3435; 38B Trill Rd, Observatory; mains R30-40; ☺ 6-11.30pm Mon-Sat

Sample pap (maize porridge) and veg, grilled springbok or lamb curry at this funky hang-out, where junkyard décor and matchbox-label wallpaper create that chic-shack look.

CAPERS Map p256 · Modern South African $$

☎ 021-448 4038; Black River Park North, Link Rd, Observatory; mains R50; ⏱ 8am-3.30pm Mon-Fri

Head into the business park to find this extremely good breakfast and lunch place, staffed by graduates from the nearby chefs academy. The chic pink-and-white décor is lovely, and the food is great value and of a high standard.

DIVA Map p256 · Italian $$

☎ 021-448 0282; 88 Lower Main Rd, Observatory; mains R50; ⏱ 10am-11.30pm

Diva's thin-crust pizzas are excellent (the Mediterranean with wine-soaked aubergine is a favourite) and it does plenty of other Italian goodies in a faded Venetian-style atmosphere.

CONSTANTIA

JONKERHUIS Map pp244-5 · Brasserie $$

☎ 021-794 6255; Groot Constantia, Constantia; mains R50-80; ⏱ 10am-10pm Mon-Fri, 9am-10pm Sat, 9am-4pm Sun

A change of management has led to a more-casual brasserie style at this atmospheric restaurant, with its pleasant vine-shaded courtyard. Sample cured meats with a glass or two of the local wines, or you can satisfy your sweet tooth with the desserts.

RIVER CAFÉ

Map pp244-5 · Modern South African $$$

☎ 021-794 3010; Constantia Uitsig, Spaanschemat River Rd, Constantia; mains R60; ⏱ 8.30am-5pm

At the entrance to the Constantia Uitsig estate, this delightful and popular café serves big portions of food made with organic and free-range products. A booking is essential, especially for weekend brunch.

LA COLOMBE Map pp244-5 · French $$$

☎ 021-794 2390; Constantia Uitsig, Spaanschemat River Rd, Constantia; mains R90; ⏱ 12.30-2.30pm & 7.30-9.30pm

Booking is essential at this highlight of the Constantia dining scene. The shady garden setting is one of Cape Town's nicest and the service exceptional, but it's chef Franck Dangereaux' fine touch on his Provençal-style dishes that really impresses at this hugely decadent restaurant.

NEWLANDS

KIRSTENBOSCH TEA ROOM

Map pp244-5 · Café $

☎ 021-797 4883; Kirstenbosch Botanical Gardens, Rhodes Dr, Newlands; mains R25-35; ⏱ 8am-5pm

Fresh breads and cakes baked on the premises are available at this popular café at the top entrance to the gardens. For more of a fancy meal on a crisp, white tablecloth try the Silver Tree (☎ 021-762 9585; ⏱ 8am-10pm), near the gardens' main gate. The attached Fynbos Food Court is good for take-away food and sells beer and wine.

GARDENER'S COTTAGE

Map pp246-7 · Café $

☎ 021-689 3158; Montebello Craft Studios, 31 Newlands Ave, Newlands; mains R40; ⏱ 8am-4.30pm Tue-Sun

After exploring the Montebello craft studios (p169), head for this lovely café and tea garden in the grounds. It serves simple, hearty meals in a relaxed atmosphere.

OTHER SUBURBS

FAT CACTUS Map pp246-7 · Mexican $$

☎ 021-685 1920; 47 Durban Rd, Mowbray; mains R50; ⏱ 11am-11pm

All the usual Mexican suspects are on the menu at this fun café-bar, where the combo platter is big enough to share. There's also a kids' menu. Across the road is the owner's wife's appealing Greek restaurant, simply called Greek! (☎ 021-686 4314).

PERIMA'S Map pp246-7 · Indian $$

☎ 021-671 3205; 3 Newmarket Pl, Belvedere Rd, Claremont; mains R40-60; ⏱ noon-10.30pm Mon-Sat

It's worth venturing into the suburbs to sample Perima's authentic South Indian cuisine, served in a colourfully decorated room that avoids the usual clichés of the genre. The spicy curries will have your taste buds swaying in time to the Bollywood soundtrack.

LUPO'S Map pp244-5 · Italian $$$

☎ 021-762 3855; 19 Wolfe St, Wynberg; mains R70; ⏱ 7.30am-4pm & 6.30-10pm

In the heart of the picturesque area known as Chelsea Village, Lupo's offers a very tempting buffet of home-style Italian dishes, as well as à la carte dishes. At lunch it costs R10 per 100g, while for dinner it's a flat R93.

FALSE BAY & SOUTHERN PENINSULA

If anything should convince you to spend a bit more time around False Bay it should be the following selection of restaurants and cafés. Kalk Bay's Main Rd has long runneth over with appealing cafés, but Muizenberg now competes as a convivial dining destination. St George's St is home to the bulk of Simon's Town's dining options, but there are a few other good places just out of town, including decent cafés at both the **Boulders Beach Lodge** (p183) and the **Southern Right Hotel** (p183). Elsewhere in the southern peninsula, you can get a good meal in Noordhoek and on the way to Kommetjie.

MUIZENBERG

OLIVE STATION Map p257   Deli/Café $$
☎ 021-788 3264; 165 Main Rd, Muizenberg; mains R40-50; 🕙 8am-5pm Mon-Wed, Fri & Sat, 8am-9pm Thu, 9am-5pm Sun
Dine on Lebanese dishes at the relaxed café overlooking the sea or in a wind-sheltered courtyard. The olives sold in the attached deli are grown locally and cured in wooden barrels. Try the Middle Eastern–style *throubs* (dry cured olives) and the olives with roasted garlic.

EMPIRE CAFÉ Map p257   Café $$
☎ 021-788 1250; 11 York Rd, Muizenberg; mains R50; 🕙 7am-4pm Mon-Sat, 8am-4pm Sun
The surfies' favourite hang-out is a great place for breakfast or a lunch of well-made pasta dishes and salads. Local art exhibitions enliven the walls. Call to see if it's open for dinner on Thursday and Saturday.

KALK BAY

OLYMPIA CAFÉ & DELI
Map p257   Bakery & Café $$
☎ 021-788 6396; 134 Main Rd, Kalk Bay; mains R40-75; 🕙 7am-9pm
Still setting the standard for relaxed rustic cafés by the sea, Olympia has now opened a branch in the City Bowl (Map pp248–9; Shortmarket St). Breads and pastries made on the premises are great for breakfast, and its Mediterranean-influenced main dishes are generally delicious, too.

LIVE BAIT Map p257   Seafood $$$
☎ 021-788 4133; Kalk Bay harbour, Kalk Bay; mains R60; 🕙 noon-4pm & 6-10pm
Sit within arm's reach of the crashing waves and the bustle of the Kalk Bay harbour at this breezy, Greek-island-style fish restaurant, the less-fancy but equally appealing sibling of **Harbour House** (☎ 021-788 4133; mains R70-90; 🕙 noon-4pm & 6-10pm), upstairs.

SIMON'S TOWN

SWEETEST THING Map p258   Café $
☎ 021-786 4200; 82 St George's St, Simon's Town; mains R20; 🕙 8am-6pm Mon-Fri, 9am-6pm Sat & Sun
The quiches, cakes and biscuits are all freshly made at this adorable patisserie. Worth dropping by for afternoon tea with scones, if nothing else.

TIBETAN TEAHOUSE Map p258 Tibetan/Café $
☎ 021-786 1544; www.sopheagallery.com; 2 Harrington Rd, Seaforth; mains R30-40; 🕙 10am-5pm
Attached to the Sophea Gallery of Tibetan and Tibetan-inspired arts and crafts, this is a lovely café in which to revive, with its view across the bay. All the food is vegetarian and there are some vegan dishes.

MEETING PLACE Map p258   Café $
☎ 021-786 1986; 98 St George's St, Simon's Town; mains R40; 🕙 9am-4pm Mon, 9am-9pm Tue-Sun
There are lots of appealing menu items at this café, deli and interior-design shop,

Eating

FALSE BAY & SOUTHERN PENINSULA

which has a distinct Martha Stewart feel. Sit on the balcony overlooking Simon's Town's main street.

BERTHA'S Map p258   Seafood $$$

☎ 021-786 2138; Quayside Centre, 1 Wharf Rd, Simon's Town; mains R55-90; ⏰ 7am-10pm
This long-running crowd pleaser is about as close to dining by the water as you'll get in Simon's Town. Indulge in a seafood platter (R155) and watch the boats come and go across the harbour.

BON APPETIT Map p258   French $$$

☎ 021-786 2412; 90 St George's St, Simon's Town; mains R80-90; ⏰ noon-2pm & 6.30-10pm Tue-Sat
Fine French dining doesn't get much better than that on offer at this intimate bistro. In the evenings enjoy a set menu for R155 or R175.

NOORDHOEK

NOORDHOEK VILLAGE FARMSTALL

Map pp244-5   Deli/Café $
☎ 021-789 1317; www.noordhoekvillage.co.za; cnr Noordhoek Main Rd & Village Lane, Noordhoek; mains R30-40; ⏰ 8am-6pm
There are several places to eat at this faux-village complex, but the best is the farm stall. It does great sandwiches, salads made from its organic vegetables, and baked goods. Take a seat under the shady oaks outside or in the coffee shop inside.

TOWNSHIP DINING

You don't go to the townships for fine dining, but there are a few restaurants where you can try traditional Xhosa cuisine (see p17 for some examples). **Dinner@Mandelas** (see p82) is a great option, or you can arrange to visit the following eateries with a tour company or private guide:

Eziko (Map pp244-5; ☎ 021-694 0434; cnr Washington St & Jungle Walk, Langa; mains R30-40; ⏰ 9am-6pm Mon-Fri, 9am-10pm Sat) Offers simple, good food in a pleasant setting; try the chef's special fried chicken or the breakfast.

Lelapa (Map pp244-5; ☎ 021-694 2681; 49 Harlem Ave, Langa; buffet R85) Sheila has been so successful with her delicious African-style buffets that she's taken over the neighbours, extending the once-cosy home restaurant into a space for big tour groups. You need to book as there are no set opening hours at this place.

KOMMETJIE

MNANDIS Map pp244-5   Modern South African $$

☎ 021-785 3248; Solole Game Reserve, 6 Wood Rd, Sunnydale; mains R55-85; ⏰ 9am-11pm Tue-Sat, 9am-5pm Sun
Even if you're not touring the game reserve (see p110), this very stylish restaurant set in a historic homestead is a great place for a meal. The wine list has hilarious descriptions and a local marimba group plays in the convivial bar every Friday night.

Entertainment

Entertainment

Cape Town didn't become known as the 'Tavern of the Seven Seas' for nothing. Head out on a Friday or Saturday night to Long St, the Waterkant or Camps Bay for an eye-opening experience of how the locals like to party (or 'jol', as they say in South Africa).

Curiously, on other nights – with the exception of Wednesday – Cape Town's nightspots can be less than pumping, although during the long, warm summer nights chances are you'll always find some convivial place to while away the evening. There's certainly no shortage of bars with stunning views of either beach or mountain and, if getting a workout on the dance floor is more your thing, then there's bound to be a club to suit.

It's not all about drinking and dancing. Cape Town has a decent range of cinemas and theatres, while live music spans the gamut from classical to rock via jazz and marimba. Free live music is a feature of the Waterfront, in particular.

Check the weekly arts guide in the **Mail & Guardian** (www.chico.mweb.co.za/art/daily/menu -guide.htm) to find out what's going on, and the daily *Cape Argus*' **Tonight** (www.tonight .co.za) section, too. The bimonthly magazine **Cape etc** (www.capeetc.com) is also good for listings.

Tickets & Reservations
COMPUTICKET
☎ 083 915 8000; www.computicket.co.za;
🕙 9am-5pm Mon-Fri, 9am-6pm Sat
Cape Town's computerised booking agency handles ticketing for all major sporting events. There are outlets in the **Golden Acre Centre** (Map pp248–9; Adderley St, City Bowl), at the **Waterfront** (Map pp252–3; Victoria Wharf), in the **Gardens Centre** (Map p254; Mill St, Gardens) and in Sea Point's **Adelphi Centre** (Map p255; Main Rd, Sea Point), as well as other places.

DRINKING
As in other major party cities, the line between bar and club in Cape Town has become increasingly blurred; long opening hours (until 4am on Wednesday, Friday and Saturday) and DJs can be found at both. Generally, though, clubs will charge an entrance fee. Long and Kloof Sts, the Waterkant (where you'll find the bulk of Cape Town's gay bars) and Camps Bay pump late into the night on summer weekends, as does the Waterfront. Rest assured though, there are still plenty of regular pubs where you can have a quiet drink. Most open around 3pm and close after midnight, but some stay open much later. Where opening times do not fit these standards, we have listed them in the reviews in this chapter.

CITY BOWL
CAFÉ DU SÜD Map pp248-9
☎ 021-422 0500; 107-109 Loop St, City Bowl;
🕙 10am-11pm Mon-Sat
With its quirky mix of wall maps, globes and retro furnishings (all for sale), Café du Süd is a mecca for the style set. The food is unmemorable but the drinks divine – sink into the leather sofa for afternoon tea or late-night cocktails.

CASTLE HOTEL Map pp248-9
☎ 021-461 4946; cnr Canterbury & Constitution Sts, City Bowl
This historic pub, dating from 1900, has three rooms once frequented by the lawyers, police and criminals who lived and worked in the area that it once bordered: District Six. Expect political incorrectness, nicotine-stained walls and cheap booze. There's a surprisingly smart restaurant upstairs (see p125).

TOP FIVE BARS & PUBS
- Marvel (opposite)
- Café du Süd (above)
- Relish (p139)
- Nose Wine Bar (p138)
- Alba Lounge (p139)

CAVEAU Map pp248-9
☎ 021-422 1367; www.caveau.co.za; Heritage Sq,
92 Bree St; ⏱ 7am-11.30pm Mon-Sat
Cape Town should have more wine bars,
so this one is a welcome addition to the
handsome Heritage Sq. It has a goodly
selection of local drops. The tapas dishes
are tasty, too.

COOL RUNNINGS Map pp248-9
☎ 021-426 6584; 227 Long St, City Bowl
Now with a café at street level, the reggae-
themed bar's long balcony on the 1st floor
remains the chill-out place of choice for the
backpacker set. Catch the breeze and the
Caribbean vibe. The original branch is in
Observatory (Map p256; ☎ 021-448 7656; 96
Station St, Observatory).

FIREMAN'S ARMS Map pp248-9
☎ 021-419 1513; 25 Mechau St, City Bowl
Boxed in by new apartment blocks, this
old-time survivor (here since 1906) is likely
to be around for a while longer. Inside,
the Rhodesian and old South African flags
remain pinned up alongside a collection of
firemen's helmets. Come to watch rugby
on the big-screen TV, grab some seriously
tasty pizza or just down a lazy pint or two.

GALLERY BAR Map pp248-9
☎ 021-423 2086; www.urbanchic.co.za;
cnr Long & Pepper Sts, City Bowl
The chic, urban black set gather beneath
the Urban Chic hotel at this sophisticated
bar with squishy sofas, windows opening
onto Long St and a nice line in cocktails. It's
one of the more-relaxed inner-city bars.

JO'BURG Map pp248-9
☎ 021-422 0142; 218 Long St, City Bowl
You haven't really partied on Long St until
you've moved to the Jo'burg beat. Little
has changed here in years – there's still
the pool table at the back, there's still that
cheeky Bart Simpson light sculpture on the
wall, and there's still that infectious blend
of funky music, groovy patrons and free-
flowing drinks.

M BAR Map pp248-9
☎ 021-423 7247; www.metropolehotel.co.za;
38 Long St, City Bowl
Did someone mention Versace? The glitzy
Italian designer would be proud of how his
fabric designs on the sofa blend into the
brash bordello opulence of the M Bar. A
DJ is on hand to keep the posing models
entertained.

MARVEL Map pp248-9
☎ 021-426 5880; 236 Long St, City Bowl;
⏱ 1pm-4am
Stuffed as a sardine, Marvel is a fantastic
bar where cool kids of all colours rub shoulders (not to mention practically everything
else). If you can, grab one of the cosy
booths at the front, or linger on the pavement and enjoy the foot-tapping grooves
from the DJ.

ORCHARD BANK Map pp248-9
www.orchardbank.co.za; 229B Long St, City Bowl
One of Long St's more interesting and laid-
back venues, with a roster of events including stand-up comedy. The comfy sofas are
a good place from which to put a dent into
the jugs of cocktail mixes.

PO NA NA SOUK BAR Map pp248-9
☎ 021-423 4889; Heritage Sq, 100 Shortmarket
St, City Bowl; ⏱ noon-2am Mon-Sat year-round,
5pm-1am Sun Dec-Mar
Head inside Heritage Sq to discover a sultry
slice of Marrakech at this trendy bar. It has
plump cushions, low tables and balconies
overlooking the restored courtyard.

Jo'burg (left)

SAINTS Map pp248-9

☎ 021-424 1007; 110 Bree St, City Bowl;
🕒 5pm-2am Wed-Sat

At the southern end of St Stephen's Church, a flight of stone steps leads up to this sophisticated cocktail bar decorated with colourful graphic paintings. It sometimes hosts live jazz and comedy performances.

SHOGA Map pp248-9

☎ 021-426 2369; 121 Castle St, Bo-Kaap;
🕒 6pm-2am Mon-Sat

This bar and Asian brasserie is cut from the same classy mould as **Ginja** (p126) on the ground floor. Order a cocktail and a snack at the long bar or relax in the oversized chairs and low sofas.

WATERKANT

BAR CODE Map pp248-9

☎ 021-421 5305; www.leatherbar.co.za;
18 Cobern St, Waterkant; 🕒 10pm-3am Sun-Thu, 10pm-4am Fri & Sat

Into leather and latex? Then this is the bar for you. Dress appropriately otherwise you won't be let in, and don't be shocked if you stumble into something stronger than the drink in the dark room.

BRONX Map pp248-9

☎ 021-419 9219; www.bronx.co.za;
35 Somerset Rd, Waterkant; 🕒 8pm-4am

People of all shapes, sizes and sexual persuasions pack out this fun bar, where buff bare-chested barmen and DJs keep patrons dancing until dawn. Flex your vocal chords at the Monday-night karaoke session.

CAFE MANHATTAN Map pp248-9

☎ 021-421 6666; www.manhattan.co.za;
74 Waterkant St, Waterkant; 🕒 9.30am-2am

Give thanks to the far-sighted proprietor of Cafe Manhattan since he kick-started the gay quarter a decade or so ago by opening this popular bar and restaurant. An enlarged deck makes it even easier to check out the area's human traffic.

CAPELLA Map pp248-9

☎ 021-425 0439; 21 Somerset Rd, Waterkant;
🕒 noon-midnight

From the same stable as the equally lavish Cruz and Opium comes this Afro-chic venue with ostrich-egg chandeliers, zebra-

---

hide upholstery and an intricately carved Indian doorway. Avoid the so-so food and head to the bar for the excellent cocktails.

CRUZ Map pp248-9

☎ 021-421 5401; www.cruzcapetown.co.za;
21B Somerset Rd, Waterkant; 🕒 8pm-4am

They may tell you that it's the glitzy décor and handsome clientele that make this the hot gay bar of the moment, but we know that the real draw is its troupe of brief-clad go-go boys shaking their stuff on the podiums. How else could you endure dancing to a disco version of the theme from *The Love Boat*?

LIPSTICK LOUNGE Map pp248-9

☎ 082 738 3612; www.lipstickcapetown.co.za;
2 Lelie Lane, Waterkant; 🕒 5pm-2am Fri, 8pm-3pm Sat

At last, a stylish, exclusively female hangout in the Waterkant. Find it behind 54 Waterkant St, and check the website for details of the special events it hosts around town.

NOSE WINE BAR Map pp248-9

☎ 021-425 2200; www.thenose.co.za;
Cape Quarter, Dixon St, Waterkant

No longer the city's only wine bar, but still a great place to pass an evening. Match around 40 of the Cape's best wines with some top-notch cooking, which includes inventive use of local ingredients (carpaccio of giraffe is lovely). It also runs wine-tasting courses (see p40).

ROSIE'S Map pp248-9

☎ 021-421 6666; 125A Vos St, Waterkant

There's no room for airs and graces, or need for fashionable attire, at this cosy pool bar, which attracts an older, racially mixed crowd.

GARDENS & SURROUNDS

CAFÉ VESPA Map p254
☎ 021-426 5042; www.cafevespa.com;
108 Kloof St, Tamboerskloof; ☺ 9am-midnight
As well as hiring out Vespas (see p211), this hipster hang-out does a mean line in cocktails, coffee and tapas, all of which can be enjoyed on the terrace, which has a grandstand view of Table Mountain.

PERSEVERANCE TAVERN Map p254
☎ 021-461 2440; 83 Buitenkant St, Zonnebloem
Flickering candles in a dim interior give plenty of atmosphere to the heritage-listed pub Cecil Rhodes called his local. There are four beers on draught and you can order decent pub grub, such as a grill (R52) or fish and chips (R32).

PLANET Map p254
☎ 021-483 1864; Mount Nelson Hotel,
76 Orange St, Gardens
The old Nellie goes for contemporary cool in its silver-coated champagne and cocktail bar. Join the fashion crowd to enjoy some 250 different bubblies and 50-odd alcoholic concoctions.

RAFIKI'S Map p254
☎ 021-426 4731; 13B Klook Nek Rd, Tamboerskloof
A long, wrap-around balcony, with its view out to Table Bay, draws the crowds to this relaxed bar and restaurant, where you can occasionally catch live music shows.

RELISH Map p254
☎ 021-422 3584; www.relish.co.za;
70 New Church St, Tamboerskloof; ☺ noon-2am
Mon-Fri, 5pm-2am Sat & Sun
Few bars afford such a panoramic view of Table Mountain and Lion's Head as this trendy place. It rises up three glass-fronted floors, leading onto a wide balcony. The food is good and during happy hour (6pm to 7pm) cocktails are only R12.

RICK'S CAFÉ AMERICANE Map p254
☎ 021-424 1100; 2 Park Lane, Gardens
No Sam to play it again, but everything else looks like it could be straight from Casablanca (including the famous neon sign) at this movie-themed bar and restaurant. Wear a fedora and make like Bogie and Bergman.

SHACK Map p254
☎ 021-461 5892; 43-45 De Villiers St, Zonnebloem
A laid-back hang-out for a young, studenty crowd. It's a bit of a maze, spread across several levels, and includes a pool hall and a room for table football, all part of a complex of venues.

GREEN POINT & WATERFRONT

ALBA LOUNGE Map pp252-3
☎ 021-425 3385; www.albalounge.co.za; 1st fl,
Hildegards, Pierhead, Waterfront
Easily the most stylish place for cocktails at the Waterfront. The views across the harbour are seductive, the cocktails inventive and there's a roaring fire in winter to add to that inner alcoholic glow.

BASCULE BAR Map pp252-3
☎ 021-410 7082; Cape Grace, West Quay,
Waterfront; ☺ 11am-1am
Some 480 varieties of whisky are served at the Grace's sophisticated bar, and there're still a few slugs of the 50-year-old Glenfiddich (just R15,200 a tot) left. Outdoor tables facing onto the marina are a pleasant spot away from the madness of the Waterfront.

BELTHAZAR Map pp252-3
☎ 021-421 3753; www.belthazar.co.za; Shop 153,
Victoria Wharf, Waterfront
Claiming to be the world's biggest wine bar, Belthazar offers 600 different South African wines, 170-odd of which you can get by the (Riedel) glass. The restaurant specialises in top-class Karan beef and it also does plenty of seafood dishes, too.

BUENA VISTA SOCIAL CAFÉ Map pp252-3
☎ 021-433 0611; Exhibition Bldg, 81 Main Rd,
Green Point
A nice mojito is mixed at this Cuban-themed bar and restaurant, which takes its inspiration from the famous CD. Book a seat on the airy balcony and come on Sunday if you want to salsa dance.

MITCHELL'S SCOTTISH ALE HOUSE & BREWERY Map pp252-3
☎ 021-419 5074; www.mitchellsbreweries.co.za;
East Pier Rd, Waterfront; ☺ 11am-2am
Check all pretensions at the door of this traditional pub, which shares a building with the Ferryman's Tavern and serves a variety of freshly brewed beers and good-value meals.

Entertainment

DRINKING

MONK BAR Map pp252-3

☎ 021-439 6306; Zero Nine Three Two,
79 Main Rd, Green Point

Work your way through the many bottled Belgium brews, or the Hoegaarden, Leffe and Stella beers on tap, at this stylish DJ bar over the trendy 0932 Belgian restaurant.

TOBAGO'S Map pp252-3

☎ 021-441 3412; Radisson Hotel Waterfront, Beach Rd, Granger Bay; ⏰ 6.30am-10.30pm

Walk through the hotel to the spacious deck bar with a prime Table Bay position. It's a great place to enjoy a sunset cocktail and you can take a stroll along the break-water after.

ATLANTIC COAST BEACHES & SUBURBS

BARAZA Map p256

☎ 021-438 1758; www.blues.co.za; the Promenade, Victoria Rd, Camps Bay

Inspired by the chilled vibe of Zanzibar, this cocktail bar overlooking the beach is an understandably popular spot. The electro-jazz duo Goldfish play here on Thursday.

BLUE PETER

☎ 021-554 1956; Popham St, Bloubergstrand; ⏰ 11am-11pm

At this perennial favourite, around 15km north of the city centre, the deal is grab a beer, order a pizza and plonk yourself on the grass outside to enjoy the classic views of Table Mountain and Robben Island.

CAFÉ CAPRICE Map p256

☎ 021-438 8315; 37 Victoria Rd, Camps Bay; ⏰ 9am-2am

The bronzed and beautiful gather at this café-bar, which is as popular for breakfast as it is for sundowner drinks. Grab a pavement table for the best view.

CHAPMAN'S PEAK HOTEL Map p258

☎ 021-790 1036; Main Rd, Hout Bay

If the drive along Chapman's Peak Dr has made you a little weak at the knees, rest at this convivial historic pub and restaurant. There's a broad outdoor deck overlooking the bay and decent hotel rooms (single/double including breakfast R600/800) if you decide to linger longer.

IGNITE Map p256

☎ 021-438 7717; 2nd fl, the Promenade, Victoria Rd, Camps Bay

New name and a slight makeover for this slick venue, with a broad terrace and dress-circle views of the beach. Events are often held here, including stand-up comedy.

LA MED Map p256

☎ 021-438 5600; Glen Country Club, Victoria Rd, Clifton

This eternal alfresco bar gets its cred from its killer view down the length of the Twelve Apostles. Sinking a sundowner here is a Cape Town rite of passage. Keep an eye out for the easily missed turn-off, on the way to Clifton from Camps Bay.

LA VIE Map p255

☎ 021-439 2061; 205 Beach Rd, Sea Point; ⏰ 7.30am-midnight

One of the very few places you can have anything from breakfast to late-night cock-tails within sight of Sea Point promenade. Lounge on the outdoor terrace and enjoy the thin-crust pizza.

SOUTHERN SUBURBS

A TOUCH OF MADNESS Map p256

☎ 021-448 2266; www.cafeatom.co.za; 12 Nuttall Rd, Observatory; ⏰ noon-late Mon-Sat, 7pm-late Sun

This long-running bar and restaurant offers an eclectic art-house atmosphere, dressed up in purple with lace trimmings. Wannabe poets should check out the Monday-night open-mike poetry fests.

BARRISTERS Map pp246-7

☎ 021-674 1792; cnr Kildare Rd & Main St, Newlands; ⏰ 9.30am-10.30pm

Upmarket Newlands' favourite watering hole offers up a series of cosy rooms hung with an eye-catching assortment of items in ye-olde-country-pub style. Has a very decent menu, too (mains R70).

CAFÉ CARTE BLANCHE Map p256

☎ 021-447 8717; 42 Trill Rd, Observatory; ⏰ 6pm-2am

Candles, cosy nooks and crannies, and avant-garde music set the scene at this tiny café-bar, a favourite with the Obs alternative set.

CAFFÉ VERDI Map pp244-5

☎ 021-762 0849; 21 Wolfe St, Wynberg
This handsome café-bar, set in a 110-year-old house with a pretty courtyard, is a pleasant place to retire for a drink after exploring Maynardville and Chelsea Village.

DON PEDRO'S Map pp246-7

☎ 021-447 4493; 113 Roodebloem Rd, Woodstock
It's a longtime favourite with white liberals for a boozy late night out, and is now popular with the yuppies moving into the area.

FORRESTER'S ARMS Map pp246-7

☎ 021-689 5949; 52 Newlands Ave, Newlands;
🕙 11am-11pm Mon-Sat, 10am-6pm Sun
The very-English-style pub Forries has been around for over a century. It offers a convivial atmosphere, good pub meals, including wood-fired pizza, and a pleasant beer garden.

PEDDLARS ON THE BEND Map pp244-5

☎ 021-794 7747; Spaanschemat River Rd
Cool off with a beer in the shaded garden of this lively pub. If you don't fancy all that highfalutin wine-estate fodder, the hearty dishes (mains R50 to R60), such as chicken pie and *eisbein* (pork knuckle), should suit you fine.

SOBHAR Map pp246-7

☎ 021-674 3377; www.sobhar.co.za;
1 Letterstedt House, Main Rd, Newlands;
🕙 4pm-2am Mon, Tue & Sat, noon-2am Wed-Fri
There are comedy shows every Thursday (R20; booking essential) and salsa classes (usually on Monday and Wednesday) at this lively cocktail bar that's big with the preppy Newlands set.

FALSE BAY & SOUTHERN PENINSULA

BRASS BELL Map p257

☎ 021-788 5455; Kalk Bay train station, Main Rd, Kalk Bay; 🕙 11am-10pm
Take the tunnel beneath the train tracks to reach this Kalk Bay institution overlooking the fishing harbour. On a sunny day there are few places better to drink and eat (mains R50 to R80) by the sea.

COBBS Map pp244-5

☎ 021-780 1480; www.cobbs.co.za; Main Rd, Scarborough; 🕙 9am-10pm Tue-Thu, 9am-11pm Fri & Sat, 9am-8pm Sun
Don't rush back to the city after your visit to Cape Point. Swing by this welcoming bar and restaurant where you can relax on the upper level with a view of the Atlantic surf.

POLANA Map p257

☎ 021-788 7162; Kalk Bay harbour, Kalk Bay
Yet another very tempting reason to hang out in Kalk Bay is this great-looking bar, right on the water. It serves Portuguese-style seafood – sardines, langoustines and *lulas* (baby calamari).

SKEBANGA'S BAR Map pp244-5

☎ 021-789 1783; cnr Beach & Pine Rds, Noordhoek
If you're down this way, say after a drive along Chapman's Peak Dr, the bar above the Red Herring restaurant is a pleasant place for a drink or a bite to eat. There's a good view of the beach from the terrace.

Drinking by the ocean at Brass Bell (left)

CLUBBING

House, R&B and hip-hop – these are the sounds you're most likely to hear in Cape Town's clubs. Break beats, lounge and electronica are also popular. Local DJs of note include Craig da Souza (tech house), Ready D (hip-hop), Leighton Moody (deep house), as well as the fantastic electro-jazz mixmasters Goldfish. Cape Town's club scene is also firmly plugged into the global dance network, so expect star appearances by the likes of Basement Jaxx and Paul Oakenfield.

Long St and its immediate surroundings are the epicentre of the city's club scene, with Waterkant also a busy clubbing area. Trance parties, such as Vortex and Alien Safari, held outdoors an hour or so from the city centre, still happen through summer; check the websites www.3am.co.za and www.aliensafari.co.za for details or make inquiries at the main backpacker hostels.

Admission charges range from R10 to R50 and most places don't really get going until after midnight, with a notional 4am closing time. Check listings in the *Cape Argus'* **Tonight** (www.tonight.co.za) section and in the **Mail & Guardian** (www.chico.mweb.co.za/art/daily/menu-guide.htm), as well as the **Thunda.com** (www.thunda.com) and **Rage** (www.rage.co.za) websites for details of coming events and the latest venues.

DELUXE Map pp248-9
☎ 021-422 4832; Unity House, cnr Long & Longmarket Sts, City Bowl; admission R40
Come on Friday and Saturday night to join the musically sophisticated, mixed and gay crowd at this long-running minimalist venue that specialises in house and tribal trance.

GALAXY Map pp244-5
☎ 021-637 9132; College Rd, Ryelands, Athlone; admission R30
Get down to R&B, hip-hop and live bands at this longtime Cape Flats dance venue, which attracts a black and coloured crowd. The equally legendary jazz venue **West End** (p145) is next door.

GALLERY Map pp246-7
☎ 021-461 9649; www.thegalleryonline.co.za; 84 Sir Lowry Rd, Zonnebloem; admission R40-80
Only open Friday and Saturday, the Gallery has cornered the market on hard dance and is the place to catch visiting big-shot DJs from the UK and Germany.

HECTIC ON HOPE Map p254
☎ 021-465 4918; 69 Hope Lane, Gardens; admission R10
Studiedly untrendy, school-hall-style venue above an old boozer. New wave, electronica and alternative dance hits from recent decades are what draw the studenty, screw-fashion crowd.

HEMISPHERE Map pp248-9
☎ 021-421 0581; www.hemisphere.org.za; 31st fl, ABSA Centre, Riebeeck St, City Bowl; admission R50; ⏰ 9pm-3am Tue-Sat
Twinkling views of the city are part of the deal at this super-stylish club atop the ABSA Centre. It's real velvet-rope-and-glamour-model stuff, so dress to the nines and pack that shoulder chip of attitude and you'll fit in fine. While up here also check out the equally swank bar at **Antique** (Map pp248–9; ☎ 021-419 0762; ⏰ 7pm-midnight).

LUSH Map pp248-9
☎ 082 565 6174; www.lushcapetown.co.za; Sliver, 27 Somerset Rd, Waterkant; admission R20; ⏰ 9pm-2am every second Sat
Veteran party organiser Myrna runs this Sapphic dance night. Lush takes place every second Saturday of the month and is held upstairs at Sliver. Well-behaved gay men will also be let in with their lesbian sisters.

MERCURY LOUNGE Map p254
☎ 021-465 2106; www.mercuryl.co.za; 43 De Villiers St, Zonnebloem; admission R10
Friday's 'Shaken not Stirred' offers relaxed lounge sounds with the occasional foot-tapping hit from the '70s and '80s. A similarly funky vibe reigns at the Saturday night's 'Straight no Chaser' session. Also watch out for the 'What a Feeling' '80s DJ nights.

MIAN MIAN Map pp248-9
☎ 021-422 5823; 196½ Long St, City Bowl; admission R30
Lofty palms, twinkling fairy lights and a spacious bar and dance space are hidden in a narrow alley between 196 and 198 (hence the ½ in the address). It aims for a sophisticated vibe but somehow the try-too-hard crowd doesn't fit.

OPIUM Map pp248-9

☎ 021-425 4010; www.opium.co.za; 6 Dixon St, Waterkant; admission R40

With three dance floors, big bars, plush décor and a too-cool-for-school attitude, its no surprise that Opium has been such a big hit on the Cape Town clubbing scene. Come to see model types practise their catwalk strut and pout.

QUE PASA Map pp248-9

☎ 083 556 7466; www.quepasa.co.za; 7-9 Bree St, City Bowl; admission R20-40

Salsa is all the rage in Cape Town and this is one of the top clubs at which to practise. Classes are held on Monday, Tuesday, Thursday and Saturday, when the club has a regular party night, too.

RHODES HOUSE Map pp248-9

☎ 021-424 8844; www.rhodeshouse.com; 60 Queen Victoria St, City Bowl; admission R50

Not quite as hot as it once was, this luxurious venue, spread over a grand old house, can still provide a good dance night out. Thursday is R&B night.

SLIVER Map pp248-9

☎ 021-421 4798; www.sliver.co.za; 27 Somerset Rd, Waterkant; admission R20

A gay and gay-friendly crowd fill this spacious, fun venue with a fairy-light-festooned courtyard and rooftop chill-out areas. Upstairs thudding-hard house and bare chests are the go, while downstairs, house and anthems keep the dance floor crowded.

SNAP Map pp248-9

☎ 083 940 3983; 6 Pepper St, City Bowl; admission R20

Dance to music from across Africa at this urban African club. It has a welcoming, predominantly black audience.

ZULA SOUND BAR Map pp248-9

☎ 021-424 2442; 194 Long St, City Bowl; admission R20

Hosts an interesting range of events including live bands, DJs and even open-mike poetry sessions. The long balcony is the place to watch Long St go by.

LIVE MUSIC

Music in all its forms is the very fabric of Cape Town. There are plenty of free or cheap opportunities to enjoy music all over the city, from buskers at the Waterfront or in Greenmarket Sq to the much celebrated Sunday-afternoon concerts at Kirstenbosch (p11). Live bands play in many restaurants and bars, and concerts don't get any bigger than those held at Green Point Stadium, location of 2003's huge Nelson Mandela concert and 2006's South African debut by Robbie Williams.

JAZZ

It's no accident that many world-renowned jazz artists began their careers in Cape Town. The free-flowing nature of jazz is well suited to the relaxed, cosmopolitan nature of the city. Although there are few permanent jazz venues, the music is performed frequently around the city.

Entertainment

LIVE MUSIC

EVOLUTION OF THE MCQP

It's a safe bet to say that there's no costume party in the world quite like the Mother City Queer Project (MCQP). What began in 1994 as a small-scale tribute by 'party architect' André Vorster (who really is an architect) to his deceased lover has grown into one of Cape Town's major annual events, held every December and attracting some 4500 revellers.

Every party has a theme and is always held in an interesting venue: in 2005 it was 'It's a Circus' and the location Ratanga Junction (p148). You have to come in costume (if you don't you won't be let in) which means everyone – gay, straight and everything in-between – joins in the fun with abandon.

In 2005 Vorster sold the MCQP brand to a quintet of local movers and shakers who aim to grow the event from one night into a week-long happening. Innovations already include more nondance-type activities at the party and major sponsorship that has allowed bigger prizes for winners of the costume competition. The new promoters are keen for the party to keep it's original community edge, though. You can buy tickets online, or get them in their collectable 3-D-design form from outlets around the city: see www.mcqp.co.za for details.

A night at a Cape Flats jazz club, such as **Duma's Falling Leaves** (☎ 021-426 4260) in Guguletu, is an unforgettable experience, but you are strongly advised not to go alone. Contact companies organising township tours, eg **Coffee Beans Routes** (p82), which has a Monday-night jazz safari to Swingers.

Jazz-festival highlights include January's **Standard Bank Cape Town Jazzathon** (www.jazzathon.co.za; p9), a free event at the Waterfront, and the two-day **Cape Town International Jazz Festival** (www.capetownjazzfest.com; p10) held at the end of March at the Cape Town International Convention Centre, with a free concert in Greenmarket Sq.

DISTRIX CAFÉ ON HANOVER Map pp248-9
☎ 021-426 7118; 106 Darling St, Zonnebloem; ☻ 9am-10pm Mon-Sat
This revitalised café-bar, on the edge of District Six, has jazz and other live music events in the evenings. It's also worth visiting to admire its imaginatively designed rock garden courtyard.

DIZZY'S JAZZ CAFÉ Map p256
☎ 021-438 2686; www.dizzys.co.za; 41 the Drive, Camps Bay; admission on weekends R20
There's live jazz on Friday and Saturday, and other types of music the rest of the week at this restaurant (specialising in seafood platters). It's also getting a reputation as a backgammon venue – competitions are held on Monday nights during the low season (March to November).

GREEN DOLPHIN Map pp252-3
☎ 021-421 7471; www.greendolphin.co.za; Victoria & Alfred Arcade, Pierhead, Waterfront; obstructed/unobstructed view R20/25
This upmarket jazz venue and restaurant at the Waterfront holds the *Guinness Book of Records* award for highest number of consecutive nights of jazz. Shows kick off at 8.15pm. If you don't mind an obstructed view, the admission charge is a little lower.

HANOVER STREET Map pp244-5
☎ 021-505 7777; www.grandwest.co.za; GrandWest Casino, 1 Vanguard Dr, Goodwood; admission R30; ☻ 9pm-late Wed, Fri & Sat
It aims to re-create the jazz spirit of New Orleans (as if Cape Town's wasn't strong enough) at this classy venue in the casino. Jazz fans, however, appreciate its programme of top acts.

MANNENBURG'S JAZZ CAFÉ
Map pp252-3
☎ 021-421 5639; Clock Tower Centre, Waterfront; admission R30-80
Swing to jazz and African jive at this famed jazz club that seems to have survived its move to the Waterfront. On Friday and Saturday it's free to see bands playing the sundowner set from 5pm to 7pm, but an admission charge kicks in later.

MARIMBA Map pp248-9
☎ 021-418 3366; www.marimbasa.com; Cape Town International Convention Centre, City Bowl; diners/nondiners R20/30
Yes, there is a marimba band playing occasionally at this slick Afro-chic venue that's part of the Cape Town International Convention Centre. There's also a packed schedule of other jazz artists. The food is good and music sets kick off at 8pm.

SWINGERS Map pp244-5
☎ 021-762 2443; Dolphin Way, Lansdowne; admission R20
While it's 'grab a granny' most nights of the week, you'll need to book ahead for a table at the renowned Monday-night jam sessions hosted by Alvin Dyers, leader of the house jazz band, at this legendary Cape Flats venue.

Musician, Green Dolphin (left)

WEST END Map pp244-5

☎ 021-637 9133; Cine 400 Bldg, College Rd, Ryelands; admission R30; ☺ 8pm-late Fri & Sat
Mainstream jazz is the name of the game here. One of the city's top venues, it attracts a well-heeled clientele and top performers. There's plenty of security, if you drive.

ROCK & AFRICAN

ACCOUSTIC MUSIC CAFÉ Map p257

☎ 021-788 1900; www.acousticcafe.co.za; 120 Main Rd, Muizenberg; admission R20
At South Africa's only totally vegetarian pub, drumming workshops are hosted every Monday at 7pm (R30 lesson, R20 drum hire), and there's an open-mike night on Tuesday. The rest of week there's usually a live rock band playing.

DRUM CAFÉ

☎ 021-462 1064; www.thedrumcafe.com; admission plus drum hire Mon, Wed & Fri R60/80
Check the website or call for details of where this long-established drumming circle will be holding its regular sessions now that it's had to move out of its old home.

MAMA AFRICA Map pp248-9

☎ 021-426 1017; 178 Long St, City Bowl; diner/nondiner R10/15
Live marimba and other swinging African sounds fuel the atmosphere at this eternally popular tourist venue, where you can dine on a range of game dishes (mains R70). Bookings are essential at weekends, otherwise squeeze into a spot by the bar.

MARCO'S AFRICAN PLACE Map pp248-9

☎ 021-423 5412; 15 Rose Lane, Bo-Kaap; admission R10; ☺ noon-11pm
Marco Radebe's African restaurant feels a whole lot more authentic than Mama Africa. The food's good (mains R60 to R70) and when the band starts expect to start dancing with the waiters.

MERCURY LIVE Map p254

☎ 021-465 2106; www.mercuryl.co.za; 43 De Villiers St, Zonnebloem; admission R20-40
Cape Town's premier rock venue plays host to top South African bands and overseas visitors. The sound quality is good and if you don't like the band, there's always the DJ bar Mercury Lounge, below, and the Shack bar, next door.

CLASSICAL

As well as performing many concerts at all kinds of venues throughout the year, the Cape Philharmonic Orchestra (www.cpo.org.za) has been working hard to ensure its musicians will reflect the ethnic breakdown of the Western Cape more closely. To this end it has formed the Cape Philharmonic Youth Orchestra and the Cape Philharmonic Youth Wind Ensemble, with around 80% of members coming from disadvantaged communities. As if that wasn't enough, the Philharmonic also teams up with Cape Town Opera (www.capetownopera.co.za) and Cape Town City Ballet (www.capetowncityballet.org.za), both of which usually perform at Artscape. There also are a couple of monthly classical recitals at the Joan St Leger Lindbergh Arts Centre (p107) in Muizenberg, which are very popular, so book well ahead.

ARTSCAPE Map pp248-9

☎ 021-410 9800; www.artscape.co.za; 1-10 DF Malan St, Foreshore
Consisting of three different-sized auditoriums (including the studio On The Side), this is the city's premier arts complex. You can catch regular classical concerts here, as well as ballet, opera, theatre and cabaret shows. Walking around this area at night is not recommended; book ahead for a nonshared taxi since there are none to be found on the streets. There's plenty of secure parking.

CITY HALL Map pp248-9

☎ 021-410 9809; www.cpo.org.za; Darling St, City Bowl
Every Thursday the Cape Philharmonic Orchestra plays in the auditorium of the grand 1905 former City Hall. There are good acoustics (particularly in the main balcony seats), but no air conditioning so expect to sweat it out. Concerts often sell out, but it's usually possible to get a space on the choir benches behind the orchestra at the last minute.

ST GEORGE'S CATHEDRAL Map pp248-9

☎ 021-424 7360; www.stgeorgescathedral.com; Wale St, City Bowl
Check the website for the programme of classical music performed at the people's cathedral, including orchestral works by the greats, usually on the last Sunday of the month. It's worth coming to hear the cathedral's magnificent organ.

THEATRE, CABARET & COMEDY

What Cape Town's theatre scene lacks in size it certainly makes up for in ambition. There's often something interesting to catch beyond the blockbusters that check into Artscape (p145) and the Cape Town International Convention Centre. See p36 for more about Capetonian theatre. For details of the theatre festivals at Spier and Oude Libertas in Stellenbosch, see the boxed text, p192.

There isn't a dedicated venue for comedy in town at present, but shows do happen regularly at places such as On Broadway, home of the hilarious drag duo Mince, Muizenberg's Masque Theatre and Obz Café. There's also **Theatresports** (www.improvision.co.za), a local version of *Whose Line Is It Anyway*, held Tuesday and Thursday at Artscape's On The Side venue.

Good comedians whose shows you should keep an eye out for include TV star **Marc Lottering** (www.marclottering.com); **Mark Sampson** (www.samp.co.za), a founder of the Cape Comedy Collective whose show Missing Links scored a hit at the 2005 Edinburgh Fringe Festival; tattooed funny guy Cokey Falkow; and international sensation Pieter-Dirk Uys (see the boxed text, below).

BAXTER THEATRE Map pp246-7

☎ 021-680 3989; www.baxter.co.za; Main Rd, Rondebosch

Since the 1970s the Baxter has been the focus of Capetonian theatre. There are three venues here – the main theatre, the concert hall and the studio – and between them they cover everything from kids' shows to African dance spectaculars.

CAPE TOWN INTERNATIONAL CONVENTION CENTRE Map pp248-9

CTICC; ☎ 021-410 5000; www.cticc.co.za; 1 Lower Long St, City Bowl; Ⓟ

The CTICC has been so successful since it opened in mid-2003 that it's busy adding a further 1200 sq metres of exhibition space to the existing 10,000 sq metres. As well as big theatre productions, major events such as the **Cape Town International Jazz Festival** (p10) and the **Design Indaba** (p9) are held here. If nothing else, step inside to admire the giant relief sculpture in the main hall, *Baobabs, Stormclouds, Animals and People*, a collaboration between Brett Murray and the late San artist Tuoi Steffaans Samcuia.

EVITA SE PERRON

Evita's Platform; ☎ 022-492 2851; www.evita.co.za; Darling; tickets R50-80; ⊙ performances 2pm & 8pm Sat, 2pm Sun

This cabaret-style theatre and dining venue in Darling, 75km north of Cape Town, is where you can see the frequently hilarious and often thought-provoking shows of satirist Pieter-Dirk Uys. His characters touch on everything from South African politics and history to ecology. Nothing is off-limits, including the country's struggle with racism. See the boxed text, below, for more.

INDEPENDENT ARMCHAIR THEATRE Map p256

☎ 021-447 1514; www.armchairtheatre.co.za; 135 Lower Main Rd, Observatory

This bar and casual theatre-cum-lounge has an eclectic range of other events, including comedy, short dramas and band gigs. Monday night see a movie and eat pizza for R30; doors open 8pm, movie starts 9pm.

SOUTH AFRICA'S MOST FAMOUS WHITE WOMAN

Regardless of their political views, most South Africans (and many foreigners) have a soft spot in their hearts for Evita Bezuidenhout, the republic's own Dame Edna Everage, or as she'd prefer to be known, 'the most famous white woman in Africa'. Quite the cultural icon, Evita has had her own TV chat show, as well as a perfume and wine named after her.

Evita is one of several wonderful comic creations of actor and writer **Pieter-Dirk Uys** (www.pdu.co.za). An audience with her is granted in the long-running show *Tannie Evita Praat Kaktus* (Aunty Evita Talks Cactus), regularly performed at Uys' wonderfully kitsch theatre in Darling. It's an understandable and very funny mixture of English and Afrikaans, covering a variety of pertinent topics, not least her own role in the end of apartheid and the process of reconciliation.

A longtime campaigner for civil and gay rights, Uys' many shows fearlessly tackle all the hot-button issues of South Africa, including AIDS – his AIDS awareness show *For Facts Sake!* has been performed at over 500 schools to more than one million school kids. To find out more about Uys' fascinating career – not to mention that of Evita – read his memoir *Between the Devil and the Deep*.

Sign for Independent Armchair Theatre (opposite)

LITTLE THEATRE & ARENA THEATRE
Map p254

☎ 021-480 7129; www.drama.uct.ac.za; University of Cape Town Hiddingh Campus, Orange St, Gardens
Read the reviews before going to see the productions of widely varying quality and content from students at the University of Cape Town's drama department, which are staged in these two small venues.

MASQUE THEATRE Map p257

☎ 021-788 1898; www.muizenberg.info; 37 Main Rd, Muizenberg
The programme at this small theatre changes on a pretty regular basis, veering from one-man comedy shows to musical reviews and more-serious plays.

MAYNARDVILLE OPEN-AIR THEATRE
Map pp244-5

☎ 021-421 7695; www.artscape.co.za; cnr Church & Wolfe Sts, Wynberg
It wouldn't be summer in Cape Town without a visit to Maynardville's open-air theatre to see Shakespeare; 2006's *Much Ado About Nothing* was excellent. Bring a blanket, pillow and brolly, though, as the weather can be dodgy and the seats are none too comfy. At other times of the year, dance, jazz and theatre performances also take place here.

OBZ CAFÉ Map p256

☎ 021-448 5555; www.obzcafe.co.za; 115 Lower Main Rd, Observatory; admission R20-50
As if the human theatre of Lower Main Rd wasn't enough, inside this spacious café-

bar is a separate performance space where you can catch all manner of shows, including comedy and cabaret.

OLD ZOO Map pp246-7

☎ 083 915 8000; Groote Schuur Estate, Princess Anne Ave, Newlands
The wonderfully inventive Theatre of Africa has started using the lion's den in the ruins of Cecil Rhodes' zoo on the southern slopes of Devil's Peak as a highly atmospheric venue for its music, mime and drama works. Don't miss the chance to catch a performance here, which may even include dinner beforehand in the former animal cages!

ON BROADWAY Map pp248-9

☎ 021-424 0250; www.onbroadway.co.za; 88 Shortmarket St, City Bowl; tickets R70-75; ☼ shows 8.30pm
A move into spacious and slickly decorated premises in the City Bowl has done wonders for this hugely popular cabaret-supper venue. Certainly book well ahead for resident drag and comedy duo Mince, who strut their glamorous stuff Sunday and Monday nights. Other nights see a variety of musical and comedy acts.

THEATRE ON THE BAY Map p256

☎ 021-438 3301; www.theatreonthebay.co.za; 1 Link St, Camps Bay
Camp's Bay is the last place where you'd expect anything avant-garde or challenging on stage to have a ready audience, so the programme here sticks with the conventional play or a one-person show.

CINEMAS

There's no shortage of cinemas in Cape Town showing all the latest international releases, as well as a decent selection of art-house movies. Big multiplexes – run by Ster Kinekor and Nu Metro – can be found at the **Waterfront** (Map pp252–3), **Cavendish Square** (Map pp246–7; Cavendish St, Claremont), **Canal Walk** (Map pp244–5) and **Longbeach Mall** (Map pp244–5; Sunnydale Rd, Sun Valley) near Noordhoek. For the multiplexes the best night to go is Tuesday when the usual R35 entry price drops by half to R18. See the local press for listings of films and where they are showing.

CAVENDISH NOUVEAU Map pp246-7

☎ 086 130 0444; Cavendish Sq, Cavendish St, Claremont; tickets R35

With its sibling Cinema Nouveau Waterfront (Map pp252–3; Victoria Wharf), this classy multiplex showcases the best of independent and art-house movies. The facilities are good, but check first whether the same movies are playing at the Labia, since tickets are much cheaper there.

CINE 12 Map p256

☎ 021-437 9000; www.12apostleshotel.com; Victoria Rd, Camps Bay; admission free with dinner

There are just 16 luxurious red-leather-upholstered seats in the Twelve Apostles Hotel's private cinema, where one of some 240-plus DVDs are screened each night. If you want, you can hire the whole place out. Otherwise, come to the hotel's restaurant for dinner and check out what's screening afterwards.

LABIA Map p254

☎ 021-424 5927; www.labia.co.za; 68 Orange St, Gardens; tickets R25

Now stop that sniggering! This lifeline to the nonmainstream movie fan is named after the old Italian ambassador and local philanthropist Count Labia. It is Cape Town's best cinema in terms of price and programming. The African Screen programme is one of the rare opportunities

FILM FESTIVALS

Apart from at the Labia's African Screen, it's uncommon for locally made films to be screened generally in Cape Town. One opportunity you will have to see African cinema, though, is at the following film festivals:

Encounters (www.encounters.co.za) A documentary film festival held in July.

Out in Africa: SA International Gay & Lesbian Film Festival (www.oia.co.za) Usually in February or March.

South African World Film Festival (www.sithengi .co.za) Held in November/December.

you'll have to see locally made films. Also check out what's playing at the two-screen **Labia on Kloof** (☎ 021-424 5727), in the Lifestyles on Kloof centre around the corner.

CASINO

GRANDWEST CASINO Map pp244-5

☎ 021-505 7174; www.suninternational.com /resorts/grandwest/; 1 Vanguard Dr, Goodwood

Cape Town's long-gone Victorian post office served as the model for the florid façade of this casino. Even if gambling isn't your thing, there's plenty to keep you entertained, including a state-of-the-art cinema, many restaurants, a food court, an Olympic-sized ice rink (p152), a kids' theme park and music shows.

AMUSEMENT PARK

RATANGA JUNCTION Map pp244-5

☎ 021-550 8504; www.ratanga.co.za; Century City, Milnerton; adult/child R95/45; ⏰ 10am-5pm Fri-Sun, all week during school holidays

Open from November to July, this African-themed amusement park is next to Canal Walk shopping centre. The entry fee covers all rides, which include the usual collection of roller coasters and stomach churners. You'll pay R35 extra per ride for the Slingshot.

Activities

Activities

You want to get active? You've come to the right place. Cape Town is nirvana for the outdoor thrill seeker, with plenty of operators around to ensure that you don't go home without having experienced a heart-pumping adventure. With wind-whipped waves and Table Mountain on hand, surfing, walking and rock climbing are hugely popular and can easily be organised. For more-extreme adventures, such as shark-cage diving or paragliding, you'll need to travel out of the city or wait for the ideal weather conditions.

It's not all about adrenaline. Cape Town is an ideal location for a leisurely game of golf, practising your yoga moves, a spot of pampering at the spa, or just kicking back and watching sport in a luscious setting.

HEALTH & FITNESS

ALTERNATIVE THERAPIES

Observatory is the Cape Town apex of alternative lifestyles. On the first Sunday of the month a **Holistic Lifestyle Fair** (Map p256; ☎ 021-788 8088) takes place at the Observatory Recreation Centre, on the corner of Station and Lower Main Rds.

CHINESE MARTIAL ARTS & HEALTH CENTRE Map p256

☎ 021-448 2594; www.cmahc.co.za; 85 Station Rd, Observatory; ⏰ 5-9.30pm Mon-Thu

Come here to practise the oriental martial and meditation arts of Kung Fu, Tai Chi and the Purple Cloud Chi Kung. Everyone is welcome to watch the beginners' classes.

NIA TECHNIQUE Map p256

☎ 021-674 3747; www.niasouthafrica.co.za; 10 Anson Rd, Observatory

An acronym for Neuromuscular Integrative Action, Nia (which also means 'With Purpose' in Swahili) is a cardiovascular blend of dance, yoga, martial arts and the healing arts. Check the website for the daily schedule of classes (R60 per class, R395 per month).

CYCLING

Despite the mountainous territory and the lack of dedicated cycling paths, cycling is a popular activity in Cape Town. You'll find several places here where you can hire bicycles (see p208), including mountain bikes.

The City Bowl is a relatively flat area for cycling, as are the coastal roads leading to the Waterfront and around to Camps Bay. For mountain biking there are the paths leading off the lower slopes of Table Mountain, as well as those in the Tokai Plantation (see p71), which has a technical single-track. The Cape of Good Hope Nature Reserve (Cape Point) is also recommended; both **Day Trippers** (p91) and the **Baz Bus** (☎ 021 439 2323; www.bazbus.com) offer tours here that include cycling.

Since 1977 the **Pick 'n' Pay Cape Argus Cycle Tour** (☎ 083 910 6551; www.cycletour.co.za) around the peninsula has been held on a Saturday in the middle of March. With more than 30,000 entrants each year, it is the largest bicycle race in the world. Another race to watch out for is the **Cape Epic** (☎ 021-426 4373; www.cape-epic.com), an eight-day event covering 900km, from Knysna on the Garden Route to the Spier wine estate just outside of Stellenbosch.

Also check the website of South Africa's top cycling organisation **Pedal Power Association** (☎ 021-689 8420; www.pedalpower.org.za) for details of races and cycle tours around the Cape.

DOWNHILL ADVENTURES Map p254

☎ 021-422 0388; www.downhilladventures.com; cnr Orange & Kloof Sts, Gardens

A variety of cycling trips and adventures are available from this long-established outfit. Try a thrilling mountain-bike ride down from the lower cable station on Table Mountain (R350), or ride through the Constantia Winelands and the Cape of Good Hope (R500). You can also hire bikes (R100 per day).

GOLF

Golf tourism is a big deal in the Cape, and there are some 55 courses dotted around the city. Some are superb and many welcome visitors (but you should book and will need to dress appropriately). For details of fees etc, contact the **Western Province Golf Union** (☎ 021-686 1668; www.wpgu.co.za).

LOGICAL GOLF ACADEMY Map p256

☎ 021-448 6358; www.logicalgolf.co.za;
River Club, Observatory Rd, Observatory
Behind the River Club is this driving range and golf school where you can practise your swing to perfection. A 30-minute lesson is R150, while the golfer breakfast every weekend gives you a full breakfast plus 50/100 balls for R60/75.

MILNERTON GOLF CLUB Map pp244-5

☎ 021-434 7808; www.milnertongolfclub.co.za;
Tanglewood Cres, Milnerton; visitor per 18 holes R320
About 12km north of the city centre along the R27, the 18-hole, par 72 Milnerton has a magnificent position overlooking Table Bay and great views of Table Mountain. Wind can be a problem, though.

MOWBRAY GOLF CLUB Map pp244-5

☎ 021-685 3018; www.mowbraygolfclub.co.za;
Raapenberg Rd, Mowbray
Established in 1910, Mowbray is considered by some as the best in-town course for its rural setting and abundant birdlife. It certainly has a lovely view of Devil's Peak.

GYMS

Virgin Active (www.virginactive.co.za), which is South Africa's largest chain of gyms, has several well-equipped branches around Cape Town; convenient ones are located at **Green Point** (Map pp252–3; ☎ 021-434 0750; Bill Peters Dr), the **Foreshore** (Map pp248–9; ☎ 021-421 5857; Lower Long St) and **Gardens** (Map p254; ☎ 021-462 6239; Wembley Sq, Glynn St). Daily rates are R80 and a monthly pass costs R435.

GYM ON THE BAY Map p256

☎ 021-438 6085; 1 Link St, Camps Bay; ☷ 6am-8pm Mon-Fri, 7am-5pm Sat, 9am-5pm Sun; per day R120
Above the Theatre on the Bay, this is the most convenient gym if you're camped out

COOKERY COURSES

If you're impressed by the some of the unique dishes of the Cape and want to learn how to cook them, help is on hand. The tour company **Andulela** (☎ 021-790 2592; www.andulela.com) offers both a half-day Cape Malay cookery course (R295) in the Bo-Kaap every Saturday, and an African cooking safari (R295) in the township of Kayamandi, near Stellenbosch, where you can learn to prepare traditional Xhosa foods.

The ebullient Thope Lekau offers a half-day Cook Up (R150) at her Khayelitsha-based B&B **Kopanong** (p184), where you can learn to cook like an African mama.

Michelin Star chef Conrad Gallagher runs **Cooking with Conrad Gallagher** (☎ 021-794 0111; www.conradgallagherfood.com), a two-day gourmet cooking course (R1850) in Constantia, covering not only everything from breakfasts to braais but also table dressings and flower arrangements. His 'Desperate Housewives' one-day course (R1000) for 'ladies of leisure' is on the first and last Saturday of the month.

at Camps Bay. If you want a trainer to help you get that glam Camps Bay figure you're looking at an extra R180 per session.

SPORTS SCIENCE INSTITUTE OF SOUTH AFRICA Map pp246-7

☎ 021-659 5600; www.ssisa.com; Boundary Rd, Newlands; ☷ 5.30am-9pm Mon-Fri, 6.30am-12.30pm & 4-7pm Sat, 8am-12.30pm & 4-7pm Sun
This world-class facility is where many of the country's top professional sportspeople train. Amenities include a 25m pool, an indoor running track and a crèche. Day visitors are welcome. It's sandwiched between the Newlands cricket and rugby stadiums.

ZONE ON KLOOF Map p254

☎ 021-426 5706; www.zonefitness.co.za; 1st fl, Lifestyles on Kloof, 50 Kloof St; per day R75
A convenient gym if you're staying in the Gardens area or on Long St. A month's membership is also a good deal at R350, and it offers a range of classes, including yoga.

HEALTH & DAY SPAS

Head to Cape Town's top-end hotels to find the most luxurious spas. All offer the usual range of facial and body treatments, including various forms of massage and day-long packages. Women should also check out the massage at **Long St Baths** (p152).

ALTIRA SPA Map pp248-9

☎ 021-412 8200; www.altiraspa.com; Arabella Sheraton Grand Hotel, Convention Sq, Lower Long St, Foreshore; ✆ 8am-8pm
Floor-to-ceiling windows afford great views at this sleek spa; you can swim laps looking out at the Waterfront or relax in the Jacuzzi while gazing up at Table Mountain. There's a full gym, a sauna, a steam room and foot baths.

ANGSANA SPA Map pp246-7

☎ 021-674 5005; www.angsanaspa.com; Vineyard Hotel & Spa, Colinton Rd, Newlands; ✆ 10am-8pm
Take one tired body. Massage till tender with lemongrass- and sesame-scented oil. Steam till sweaty, then scrub down with jasmine and frangipani salts. Finally, rinse with an invigorating full-body shower and relax. Result: instant revival at what is Cape Town's most stylish spa.

CAPE GRACE SPA Map pp252-3

☎ 021-410 7140; www.capegrace.com/spa; Cape Grace, West Quay, Waterfront; ✆ 8am-8pm
Decorated in vibrant, warm and earthy colours, there're both African and spice-route themes going on here. Some massages incorporate traditional San methods; try the African Cape massage (R695 for one hour and 10 minutes) using a *fynbos* rub (made from the native vegetation of Cape Town) and nut butter from the shea tree. The treatment rooms overlook Table Mountain.

SANCTUARY SPA Map p256

☎ 021-437 9000; www.12apostleshotel.com/spa .htm; Twelve Apostles Hotel, Victoria Rd, Camps Bay; ✆ 8am-8pm
The spa occupies a mock cave that could be the set from a James Bond movie, a feeling that is compounded by the state-of-the-art contraptions in the treatment rooms. It offers Cape Town's only *rasul* chamber (a Middle Eastern sauna), as well as a flotation pool.

SANTÉ WELLNESS CENTRE Map p49

☎ 021-875 8100; www.santewellness.co.za; Winelands Hotel, Klapmuts; ✆ 8am-8pm
An hour's drive northwest of the city near Paarl, this large spa makes much of its vinotherapy regimen (R1350 with lunch),

which includes a shiraz body rub, chardonnay cocoon wrap and cabernet sauvignon bath! There are lots of other treatments available, as well as a gym, and indoor and outdoor pools.

SOLOLE WELLNESS CENTRE
Map pp244-5

☎ 021-785 3248; www.solole.co.za; 6 Wood Rd, Sunnydale; ✆ 9.30am-5.30pm Mon-Fri, 9am-5pm Sat & Sun
One of the more interesting wellness centres in Cape Town is based in four traditionally constructed, thatched-roof rondavels at the Solole Game Reserve. The interiors are surprisingly cool even on the hottest of days, and make for relaxing venues for a range of massages and body therapies performed by a team of specialists. Afterwards you can swim in the complex's outdoor pool.

ICE-SKATING
ICE STATION Map pp244-5

☎ 021-535 2260; www.icerink.co.za; GrandWest Casino, 1 Vanguard Dr, Goodwood; admission depending on day & size of rink R18-28
One of the few good reasons to head out to the casino is to take advantage of its Olympic-sized ice rink. Call up for the opening hours since they change frequently.

SWIMMING

There's also a good indoor pool at the Sports Science Institute of South Africa (p151).

LONG ST BATHS Map pp248-9

☎ 021-400 3302; cnr Long & Buitensingle Sts; adult/child R9/6; ✆ 7am-7pm
Dating from 1906, these nicely restored baths, featuring painted murals of city-centre life on the walls, are heated and very popular with the local community. The separate Turkish steam baths (R52) are a great way to sweat away some time, especially during the cooler months. Women are admitted 8.30am to 7.30pm Monday and Thursday, 9am to 6pm Saturday; men 1pm to 7.30pm Tuesday, 9am to 7.30pm Wednesday and Friday, and 8am to noon Sunday. Massages are available for women (R39 massage only, R73 massage and Turkish steam bath).

SEA POINT PAVILION Map p255

☎ 021-434 3341; Beach Rd, Sea Point; adult/child R9.50/6; ⏱ 7am-6.50pm Oct-Apr, 8.30am-5pm May-Sep

This huge outdoor pool complex is a Sea Point institution and has some lovely Art Deco decoration. It gets very busy on hot summer days, not surprisingly, since the pools are always at least 10ºC warmer than the always-frigid ocean.

YOGA & PILATES

For listings of Pilates instructors and classes check www.pilatesafrica.co.za.

BKS IYENGAR YOGA CENTRE Map p256

☎ 021-438 3383; www.capetownyoga.com; 15A the Drive, Camps Bay

Ninety-minute Iyengar yoga classes run from either 9am or from 6pm Monday to Friday, with an 11am session on Saturday. You can take five classes over two weeks and pay R160, otherwise there's a R200 membership fee and classes from R70 per session.

MOKSHA Map p254

☎ 021-465 1733; www.moksha.biz; 16 Mill St, Gardens; ⏱ 9am-8pm

Ashtanga yoga and a host of other courses are on offer at this stylish, centrally located, very business-minded studio, which even offers its own range of yoga clothing. Nonmembers pay R75 per class, or R650 for unlimited visits over a month.

OUTDOOR ACTIVITIES

ABSEILING & KLOOFING

Apart from the main abseiling site on Table Mountain, abseiling is also part of kloofing (canyoning) trips around Cape Town. The sport of clambering into and out of kloofs (cliffs or gorges) also entails climbing, hiking, swimming and jumping. It's great fun, but can be dangerous so check out operators' credentials carefully before signing up; two long-running operators are Abseil Africa and Day Trippers (p91).

180º ADVENTURES

☎ 021-462 0992; www.180.co.za

Mainly involved in arranging corporate training exercises, this outfit is experienced at running kloofing trips and also

offers an interesting Cape Town–based variation: a 2.3km 'walk' from Deer Park to the castle through the stormwater canals running under the city. It only runs during the dry summer months, needs eight people to go ahead and costs R280 per person.

ABSEIL AFRICA Map pp248-9

☎ 021-424 4760; www.abseilafrica.co.za; 1 Vredenburg Lane, City Bowl; abseil off Table Mountain R295; ⏱ 10am-6pm

The 112m drop off the top of Table Mountain is a guaranteed adrenaline rush, and the cheapest place to book it is direct with the operator, whose office is just off Long St. Don't even think of tackling it unless you've got a head (and a stomach) for heights. Take your time, because the views are breathtaking. The kloofing trips to gorges around Gordon's Bay involve jumps varying between 3m and 22m.

DIVING & SHARK-CAGE DIVING

Corals, kelp beds, wrecks, caves, drop-offs, seals and a wide variety of fish are some of the attractions that make Cape Town a great diving location. The best time is from June to November, when the water on the False Bay side is warmer and visibility is greater. Diving any time of the year off the Atlantic coast will require a 5mm wet suit.

Shark-cage diving is heavily promoted in Cape Town, even though the action is at Gansbaai, 175km southeast of the city. The closest town to Gansbaai is Hermanus, where several operators vie for trade. This popular but controversial activity (see the boxed text, p154) costs around R1100 for a day trip from Cape Town; in Hermanus you'll pay roughly R300 less and you won't have to get up at the crack of dawn. Tours, which you will need to book in advance,

Activities

OUTDOOR ACTIVITIES

CAPE TOWN'S TOP FIVE ADRENALINE RUSHES

- Abseil off Table Mountain (left).
- Fly over the peninsula in a helicopter (p155).
- Paraglide down to La Med (p156).
- Dive with sharks at the Two Oceans Aquarium (p154).
- Surf at Kommetjie (p157).

THE TROUBLE WITH SHARK DIVING

Shark attacks have been on the rise of late in Cape Town, and many Capetonians are linking this with the growing popularity of shark-cage diving. Operators use bait to attract the sharks. The theory, according to opposers of the activity, is that these killer fish are being trained to associate the presence of humans with food. There's still no hard evidence linking the two, but don't be surprised to find resistance to, as well as support for, your decision to have a *Jaws*-like encounter.

generally include breakfast, lunch and diving gear. Most operators will require divers to hold an internationally recognised diving qualification to take part, although some allow snorkellers into the cage. Take note: your chances of spotting sharks are much lower in the warmer summer months.

PRO DIVERS Map p255

☎ 021-433 0472; www.prodiverssa.co.za; 88B Main Rd, Sea Point; ☽ 9am-3pm Mon, 9am-6pm Tue-Sun

This recommended operator is conveniently located near Sea Point's hostels and guesthouses. Open-water PADI courses run at R2600. Dives kick off at R100 for a shore dive and R150 for a boat dive. Gear hire is R260.

SHARK-CAGE DIVING.NET

☎ 083 300 2138; www.sharkcagediving.net; trips R800

In his time Brian McFarlane caught 33 great whites. The hunter has now turned conservationist and is one of the most highly recommended operators in Hermanus. Add R250 for return transport from Cape Town.

SHARK LADY ADVENTURES Map p199

☎ 028-312 3287, 028-312 4529, 083 746 8985; www.sharklady.co.za; 61 Marine Dr, Hermanus; trips R850

Kim Maclean is the shark lady in question, and has been running trips for over 10 years. Ask about the spherical crystal cage dive (R1700), which gets you even closer to the fish and is strictly for divers only.

TABLE BAY DIVING Map pp252-3

☎ 021-419 8822; www.tablebaydiving.com; Shop 7, Quay 5, Waterfront

This reputable operator is based at the Waterfront. Shore dives are R200, boat dives R300, and full equipment hire R300. Its open-water PADI course is R3250 and it can also arrange shark-cage diving trips to Gansbaai.

TWO OCEANS AQUARIUM Map pp252-3

☎ 021-418 3823; www.aquarium.co.za; Dock Rd, Waterfront; dives R400

A guaranteed way to swim with sharks is to dive in the tanks at the Two Oceans Aquarium. No great whites, but several raggedtooth sharks, a 150kg short-tailed stingray, other predatory fish and a turtle make for a delightful diving experience. The cost includes hire of diving gear, and you need to be a certified diver. If not, one-day resort courses can be arranged. It also offers the chance to dive in the aquarium's kelp forest tank (R400), or to dive in an Imperial Navy diving suit with lead boots and an 18kg copper helmet (R650).

Marine life, Two Oceans Aquarium (above)

FLYING & MICROLIGHTING

There's no shortage of ways to get a bird's-eye view of the Cape in a range of machines, from microlights to ex-Vietnam helicopters. If there are no operational hours listed with the following reviews, you'll need to call to make a booking.

AQUILA MICROLIGHT SAFARIS
☎ 021-712 1913, 083 580 7250;
http://home.mweb.co.za/ts/tskorge
Trygve Skorge is the unlikely sounding name of an enthusiast who offers tours in his motor-powered microlight at Wintervogel Farm, about 40km north of the city. For a 30-minute/one-hour flight it's R454/707.

HOPPER Map pp252-3
☎ 021-419 8951; www.thehopper.co.za;
Shop 6, Quay 5, Waterfront
Rates of this helicopter operation start at R400 per person for a 15-minute flight over either Sandy Bay or out to the Twelve Apostles at 4pm daily. A 30-minute flight to see both oceans is R900.

HUEY EXTREME CLUB Map pp252-3
☎ 021-418 0207, 072 118 2627; Waterfront;
flights from R875
At a booth next to Cape Union Mart at the Waterfront, you can book an exhilarating ride on an ex-Vietnam US Marine Corps Huey chopper. It flies with open doors for that authentic *Apocalypse Now* experience – a hell of a lot more exciting than other helicopter rides.

THUNDERCITY Map pp244-5
☎ 021-934 8007; www.thundercity.com; Tower Rd, Cape Town International Airport; ⊗ 10am-5pm
Hawker Hunters, BAe Buccaneers, and the supersonic interceptor English Electric Lightnings – all these big boys' toys are available for daredevil wannabe pilots with plenty of spare rand.

HIKING & CLIMBING

The mountainous spine of the Cape Peninsula is a rock-climbing paradise, though it's not without its dangers, chief of which are the capricious weather conditions (see p70). Mountain rescues, and climbing fatalities, seem to occur on a weekly basis. Finding a guide or someone to climb with is always recommended. For details of guided hikes throughout the Table Mountain National Park, see p74.

CITY ROCK Map p256
☎ 021-447 1326; www.cityrock.co.za;
cnr Collingwood & Anson Rds, Observatory;
⊗ 11am-9pm Mon-Thu, 10am-6pm Fri-Sun
This popular indoor climbing gym offers climbing courses (from R99), and hires out and sells climbing gear. A day pass for the climbing wall is R55.

MOUNTAIN CLUB OF SOUTH AFRICA
Map p254
☎ 021-465 3412; www.mcsa.org.za;
97 Hatfield St, Gardens
This club, which can recommend guides to serious climbers, also has a climbing wall (R5; ⊗ 10am-2pm Mon-Fri, 6-9pm Tue & Wed).

HORSE RIDING

The beach at Noordhoek is the most popular Cape Town location for horse riding. Nearby at Imhoff Farm (see p109), on the way to Kommetjie, there's the novelty of camel rides – a great distraction if you're travelling with kids. Head out to the Winelands to take horseback tours both at Mont Rochelle Equestrian Centre (Map p193; ☎ 083 300 4368) in Franschhoek and Spier (p47).

FYNBOS TRAILS
☎ 082 335 8132; www.fynbostrails.com
This operation has half-/full-day horseback tours of the Winelands for experienced riders for R550/800, including all tastings and lunch on the full-day tour. For a two-day tour along the Berg River it's R1600.

OUDE MOLEN STABLES Map p256
☎ 072 199 7395; Violet Bldg, Oude Molen Eco Village, Alexandria Rd, Pinelands; per hr R100
Contact Kendre about horse riding at this eco-village where you'll also find a number of other interesting operations (see p104).

SLEEPY HOLLOW HORSE RIDING
Map pp244-5
☎ 021-789 2341, 083 261 0104; Noordhoek;
⊗ by appointment
This reliable operation can arrange horse riding along the wide, sandy Noordhoek beach, as well as in the mountainous hinterland.

Activities

OUTDOOR ACTIVITIES

HOT-AIR BALLOONING

WINELAND BALLOONING Map p196

☎ 021-863 3192; 64 Main St, Paarl; per person R1550
A predawn wake-up call is necessary if you take a hot-air balloon trip over the Winelands, but the experience will be unforgettable. Contact Carmen or Udo who run trips between November and April, but only when the weather conditions are right.

KAYAKING

The **African Paddling Association** (☎ 021-683 3698; www.apa.org.za) has a list of certified kayaking operators, and gives a lowdown on canoeing, sea kayaking and white-water paddling in the Cape region. Also see the website of **TASKS** (www.tasks.co.za), the African Sea Kayak Society.

REAL CAPE ADVENTURES

☎ 021-790 5611, 082 556 2520;
www.seakayak.co.za; ✆ by appointment
Apart from making and selling its own kayaks, this Hout Bay–based company runs a variety of kayaking trips around the Cape and further afield for paddlers of all levels. The half-day Hout Bay paddle, good for novice kayakers, kicks off at R200.

SEA KAYAK SIMON'S TOWN Map p258

☎ 082 501 8930; www.kayakcapetown.co.za;
Wharf Rd, Simon's Town
Paddle out to the penguins at Boulders (R200) with this Simon's Town–based operation. It also offers a variety of other tours, including one to Cape Point (R650), whale-watching from kayaks off Glencairne and overnight kayaking safaris.

WALKER BAY ADVENTURES

☎ 028-314 0925, 082 739 0159; www.walkerbay adventures.co.za; Prawn Flats, Hermanus
This Hermanus-based operation running sea-kayaking tours (R150) gives you the opportunity to see whales up close and personal. It also does lagoon cruises and hires out kayaks and boats.

PARAGLIDING

Feel like James Bond as you paraglide off Lion's Head, land at the Glen Country Club in Clifton, and then sink a beer at **La Med** (p140). Total novices are welcome to take a tandem flight, but should be prepared to lug their paraglider up the mountain. Make an inquiry on your first day in Cape Town – the weather conditions have to be just right.

The **South African Hang-Gliding & Paragliding Association** (☎ in Pretoria 012-668 1219; www .sahpa.co.za) can provide the names of operators and schools that offer paragliding courses for beginners.

AIR TEAM

☎ 082 727 6584; www.tandemparagliding.co.za;
flights from R750
The telephone number above puts you through to Ian Willis, who is part of a collective of paragliding instructors and enthusiasts offering tandem flights in and around Cape Town. As well as launches off Lion's Head, Air Team offers options to fly from Silvermine over False Bay, and from the mountains overlooking Hermanus.

SAILING

As South Africa gears up for its first ever America's Cup challenge in 2007, the focus will be on Cape Town where *Shosholoza*, the boat on which the nation's hopes rest, is moored: you can see her opposite the Cape Grace at the Waterfront.

CLASSIC CAPE CHARTERS

☎ 021-418 0782; www.capecharters.co.za
As well as giving you the opportunity to rent its luxury motor yacht *La Famiglia*, this company can arrange a host of other waterborne activities, including jet-skiing, tubing and rubber ducking.

OCEAN SAILING ACADEMY Map pp252-3

☎ 021-425 7837; www.oceansailing.co.za; West Quay Bldg, Waterfront; ✆ 8.30am-5pm Mon-Fri, 8.30am-1pm Sat
Contact the only Royal Yachting Association (RYA) school in South Africa to find out about its sailing courses, tailored to all skill levels.

ROYAL CAPE YACHT CLUB Map pp246-7

☎ 021-421 1354; www.rcyc.co.za; Duncan Rd, Foreshore
Races known as the 'Wags' are held every Wednesday afternoon at the club. Get here at 4.30pm if you want to take part, otherwise it's a 6pm start. Anyone with sailing knowledge can participate – you'll be assigned to a boat.

SKYDIVING

Cape Town is one of the cheapest places for you to learn to skydive or do a tandem dive. The view over Table Bay and the peninsula alone makes it worth it.

SKYDIVE CAPE TOWN

☎ 082 800 6290; www.skydivecapetown.za.net
Based about 20km north of the city centre in Melkboshstrand, this experienced outfit offers skydives for R1200 per person.

SURFING & SANDBOARDING

The surf scene is huge in Cape Town, with surfing possibilities ranging from gentle shore breaks that are ideal for beginners to 3m-plus monsters for experts only. There are breaks that work on virtually any combination of wind, tide and swell direction: for tips on choosing one, see the boxed text, below, and check out the **daily surf report** (☎ 082 234 6353; www.wavescape.co.za) for more details.

A couple of the surfing operators also offer sandboarding, which is just like snowboarding, except on sand dunes. It's huge fun but also, because of all that climbing up and down the sand dunes, a terrifically punishing work-out; expect muscles to ache where you never knew you had them.

DOWNHILL ADVENTURES Map p254

☎ 021-422 0388; www.downhilladventures.com; cnr Orange & Kloof Sts, Gardens
This totally adrenaline-focused company got the craze for sandboarding going in the Cape, and its trip to Atlantis, north of the city centre, is R500. It also runs a regular surf school with half-day introductory courses for R350.

GARY'S SURF SCHOOL Map p257

☎ 021-788 9839; www.garysurf.co.za; Surfer's Cnr, Beach Rd, Muizenberg; ☽ 8.30am-5pm
If genial surfing coach Gary Kleinhan can't get you to stand on a board within a day, you don't pay for the two-hour lesson (R380). His shop, the focus of Muizenberg's surf scene, hires out boards and wet suits for R100 each per day. It also runs sandboarding trips to the dunes at Kommetjie (R250).

ROXY SURF CLUB Map p257

☎ 082 562 8687, 072 586 0905; roxy@mobileemail.vodafonesa.co.za; 4 York Rd, Muizenberg
Roxy Towill began Cape Town's only women-only surf club to encourage more girls to get into the male-dominated sport. If you join the club, it's R200 per month for four lessons of 1½ hours each. A private lesson including board is R250, while individual group lessons are R75 per person.

SUNSCENE OUTDOOR ADVENTURES

☎ 021-783 0203, 083 517 9383;
www.sunscene.co.za
A two-hour sandboarding lesson with the expert guys from Sunscene, based near Kommetjie, will cost R250 including refreshments (essential!). Lessons are held in the sheltered environment of the Fish Hoek sand dunes, beneath Peer's Cave. The company also offers traditional surfing lessons and trips, along with fishing trips from Kalk Bay and a host of other adrenaline-pumping activities.

Activities

OUTDOOR ACTIVITIES

WEATHER TIPS FOR BEACH BABES & SURFERS

The following are some local tips if the wind is up and you're deciding which beach to sun on or surf off:

- If the wind is a northerly or northeasterly (mainly from April to September), head to the Bloubergstrand area. You'll avoid the cloud and rain, usually closer to Table Mountain, and the beaches are more pleasant because the wind is offshore and cooling, rather than chilly.

- During the westerlies (from November to March), the coastal area between Muizenberg and Simon's Town is shielded from the worst of the wind by the mountains.

- If the wind is a southerly or southwesterly (throughout the summer), head for Llandudno and Sandy Bay. Sandy Bay, in particular, is shielded by the Sentinel (the tall mountain to the south), and can be gloriously warm when everywhere else is miserable.

- The most famous wind, the Cape doctor, is lifted by Table Mountain, so beaches on the western seaboard, such as Camps Bay and Llandudno, are protected. Kalk Bay is also protected from the Cape doctor. A 'bubble' seems to form against the mountain and creates an area of calm, while just down the road in Fish Hoek, the wind howls onshore.

WINDSURFING & KITE BOARDING

With all that summer wind, it's hardly surprising that the Cape coast is a favourite spot for windsurfers and kite boarders. Blouberg-strand is a popular location, as is the lagoon in Langebaan (Map p186), further north.

CAPE SPORT CENTRE

☎ 022-772 1114; www.capesport.co.za
Based in Langebaan, Cape Sport Centre has more than 10 years' experience and can arrange windsurfing, kite boarding and kayaking.

WINDSWEPT

☎ 082 961 3070; www.windswept.co.za
Philip Baker runs windsurfing and kite-boarding camps out of his base in Blou-bergstrand. A three-hour beginner's course costs R450, or if you know the ropes you can hire a board from R250. Packages including accommodation are available.

WATCHING SPORT

Tickets & Reservations
COMPUTICKET

☎ 083 915 8000; www.computicket.co.za;
☺ 9am-5pm Mon-Fri, 9am-6pm Sat
Cape Town's computerised booking agency handles ticketing for all major sporting events. There are outlets in the Golden Acre Centre (Map pp248–9; Adderley St, City Bowl), at the Waterfront (Map pp252–3; Victoria Wharf), in the Gardens Centre (Map p254; Mill St, Gardens) and in Sea Point's Adelphi Centre (Map p255; Main Rd), among other places.

CRICKET
NEWLANDS CRICKET GROUND

Map pp246-7
☎ 021-657 3300, ticket hotline 021-657 2099;
Camp Ground Rd, Newlands
If it wasn't for nearby South African Breweries messing up the view towards the back of Table Mountain, Newlands would be a shoe-in for the title of world's prettiest cricket ground. There's room for a crowd of

25,000, so this is where all of the Protea's international matches are held. The cricket season runs from September to March with the day–night matches drawing the biggest crowds. Grab a spot on the grass bank to soak up the festive atmosphere. Tickets cost about R50 for local matches and up to R200 for internationals.

SOCCER

With tickets costing just R20, attending a soccer game is not only cheap, it's also a hugely fun night out with Capetonian supporters taking every opportunity to blow their plastic trumpets – bring your earplugs!

The season runs from August to May. Ajax Cape Town, who is affiliated with the Dutch club Ajax Amsterdam, sometimes plays matches at Newlands Rugby Stadium (below). Matches are also played at Green Point Stadium (Map pp252–3), off Fritz Sonnenberg Rd in Green Point, and Athlone Stadium (Map pp244–5), off Klipfontein Rd in Athlone. This last stadium is home to Santos soccer team. Tickets can be purchased through Computicket.

HORSE RACING

If you like to watch or bet on the horses, races are held every Wednesday and Sunday. For more information contact the Western Province Racing Club (☎ 021-551 2110).

KENILWORTH RACE COURSE

Map pp244-5
☎ 021-700 1600; Rosemead Ave, Kenilworth
There's year-round racing here. The main event to put down in your diary is the J&B Met (p9), South Africa's equivalent of Ladies Day at Ascot.

RUGBY
NEWLANDS RUGBY STADIUM

Map pp246-7
☎ 021-659 4600; www.wprugby.com;
Boundary Rd, Newlands
Home to the Stormers, this is the hallowed ground of South African rugby. Tickets for Super 12 games cost at least R85 in seats, R35 to R45 in the stands. Tickets for international matches cost about R325.

Shopping

Shopping

Bring an empty bag with you to Cape Town because chances are that you'll be leaving laden with local booty. The city's irresistible range of products – from modern African beadwork to fine wines – is guaranteed to turn the most consumer-averse visitor into a shopaholic.

Local design and fashion are really taking off (see p18), so if you want to give your wardrobe or home that contemporary African look, Cape Town is the place to go shopping. The city also acts as a clearing house for antiques and curios from all over Africa and you'll find some amazing pieces here – as well as plenty of fakes! If you're looking for simple gifts but don't want tacky touristy stuff (of which there's also plenty), go for township-produced crafts made from recycled bottles, cans and old food labels; you'll often be helping people who are struggling with poverty and HIV/AIDS. For other ideas, see below.

For one-stop shopping you still can't beat the mega malls such as the Waterfront's **Victoria Wharf** (Map pp252–3; ☎ 021-408 7600; www.waterfront.co.za; Waterfront; ⊙ 9am-9pm), **Canal Walk** (Map pp244–5; ☎ 0860 101 165; www.canalwalk.co.za; Century Blvd, Century City, Milnerton; ⊙ 9am-9pm), or **Cavendish Square** (Map pp246–7; ☎ 021-671 8042; www.cavendish.co.za; Cavendish St, Claremont; ⊙ 9am-6pm Mon-Thu, 9am-9pm Fri, 9am-6pm Sat, 10am-4pm Sun), all hugely popular for their range of shops, long opening hours and cheap or free parking. The increase in residential units in the City Bowl also means there's an increasingly lively shopping scene there; watch out for developments around the new Rhodes Mandela Place (Map pp248–9). And don't miss out on sampling one of Cape Town's several lively craft and flea markets (see the boxed text, p162).

Opening Hours

Most shops, particularly those in the City Bowl area, open from 8.30am to 5pm Monday to Friday and 8.30am to 1pm Saturday. If opening hours are not given in the listings in this chapter you can assume these hours apply. Shopping centres keep longer hours and are often open daily.

Consumer Taxes

South Africa has a value-added tax (VAT) of 14%. Foreign visitors can reclaim some of their VAT expenses on departure. For details, see p218.

Bargaining

When buying handicrafts from street hawkers and at some market stalls, bargaining is expected but isn't the sophisticated game that is often played in Asia. Don't press too hard.

TOP FIVE BEST BUYS

There are some brilliant original designer goods on sale in the Mother City. If we had to choose only five to take home, the following would be on our shopping list:

- Heath Nash lampshades (p168) – Nash's Flowerball and Curl lampshades elevate recycled plastic to an arty level. Also check out his wirework Soccerbowls and Life is Beautiful Here coat rack.
- Imagenius baby booties (p162) – if only these adorably cute dyed-buckskin baby booties came in adult sizes!
- Monkeybiz beadwork – we defy you to leave Cape Town without one of Monkeybiz' colourful dolls, animals or placemats. Hand over your credit card at the Bo-Kaap shop (p162) or at Carrol Boyes (p166) at the Waterfront.
- Nguni Cows from Streetwires (p163) – more brilliant beadwork in these richly patterned cow sculptures designed by Elias Kahari and Michaela Howse.
- Philippa Green bracelet (p165) – the embroidered Perspex cuffs of this young jewellery designer are seen on the smartest of Capetonian wrists. Also on sale at Monkeybiz (p162) and Africa Nova (p163).

CITY CENTRE

CITY BOWL & BO-KAAP

Pedestrianised St George's Mall, thronged with stalls selling art and fashion, is always an interesting browse. Adderley St, once Cape Town's principal shopping strip, is coming back to life, while the southern end of Long St is the place to head for second-hand books, antiques and streetwear boutiques. There are plenty of interesting galleries (see the boxed text, p164) to explore in the City Bowl. The whole area is best explored during the week though; it's dead from Saturday afternoon to Monday morning.

AFRICAN IMAGE Map pp248-9   Arts & Crafts
☎ 021-423 8385; www.african-image.co.za; cnr Church & Burg Sts, City Bowl
Fab range of new and old crafts and artefacts at reasonable prices. You'll find a lot of township crafts here, as well as wildly patterned shirts. Buy a can of Afro Coffee from **Café African Image** (p124) next door.

AFRICAN MUSIC STORE
Map pp248-9   Music
☎ 021-426 0857; 134 Long St, City Bowl
The prices are higher than in chain CD shops, but the range of local music, including all top jazz, *kwaito* (a form of township music), dance and trance recordings, can't be surpassed. The staff are knowledgeable about the music scene.

ATLAS TRADING COMPANY
Map pp248-9   Food
☎ 021-423 4361; 94 Wale St, Bo-Kaap
The pungent smell of over 100 different herbs, spices and incense perfumes the air at this cornerstone of the Bo-Kaap's Cape Muslim community. It's a wonderfully atmospheric place and the proprietors will happily share some local recipes with you.

BEAD CENTRE OF AFRICA
Map pp248-9   Jewellery
☎ 021-423 4687; www.beadmerchantsofafrica .com; 207 Long St, City Bowl
Beads of every shape and shade are sold here. Head to the rear to peruse the excellent selection of 'how to' books, Zulu-inspired bead jewellery by Abacus, Indian beaded slippers and stringed trade beads.

There is also another outlet in the **City Bowl** (Map pp248-9; 223 Long St), and the company runs the bargain bead store **KgB** (Map pp248-9; cnr Bree & Dorp Sts). Check the website for details of the regular beading classes (from R100).

BEINKINSTADT Map pp248-9   Judaica
☎ 021-461 2431; 38 Canterbury St, City Bowl; 🕙 9am-5pm Mon-Fri
Bordering the old District Six, this marvellous Judaica emporium is run by Michael and Fay Padowich, the third generation of original owners. Inside and out, hardly anything seems to have changed since it opened in 1903. Good souvenirs include CDs of Jewish music from South Africa, and locally made challah covers and yarmulkes.

CLARKE'S Map pp248-9   Books
☎ 021-423 5739; www.clarkesbooks.co.za; 211 Long St, City Bowl
Clarke's stocks the best range of books on South Africa and the continent, and has a great second-hand section. If you can't find what you're looking for here, it's unlikely to be at the many other bookshops along Long St (although there's no harm in browsing).

Mosaic of Nelson Mandela, African Image (left)

Shopping

CITY CENTRE

8-9   Clothing, Arts & Crafts
ꞁagenius.co.za;

ꞁis treasure-trove of
offers up an eclec-
ꞁamics, beachwear,
e buckskin baby
stylish gift cards, boxes
and wrapping, too.

MEMEME Map pp248-9   Clothing & Accessories
☎ 021-424 0001; 121 Long St, City Bowl;
🕑 9.30am-5.30pm Mon-Sat

A forerunner of the funky boutiques bloom-
ing along Long St, Mememe is a showcase
for young Capetonian designers, such as

Richard de Jager, Carine Terreblanche and
the owner Doreen Southwood. You'll also
find works here by artists such as Heath
Nash (see p168).

MONKEYBIZ Map pp248-9   Arts & Crafts
☎ 021-426 0145; www.monkeybiz.co.za;
65 Rose St, Bo-Kaap

You won't miss this yellow building painted
with red monkeys! Equally colourful beadwork products are found inside, all made
by township women. The shop also stocks
funky jewellery by Philippa Green and Ida-
Elsje (see p165) and gifts by other quirky
Capetonian designers. Profits from the beadwork support the Monkeybiz Wellness Clinic
for HIV/AIDS-affected women held upstairs

TOP FIVE MARKETS

You'll have fun hunting through Cape Town's many craft markets for the authentic, quality items amid the piles of cheap tourist-trade stuff. The Market at Grand Parade (Map pp248-9) on Wednesday and Saturday doesn't sell much of interest to visitors, but it's certainly lively, with people scrambling for bargains, mainly clothing.

Green Point Market (Map pp252-3; Green Point Stadium, Western Blvd, Green Point; 🕑 8.30am-6pm Sun) Held in the main parking lot in front of the stadium, this craft market is one of the best places to hunt for inexpensive African art, fabrics and clothes.

Greenmarket Square (Map pp248-9; cnr Shortmarket & Berg Sts, City Bowl; 🕑 9am-4pm Mon-Sat) Masks, jewellery, bargain CDs, pottery and the satirical, anticorporate T-shirts of Laugh It Off are just some of the finds at this market, held in cobbled Greenmarket Sq.

Hout Bay Craft Market (Map p258; ☎ 021-790 3474; Baviaanskloof Rd, Hout Bay; 🕑 10am-5pm Sun) Held on the village green, this is a great alternative to Green Point Market, offering lots of great crafts made by local people, including the paper products of Iziko lo Lwazi (p168).

Kirstenbosch Craft Market (Map pp244-5; ☎ 021-671 5468; cnr Kirstenbosch & Rhodes Drs, Newlands; 🕑 9am-5pm last Sun of month) Proceeds from this craft market go to the development fund for Kirstenbosch Botanical Gardens. Mr Mather's handmade wooden toys are worth looking out for.

Milnerton Flea Market (Map pp244-5; ☎ 021-550 1383; Racecourse Rd, Milnerton; 🕑 7am-3pm Sat & Sun) Hunt for genuine antiques at bargain prices at this car-boot sale in an industrial corner of Cape Town. With patience and luck you'll find collectable china, glass and furnishings.

Painted ostrich eggs, Greenmarket Square (above)

here every Friday, the same day women artists pack the street outside the **head office** (Map pp248–9; 43 Rose St; Bo-Kaap) to sell their beadwork – it's a very lively scene. You'll also find Monkeybiz products for sale at **Carrol Boyes** (p166) at the Waterfront.

PAN AFRICAN MARKET

Map pp248-9   Arts & Crafts
☎ 021-426 4478; www.panafrican.co.za; 76 Long St, City Bowl
A microcosm of the continent with a bewildering range of arts and crafts. There's also a cheap café and music store packed into its three floors, and you can have an African outfit made up here.

SHAP'S CAMERALAND

Map pp248-9   Photography
☎ 021-423 4150; 66 Long St
There are several places to buy cameras and get your photos developed or burned to disc along Long St; Shap's is a reliable place with competitive prices and efficient service.

SKINZ Map pp248-9   Leather Goods

☎ 021-424 3978; 86 Long St, City Bowl
If you want a little something made from exotic leather or animal skins – think zebra, springbok, crocodile and ostrich – then this is your place. It does regular cow-hide leather too, but doesn't that sound boring compared to purple-dyed springbok? A whole zebra skin goes for between R5000 and R11,000, depending on the grade.

STREETWIRES Map pp248-9   Arts & Crafts

☎ 021-426 2475; www.streetwires.co.za; 77-79 Shortmarket St, Bo-Kaap
The motto is 'Anything you can dream up in wire we will build'. And if you visit this social project designed to uplift young blacks and coloureds to see the wire sculptors at work, you'll see what that means! It stocks an amazing range, including working radios and chandeliers as well as artier products such as the Nguni Cow range, which you'll also find sold at upmarket craft shops such as **Africa Nova** (right).

SURF ZONE Map pp248-9   Surf & Swimwear

☎ 021-426 4226; 45 Castle St, City Bowl
All the usual international labels, including Rip Curl and Billabong, in what is claimed to be the biggest range of surfwear, wet suits and boards in Africa.

VIBRATIONS Map pp248-9   Musical Instruments

☎ 021-461 2385; www.vibrationstudio.com; 129 Longmarket St, City Bowl
The vibrant sound of African music drifts from this 1st-floor shop and recording studio, where you can pick up an authentic range of African instruments, including buckskin covered *goema* drums for R250.

WOLA NANI Map pp248-9   Arts & Crafts

☎ 021-423 7385; www.wolanani.co.za; 76 Long St, City Bowl
Wola Nani, Xhosa (isiXhosa) for 'We Embrace and Develop Each Other', is an NGO that addresses the needs of those infected with HIV and AIDS. You'll find its label-covered picture frames and papier-mâché bowls, as well as other products, on sale here at its head office, and at many other Cape Town craft shops.

WATERKANT

The shopping complex **Cape Quarter** (Map pp248–9; 72 Waterkant St) remains a huge hit with both locals and visitors alike – you'll find the deli-café **Andiamo** (p127) here, as well as furniture, jewellery and homewares stores. There's also a branch of the eclectic interior-design store **Cape to Cairo** (p170), opposite, on Waterkant St.

AFRICA NOVA Map pp248-9   Arts & Crafts

☎ 021-425 5123; Cape Quarter, 72 Waterkant St, Waterkant; ☿ 9am-5pm Mon-Fri, 10am-2pm Sat & Sun
One of the most stylish and desirable collections of contemporary African textiles, arts and crafts. You'll find potato-print fabrics made by women in Hout Bay, Karin Dando's mosaic trophy heads, Jordaan's handmade felt rock cushions (which look like giant pebbles), and a wonderful range of ceramics and jewellery.

BIG BLUE Map pp248-9   Clothing

☎ 021-425 1179; www.bigblue.co.za; Somerset Rd, Waterkant
A good boutique for picking up some fun clubbing gear or beachwear by South African designers, including Jo Soap, Karen Frazer, Amanda Laird Cherry, Cuba Vera and Gottalotalove. There's also a branch in **Cavendish Square** (Map pp246–7; Cavendish St, Claremont).

GALLERY CRAWL

There're some very talented artists at work in Cape Town (see p32) and a day spent exploring the following centrally located galleries is a rewarding experience. Keep an eye out in the local press for exhibition openings, when it's possible to drop by and mingle with the art set over drinks and nibbles. The annually updated *Arts & Crafts Cape Town Map*, available free at Cape Town Tourism offices (p219), is a useful resource. Unless otherwise mentioned, opening hours are 10am to 5pm Monday to Friday and 10am to 3pm Saturday.

34 Long (Map pp248–9; ☎ 021-426 4594; www.34long.com; 34 Long St, City Bowl; ⏱ 9am-5pm Tue-Fri, 10am-2pm Sat) New gallery space hosting interesting exhibitions: a recent one compared the work of cutting-edge and established South African artists, such as Matthew Hindley and William Kentridge, with those from China and Japan.

AVA Gallery (Map pp248–9; ☎ 021-424 7436; www.ava.co.za; 35 Church St, City Bowl) Exhibition space for the nonprofit Association for Visual Arts (AVA), which shows some very interesting work by local artists. Browse the room at the front for a selection from former exhibitions.

Bell-Roberts Art Gallery (Map pp248–9; ☎ 021-422 1100; www.bell-roberts.com; 89 Bree St, City Bowl) A move to larger, light-filled premises has allowed this gallery and art-book publisher wider scope for its exhibitions. Well worth a browse to discover who's on the up in the Cape Town art world.

Everard Read (Map pp252–3; ☎ 021-418 4527; www.everard-read-capetown.co.za; 3 Portswood Rd, Waterfront; ⏱ 9am-6pm Mon-Fri, 9am-4pm Sat) Very classy gallery showcasing the best of contemporary South African art, including works by John Meyer and Velaphi Mzimba.

João Ferreira Gallery (Map pp248–9; ☎ 021-423 5402; www.joaoferreiragallery.com; 80 Hout Lane, City Bowl; ⏱ 10am-5pm Tue-Fri, 10am-2pm Sat) One of the city's top galleries representing many established and up-and-coming artists.

Michael Stevenson Gallery (Map pp248–9; ☎ 021-421 2575; www.michaelstevenson.com; Hill House, De Smidt St, Waterkant) One of the city's best exhibition spaces where you'll find works by Hilton Neil, Bernie Searle and Brett Murray, as well as many others. The catalogues, art books and posters are a good buy, if you can't afford the art itself.

Photographers Gallery (Map pp248–9; ☎ 021-422 2762; www.erdmanncontemporary.co.za; 63 Shortmarket St, City Bowl; ⏱ 10am-5pm Tue-Fri, 10am-1pm Sat) As well as representing the fine work of many top South African photographers, this gallery shows pieces by artists Lien Botha and Conrad Botes (see the boxed text, p33).

What If The World (Map pp248–9; ☎ 021-461 2573; www.whatiftheworld.com; 11 Hope St, City Bowl; ⏱ 10am-6pm Mon-Sat) Edgy little gallery and design collective that has exhibitions by emerging artists and quirky events, including an annual T-shirt-design festival. Check out the Neighbour Goods event, a creative market and studio sale usually held for 24 hours on the last Monday of the month.

HAND Map pp248-9   Clothing & Accessories

☎ 021-425 9912; www.hand.net; 28 Hudson St, Waterkant; ⏱ 9.30am-6pm Mon, Tue, Thu & Sat, 9.30am-8pm Wed & Fri

A one-stop fashion experience. Get your locks trimmed (R80 to R150), browse the boutique of designer clothes, jewellery and art, and have an ostrich sandwich (R25) and cappuccino (R10) at the café.

GARDENS & SURROUNDS

Kloof St is the Gardens' principal shopping drag, stacked with interesting outlets and anchored by the shopping centre **Lifestyles on Kloof** (Map p254; 50 Kloof St), where you'll find some good fashion and footwear boutiques, branches of Exclusive Books and Woolworths, as well as the Labia on Kloof cinema (p148) and a gym (p151). Another

useful Gardens shopping mall is the Gardens Centre (opposite). Also keep an eye out for shops opening in the new **Wembley Centre** (Map p254; Glynn St).

AFROGEM Map p254   Jewellery

☎ 021-424 8048; 64 New Church St, Gardens; ⏱ 8.30am-6pm Mon-Fri, 8.30am-5pm Sat & Sun

Diamonds, aquamarines, topazes – you name the gem, chances are this company makes gold or silver jewellery using it. See how it's done on a free guided tour.

BE MUSE Map p254   Clothing & Accessories

☎ 021-422 3788; cnr Park Lane & New Church St, Gardens

Lots of pretty items for sale, nearly all by South African designers, at this fashion and interior-design boutique that's a slight cut above several similar places in the Gardens area.

GALLERY ZOOM Map p254 | Homewares
☎ 021-422 5222; 24 Kloof St, Gardens
Eddie Zoom's jumble sale of retro furnishings from the 1950s to the 1980s is where you can also get newly made Tretchikoff prints on canvas or paper (from R200). Ask to flip through the catalogue for the iconic image of your choice.

GARDENS CENTRE Map p254 | Shopping Centre
☎ 021-465 1842; Mill St, Gardens
Very handy mall that covers all the bases with good cafés, bookshops, an Internet café, Pick 'n' Pay and Woolworths supermarkets, a Flight Centre and a Cape Union Mart camping-supplies shop.

HEARTWORKS Map p254 | Arts & Crafts
☎ 021-424 8419; 98 Kloof St, Gardens; ☽ 9am-5pm Mon-Fri, 9.30am-3pm Sat, 9.30am-2pm Sun
Browse Heartworks' varied range of crafts, including Wola Nani goods, Mealie bags made in Hout Bay, telephone-wire baskets from Natal, and Mustardseed and Moonshine ceramics. There's also a branch in the Gardens Centre (Map p254; ☎ 021-465 3289; Mill St, Gardens).

LIM Map p254 | Homewares
☎ 021-423 1200; www.lim.co.za; 86A Kloof St, Gardens
The shop's name is an acronym for 'less is more', which sums up the stylish, pared-back selection of homewares, including many cute fashion accessory items made from buckskin.

PHILIPPA GREEN & IDA-ELSJE
Map p254 | Jewellery
☎ 021-424 1101; 79 Kloof St, Gardens; ☽ 9am-5pm Mon-Fri
At the studio of Philippa Green (www.philippagreen.com) and Ida-Elsje (www.olivegreencat.com), you'll find the work of two very talented young jewellery designers, both of whom are catching international attention. Green's signature pieces are her chunky Perspex cuffs, hand-stitched with patterns and graphic text, while Elsje specialises in delicate earrings and necklaces. They also collaborate on the striking Situ range of diamond jewellery.

READERS PARADISE Map p254 | Books
☎ 021-424 4335; 71A Kloof St, Gardens; ☽ 9am-9pm Mon-Sat, 10am-3pm Sun
Longer-than-usual opening hours and a decent discount on prices make this reasonably stocked shop a favourite of Capetonian bibliophiles.

RELIGION Map p254 | Clothing
☎ 021-423 8538; 43 Kloof St, Gardens
Apart from its own brand of unisex fashion for the streetwise, this interesting boutique stocks clothing by the likes of Jacob Kimmie and Craig Native, whose T-shirts, printed with bull's-eye designs of Africa, you'll see everywhere in Cape Town.

WINE CONCEPTS Map p254 | Wine
☎ 021-426 4401; www.wineconcepts.co.za; Lifestyles on Kloof, 50 Kloof St, Gardens; ☽ 10am-7pm Mon-Wed, 10am-8pm Thu & Fri, 9am-5pm Sat
You'll get expert advice on a broad range of local wines at this small but appealing cellar. Free wine tastings are held Thursday to Saturday. It also has a branch in Newlands (Map pp246–7; cnr Kildare Rd & Main St), next to Barristers.

ATLANTIC COAST

Not everywhere along the coast is a shopping paradise; Sea Point and Camps Bay, for example, have few unique stores. However, expect the already-heavy crowds at mega shopping complexes, such as the Waterfront and Canal Walk, to swell at the weekends.

The Waterfront's main mall is Victoria Wharf (Map pp252–3; ☎ 021-408 7600; www.waterfront.co.za; Waterfront; ☽ 9am-9pm), and it's where you'll find all the big names of South African retail. In Green Point, the new development Portside (Map pp252–3; Main Rd) is worth checking out.

GREEN POINT & WATERFRONT
AFRICAN ART FACTORY
Map pp252-3 | Arts & Crafts
☎ 021-421 9910; www.africanartfactory.co.za; Block E, Old City Hospital Complex, 2 Portswood Rd, Waterfront; ☽ 8am-4.30pm Mon-Fri, 8am-1pm Sat
This partnership project of designers and craftspeople produces colourful ceramics, wireworks and other items within the old City Hospital grounds. An example is

Luvuyo Nyathi who recycles tin drink cans and bottle tops into decorative flowers, picture frames, bags and boxes.

CAPE UNION MART ADVENTURE CENTRE Map pp252-3 Outdoor Gear

☎ 021-425 4559; www.capeunionmart.co.za; Quay 4, Waterfront; 8.30am-11pm

This impressive outdoors shop offers practically everything you'd need for anything from a hike up Table Mountain to a Cape-to-Cairo safari. The shop includes a café, climbing wall, hiking-boot testing station and cold-weather chamber (to assess those thermals!). There's also a smaller branch in Victoria Wharf (Map pp252–3; Waterfront) and one at the Gardens Centre (Map p254; Mill St, Gardens).

CARROL BOYES Map pp252-3 Homewares

☎ 021-418 0595; www.carrolboyes.co.za; Shop 6180, Victoria Wharf, Waterfront; 9am-9pm

Carrol Boyes' sensuous designs in pewter and steel give a fun feel to cutlery, kitchen products and homewares. You also find Monkeybiz' rainbow-hued beadworks on sale here (see p162).

CD WHEREHOUSE Map pp252-3 Music

☎ 021-425 6300; www.cdwherehouse.co.za; Dock Rd, Waterfront; 9am-9pm

You'll find a good selection of local artists at the Waterfront's biggest collection of CDs and DVDs. Prices are reasonable.

EXCLUSIVE BOOKS Map pp252-3 Books

☎ 021-419 0905; www.exclusivebooks.co.za; Victoria Wharf, Waterfront; 9am-9pm

This chain bookshop has a great selection of titles and comfy surroundings in which to browse before you buy. There are also branches at Cavendish Square (Map pp246–7; Cavendish St, Claremont) and Lifestyles on Kloof (Map p254; 50 Kloof St, Gardens).

KLÛK & CGDT Map pp252-3 Clothing

☎ 083 377 7780; ww.kluk.co.za; cnr Main & Upper Portswood Rds, Green Point; 9.30am-8pm Mon-Fri, 10am-4pm Sat, 11am-3pm Sun

The stylish boutique of local designers Malcom Klûk (former apprentice to John Galliano) and Christiaan Gabriel du Toit. Their range features lots of natural fibres and they also stock other designers clothes, including the glam party dresses of Kelly Bloom.

KRAAL GALLERY Map pp252-3 Rugs

☎ 021-421 1600; www.thekraalgallery.co.za; Dock Rd, Waterfront; 9am-9pm

See weavers in action creating multicoloured, uniquely designed rugs and wall hangings at this stand-alone shop, behind the Mitchell Brewery on the Waterfront.

LAVA LAVA Map pp252-3 Clothing

☎ 021-425 5065; Shop 10, Alfred Mall, Waterfront; 9am-9pm

Make an African fashion statement by wearing one of Lava Lava's brightly patterned shirts or sarongs, or buy one of its fabric swatches.

NAARTJIE Map pp252-3 Children's Clothing

☎ 021-421 5819; www.naartjie.homestead.com; Shop 117, Victoria Wharf, Waterfront; 9am-9pm

This attractive range of designer cotton children's clothing has grown from a stall on Greenmarket Sq to a global brand. There's also a branch in Cavendish Square (Map pp246–7; ☎ 021-683 7184; Cavendish St, Claremont) and a factory shop in Hout Bay (Map p258; ☎ 021-790 3093; 46 Victoria Ave).

RED SHED CRAFT WORKSHOP

Map pp252-3 Arts & Crafts

☎ 021-408 7847; Victoria Wharf, Waterfront; 9am-9pm Mon-Sat, 10am-9pm Sun

This permanent market focuses on local crafts, including ceramics and textiles. Look for the delicate jewellery of Get Wired, made by women in Crossroads; the colourful textile products of Ikamva Labantu (p168); and the stationary products of T-Bag Designs (www.tbagdesigns.co.za) from Hout Bay.

SHIMANSKY Map pp252-3 Jewellery

☎ 021-421 2788; www.shimansky.co.za; top fl, Clock Tower Centre, Waterfront; 9am-9pm

Diamonds are synonymous with South Africa and here you'll find plenty of them set in a range of jewellery designs. There's also a workshop where you can take a peek at how all that bling is put together and choose some stones of your own.

SUN GODDESS Map pp252-3 Clothing

☎ 021-421 7620; www.sungoddess.co.za; Shop 230, Victoria Wharf, Waterfront; 9am-9pm

The inspiration for Sun Goddess' range is traditional African culture, but the daring

Red Shed Craft Workshop (opposite)

design combinations with modern fabrics and embellishments make them fun and contemporary. The clothes are mainly for women, but there are also some surprisingly groovy, beaded kaftan-style garments for men.

TRAVELLERS BOOKSHOP

Map pp252-3   Books

☎ 021-425 6880; Victoria Wharf, Waterfront; ☽ 9am-9.30pm

Cape Town's only dedicated travel bookshop stocks all the practical reading material you might need for your travels in Africa and further afield. It also has a good range of general books on Cape Town and South Africa.

ULTRA LIQUORS Map pp252-3   Wine

☎ 021-434 4838; 122 Main Rd, Green Point; ☽ 9am-6pm Mon-Thu, 9am-6.30pm Fri, 8.30am-5pm Sat

Pile 'em high, sell 'em cheap is the deal at this liquor warehouse chain – don't expect much in the way of expert advice, but the range is wide and the prices can seldom be beat, even at the cellar door.

VAUGHAN JOHNSON'S WINE & CIGAR SHOP Map pp252-3   Wine

☎ 021-419 2121; www.vaughanjohnson.com; Dock Rd, Waterfront; ☽ 9am-6pm Mon-Fri, 10am-5pm Sat & Sun

Selling practically every South African wine you could wish to buy (plus a few more from other countries), it's open, unlike most wine sellers, on Sunday.

WALLFLOWER

Map pp252-3   Interior Design & Gifts

☎ 021-434 8265; 1st fl, Portside, Main Rd, Green Point; ☽ 9am-8pm

Follow the trail of rose petals up the stairs to this interior-design boutique, which stocks a fine selection of gifts. Choose from handmade candles, body products (which you can test) and delicate ceramics by the likes of Lisa Firer and Heather Mills, whose studio you can visit at Imhoff Farm (p109).

WATERFRONT CRAFT MARKET

Map pp252-3   Arts & Crafts

☎ 021-408 7842; Dock Rd, Waterfront; ☽ 9.30am-6pm

Also known as the Blue Shed, this eclectic arts-and-crafts market, between Two Oceans Aquarium and CD Wherehouse, harbours some great buys. Search out Waterfront Music (☎ 021-438 1125; www.townshipguitars .com), which makes and sells the all-electric township 'blik' guitars made from oil cans, wood and fishing wire (R1600 to R3200).

BEACHES & SUBURBS

CANAL WALK Map pp244-5   Shopping Centre

☎ 0860 101 165; www.canalwalk.co.za; Century Blvd, Century City, Milnerton; ☽ 9am-9pm

With some 450 shops, 50-odd restaurants and 18 cinema screens you'd be a fool to argue with its claim of being the largest mall in Africa. The food court is so big that acrobatics shows are often held over the diners. Drive here along the N1, or check the website for details of a shuttle bus service from the Waterfront and the City Bowl.

IZIKO LO LWAZI Map p258   Arts & Crafts

☎ 021-790 2123; Hout Bay Community Cultural Centre, Baviaanskloof Rd, Hout Bay; ⏱ 9.30am-1pm Mon-Fri

What began as an adult-literacy programme has morphed into a craftwork collective producing creative recycled-paper products. The Uxolo range of beaded cards is delightful. You can also see the work at the **Hout Bay Craft Market** (p162).

SOUTHERN SUBURBS

Claremont is the main shopping area of the Southern Suburbs; this is where you will find **Cavendish Square** (Map pp246–7; ☎ 021-671 8042; www.cavendish.co.za; Cavendish St, Claremont; ⏱ 9am-6pm Mon-Thu, 9am-9pm Fri, 9am-6pm Sat, 10am-4pm Sun), a top-class shopping mall with outlets of many of Cape Town's premier fashion designers, as well as supermarkets, department stores and two multiplex cinemas. In Woodstock and Observatory you'll find several more-craft-focused shops.

CLOTHING SIZES

Measurements approximate only, try before you buy

Women's Clothing

Aus/UK	8	10	12	14	16	18
Europe	36	38	40	42	44	46
Japan	5	7	9	11	13	15
USA	6	8	10	12	14	16

Women's Shoes

Aus/USA	5	6	7	8	9	10
Europe	35	36	37	38	39	40
France only	35	36	38	39	40	42
Japan	22	23	24	25	26	27
UK	3½	4½	5½	6½	7½	8½

Men's Clothing

Aus	92	96	100	104	108	112
Europe	46	48	50	52	54	56
Japan	S		M	M		L
UK/USA	35	36	37	38	39	40

Men's Shirts (Collar Sizes)

Aus/Japan	38	39	40	41	42	43
Europe	38	39	40	41	42	43
UK/USA	15	15½	16	16½	17	17½

Men's Shoes

Aus/UK	7	8	9	10	11	12
Europe	41	42	43	44½	46	47
Japan	26	27	27½	28	29	30
USA	7½	8½	9½	10½	11½	12½

HABITS Map pp246-7   Clothing & Accessories

☎ 021-671 7330; www.habits.co.za; 1 Cavendish Close, Cavendish St, Claremont

The women's clothes designed by Jenny le Roux are classical and practical, made from linen, cotton and silk. Her Bad Habits label is for younger women. Bored partners can crash on the sofa, watch TV and sip complimentary iced tea.

HEATH NASH Map pp246-7   Interior Design

☎ 021-447 5757; www.incapetown.com /heathnash; 2 Mountain Rd, Woodstock; ⏱ 8am-5pm

Give the current young darling of the Cape Town arts-and-crafts scene a call before visiting his Woodstock studio, in an unmarked building just off Victoria Rd. Here you'll find his full range of fab Flowerball shades made from recycled plastics, wirework fruit bowls, candelabra and coat racks, plus new products in the making.

HIP HOP Map pp246-7   Clothing

☎ 021-674 4605; 12 Cavendish St, Claremont; ⏱ 9am-5.30pm Mon-Fri, 9am-4pm Sat, 10am-2pm Sun

Hip Hop is another Cape Town fashion success story. The women's clothes look good on all shapes and sizes and are suitable for a range of occasions. Drop by the factory outlet in the **City Bowl** (Map pp248–9; ☎ 021-465 0352; 35B Buitenkant St; ⏱ 9am-5pm Mon-Fri, 9am-1pm Sat) for bargains.

IKAMVA LABANTU

Map pp246-7   Arts, Crafts & Clothing

☎ 021-461 8338; www.ikamva.com; Buchanan Sq, 160 Sir Lowry Rd, Woodstock; ⏱ 8.30am-4.30pm Mon-Thu, 8.30am-3pm Fri

Wonderful fabric products, including stuffed animal toys, Nelson Mandela dolls and kids' backpacks and clothes are made by the people with disabilities who are employed here. This is the factory shop and there's also an outlet in the **Red Shed Craft Workshop** (p166) at the Waterfront.

INDIA JANE: THE SECRET ROOM

Map pp246-7   Clothing & Accessories

☎ 021-683 7607; www.indiajane.com; 14 Cavendish Close, Cavendish St, Claremont; ⏱ 10am-5.30pm Mon-Fri, 9.30am-4pm Sat

The sexy, silky clothes at India Jane's boutiques reflect the stylish, laid-back atmosphere of the city and include designs by Miss Moneypenny (a label designed by Durbanite Emma Jackson) and the peasant skirts of Anthea Mooney. Other branches are in **Kalk Bay** (Map p257; Main Rd) and in **Cavendish Square** (Map pp246–7; Cavendish St, Claremont).

LUNAR Map pp246-7   Clothing & Accessories
☎ 021-674 6871; Kildare Centre, 62 Main St, Newlands

Karen Termorshuizen uses lots of light, natural-coloured fabrics in her appealing collection, tailored to the cultivated tastes of this ritzy corner of Cape Town. You'll find very good quality leather and animal-skin bags and accessories here, too.

MNANDI TEXTILES & DESIGN
Map p256   Clothing & Textiles
☎ 021-447 6814; 90 Station Rd, Observatory

Mnandi sells cloth from all over Africa as well as clothing printed with everything from ANC election posters to animals and traditional African patterns. You can also have clothes tailor-made. The Xhosa women and Desmond Tutu cloth dolls (R200) are darling.

MONTEBELLO Map pp246-7   Arts & Crafts
☎ 021-685 6445; www.montebello.co.za; 31 Newlands Ave, Newlands; 9am-5pm Mon-Fri, 9am-4pm Sat, 9am-3pm Sun

This development project has helped several great craftspeople and designers along the way. In the leafy compound, check out the colourful bags made from recycled materials, the fashions of **Miele** (www.miele.co.za), and Thando Papers, started by Joseph Diliza who had the idea of turning invasive reeds from urban rivers into exclusive paper products. On weekdays you can visit the artists' studios. There's also a good café, the **Gardener's Cottage** (p132).

SPACE Map pp246-7   Clothing & Accessories
☎ 021-674 6643; Shop L69, Cavendish Square, Cavendish St, Claremont; 9am-6pm Mon-Thu & Sat, 9am-9pm Fri, 10am-4pm Sun

Check out cool South African designer wares by the likes of Amanda Laird Cherry at this cute boutique in the bowels of Cavendish Square.

YOUNG DESIGNERS EMPORIUM
Map pp246-7   Clothing & Accessories
☎ 021-683 6177; Shop F50, Cavendish Square, Cavendish St, Claremont

It's a bit of a jumble, but you'll most likely find something groovy to suit at YDE among the street clothes and accessories for both sexes by new South African designers.

FALSE BAY & SOUTHERN PENINSULA

You could spend all day browsing the antique shops and galleries of Kalk Bay's Main Rd. Simon's Town's St George's St is also a fruitful shopping strip, especially if you're into naval memorabilia, available by the bucket load at the antique shops here. The southern peninsula's main shopping centre is **Longbeach Mall** (Map pp244–5; ☎ 021-785 5955; Sunnydale Rd, Sun Valley; 9am-6pm Mon-Fri, 8.30am-4pm Sat & Sun), between Noordhoek and Kommetjie, where you'll find all the usual supermarkets and a multiplex cinema.

ARTVARK Map p257   Arts & Crafts
☎ 021-788 5584; www.artvark.org; 48 Main Rd, Kalk Bay; 10am-6pm

This store stocks a wide range of interesting arts and crafts by local artists, including paintings, pottery and jewellery. It also sells goods from India and Central America.

BELLE OMBRE ANTIQUES
Map p257   Antiques & Crafts
☎ 021-788 9802; 19 Main Rd, Kalk Bay; 9am-5pm Mon-Fri, 10am-5pm Sat & Sun

Appealing Cape country antiques and African pieces, including wood carvings from Ethiopia and Namibia, are sold here. In a shady garden behind, you'll find the Blue Brinjal restaurant, a rustic place for lunch or a snack while you're doing the shopping rounds.

CAPE TO CAIRO

Map p257   Interior Design & Gifts

☎ 021-788 4571; 100 Main Rd, Kalk Bay;
⊗ 9.30am-5.30pm

Quirky interior design items and gifts from around Africa and overseas are jumbled up in this Aladdin's cave of a store. There's also a branch in the **Waterkant** (Map pp248–9; ☎ 021-421 3518; Upper Waterkant St).

CLEMENTINA CERAMICS & A.R.T. GALLERY Map p257   Arts & Crafts

☎ 021-788 8718; www.clementina.co.za;
20 Main Rd, Kalk Bay; ⊗ 10am-5pm Tue-Sun

There's a continuously changing display of one-off works by Clementina van der Walt and other artists here, as well as a full selection of Clementina's distinctive tableware, hand-painted in bright colours. Attached is the relaxed Café des Arts where you can take tea in a courtyard overlooking the bay.

KALK BAY MARKET

Map p257   Clothing & Interior Design

Belmont Way, Kalk Bay; ⊗ 10am-5pm

It's worth browsing through this collection of likeminded shops showcasing designer clothes, preloved garments, African beadwork and the furnishing designs of **Urban Being** (www.urbanbeing.co.za).

KALK BAY MODERN Map p257   Arts & Crafts

☎ 021-788 6571; Windsor House, 150 Main Rd, Kalk Bay; ⊗ 9am-5pm

Wander through the pretty garden to this house stocked with an eclectic and highly appealing range of arts and crafts. There are often special exhibitions by local artists showing here. Check out the collection of potato-print cloth products from the locally produced **Kudinda range** (www.kudinda.co.za).

KALK BAY QUARTER Map p257   Crafts & Gifts

☎ 021-788 6312; 58 Main Rd, Kalk Bay;
⊗ 9am-5pm Mon-Fri, 9.30am-5pm Sat & Sun

A good place to rummage for gifts. Have a look at the ceramics by Tessa Gawith, the traditional-style confectionary of Sweet & Salty Mason's, and Brett Murray's Boogie Lights series of wall lamps.

LIGHT Map p258   Arts & Crafts

☎ 021-786 5877; www.lightonline.co.za;
St George's St, Simon's Town; ⊗ 10.30am-5pm Tue-Sun

At this stylish gallery you'll find the handmade paper art and décor of Cathy Stanley, as well as a great selection of weathered wooden frames and furniture made from driftwood.

POTTER'S SHOP & STUDIO

Map p257   Arts & Crafts

☎ 021-788 7030; 6 Rouxville Rd, Kalk Bay;
⊗ 9am-4pm Mon-Sat, 10am-4pm Sun

Jo'burger Chris Silverston started her pottery business back in 1986 and has since nurtured many talented Xhosa and coloured artists, such as Majolandile Dyalvane and Madoda Fani. Watch them at work in the studio in **Muizenberg** (Map p257; ☎ 021-788 8737; 9 Atlantic Rd; ⊗ 9am-4pm Mon-Fri). Their products are sold all across the Cape.

QUAGGA ART & BOOKS Map p257   Books

☎ 021-788 2752; 84 Main Rd, Kalk Bay;
⊗ 9.30am-5pm Mon-Sat, 10am-5pm Sun

It's hard to pass this appealing bookshop by if you're looking for old editions and antiquarian books, as well as local art, and tribal art and artefacts.

Sleeping

Sleeping

Whether you're in search of a lively hostel, a characterful guesthouse or desire serious pampering, the Mother City has the perfect spot for you. What follows is a selection of the better places we've come across from a very crowded market.

Remember location is everything here. If beaches are your thing, suburbs along the Atlantic or False Bay coasts make better sense than, say, Gardens or City Bowl. If you have transport, then anywhere is OK, but remember to inquire about the parking options when making a booking and check whether there's a charge (anything from R20 to R50 per day for city-centre hotels). If secure parking is available, we've noted how much it costs per day.

Price Ranges

We quote the rack rates here for rooms with private bathrooms, during high season and including VAT of 14%. Hotels are listed in order of the cheapest to most expensive double room. Hostels typically don't include breakfast in their rates, but unless otherwise mentioned, rates elsewhere do include breakfast. A 1% tourism promotion levy is usually added to the bill, but some places, particularly the budget ones, include this in the room rates. Special deals will often be available and rates for longer stays are definitely negotiable.

Reservations

If there's somewhere you particularly want to stay, it's essential to make a reservation as far in advance as you can, especially if you're visiting during school holidays from mid-December to the end of January and at Easter when many places are fully booked several months in advance.

Longer-Term Rentals

In addition to the rental businesses listed below, check the rental ads in the local newspapers (see p217) or inquire at Cape Town Tourism (p219) about what deals may be available on serviced apartments.

ACCOMMODATION SHOP

☎ 021-439 1234; www.accommodationshop.co.za
Offers a vast range of accommodation, from studios to multibedroom apartments and houses all around the city.

CAPE CONCIERGE

☎ 021-447 5057; www.capeconcierge.co.za
This friendly outfit offers top-notch properties on both a short- and long-term basis. The website has useful info and it sends out a regular newsletter on local events.

VILLAGE & LIFE Map pp248-9

☎ 021-430 4444; www.villageandlife.com;
1 Loader St, Waterkant
This long-established property company has many accommodation options around the Waterkant, as well as out at Camps Bay and Mouille Point.

CITY CENTRE
CITY BOWL & BO-KAAP

Increasingly the des res location, but at weekends (particularly Sunday), the City Bowl remains dead as practically all the businesses are shut. The concrete-bound Foreshore continues to sprout hotels and there are a couple of options in the colourful Bo-Kaap.

LONG ST BACKPACKERS

Map pp248-9   Hostel $
☎ 021-423 0615; www.longstreetbackpackers.co.za;
209 Long St, City Bowl; dm/s/d R80/120/160
Backpackers dot the length of Long St, but the best remains this, the longest running.

In a block of 14 small flats, with four beds and a bathroom in each, accommodation is arranged around a leafy, quiet courtyard decorated with funky mosaics.

ST PAUL'S B&B GUEST HOUSE

Map pp248-9   B&B $

☎ /fax 021-423 4420; stpaul@absamail.co.za; 182 Bree St, City Bowl; s/d R150/250; P

This spotless B&B, in a very handy location, is a quiet alternative to a backpackers. The simply furnished and spacious rooms have high ceilings and there's a vine-shaded courtyard where you can relax or take breakfast.

INN LONG STREET Map pp248-9   Hostel $

☎ 021-424 1660; innlongstreet@ataris.co.za; 230 Long St, City Bowl; dm R75, d with/without bathroom R290/240; P

There's a calm vibe at this backpackers, despite it being in the thick of Long St. It's set in a nice old building, with wooden floors and a wrap-around balcony that all rooms access. A recent paint job and funky lights give it some style. Parking is R20 per day.

PARLIAMENT HOTEL Map pp248-9   Hotel $

☎ 021-461 6710; www.parliamenthotel.co.za; 9 Barrack St, City Bowl; s/d from R250/400; P

Hardly flash, but this place continues to be one of the best-value City Bowl hotels. The clean, good-sized rooms have great views on the upper levels, staff are friendly and there's a café where you can get breakfast (R50 extra). Parking costs R40 per day.

ROSE LODGE Map pp248-9   B&B $

☎ 021-424 3813; www.rosestreet28.com; 28 Rose St, Bo-Kaap; s/d R220/400

Inside a grey-painted corner house in the Bo-Kaap is this cute B&B. The Canadian owner likes to play the grand piano and has two adorable dogs. There are just three

cosy rooms (with private bathrooms), all decorated in contemporary style.

CAPE DIAMOND HOTEL

Map pp248-9   Hotel $$

☎ 021-461 2519; www.capediamondhotel.co.za; cnr Longmarket & Parliament Sts, City Bowl; s/d from R370/530; P

Great-value new hotel that has retained features of its Art Deco building, such as the wood-panelled floors. Boxed in by tower blocks, it's short on natural light, but in compensation there's a rooftop Jacuzzi with a view to Table Mountain. Breakfast is R45 extra and parking is R45 per day.

DADDY LONG LEGS

Map pp248-9   Boutique Hotel $$

☎ 021-422 3074; www.daddylonglegs.co.za; 134 Long St, City Bowl; r R750;

This boutique hotel-cum-art installation is what you get when artists are given free rein to design the boudoirs of their dreams. The results range from a bohemian garret to a hospital ward! Our favourites include the karaoke room (with a mike in the shower), and the cartoon-decorated room designed by pop group Freshly Ground. There's nowhere to put your luggage – hey, these are artists not hoteliers! – but a stay here is anything but boring. It also offers superstylish apartments (same price) at 263 Long St, an ideal choice if you crave hotel-suite luxury and want to self-cater.

TOWNHOUSE Map pp248-9   Hotel $$

☎ 021-465 7050; www.townhouse.co.za; 60 Corporation St, City Bowl; s/d from R572/1045; P

Sharing the good service and high standards of its big sister the Vineyard Hotel & Spa (p181), this is a popular inner-city choice. The cheaper old-style rooms are fine, but it's worth paying slightly more for the smartly renovated deluxe ones (and ask for

TOP FIVE SLEEPS

- backpackers – the Backpack (p176)
- guesthouse – An African Villa (p176)
- luxury hotel – Vineyard Hotel & Spa (p181)
- boutique hotel – Alta Bay (p177)
- self-catering – Daddy Long Legs (above)

one with a view of the mountain). The pool is tiny, as is the gym. Parking is R35 per day.

CAPE TOWN HOLLOW

Map pp248-9   Hotel $$

☎ 021-423 1260; www.capetownhollow.co.za; 88 Queen Victoria St, City Bowl; s/d R745/1060; P ✗ 🖳 📶

Overlooking the Company's Gardens, this good-value midrange hotel has pleasant rooms and decent facilities, including a minuscule pool, small gym, business centre and restaurant with leafy aspect. Parking is R30 per day.

CAPE HERITAGE HOTEL

Map pp248-9   Boutique Hotel $$

☎ 021-424 4646; www.capeheritage.co.za; 90 Bree St, City Bowl; s/d from R825/1190, ste s/d R1325/1905; P ✗ 🖳

Gracious service matches the Cape Dutch style of this elegant boutique hotel, which is part of the Heritage Sq redevelopment of 18th-century buildings. Each of the 15 rooms has its own character (some have four-poster beds) and plenty of modern conveniences (such as satellite TV and clothes presses). Parking is R25 per day.

METROPOLE HOTEL

Map pp248-9   Boutique Hotel $$

☎ 021-424 7247; www.metropolehotel.co.za; 38 Long St, City Bowl; s/d/ste from R600/1200/1650; P ✗ 🖳

This central boutique hotel, all minimalist lines and soothing colours, is unashamedly aimed at the gay and *wallpaper**-reader market. Go for the larger superior rooms with their ostrich-leather-trimmed bed-steads. The stylish restaurant Veranda (p126) and bar M Bar (p137) remain deservedly popular. Parking is R50 per day.

URBAN CHIC Map pp248-9   Boutique Hotel $$

☎ 021-423 2086; www.urbanchic.co.za; cnr Long & Pepper Sts, City Bowl; r R1242; P ✗ 🖳

Ask for one of the corner rooms with the fabulous floor-to-ceiling views towards Table Mountain. All the rooms at this stylish boutique hotel are an extension of the art gallery below. The ground-floor Gallery Bar (p137) is currently a very hip watering hole. Parking is R40 per day.

LIGHTING UP?

Most midrange and top-end hotels in Cape Town have nonsmoking rooms, and some even have nonsmoking floors. Most B&Bs and backpackers are also nonsmoking, at least in the bedrooms, although some provide a smoking area.

PROTEA HOTEL NORTH WHARF

Map pp248-9   Self-Catering $$

☎ 021-443 4600; www.proteahotels.com; 1 Lower Bree St, Foreshore; apt s/d R1350/1500; P ✗ 🖳 📶

Huge, well-equipped and stylish self-catering apartments are great value compared to what you'd pay for similar facilities elsewhere. The air-con in each room is individually adjustable, the kitchens are first-rate and there's a decent-sized rooftop pool and small gym. Rates don't include breakfast, although this is available in the hotel's restaurant.

ARABELLA SHERATON GRAND HOTEL Map pp248-9   Hotel $$$

☎ 021-412 9999; www.sheraton.com /capetown; Convention Sq, 1 Lower Long St, Foreshore; s/d/ste from R3210/3510/8415; P ✗ 🖳 📶

The glass box attached to the Cape Town International Convention Centre contains a sleek, contemporary, business-focused hotel. The corporate feel is softened by warmer colours in the rooms and sweeping views. Excellent facilities include the rooftop Altira Spa (p152). Parking is R25 per day.

MUTUAL HEIGHTS

Map pp248-9   Self-Catering $$$

☎ 021-794 3140; simonhudson@mweb.co.za; cnr Parliament & Darling Sts, City Bowl; apt for 4 people R5000; P ✗ 🖳

Indulge your inner Batman in the astonishing penthouse of Mutual Heights, the Art Deco design inspired by Amsterdam's Tuschinski Theatre. With four double bedrooms, a 14m-high ceiling over the lounge, and a kitchen made for entertaining, this is the ultimate slumber-party venue: grab your Robin or Cat Woman and come play!

WATERKANT

Lovely as many of the properties are in the Waterkant, the apex of gay Cape Town is not a location for those looking for assured peace and serenity. Also, security is an issue – we've heard stories of break-ins at guesthouses here, so keep your windows locked.

DE WATERKANT PLACE

Map pp248-9   B&B $$

☎ 021-419 2476; www.dewaterkantplace.com; 35 Dixon St, Waterkant; s/d from R500/600; 🖵
This appealing guesthouse with just five antique-decorated rooms offers fine value for what is generally a pricey area. Guests are free to use the kitchen and there's a lovely view from the roof.

DE WATERKANT HOUSE

Map pp248-9   Boutique Hotel/Serviced Apartments $$

☎ 021-409 2500; www.dewaterkant.com; cnr Napier & Waterkant Sts, Waterkant; s/d R470/720; 🖵 🖵
Run by Village & Life (see p172), this pleasant B&B, with its plunge pool and rooms with glossy-magazine-style furnishings, is in the heart of the gay village. Village & Life also has a wide range of apartments in the area, kicking off at R650 for a single and R950 for a double, as well as the popular budget-level 'crash pads' (single/double R280/400), which are not nearly as shabby as they sound.

RESPONSIBLE LUXURY

Following the success of his novels *The Drowning People* and *Us*, young South African author Richard Mason set up the Kay Mason Foundation (KMF; www.kaymasonfoundation.org), a charitable trust to fund the high-school education of poor but talented Capetonian kids. He also bought the Pinnacle (Map pp248–9; ☎ 072 740 4884; www.thepinnacle .co.za; 1011 Manhattan Pl, 103 Bree St, City Bowl; apt US$445; 🅿 🖵 🖵 🖵), a penthouse apartment overlooking the Bo-Kaap. It's a gorgeous four-level, industrial-style space with two bedrooms, beautifully decorated with an elegant selection of antiques and modern furnishings. A lovely housekeeper, Nelly, takes care of your needs. Ten percent of the profits goes towards the foundation. This 'responsible luxury', as Mason calls it, has so far helped some 60 children get the best education possible; several KMF graduates have since gone on to university.

VILLAGE LODGE Map pp248-9   B&B $$

☎ /fax 021-421 1106; www.thevillagelodge.com; 49 Napier St, Waterkant; s/d R750/1220; 🖵 🖵 🖵
The main location of this chic guesthouse is on Napier St. Rooms are smart if somewhat cramped. The rooftop pool is a prime spot for guests to check each other out, as is the good Thai restaurant, Soho. The interior-design accessories (many from Poland) are sold at the lodge's shop on Waterkant St, which doubles as a reception for the other cottages and apartments it rents out in the area.

VICTORIA JUNCTION

Map pp248-9   Hotel/Serviced Apartments $$

☎ 021-418 1234; www.proteahotels.co.za; cnr Somerset St & Ebenezer Rd, Waterkant; s/d R1085/1550, apt s/d R1720/2110; 🅿 🖵 🖵 🖵
Hard to believe that this arty hotel is part of the Protea chain. Style mavens will be happy with the industrial loft-style rooms and self-catering apartments with exposed brick walls. There's a reasonably sized lap pool and some neat artwork in the lobby, including *32 Reasons Why I Love Cape Town* by Gordon Radowsky. Parking is R30 per day.

GARDENS & SURROUNDS

Gardens and the attendant mountainside suburbs are the domain of the boutique guesthouse, a type of accommodation in which Cape Town has cornered the market. If you don't have wheels or don't fancy the slog up and down the hill each day, it's better to stay in Gardens with its easier access to the city.

CAPE TOWN BACKPACKERS

Map p254   Hostel $

☎ /fax 021-426 0200; www.capetown backpackers.com; 81 New Church St; dm/s/d with shared bathroom R90/180/220, guesthouse s/d R275/320; 🅿 🖵
The backpacker hostel grows up at this stylish place. It offers both pleasant dorms and a guesthouse with en suite rooms on neighbouring Kohling St that puts many midrange hotels to shame. Mama Fefe, who looks after the equally stylish branch in Sea Point (see p179), cooks up a Xhosa dinner on Wednesday nights. Parking costs R10 per day.

ASHANTI LODGE Map p254 — Hostel $

☎ 021-423 8721; www.ashanti.co.za;
11 Hof St, Gardens; dm/d with shared bathroom
R90/250, guesthouse d R370; Ⓟ ⌨ ☎
Ashanti continues to be one of Cape
Town's premier party hostels, with much
of the action focused on its lively bar and
deck, which overlooks Table Mountain. The
big, brightly painted old house holds the
dorms and a lawn on which you can camp
(R50 per person). For something quieter,
opt for the excellent rooms (with private
bathrooms), which are situated in two
separate heritage-listed houses around the
corner.

BACKPACK Map p254 — Hostel $

☎ 021-423 4530; www.backpackers.co.za;
74 New Church St, Tamboerskloof; dm/s/d with
shared bathroom R90/250/300, s/d with private
bathroom R300/360; Ⓟ ⌨ ☎
Setting the gold standard for Cape Town's
backpackers is the Backpack. Three spacious houses are combined to create a relaxed hostel with something for everyone,
be it a lively time at the Thursday-night
African drumming sessions or just chilling
out in the chic lounge. Never one to rest on
its laurels, the Backpack recently received
Fair Trade in Tourism accreditation. Parking
is R20 per day.

BLENCATHRA Map p254 — Hostel $

☎ 021-424 9571, 073 389 0702; cnr De Hoop &
Cambridge Aves, Tamboerskloof; dm/d with shared
bathroom R120/250; Ⓟ ⌨ ☎
You're well on the way up Lion's Head at
this charming family home, which offers a
range of attractive rooms. It's the ideal spot
for those looking to escape the city and
the more-commercialised backpacker options. Owner Charles specialises in outdoor
adventure trips.

FRITZ HOTEL Map p254 — B&B $$

☎ 021-480 9000; www.fritzhotel.co.za; 1 Faure St,
Gardens; s/d from R550/600; Ⓟ ⌨
This centrally located guesthouse remains
one of our favourites. It mixes Art Deco,
1950s and modern furnishings to good effect. You'll pay slightly more for the rooms
with Juliet balconies at the rear of the
house and those that open onto its shady
garden.

AMSTERDAM GUEST HOUSE

Map p254 — B&B $$
☎ 021-461 8236; www.amsterdam.co.za; 19 Forest
Rd, Oranjezicht; s/d from R596/695; Ⓟ ✕ ⌨ ☎
It's men only at this convivial gay guesthouse
that's notable for its good range of com-
fortable rooms, decent-sized pool, Jacuzzi,
sundeck and sauna. If that's not enough, it
also has all 169 episodes of *I Love Lucy* on
video, plus hundreds of other movies.

GUESTHOUSE ONE BELVEDERE

Map p254 — B&B $$
☎ 021-461 2442; www.onebelvedere.co.za;
1 Belvedere Ave, Oranjezicht; s/d R525/750;
Ⓟ ⌨ ☎
Rob and Charl run this gay-friendly B&B,
which offers six pleasant rooms with private bathrooms. The heritage-listed home
features a handsome wrought-iron veranda.
The small pool is solar heated and there's a
Jacuzzi and steam room.

AN AFRICAN VILLA Map p254 — B&B $$

☎ 021-423 2164; www.capetowncity.co.za/villa;
19 Carstens St, Tamboerskloof; s/d from R640/800;
⌨ ☎
There's a sophisticated and colourful
'African Zen' look at this highly appealing
guesthouse sheltering behind the façade
of three 19th-century terrace houses.
Relax in the evening in one of two comfy
lounges while sipping the complimentary
sherry.

DUNKLEY HOUSE Map p254 — B&B $$

☎ 021-462 7650; www.dunkleyhouse.com; 3B
Gordon St, Gardens; d/ste from R700/990; ⌨ ☎
This ultrastylish guesthouse, close to the
Company's Gardens, is tucked away on a
quiet street. Neutral-toned rooms feature
CD players and satellite TV, and there's a
plunge pool in the courtyard. At the time
of writing there were plans to add more
rooms in the neighbouring property.

HIPPO BOUTIQUE HOTEL

Map p254   Boutique Hotel $$

☎ 021-423 2500; www.hippotique.co.za; 5-9 Park Lane, Gardens; s/d R800/1200; Ⓟ 🅧 🖳 🖭

Even though it's situated beside Kloof St with its plethora of restaurants, this appealing boutique property offers spacious, stylish rooms with a small kitchen for self-catering. Gadget-lovers will also be pleased with the DVD player and music system.

ABBEY MANOR Map p254   B&B $$

☎ 021-462 2935; www.abbey.co.za; 3 Montrose Ave, Oranjezicht; s/d from R995/1290; Ⓟ 🅧 🖳 🖭

This luxurious guesthouse occupies a grand Arts and Crafts–style home, built in 1905 for a shipping magnate. Fine linens, antique furnishings, a roomy pool and courteous staff enhance the experience.

CAPE MILNER Map p254   Hotel $$

☎ 021-426 1101; www.threecities.co.za; 2A Milner Rd, Tamboerskloof; s/d/ste R995/1300/2140; Ⓟ 🅧 🖳 🖭

Silks and velvets in metallic colours add a sophisticated touch to the contemporary-style rooms here. Friendly service and sweeping views of Table Mountain from the luxurious suites and pool deck area are other pluses. Parking is R25 per day.

CAPE CADOGAN

Map p254   Boutique Hotel/Serviced Apartments $$

☎ 021-480 8080; www.capecadogan.com; 5 Upper Union St, Gardens; d/apt from R1350/1875; Ⓟ 🖳 🖭

The *Gone with the Wind*–style heritage-listed villa on Upper Union St is the main guesthouse of this very classy boutique operation, which also embraces several appealing self-catering apartments in the mews of nearby Nicol St.

FOUR ROSMEAD Map p254   B&B $$

☎ 021-480 3810; www.fourrosmead.com; 4 Rosmead Ave, Oranjezicht; d/ste from R1430/2000; Ⓟ 🅧 🖳 🖭

A heritage-listed building dating from 1903 has been remodelled into this luxury B&B. Special touches include a saltwater swimming pool and a fragrant Mediterranean herb garden. The pool-house suite with lofty ceiling is great if you want extra privacy.

ALTA BAY Map p254   Boutique Hotel $$$

☎ 021-487 8800; www.altabay.com; 12 Invermark Cres, Higgovale; d R2100; Ⓟ 🅧 🖳 🖭

Cascading down the hillside, Alta Bay is a haven of tranquillity, as well as a designer heaven. The six luxury rooms are adorable, mixing locally handcrafted furnishings (including huge king-size beds) with European artworks.

HEMINGWAY HOUSE & LODGE

Map p254   B&B $$$

☎ 021-461 1857; www.hemingwayhouse.co.za; 1 Lodge Rd, Oranjezicht; d R2500; Ⓟ 🖳 🖭

Flip a coin to choose between the two glamorous options here. Hemmingway House, set in a former masonic lodge, offers four bohemian-glitz-styled rooms around a vine-shaded courtyard with a sunken pool. Across the road, the Lodge is fantastically modern – think *Elle Décor* does Africa.

KENSINGTON PLACE

Map p254   Boutique Hotel $$$

☎ 021-424 4744; www.kensingtonplace.co.za; 38 Kensington Cres, Higgovale; d incl breakfast R2550; Ⓟ 🅧 🖳 🖭

This continues to be one of Cape Town's finest boutique properties. Nestled discreetly in wind-free Higgovale, it offers eight spacious and tastefully decorated rooms, all with balconies and beautifully tiled bathrooms. Added extras are free Internet access, fresh fruit and flowers, a small pool and faultless service.

Sleeping

CITY CENTRE

Kensington Place (above)

177

MOUNT NELSON HOTEL

Map p254   Hotel $$$

☎ 021-483 1000; www.mountnelsonhotel
.orient-express.com; 76 Orange St, Gardens;
s/d from R5395/5535, ste s/d from R8165/8305;
P ⊠ ⊡ ⊠

Painted sugar-pink and reassuringly expensive, the Nellie is a time capsule of the colonial era, down to the doormen in pith helmets. Surprisingly it's a great place to bring the family since it pushes the boat out for the little ones, with kid-size robes and free cookies and milk at bedtime, not to mention the big pool and 3 hectares of gardens for splashing in and running around. At the very least, drop by for afternoon tea (see p129).

ATLANTIC COAST
GREEN POINT & WATERFRONT

The attractions of the Waterfront area need little further elaboration, however, if you want to escape the crowds but still be reasonably close to both the city and the beaches, Green Point makes a pretty good compromise.

BIG BLUE Map pp252-3   Hostel $

☎ 021-439 0807; www.bigbluebackpackers.hostel
.com; 7 Vesperdene Rd, Green Point; dm/s/d with
shared bathroom R85/220/270, d with private
bathroom R320; ⊡ ⊠

This brightly painted hostel remains a leading light of the Cape Town backpacking scene – come enjoy its grand hallway, spacious dorms, Zen garden and friendly atmosphere.

HOUSE ON THE HILL

Map pp252-3   Self-Catering $

☎ 021-439 3902; www.houseonthehillct.co.za;
25 Leinster Rd, Green Point; d/tr with shared
bathroom R260/315, d/tr with private bathroom
R265/385

Handy for the restaurants and bars of Green Point, this self-catering house is a fine alternative to the bigger backpacker hostels. Book ahead for the five rooms, which are very pleasantly furnished in African style, with the bonus of a TV and CD player.

WILTON MANOR

Map pp252-3   Boutique Hotel $$

☎ 021-434 7869; www.wiltonmanor.co.za;
15 Croxteth Rd, Green Point; s/d from R550/600;
P ⊡ ⊠

This charming two-storey house, dating from 1886 and featuring a wooden veranda, has been converted into a very stylish guesthouse. Each of the seven rooms is individually decorated and guests are free to use the kitchen. The owners also run the more-contemporary Wilton Place higher up Signal Hill, as well as Altona Lodge, a budget guesthouse that's also on Croxteth Rd – check the website for further details.

HEAD SOUTH LODGE

Map pp252-3   Boutique Hotel $$

☎ 021-434 8777; www.headsouth.co.za;
215 Main Rd, Green Point; s/d incl breakfast R650/750;
P ⊠ ⊡ ⊠

A fabulous homage to the 1950s with its retro furnishings and collection of Tretchikoff prints hung en masse in the bar. The 15 rooms are spacious and decorated with modern art by Phillip Briel, the location is good and there's a tiny plunge pool in the front garden.

CAPE STANDARD

Map pp252-3   Boutique Hotel $$

☎ 021-430 3060; www.capestandard.co.za;
3 Romney Rd, Green Point; s/d R750/990; P ⊡ ⊠
This secluded boutique hotel, one of Cape Town's nicest, offers whitewashed beachhouse-chic rooms downstairs or moreedgy, contemporary-style rooms upstairs. The hotel prides itself on the mosaic-tiled bathrooms with showers big enough to dance in.

VICTORIA & ALFRED HOTEL

Map pp252-3   Hotel $$$

☎ 021-419 6677; www.vahotel.co.za; Pierhead,
Waterfront; s/d from R1465/2085; P ⊠ ⊡
One of the less-pricey top-end hotels at the Waterfront has recently added a new floor of industrial-chic loft rooms. You'll pay slightly more for views towards Table Mountain, which are impressive. There's free transport to the sister hotel, the Ambassador in Sea Point, where you can use the pool. Rates don't include breakfast.

Reception at Head South Lodge (opposite)

CAPE GRACE Map pp252-3 — Hotel $$$

☎ 021-410 7100; www.capegrace.com; West Quay, Waterfront; s/d from R4360/4490; Ⓟ ☒ ▣ ▣
Former president Bill Clinton's choice when he visited the Waterfront, this luxurious hotel operates like an exclusive but very welcoming club. The best rooms face Table Mountain. Here you'll also find the excellent restaurant **One.Waterfront** (p130), the **Bascule Bar** (p139) and a colourfully decorated spa (p152).

BEACHES & SUBURBS
Sea Point & Hout Bay

Sea Point and the adjacent suburbs of Fresnaye and Bantry Bay are good choices for a seaside base, usually with more-realistic prices than Camps Bay. Hout Bay is handy for both the Atlantic coast beaches and Constantia's vineyards.

LION'S HEAD LODGE
Map p255 — Hotel/Hostel $

☎ 021-434 4163; www.lions-head-lodge.co.za; 319 Main Rd, Sea Point; d R398; Ⓟ ☒ ▣
The operators try hard to make this old-fashioned budget hotel more appealing by lowering the rates for stays longer than one night. It has a reasonably sized pool and a

bar, and does three-course Sunday lunches for R60. Sharing the hotel's facilities is the even more run-down **Aardvark Backpackers** (☎ 021-434 4172; dm/d R100/398), which has its dorms in converted flats. HI members get a 10% discount.

CAPE TOWN BACKPACKERS
SEA POINT Map p255 — Hostel $

☎ /fax 021-426 0200; www.capetownbackpackers .com; 1 Rocklands Rd; dm/d R90/400; ▣ ▣
In a nicely converted bungalow, this is easily the best budget option in Sea Point, steps away from the sea front. There's a six-bed dorm and three double rooms with private bathrooms and giant rain showers, as well as a spacious communal kitchen, all presided over by the convivial Mama Fefe.

VICTORIA VIEWS
Map p258 — B&B/Self-Catering $$

☎ 021-790 0085; www.victoriaviews.co.za; 94 Victoria Ave, Hout Bay; d R600; Ⓟ ▣ ▣
Incredible value is on offer at this new guesthouse on the main road into Hout Bay. There are three stylishly decorated double rooms and one self-catering studio, all with bamboo roofs and sweeping mountain views from the communal balcony.

AMBLEWOOD GUESTHOUSE
Map p258 — B&B $$

☎ 021-790 1570; www.amblewood.co.za; 43 Skaife St, Hout Bay; s/d from R500/790; Ⓟ ▣ ▣
Cool off in the small pool on the deck of this upmarket B&B and look out over the beautiful sweep of Hout Bay. There's a range of pleasant rooms, decorated with period furniture to match the style of the house.

HUIJS HAERLEM Map p255 — B&B $$

☎ 021-434 6434; www.huijshaerlem.co.za; 25 Main Dr, Sea Point; s/d incl breakfast R680/980; Ⓟ ▣ ▣
Get a work-out walking up one of Sea Point's steeper slopes to reach this excellent gay-friendly (but not exclusively gay) guesthouse. It comprises two houses decorated with top-quality antiques and joined by delightful gardens in which you'll find a decent-sized pool.

HOUT BAY MANOR Map p258   Hotel $$

☎ 021-790 0116; www.houtbaymanor.co.za; Baviaanskloof Rd, Hout Bay; s/d incl breakfast from R820/1220; P ⊠ 🖳 🖭

If Laura Ashley is your thing, you'll love the spacious and comfortable rooms in this building, dating from 1871 (and apparently haunted by a ghost!). Some rooms even have four-poster beds. Service is excellent.

WINCHESTER MANSIONS HOTEL

Map p255   Hotel $$

☎ 021-434 2351; www.winchester.co.za; 221 Beach Rd, Sea Point; s/d incl breakfast from R1150/1500; P ⊠ 🖳 🖭

There's a choice between classic and modern rooms – all very pleasant – at this Cape Dutch–style beauty with a prime position along the Sea Point promenade. The pool is good and the lovely courtyard **restaurant** (brunch R145; ⏲ 11am-2pm), with its central fountain, is popular for its Sunday brunch with live jazz, for which you should book ahead.

O ON KLOOF Map p255   Hotel $$

☎ 021-439 2081; www.oonkloof.co.za; 92 Kloof Rd, Bantry Bay; d from R1500; P ⊠ 🖳 🖭

Cross the mini bridge over the ornamental pool leading to this gorgeous contemporary-styled guesthouse. The cheapest of the six spacious rooms don't have full sea views but the good facilities, including a big indoor pool and gym, are ample compensation.

ELLERMAN HOUSE Map p255   Hotel $$$

☎ 021-430 3200; www.ellerman.co.za; 180 Kloof Rd, Bantry Bay; d/ste/villa from R3900/9100/25,000; P ⊠ 🖳 🖭

Imagine you've been invited to stay with an immensely rich art-collecting Capetonian friend. This mansion overlooking the Atlantic, with nine rooms, two suites and a Frank Lloyd Wright–esque villa (complete with its own spa) would be the deal. Rates include breakfast, airport transfers, laundry, all drinks (except vintage wine and champagne) and secretarial services.

Camps Bay

This is one of Cape Town's trendiest beachside suburbs and, despite the associated high prices, it gets packed, particularly in high season. There's very little in the way of budget accommodation – your best bet is to check whether Village & Life (p172) has any of its 'crash pad' rooms available here; there're a couple at Camps Bay Retreat.

CAMPS BAY RETREAT

Map p256   Boutique Hotel $$

☎ 021-437 0485; www.campsbayretreat.com; 7 Chilworth Rd, the Glen, Camps Bay; s/d from R1200/1500; P ⊠ 🖳 🖭

Based in the grand Earl's Dyke Manor (dating from 1929, although it looks older), this is a splendid option. There is a choice of 16 rooms in either the main house or the contemporary Deck House, reached by a rope bridge over a ravine. There're three pools, including one fed by a stream from Table Mountain, and a spa, as well as a couple of decent, self-catering budget rooms (R380 per person) next to the tennis court. Bicycles can be hired (R80 per day) to pedal down to the beach.

PRIMI ROYAL Map p256   Boutique Hotel $$

☎ 021-438 2741; www.primi-royal.com; 23 Camps Bay Dr, Camps Bay; d from R1500; P ⊠ 🖳 🖭

All 10 rooms are individually decorated at this comfortable, sleek hotel, which overlooks Camps Bay but is set away from the main drag. Rose petals scattered across the bed linen on welcome are a romantic touch. This place also runs the equally appealing **Primi Seacastle** (Map p256), at the opposite end of Camps Bay, overlooking the beach.

TWENTY NINE Map p256   B&B $$

☎ 021-438 3800; www.twentynine.net; 29 Atholl Rd, Camps Bay; d/ste R2000/2600; P 🖳 🖭

German guys AJ and Steven have created this utterly gorgeous gay-friendly retreat, high above Camps Bay. There are five rooms, all so tastefully decorated you'll hardly want to leave, especially as there some 600 CDs to listen to, as well as 400 DVDs to watch on the Bang & Olufsen systems.

BAY HOTEL Map p256   Hotel $$$

☎ 021-438 4444; www.thebay.co.za; 69 Victoria Rd, Camps Bay; d from R2450; P ⊠ 🖳

Part of the Village & Life accommodation group, this hang-out for the well-heeled is a stone's toss from the beach. The spacious rooms in white and earth tones are soothing; those with sea views are pricier (R3660). There's also a good-sized pool.

SOUTHERN SUBURBS

Observatory, Pinelands and Woodstock, home to bohemian types and students from the nearby university, offer a more residential side of Cape Town but are still only a few minutes from the city by car or train. For something more upscale and leafy, try the hotels in Newlands or around the vineyards at Constantia.

LIGHTHOUSE FARM LODGE

Map p256   Hostel $

☎ /fax 021-447 9177; msm@mweb.co.za; Violet Bldg, Oude Molen Eco Village, Alexandra Rd, Pinelands; dm/d with shared bathroom R60/150; P

Offering Cape Town's cheapest dorm beds, this simple and relaxed place is the better of the two hostels located on the grounds of a former hospital that is now a farm and alternative community of artists (see p104). You can pay your way at Lighthouse by working on the organic farm. It's best if you have your own transport, but the lodge is also within walking distance of Pinelands Train Station and there's good security around the complex. Breakfast is R15 to R25 extra.

DECO LODGE Map pp246-7   Hostel $

☎ 021-447 4216; www.capetowndeco.com; 22 Roodebloem Rd, Woodstock; dm/d R80/220; P

It's impossible to miss this huge purple-painted Art Deco house, which is a great alternative for the independent-minded traveller who doesn't mind being a suburb or two removed from Long St. The garden is lush, with a cooling pool, and rooms are colourfully decorated.

GREEN ELEPHANT Map p256   Hostel $

☎ 021-448 6359; greenele@iafrica.com; 57 Milton Rd, Observatory; dm/s/d with shared bathroom R85/180/280, d with private bathroom R310

The famous tree-climbing dog is getting on, but this long-running backpackers, split between two houses, remains a popular alternative to the city-centre hostels. The owners, together with the folks from Day Trippers, have helped set up the associated guesthouse Shine the Way (Map pp246–7; 17 Wesley St, Observatory), an

empowerment project with former staff, which charges the same rates.

COLETTE'S Map pp244-5   B&B $$

☎ 021-531 4830, 082 782 6349; www.colettesbb .co.za; 16 the Bend, Pinelands; s/d R400/550; P

The very charming Colette runs this women-only B&B in her spacious and pretty Pinelands home, which she shares with ducks Isabella and Ferdinand. Her two double rooms have private bathrooms and a separate entrance from the rest of the house.

VINEYARD HOTEL & SPA

Map pp246-7   Hotel $$

☎ 021-657 4500; www.vineyard.co.za; Colinton Rd, Newlands; s/d/ste from R990/1392/2880; P

Although the core of this excellent hotel is the 1799 house built for Lady Anne Barnard, a recent upgrade has given it a contemporary feel. Brand-new rooms attached to a fabulous spa (see p152) are all surrounded by lush gardens with views onto the mountain. Friendly staff, a great gym and pool complete the picture.

HUNTERS MOON LODGE

Map pp244-5   Hotel $$

☎ 021-794 5001; www.huntersmoonlodge.co.za; Southern Cross Dr, Constantia Upper; d/ste from R1820/2200; P

Honeymoon suites hardly come more romantic than the ones at Hunters Moon Lodge, set in a faux Tuscan villa surrounded by gorgeous gardens with views across Constantia's vineyards. The Antoinette suite has a four-poster bed and a bathroom big enough for a ball.

CONSTANTIA UITSIG

Map pp244-5   Hotel $$$

☎ 021-794 6500; www.uitsig.co.za; Spaansche-mat River Rd, Constantia; s/d from R1600/2400; P

Set within the vineyard of the same name (p44), this hotel offers appealing, chintzy Victorian-styled rooms, all florals and checks. There are beautiful gardens as well as three top-notch restaurants to choose from.

FALSE BAY & SOUTHERN PENINSULA

MUIZENBERG & KALK BAY

For warmer water, good surf and fewer crowds, these communities facing False Bay are ideal. Rough-edged Muizenberg is a top surf spot, while the more-genteel fishing village of Kalk Bay is tops for antique and craft shoppers.

AMBERLEY TRAVELLERS LODGE

Map p257   Self-Catering $

☎ 021-788 7032, 082 686 1864; www.amberley lodge.com; cnr Amberley & School Rds, Muizenberg; s/d/tr from R100/180/210; 🖳

Facing onto a small park, this self-catering place, in a lovely old house, is a great option for backpackers and budget travellers looking for a quieter place to stay. The rooms are generally airy and spacious.

BLUE BABOON BACKPACKERS LODGE Map p257   B&B $

☎ 021-788 3645, 083 641 6808; 136 Main Rd, Kalk Bay; s/d with shared bathroom R120/220

Above the Olympia Café & Deli, this simply furnished budget lodge offers splendid views of the harbour from the running balcony, which can be accessed from all rooms. It's the cheapest place to crash in Kalk Bay, so be sure to book ahead. Breakfast is R20 extra.

BEACH LODGE Map p257   Hostel $

☎ 021-788 1771; www.thebeachlodge.co.za; 13-19 York Rd, Muizenberg; s/d with shared bathroom R150/260; 🅿 🖳

Set in a heritage-listed building with splendid sea views, this spacious budget guesthouse is a great option for those who don't want to be more than 30 seconds from the sand. There's a huge kitchen for self-catering, a small gym and satellite TV in the comfy lounge.

SANDHILLS Map p257   B&B $$

☎ 021-788 2795; www.sandhills.co.za; 18 Beach Rd, Muizenberg; s/d incl breakfast R400/500; 🅿

Sandhills was the first of the buildings that Sir Herbert Baker designed in Muizenberg. It's now part of an arts centre (p107) and

has been converted into a lovely B&B, decorated in 1920s style. There are just two rooms either side of a spacious lounge.

BELLA EV Map p257   B&B $$

☎ 021-788 1293; www.capestay.co.za; 8 Camp Rd, Muizenberg; s/d R480/580

This charming guesthouse could be the setting for an Agatha Christie mystery, one in which the home's owner has a penchant for all things Turkish – hence the Ottoman slippers for guests' use and the Turkish-style breakfast.

INN AT CASTLE HILL Map p257   B&B $$

☎ 021-788 2554; www.castlehill.co.za; 37 Gatesville Rd, Kalk Bay; s/d R350/640; 🅿

Colourful works by local artists decorate the walls at this delightful guesthouse in a renovated Edwardian home. Some of the convivial rooms overlook the bay.

SIMON'S TOWN

Further down the False Bay coast, and a good half-hour's drive from the city centre, is the attractive naval base of Simon's Town and nearby Boulders, where you can bunk down beside the penguins. Also see p76 for details of a couple of cottages that can be rented in the Cape of Good Hope Nature Reserve.

SIMON'S TOWN BACKPACKERS

Map p258   Hostel $

☎ 021-786 1964; www.capepax.co.za; 66 St George's St, Simon's Town; dm/d R70/200; 🖳

The spacious rooms are brightly painted at this relaxed backpackers overlooking Simon's Town's harbour. There is bike hire for R80 per day and staff can help you arrange a host of activities in the area.

TOP SAIL HOUSE Map p258   B&B $

☎ 021-786 5537; www.simonstown.com/accom /topsailhouse; 176 St George's St, Simon's Town; d with/without bathroom R275/250; 🅿

The former St Joseph's Dominican Convent School, dating from the mid-1800s, houses this budget guesthouse with plain rooms and friendly owners. Its most notable feature is the 'honeymoon suite' set in the old chapel, which has the bathroom in the vestry and a tiny kitchen in the confessional.

SOUTHERN RIGHT HOTEL

Map pp244-5   Hotel $$

☎ 021-782 0314; www.southernright.info;
12-14 Glen Rd, Glencairn; s/d R375/590; **P**
A couple of kilometres before you reach
Simon's Town is this historic inn, run by
the Boulders Beach Lodge management.
The rooms are simply but appealingly
furnished, with lots of candles adding a
romantic ambience. Stay on Tuesday and it
only costs R295 for two. A restaurant, deli
and wine shop are on the premises.

BOULDERS BEACH LODGE

Map p258   B&B/Serviced Apartments $$

☎ 021-786 1758; www.bouldersbeach.co.za;
4 Boulders Pl, Boulders Beach; s/d/apt
R450/790/1500; **P** **◫**
If you'd like to share the beach with the penguins after the day-tripper crowds have gone
home, this smart guesthouse, with rooms
decorated in wicker and wood, is ideal. There
is also a range of self-catering units, as well
as a pleasant café, Penguin Point Restaurant,
which has an outdoor deck.

BRITISH HOTEL

Map p258   Serviced Apartments $$

☎ /fax 021-786 2214; www.britishhotelapart
ments.co.za; 90 St George's St, Simon's Town;
apt from R1400
These quirkily decorated apartments are
splendid value and ideal for groups of friends
or a family. They all have amazingly spacious
bathrooms, open-plan kitchens, balconies
and are set around a lovely courtyard.

NOORDHOEK & KOMMETJIE

Noordhoek offers leafy surrounds, a splen-
did (though windswept) beach and seren-
ity, while nearby Kommetjie is a chill-out
zone for surfers happy to brave the bracing
waters.

CHILL & SURF BACKPACKERS

Map pp244-5   Hostel $

☎ 021-785 4678; www.chillandsurf.co.za; 29 Kom-
metjie Main Rd, Sunnydale; camping per person R70,
dm R80, d with shared bathroom R250; **P** **◫**
Local surfer Pierre has created a very
chilled backpackers on his property, within
easy reach of Kommetjie's surfing hot
spots. The large dorm in the sandstone

house is cooler, temperature wise, than
the ones in the wooden cabins at the
back, where you'll also find the private
doubles.

MONKEY VALLEY BEACH NATURE

RESORT Map pp244-5   B&B/Serviced Apartments $$

☎ 021-789 1391; www.monkeyvalleyresort.com;
Mountain Rd, Noordhoek; s/d from R1265/1340, apt
R2785; **P** **◫** **▣**
Choose between standard B&B rooms
or spacious self-catering cottages with
thatched roofs at this imaginatively designed, rustic resort shaded by a milkwood
forest. It's a great place if you have kids,
and the wide beach is moments away.

LONG BEACH Map pp244-5   B&B $$$

☎ 021-783 4183; www.thelongbeach.com;
1 Kirsten Ave, Kommetjie; s/d R1987/2650;
P **▨** **◫** **▣**
Shut out the world while staying at this
discrete designer villa, fronting onto
stunning Long Beach. It offers five super-
spacious doubles with plenty of extras,
including use of a local mobile phone. The
management company, the Last Word (www
.thelastword.co.za), has similarly luxurious
bolt holes in Bishopscourt, Constantia and
Franschhoek.

CAPE FLATS

To get a fuller picture of life in the townships, consider bedding down in Langa or
Khayelitsha. You're no more than 20 minutes from the City Bowl by the N2 motor-
way, very close to the airport and already
well on your way to Stellenbosch. It's safe to
drive yourself to most of these places; if you
intend on using public transport, check first
with the hosts on how best to do this.

MALEBO'S Map pp244-5   B&B $

☎ 021-361 2391, 083 475 1125; www.sonke
.org/malebo.htm; 18 Mississippi Way, Graceland,
Khayelitsha; s/d with shared bathroom R180/300
In the spacious, modern home of Lydia
Masoleng there are two double rooms and
one single guest room. Dinner is available
for R80 extra. You can meet the budgie
Toosy and have a drink around the corner at Lolly's Jazz Pub, a well-established
shebeen.

Vicky's B&B (below)

MAJORO'S B&B Map pp244-5 B&B $
☎ /fax 021-361 3412, 082 537 6882; 69 Helena Cres, Graceland, Khayelitsha; s/d with shared bathroom R180/360; Ⓟ
Friendly Maria Maile is the owner of this B&B, located in a small brick bungalow in an upscale part of Khayelitsha. She can put up four people in her two homely rooms. Dinner is available for R80 and there's safe parking should you drive here.

RADEBE'S B&B Map pp244-5 B&B $
☎ 021-695 0508, 082 393 3117; radebes@ananzi .co.za; 23 Mama Way, Settlers Pl, Langa; s/d R200/360; Ⓟ ▯
The dynamic Minah Radebe brings her confident Sowetan style to the best of Langa's B&Bs. One of her three delightfully decorated guest rooms has a private bathroom and there's a nice sitting room with TV and DVD. Breakfast and other meals are served in the attached Coffee Shack restaurant.

MA NEO'S Map pp244-5 B&B $
☎ 021-694 2504, 073 146 0370; www.tiscover.co .za/maneo; Zone 7 No 30, Langa; s/d R240/360; ▯
Thandiwe Peter is 'Ma Neo'. Together with her daughter, Neo, she runs this warm and friendly B&B in Langa. There's one spacious double room in the main house as well as

a couple more in the extension at the back. All are pleasantly furnished and have TVs.

VICKY'S B&B Map pp244-5 B&B $
☎ 021-387 7104, 082 225 2986; www.vickysbandb .com; Site C-685A, Khayelitsha; s/d with shared bathroom R190/380; ▯
Vicky Ntozini's unique selling point is that she lives in a shack. Given her success she could well afford not to, but she and her extended family love it here and guests clearly enjoy the experience. There are two compact, comfy guest rooms and (rare for a shack) an inside bathroom with toilet and shower.

KOPANONG Map pp244-5 B&B $$
☎ /fax 021-361 2084, 082 476 1278; kopanong@xsinet.co.za; Site C-329 Velani Cres, Khayelitsha; s/d R290/480; Ⓟ ▯
Thope Lekau, called 'Mama Africa' for obvious reasons, runs Khayelitsha's best B&B with her equally ebullient daughter, Mpho. Her substantial brick home offers two stylishly decorated guest rooms, each with their own bathrooms. As a guide and experienced development worker, Thope will give you an excellent insight into township life, as well as cook a delicious dinner (vegetarian/meat R70/90). She also runs a cookery course on request (see the boxed text, p151).

Excursions

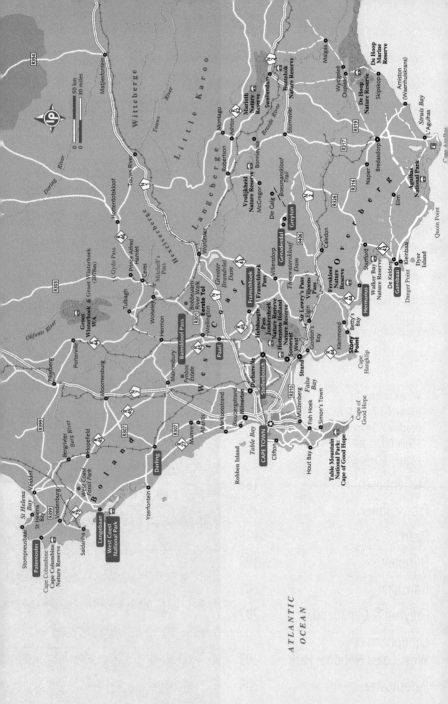

Excursions

Many people have trouble tearing themselves away from Cape Town, but if you have the time it's definitely worth escaping the city and taking a day trip. The Western Cape's excellent roads mean it takes as much time and effort to discover the neighbouring sections of the province as it does to explore the Cape Peninsula. Within two hours you can see truly beautiful scenery and interesting old towns, some tucked away in wine country first planted with vines over three centuries ago. There are also pristine, crowd-free beaches, and hikes every bit as spectacular as those of the Table Mountain National Park.

Geographically speaking, the day-trip areas surrounding Cape Town can more or less be broken up into the areas of the Boland, Overberg and West Coast.

The Boland stretches inland and upwards from Cape Town, and is the country's most famous wine-producing region. Its name means 'Upland', a reference to the dramatic mountain ranges that shoot up to over 1500m and on whose fertile slopes the vineyards form a patchwork. The Franschhoek and Bainskloof Passes that crisscross the region are among the country's most spectacular.

Heading further east, all roads from Cape Town suddenly and unforgivably come against a mountainous barrier, forcing you to hit the lower gears. Once you're up and over the top, you're 'over the mountain', the literal meaning of Overberg.

It's a gorgeous and rugged area, roughly comprising the region south and west of the Franschhoek Range, and south of the Wemmershoek and Riviersonderend Ranges, forming a natural barrier with the Breede River Valley.

Heading north of Cape Town brings you to the jagged coastline and windswept hills of the West Coast, a peaceful and undeveloped getaway with quiet whitewashed fishing villages and beautiful lagoons.

WINE COUNTRY

The most popular wine country is in the Boland, whose centuries-long history of colonial settlement has given it a European feel, particularly in French-themed culinary hot spot **Franschhoek** (p193). Lively student town **Stellenbosch** (p188) offers the most activities, while **Paarl** (p195) is a busy commercial centre with excellent estates. All three towns are within a 90-minute drive of Cape Town, although staying over is recommended. While the Winelands are busy year-round, the estates can become very crowded between November and March thanks to the popularity of picnic lunches and spit-braais held there. During winter, estates are quieter and wetter and often offer discounts on accommodation. It's worth mentioning that there are some up-and-coming estates in the **Darling** (p206) area, with none of the hype.

NATURE & HIKING

Although whales are common during the winter and spring season in **False Bay** (p109), the focus of the **whale-watching** (p201) action is at Hermanus. This pleasant coastal town is also a good base for other nature-focused adventures, including **shark-cage diving** (p153) at nearby Gansbaai and exploring the Fernkloof Nature Reserve and Walker Bay Nature Reserve. Bird-watchers will want to beat a path to the **West Coast National Park** (p203), which hosts huge numbers of migratory wading birds, as well as spectacular stretches of *fynbos* (literally 'fine bush', the vegetation of Cape Town that consists primarily of proteas, heaths and ericas). Between August and October, after good rainfall, these wild flowers bloom here and just about everywhere between Darling and Clanwilliam, 200km to the north. (Though, take note: this is the only time of year that the West Coast becomes busy.)

If you're in **Greyton** (p202) and have the time, this is a wonderful area in which to hike, the **Boesmanskloof Trail** (p203) across to McGregor being the highlight. If you're looking for a hike or mountain-bike scramble in the Winelands, drive or cycle out from Stellenbosch to the small Jonkershoek Nature Reserve, around 8km southeast of the town along the WR4.

BEACHES & SWIMMING

If you're hoping to swim in the sea rather than make a mad dash in and out of the water to avoid hypothermia (as is often a requirement at beaches such as Clifton for those without a wet suit), False Bay beaches such as **Muizenberg** (p108) offer a respite from the 13°C waters cooled by the Benguela Current, and average around 19°C. Sea temperatures rise as you head further east; the beaches around **Hermanus** (p198), such as Grotto Beach, and **Gansbaai** (p201) are lapped by the Indian Ocean and the last pleasant touches of the warm Mozambique current. For those who insist on personal refrigeration, **Langebaan** (p203) along the West Coast provides a bracing introduction to the south Atlantic.

SCENIC DRIVES

Instead of using the N2 highway to reach the Overberg, try Rte 44 from Strand, towards Hermanus around Cape Hangklip. The trip is about half an hour longer, but it's a breathtaking coastal drive in the same class as Chapman's Peak Dr in Cape Town, and incurs no toll. The Four Passes Rte, heading through Franschhoek, and the **Bainskloof Pass** (p198), northwest of Paarl, are among the most spectacular mountain passes in the country and are worth traversing back and forth to the Winelands in their own right.

VILLAGES & TOWNS

Darling (p206), a charming small town in the Swartland north of Cape Town, is best known as the home of Pieter-Dirk Uys's alter-ego **Evita Bezuidenhout** (see the boxed text, p146) and worth visiting. Further north along the West Coast is the pretty fishing village of **Paternoster** (p205), a romantic getaway famous for its golden sunsets, whitewashed houses and terrific seafood. Even more picturesque is **Greyton** (p202), in the shadow of the Riviersonderendberge, and nearby Genadendal, the oldest mission station in South Africa.

STELLENBOSCH

South Africa's second-oldest European settlement, Stellenbosch, established on the banks of the Eerste River by Governor Van der Stel in 1679, wears many faces. At times it's a rowdy joint, as University of Stellenbosch students celebrate one or another form of freedom in a series of music festivals (the Afrikaans-language University of Stellenbosch, established in 1918, continues to play an important role in Afrikaner politics and culture). At others it's a stately monument to colonial splendour, its quiet oak-lined streets featuring some of the world's finest examples of Cape Dutch, Georgian and Victorian architecture. But most times it's just plain busy, as Capetonians, wine-farm workers and tourists descend on its interesting museums, buzzing markets, quality hotels and varied eating and nightlife options.

The train station is a short walk west of the centre. The train line effectively forms the western boundary of the town, and the Eerste River, the southern. Dorp St, which runs roughly parallel to the river, is the old town's main street and is lined with numerous fine old buildings. The commercial centre lies between Dorp St and the university to the east of the Braak, the old town square. A lovely way to get acquainted with the town is to take a walking tour; ask the Stellenbosch Publicity Association for details.

Should you decide to walk around, lest you search in vain for traditional street signs, it's worth mentioning that streets in Stellenbosch are signposted by black-on-yellow pavement blocks at ground level.

TRANSPORT

Distance from Cape Town to Stellenbosch 46km
Direction East
Travel time One hour
Car Take the N2 and then Rte 310; alternatively continue to the junction with Rte 44.
Train Metro trains run roughly every 1½ hours from Cape Town to Stellenbosch (economy/1st class R7.30/12).

STELLENBOSCH

SIGHTS & INFORMATION	(p191)	De Volkskombuis.................15 A6	**SHOPPING** (p190)
Easy Rider Wine Tours.................(see 40)		Decameron.........................16 D5	Craft Market........................32 C5
Fandangos Internet Café...............1 C5		Fishmonger........................17 D5	Ex Libris...............................33 C5
Fandangos Internet Café...............(see 31)		Greengate.........................18 C4	Green Sleeves......................34 C4
Fick House............................2 B5		Java Café...........................19 C5	Oom Samie se Winkel..........35 B6
Grosvenor House.....................3 D5		L'Olive Café & Deli..............20 C5	Simonsberg Cheese Factory.....36 A3
Hospital................................4 D3		Voila! & Beads....................21 C5	
Post Office............................5 C5		Wijnhuis............................22 C5	**SLEEPING** (p192)
St Mary's on the Braak Church.....6 C5			De Goue Druif.....................37 B5
Sasol Art Museum....................7 C4		**DRINKING** (p192)	D'Ouwe Werf.......................38 C5
Standard Bank ATM..................8 C5		Binelli's..............................23 A6	Stellenbosch Hotel................39 C5
Stellenbosch Publicity Association...9 B5		Bohemia............................24 C4	Stumble Inn.........................40 B5
Toy & Miniature Museum............10 B5		De Akker............................25 B6	Wild Mushroom...................41 C5
Village Museum.......................11 D5		De Kelder...........................26 B6	
VOC Kruithuis.........................12 B5		Dros...................................27 C5	**TRANSPORT**
		Mystic Boer.........................28 C4	Minibus Taxis.......................42 C4
EATING (p191)		Nu Bar...............................29 C5	Minibus Taxis.......................43 C5
De Oewer.............................13 A6		Terrace...............................30 B5	
De Soete Inval.......................14 C5		Tollies................................31 B4	

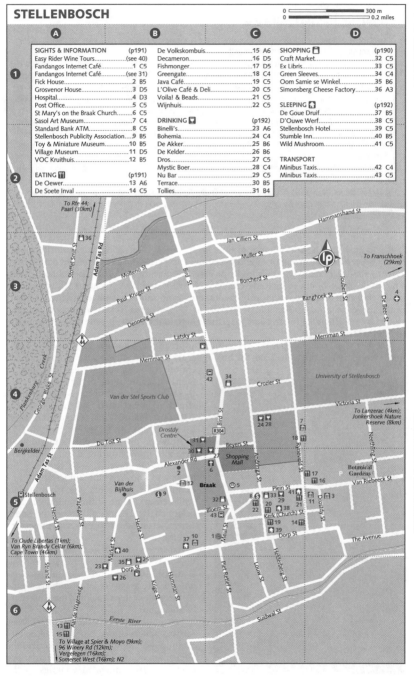

SHOPPING IN STELLENBOSCH

Stellenbosch's combination of local artists, hip students and day-trippers means it now has a booming shopping scene, with prices often a lot lower than those of similar items in Cape Town.

Apart from the daily outdoor **craft market** (Map p189; ⏰ 9am-5pm) near the Braak, which sells African curios and handmade clothing, the **Simonsberg Cheese Factory** (Map p189; ☎ 021-809 1017; 9 Stoffel Smit St; ⏰ 9am-5pm Mon-Fri, 9am-12.30pm Sat) is definitely worth a visit. There's a wonderful range here for fromage aficionados, including Camembert, Brie and a selection of blue cheeses. You can also sample the 'simonzola', a decadent blend of Gorgonzola and blue cheese. There are free tastings and the cheese is relatively inexpensive.

Oom Samie se Winkel (Uncle Sammy's Shop; Map p189; ☎ 021-887 0797; 84 Dorp St; ⏰ 8.30am-6pm Mon-Fri, 9am-5pm Sat & Sun), on the Stellenbosch map before Stellenbosch was on the map, is an unashamedly touristy general dealer but still worth visiting for its curious range of goods – from high kitsch to genuine antiques and everything else in between.

Bookshop **Ex Libris** (Map p189; ☎ 021-886 6871; 18 Andringa St) offers a solid collection of titles, including rare South African publications.

Green Sleeves (Map p189; ☎ 021-883 8374; 2 Crozier St; ⏰ 9am-5pm Mon-Fri, 9am-noon Sat) features a charming selection of retro, funky and vintage clothing; next door is a sister shop offering similar styles in furniture and homewares.

If you only have a short amount of time for historical sightseeing, your priority should be the **Village Museum**, a group of carefully restored and period-furnished houses dating from 1709 to 1850. The main entrance leads into the oldest of the buildings, the Schreuderhuis. The whole block, bounded by Ryneveld, Plein, Drostdy and Kerk (Church) Sts, is occupied by the museum and includes most of the buildings and some charming gardens. Also part of the museum, on the other side of Drostdy St, is Grosvenor House, which was commissioned by Sebastian Schröder, court magistrate here in the 1840s. It's the oldest townhouse in South Africa.

Another worthwhile stop is the delightfully surprising **Toy & Miniature Museum**. Many of the miniatures are amazingly detailed; the highlights are a model railway set and houses made entirely of icing sugar – get the guide to point out some of the best pieces.

At the north end of the Braak, an open stretch of grass, you'll find the neo-Gothic **St Mary's on the Braak Church**, completed in 1852. To the west is the **VOC Kruithuis**, built in 1777 to store the town's weapons and gunpowder, and now housing a small military museum. On the northwest corner is **Fick House**, also known as the Burgerhuis, a fine example of Cape Dutch style from the late 18th century. Most of this building is now occupied by Historical Homes of South Africa, established to preserve important architecture.

Art-lovers should not miss the **Sasol Art Museum**, which contains an irreplaceable collection of African anthropological treasures, housed here as part of an assemblage by the Anthropology department of the University of Stellenbosch.

Just outside town is the **Jonkershoek Nature Reserve**, which offers excellent hikes and mountain-biking routes, and of course the Stellenbosch area's famous vineyards. For details of recommended wineries in the area, see p45.

St Mary's on the Braak Church (right)

Sights & Information

Jonkershoek Nature Reserve (☎ 021-866 1560, 021-483 2949; car/bicycle R110/5)

St Mary's on the Braak Church (☎ 021-887 6913; Braak; admission free, only by appointment; ☻ 9am-4pm Mon-Fri)

Sasol Art Museum (Map p189; ☎ 021-808 3693; 52 Ryneveld St; adult/child R9/5; ☻ 9.30am-4.30pm Tue-Fri, 9am-4pm Sat)

Stellenbosch Publicity Association (Map p189; ☎ 021-883 3584; www.tourismstellenbosch.co.za; 36 Market St; ☻ 8am-6pm Mon-Fri, 9am-5pm Sat, 9am-4pm Sun) The staff here are extremely helpful. Pick up the excellent brochure *Discover Stellenbosch on Foot* (R3), with a walking-tour map and information on many of the historic buildings (also available in French and German). Also useful is the free brochure *Stellenbosch Wine Routes*, which gives information about opening times and tastings at many nearby wineries.

Toy & Miniature Museum (Map p189; ☎ 021-887 9433; 116 Dorp St; adult/child R10/5; ☻ 9.30am-5pm Mon-Sat, 2-5pm Sun)

Village Museum (Map p189; ☎ 021-887 2902; 18 Ryneveld St; adult/child R15/10; ☻ 9.30am-5pm Mon-Sat, 2-5pm Sun)

VOC Kruithuis (Map p189; Powder House; admission free; ☻ 9.30am-1pm Mon-Fri)

Eating

Java Café (Map p189; ☎ 021-887 6261; cnr Kerk & Andringa Sts; snacks from R15; ☻ 8.30am-11pm) A good range of drinks and snacks is available at this stylish café, with its pavement tables. It also offers Stellenbosch's cheapest Internet access (R18 per hour) and is a wi-fi hot spot.

Greengate (Map p189; ☎ 021-886 6111; 44 Ryneveld St; snacks from R20; ☻ 8am-5pm Mon-Fri, 8am-noon Sat) An organic and farm-food deli that looks good and smells terrific. It sells nuts, fruits and organic vegetables, and offers a pay-by-weight buffet at R90 per kilogram and a daily changing menu.

L'Olive Café & Deli (Map p189; ☎ 021-887 8985; Shop 1, Oude Hoek, Andringa St; snacks from R25; ☻ 8am-6pm Mon-Sat) A stylish deli offering a range of delicious snacks built around the eponymous fruit, of which it offers several varieties.

De Soete Inval (Map p189; ☎ 021-886 4842; 5 Ryneveld St; mains R50; ☻ breakfast, lunch & dinner) Known primarily for its choice of 40 different pancakes, this cheerful place also does a fine Indonesian *rijstafel* (rice with many dishes), with six dishes for R75 or a half portion for R50.

Fishmonger (Map p189; ☎ 021-887 7835; cnr Ryneveld & Plein Sts; mains R50; ☻ lunch & dinner) The choice for seafood. It's a snazzily designed place with a relaxed vibe. A platter goes for a reasonable R79.

Decameron (Map p189; ☎ 021-883 3331; 50 Plein St; mains R40-60; ☻ lunch & dinner Mon-Sat, lunch Sun) Locals are divided about whether or not cheesily designed Decameron is the town's best Italian restaurant. Arguments are commonly settled over a pizza in the outdoor seating area on a balmy summer evening.

96 Winery Rd (Map p46; ☎ 021-842 2945; Zandberg Farm, Winery Rd; mains R70; ☻ lunch & dinner Mon-Sat, lunch Sun) Off Rte 44 between Stellenbosch and Somerset West, this is one of the most respected restaurants in the area, known for its dry-aged beef. It has a relaxed style and a belief in simply cooked, real food.

De Oewer (Map p189; ☎ 021-886 5431; Aan de Wagenweg St; mains R70; ☻ lunch & dinner Mon-Sat, lunch Sun) Next to De Volkskombuis, De Oewer has an open-air section shaded by oak trees beside the river. It offers lighter meals with a more-Mediterranean emphasis.

De Volkskombuis (Map p189; ☎ 021-887 2121; Aan de Wagenweg St; mains R75; ☻ lunch & dinner Mon-Sat, lunch Sun) A local favourite that's open 365 days a year, this no-frills, atmospheric place specialises in traditional Cape Malay cuisine and features a terrace with views of the Stellenbosch Mountain Range. Note that booking is advisable.

Voila! & Beads (Map p189; ☎ 021-886 8734; cnr Kerk & Ryneveld Sts; mains R30-80; ☻ breakfast, lunch & dinner) Two fine eateries in one: in front is bustling deli Voila!, where you can create your own meal; out back is trendy à la Carte restaurant Beads, frequented by Stellenbosch's beautiful people.

Wijnhuis (Map p189; ☎ 021-887 5844; cnr Kerk & Andringa Sts; mains R50-100; ☻ lunch & dinner) One of the town's most pricey options, but well worth it. There's an extensive menu and a wine list stretching to 350 different labels. Around 20 wines are available by the glass and it does tastings. Try to get a seat in the outdoor section.

Moyo (Map p46; ☎ 021-809 1100; Rte 310, Spier, Vlottenburg; buffet R180, per kg R115; ☻ lunch & dinner) The mandatory face painting is a bit much, but this tourist-pleasing place brings a fantasy vision of Africa to the midst of the Spier wine estate, and guests love it. It's a lot of fun, with roving musicians and dancers, and alfresco dining in tents and up in the trees (you're given a blanket in winter).

Tokara (Map p46; ☎ 021-808 5959; mains R85-125; ☻ lunch & dinner) The highly renowned Tokara offers *nouvelle cuisine* in surprisingly large portions. Booking is advised.

Drinking

Binelli's (Map p189; ☎ 021-886 9009; Black Horse Centre; cnr Dorp & Market Sts) This supremely slick, New York–styled 'event bar' represents more than any other place the changing face of Stellenbosch: it offers a selection of coffees, tapas and cocktails using only high-grade ingredients.

Bohemia (Map p189; ☎ 021-882 8375; cnr Andringa & Victoria Sts) Offers live music every Tuesday, Thursday and Sunday, and hookahs (R25) with a range of different tobaccos.

De Akker (Map p189; ☎ 021-883 3512; 90 Dorp St) Has pub meals from under R30 and an upstairs cellar for live music.

De Kelder (Map p189; ☎ 021-883 3797; 63 Dorp St) A reasonably pleasant restaurant, bar and beer garden popular with German backpackers.

Dros (Map p189; ☎ 021-886 4856; Drostdy Centre, Bird St) Clustered together with the Terrace (☎ 021-887 1942) and Tollies (☎ 021-886 5497) in the complex just off Bird St and north of the Braak. These are some of the liveliest bars in town; you can eat at all of them, but that's not what most patrons have in mind.

Fandangos Internet Café (Map p189; ☎ 021-887 7501; Drostdy Centre, Bird St) A sophisticated cocktail bar and Internet café in the same complex. There's also another **branch** (Map p189; ☎ 021-887 4628; Meul St).

Mystic Boer (Map p189; ☎ 021-886 8870; 3 Victoria St) A spot favoured by cool Afrikaner kids, with surroundings perhaps best described as post-transformation era retro-Boer chic.

Nu Bar (Map p189; ☎ 021-886 8998; 51 Plein St) A place to have a beer and a boogie, with a small dance floor beyond the long bar where the DJ pumps out hip-hop and house.

Sleeping

Stumble Inn (Map p189; ☎ 021-887 4049; www.jump.to/stumble; 12 Market St; camp sites per person R40, dm R60, d with shared bathroom R160; 🖥 🍷) With a lively and welcoming atmosphere, this place is split over two old houses. One has a small pool and the other a pleasant garden, which now offers self-catering apartments for R250. The owners, travellers and wine-lovers themselves, are a good source of information and offer wine discounts for longer stays. They also run Easy Rider Wine Tours (p43) and hire out bicycles for R50 per day.

Stellenbosch Hotel (Map p189; ☎ 021-887 3644; www.stellenbosch.co.za/hotel; 162 Dorp St; s/d incl breakfast from R425/700; 🍴) A comfortable country-style hotel with a variety of rooms including some with self-catering facilities and others with four-poster beds. A section dating from 1743 houses the Jan Cats Brasserie, a good spot for a drink.

The **Oude Libertas Amphitheatre** (Map p46; ☎ 021-809 7380; www.oudelibertas.co.za) and the **Spier wine estate** (Map p46; ☎ 021-809 1100; www.spier.co.za) both hold performing-arts festivals between January and March.

The **Stellenbosch Festival** (www.stellenboschfestival.co.za), which runs for two weeks at the end of September, celebrates music and the arts in various events around the town including a street carnival. The **Wine Festival** (www.wineroute.co.za) in early August offers visitors the chance to sample up to 400 different drops in one spot, as well as attend talks and tutorials on wine.

The **Van der Stel Festival** at the end of September and early October combines with the Stellenbosch and Wine Festivals. If you're into live music, try to catch early February's **Rag Week**, where local bands vie for the attention of freshmen out to celebrate their recent student status.

De Goue Druif (Map p189; ☎ 021-883 3555; www.goueduif.hypermart.net; 110 Dorp St; s/d incl breakfast R650/700; 🍴 🖥 🍷) In a Cape Dutch building dating back to 1792, this 'Golden Grape' is a charming guesthouse run by a Belgian couple. There is a small gym and sauna.

Wild Mushroom (Map p189; ☎ 021-886 9880; 15 Ryneveld St; s/d incl breakfast R450/780; 🍴) Slap-bang in the middle of Stellenbosch's trendy restaurant zone yet surprisingly quiet, this chic multilevel guesthouse offers plush accommodation, all in very stylish shades of brown. There is also a self-catering option.

D'Ouwe Werf (Map p189; ☎ 021-887 4608; www.ouwewerf.com; 30 Kerk St; s/d incl breakfast R900/990; 🍴 🍷) This is an appealing, old-style hotel (dating back to 1802) with a good restaurant. It's worth dropping by its shady courtyard for lunch. The more expensive luxury rooms are furnished with antiques and brass beds.

Village at Spier (Map p46; ☎ 021-809 1100; www.spier.co.za; Vlottenburg; d/ste incl breakfast R1450/2500; 🍴 🍷) Forgo the usual Cape Dutch style in favour of a design copying the brightly painted houses found in Cape Town's Bo-Kaap. Rooms are large and well appointed. Spier is located 11km south of Stellenbosch on Rte 310.

Lanzerac Manor (Map p46; ☎ 021-887 1132; www.lanzerac.co.za; Jonkershoek Valley; s/d/ste incl breakfast R1700/2960/4140; 🍴 🖥 🍷) This unashamedly opulent place consists of a 300-year-old manor house and winery. Some suites have private pools. The hotel is on the Lanzerac wine estate in the Jonkershoek Valley, 5km east of town off the T16.

FRANSCHHOEK

The toughest decision you'll face in European-styled Franschhoek (literally 'French Corner'), which bills itself as the country's gastronomic capital, is where to eat. And with a clutch of wine farms and stylish guesthouses thrown in, there's a sense here that this is all too good to be true. It certainly has one of the loveliest settings in the Cape, yet it all feels a bit too much like a theme park. It's a good base from which to visit both Stellenbosch and Paarl as long as you have transport.

The town is clustered around Huguenot St. At the southern end it reaches a T-junction at Huguenot Memorial Park. Here you'll find the mildly diverting **Huguenot Memorial Museum**, which celebrates the 200 French Huguenots who settled in the region in the 17th century. It houses the genealogical records of their descendants, as well as some hefty Cape Dutch furniture. Some of the names of the original settlers, such as Malan, De Villiers, Malherbe and Roux, are among the most famous Afrikaner dynasties in the country. Behind the main complex is a pleasant café, in front is the **Huguenot Monument**, three interlocking arches symbolising the holy trinity, and across the road is the museum's annexe, with displays on the Anglo-Boer War and natural history.

Continue past the end of the town along Rte 45 until you reach the winding roads of the spectacular Franschhoek Pass. Together with the Helshoogte Pass on Rte 310, and Viljoens Pass and Sir Lowry's Pass (the most stunning of the lot) on the N2 highway, this forms part of the roughly circular **Four Pass Route** that makes for a cracking day's driving to and from Cape Town or Stellenbosch.

For details of Franschhoek's wineries, some of which can be visited on foot from the town, see p48. There's also the option of taking a horse-riding tour of the area with the **Mont Rochelle Equestrian Centre**.

Wining and dining apart, there're some decent walks in the surrounding mountains – the staff at Franschhoek Wine Valley Tourism can provide a map of suggested routes and issue permits (R10) for walks in nearby forestry areas. There are also plenty of galleries and designer shops to mop up any spare cash. In particular, visit **Huguenot Fine Chocolates**. An empowerment programme helped give the two locals who run this Belgian-style

TRANSPORT

Distance from Cape Town to Franschhoek 85km
Direction East
Travel time From Cape Town 75 minutes; from Stellenbosch or Paarl 30 minutes.
Car Follow the N2 and then stick on Rte 310 through Stellenbosch and over the Helshoogte Pass to the junction with Rte 45, where you take a right turn.
Taxi take a shared taxi from Stellenbosch to Pniel where you should be able to change to another shared taxi heading to Franschhoek from Paarl.

Excursions

FRANSCHHOEK

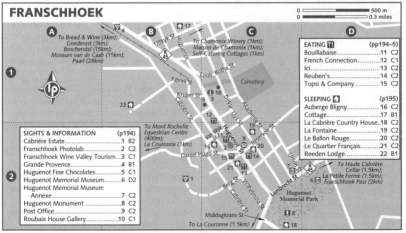

FRANSCHHOEK

0 — 500 m
0 — 0.3 miles

SIGHTS & INFORMATION (p194)
Cabrière Estate.......................1 B2
Franschhoek Photolab.................2 C2
Franschhoek Wine Valley Tourism...3 C1
Grande Provence.....................4 B1
Huguenot Fine Chocolates............5 C1
Huguenot Memorial Museum............6 D2
Huguenot Memorial Museum
  Annexe............................7 C2
Huguenot Monument...................8 C2
Post Office.........................9 C2
Roubaix House Gallery...............10 C1

EATING (pp194–5)
Bouillabaisse.......................11 C2
French Connection...................12 C1
Ici.................................13 C2
Reuben's............................14 C2
Topsi & Company.....................15 C2

SLEEPING (p195)
Auberge Bligny......................16 C2
Cottage.............................17 B1
La Cabrière Country House...........18 C2
La Fontaine.........................19 C2
Le Ballon Rouge.....................20 C2
Le Quartier Français................21 C2
Reeden Lodge........................22 B1

To Bread & Beer (3km);
Goederust (3km);
Boschendal (15km);
Museum van de Caab (15km);
Paarl (28km)

Uitkyk St
Huguenot St
Louis Botha St
Fabriek St
Cemetery
Kruger St
Cabrière St
Dirkie Uys St
Akdemie St
Reservoir St
Van Wijk St
Daniel Hugo St
Berg St
Wilhelmina St
Cabrière St
Lambrecht St
Middagkrans St
Union St
Haute Cabrière

To Chamonix Winery (1km);
Maison de Chamonix (1km);
Self-Catering Cottages (1km)

To Mont Rochelle
Equestrian Centre
(400m);
La Couronne (1km)

To Haute Cabrière
Cellar (1.5km);
La Petite Ferme (1.5km);
Franschhoek Pass (2km)

Huguenot
Memorial Park

To La Couronne (1.5km)

193

chocolate shop a leg up and now people are raving about their confections. Call in advance to arrange a tour and chocolate-making demonstration, which includes tasting of samples (R12). At the **Roubaix House Gallery**, in the beautifully restored home of Franschhoek's first teacher, you can watch David Walters, one of South Africa's most distinguished potters, at work.

Sights & Information

Franschhoek Photolab (Map p193; ☎ 021-876 4911; 28 Huguenot St; ⏰ 8am-5.30pm Mon-Fri, 8am-4pm Sat, 10am-3pm Sun) There's Internet access here at R40 per hour.

Franschhoek Wine Valley Tourism (Map p193; ☎ 021-876 3603; www.franschhoek.org.za; Huguenot St; ⏰ 9am-6pm Mon-Fri, 9am-5pm Sat, 9am-4pm Sun) Housed in a small building on the left of the main street shortly after you enter the town. Staff here can provide you with a map of the area's scenic walks and issue permits (R10) for walks in nearby forestry areas, as well as book accommodation.

Huguenot Fine Chocolates (Map p193; ☎ 021-876 4096; 62 Huguenot St)

Huguenot Memorial Museum (Map p193; ☎ 021-876 2532; Lambrecht St; adult/child R5/2; ⏰ 9am-5pm Mon-Sat, 2-5pm Sun)

Huguenot Monument (Map p193; adult/child R5/1; ⏰ 9am-5pm)

Mont Rochelle Equestrian Centre (☎ 083 300 4368; fax 021-876 2363; per hr R90)

Roubaix House Gallery (Map p193; ☎ 021-876 4304; 24 Dirkie Uys St; ⏰ 10am-6pm)

Eating

Goederust (Map p49; ☎ 021-876 3687; Main Rd, La Motte; mains R30-40; ⏰ breakfast & lunch Mon-Sun) A new take on Cape-farm kitchen food is served in this charming old-fashioned farm restaurant set in a pleasant garden. The spicy calamari salad (R40) is a knockout, as are the filled pancakes. Come on Sunday for a spit-lamb buffet (bookings essential). Goederust is easy to reach. Head 3km west out of Franschhoek and look for the large sign on Rte 45.

French Connection (Map p193; ☎ 021-876 4056; 48 Huguenot St; mains R50; ⏰ lunch & dinner) Continental no-nonsense bistro-style food using only fresh ingredients is dished up at this deservedly popular place. Chequered red tablecloths give it that *mais oui* factor.

Reuben's (☎ 021-876 3772; 19 Huguenot Rd, Franschhoek; mains R70; ⏰ noon-3pm & 7-10.30pm) It would be easy to dismiss Reuben Riffel as black empowerment's poster boy, until you taste the local chef's wonderful food combining comfort with creativity. There's hardly anything on the menu you wouldn't want to try and the chic-but-not-too-hip décor of the restaurant is a delight, too.

Bread & Wine (Map p49; ☎ 021-876 3692; Môreson Wine Farm, Happy Valley Rd, La Motte; mains R60-80; ⏰ lunch Wed-Sun) Hidden away down a dirt road as you approach town along Rte 45, this place is worth searching out. It's known for its breads, pizzas, cured meats and tasty Mediterranean-style cuisine. Try the glazed kingklip with clams and artichoke (R70). It's a winner.

Topsi & Company (Map p193; ☎ 021-876 2952; 7 Reservoir St; mains R60-85; ⏰ 12.30-3pm & 7.30-10pm Wed-Mon) Run by Topsi Venter, who should be accorded national-treasure status, this eatery is quirky and very relaxed. Topsi pops out from her open kitchen to serve the totally delicious food and chat with guests; you must BYO wine.

La Petite Ferme (☎ 021-876 3016; Franschhoek Pass Rd; mains R80; ⏰ noon-4pm) A must-visit for foodies who hanker for romantic views, boutique wines and smoked, deboned salmon trout, the restaurant's delicately flavoured signature dish. There's a helipad should you feel like choppering in from Cape Town and some luxurious rooms if you can't bear to leave.

Haute Cabrière Cellar (☎ 021-876 3688; Franschhoek Pass Rd; mains R80-90; ⏰ noon-3pm daily, 7-9pm Wed-Mon) In a dramatic dining space in a cellar cut into the mountain side. Each dish can be had either as a starter or main and all are paired with a Cabrière wine.

Franschhoek valley and surrounds

Bouillabaise (Map p193; ☎ 021-876 4430; 38 Huguenot St; mains R70-110; ☺ breakfast, lunch & dinner Mon, Wed-Sat, breakfast & lunch Sun) The Franschhoek jet set just got an upgrade, with this highly opulent champagne and oyster bar featuring blown-glass sculptures, beautiful staff, fresh seafood dishes, an excellent range of bubblies and home-made sorbets such as lime and basil or mint and mead.

Ici (Map p193; ☎ 021-876 2151; 16 Huguenot St; mains R50-R280; ☺ lunch & dinner) The restaurant of Le Quartier Français, this Franschhoek stalwart is now split into two dining options: a stylish bistro offering food such as zebra carpaccio, cape salmon and liquorice and coffee-roasted blesbok (highland antelope) loin; and a set-menu restaurant offering a four-course meal (R280). The hotel's bar does lighter meals for around R60.

Sleeping

Chamonix Guest Cottages (Map p49; ☎ 021-876 2494; www.chamonix.co.za; Uitkyk St; cottages per person from R200) Pleasant cottages sleeping up to four are set in the middle of the Chamonix vineyards, a 10-minute walk uphill, north of Huguenot St. There are considerable winter discounts (May to October).

Cottage (Map p49; ☎ 021-876 2392; thecottage55@iafrica.com; 55 Huguenot St; s/d R260/350) There is just one cottage sleeping two, or four at a pinch, but it's a beauty. It's private, quiet, just a few minutes' walk from the village centre and now has self-catering facilities.

Reeden Lodge (Map p193; ☎ 021-876 3174; www.reedenlodge.co.za; off Cabriére St; cottages from R400; ☐ ☎) A terrific option for families, with well-equipped self-catering cottages sleeping up to eight people, situated on a farm about 10 minutes' walk from town. Parents will love the peace and quiet and their kids the sheep, tree house and open space.

Le Ballon Rouge (Map p193; ☎ 021-876 2651; www.leballonrouge.co.za; 7 Reservoir St; s/d incl breakfast R500/650; ☒ ☐ ☎) A small guesthouse with good-quality rooms and stylish suites (with underfloor heating and stunning bathrooms) all opening onto a patio. It also has a popular restaurant.

Auberge Bligny (Map p193; ☎ 021-876 3767; www.bligny.co.za; 28 Van Wyk St; d from R650; ☎) Charming décor and heavy-set furniture define this guesthouse set in a Victorian homestead. Travellers, largely European, return regularly for its nine pleasant rooms and shady garden.

La Fontaine (Map p193; ☎ 021-876 2112; www.lafontainefranschhoek.co.za; 21 Dirkie Uys St; s/d incl breakfast R600/R750; ☎) Offering a quieter accommodation alternative off the town's main drag, this is a stylishly appointed family home featuring twelve spacious rooms with wooden floors and mountain views.

La Cabrière Country House (Map p193; ☎ 021-876 4780; www.lacabriere.co.za; Middagkrans Rd; d incl breakfast R1050; ☒ ☐ ☎) A modern boutique guesthouse that's a refreshing break from all that Cape Dutch architecture. There are four sumptuously decorated rooms, very personal service and sweeping views to the mountains.

La Couronne (Map p49; ☎ 021-876 2110; www.lacouronnehotel.co.za; Robertsvlei Rd; d incl breakfast from R1970; ☒ ☐ ☎) A boutique hotel-restaurant partly built into the hills, this place offers gilt-edged luxury and magnificent views across the valley.

Le Quartier Français (Map p193; ☎ 021-876 2151; www.lequartier.co.za; 16 Huguenot St; d from R2350; ☒ ☐ ☎) This is one of the best places to stay in the Winelands. Set around a leafy courtyard and pool, guest rooms are very large with fireplaces, huge beds and stylish décor. There's also a fine restaurant here.

PAARL

Less touristy and more spread out than Stellenbosch, Paarl is a large commercial centre surrounded by mountains and vineyards on the banks of the Berg River. There are several vineyards and wineries (see p51) within the sprawling town limits, including the huge Kooperatieve Wijnbouwers Vereeniging, better known as KWV.

Europeans settled the surrounding valley in the 1680s, and Paarl was established in 1720. It became a centre for wagon building, but the town is most famous for its important role in the development and recognition of Afrikaans as a language in its own right (see the boxed text, p197).

Paarl is not really a town to tour on foot, but there is still quite a lot to see and do. Main St runs 11km along the entire length of the town, parallel to the Berg River and the train line. It's shaded by oaks and jacarandas and is lined with many historic buildings. The busy commercial centre is around Lady Grey St, near where you'll find the fascinating **Paarl Museum**, housed in the Old Parsonage (Oude Pastorie), built in 1714. It has an excellent collection of Cape Dutch antiques and relics of Huguenot and early Afrikaner culture. There's a bookcase modelled on King Solomon's temple and display sections on the 'road to reconciliation', the old mosques of the local Muslim community and the Khoisan (Khoesaan).

A short walk south of the Paarl Museum is the marginally interesting **Afrikaans Language Museum**. The language's birth is chronicled in the former home of Gideon Malherbe, the

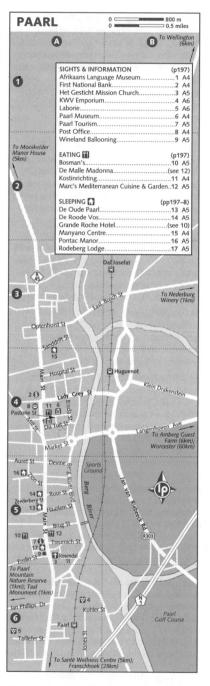

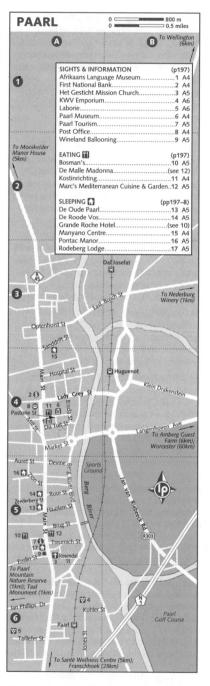

PAARL

| 0 | 800 m |
| 0 | 0.5 miles |

SIGHTS & INFORMATION (p197)
Afrikaans Language Museum................1 A4
First National Bank.............................2 A4
Het Gesticht Mission Church................3 A5
KWV Emporium................................4 A6
Laborie...5 A6
Paarl Museum..................................6 A4
Paarl Tourism.................................7 A5
Post Office....................................8 A4
Wineland Ballooning..........................9 A5

EATING (p197)
Bosman's.....................................10 A5
De Malle Madonna.........................(see 12)
Kostinrichting...............................11 A4
Marc's Mediterranean Cuisine & Garden..12 A5

SLEEPING (pp197–8)
De Oude Paarl...............................13 A5
De Roode Vos................................14 A5
Grande Roche Hotel......................(see 10)
Manyano Centre..............................15 A4
Pontac Manor................................16 A5
Rodeberg Lodge..............................17 A5

TRANSPORT

Distance from Cape Town to Paarl 56km
Direction Northeast
Travel time One hour
Car Take the N1 from Cape Town.
Bus All the major long-distance bus companies (p208) offer services passing through Paarl. The bus segment between Paarl and Cape Town costs R110, so consider taking the cheaper train to Paarl and then linking up with the buses.
Train Metro trains run roughly every hour between Cape Town and Paarl (economy/first class R8.50/14.50, 1¼ hours) from Monday to Friday. The services are less common on weekends. Take care to travel on trains during the busy part of the day, as robberies have been reported. You can travel by train from Paarl to Stellenbosch: take a Cape Town–bound train and change at Muldersvlei.

meeting place for the Association of True Afrikaners and the birthplace of the first Afrikaans newspaper. The house has been painstakingly restored.

Afrikaans is further celebrated at the giant needlelike **Taal Monument** up on the highlands overlooking the town to the west. This is the Paarl Mountain Nature Reserve, which is dominated by three giant granite domes; they apparently glisten like pearls if they're caught by the sun after rain – hence the name 'Paarl'. The reserve has mountain *fynbos* with a large number of proteas. There's a cultivated wild-flower garden in the middle that's a nice spot for a picnic, and many walks with excellent views over the valley.

Access is from the 11km-long Jan Phillips Dr, which skirts the eastern edge of the reserve. The picnic ground is about 4km from Main St. A map showing walking trails is available from Paarl Tourism.

South of the town you'll also find the luxurious Winelands Hotel containing the **Santé Wellness Centre** (p152). Also see (p156) for details of **hot-air balloon trips** you can organise out of Paarl.

Ten kilometres north of Paarl is the sedate and reasonably pretty town of **Wellington**. The Wellington Tourism Bureau, next to the Andrew Murray Church, can provide a brochure and map of the wineries in the Wellington area, which are less touristy than Paarl's, and also point you toward some places to stay. We've recommended a couple, following.

Sights & Information

Afrikaans Language Museum (Map p196; ☎ 021-872 3441; Pastorie Ave; adult/child R5/2; ⏰ 9am-1pm & 2-5pm Mon-Fri)

Paarl Museum (Map p196; ☎ 021-872 2651; www .museums.org.za/paarlmuseum; 303 Main St; adult/child R5/donation; ⏰ 10am-5pm Mon-Fri)

Paarl Tourism (Map p196; ☎ 021-872 3829; www .paarlonline.com; 216 Main St; ⏰ 9am-5pm Mon-Fri, 9am-1pm Sat, 10am-1pm Sun) Has an excellent supply of information on the whole region and helpful staff.

Santé Wellness Centre (Map p49; ☎ 021-875 8100; www.santewellness.co.za; Winelands Hotel, Klapmuts)

Taal Monument (Paarl Mountain Nature Reserve, Jan Phillips Dr; adult/child R5/2; ⏰ 8am-5pm)

Wellington Tourism Bureau (☎ 021-873 4604; www .visitwellington.com; 104 Main St, Wellington)

Eating

Kostinrichting (Map p196; ☎ 021-871 1353; 19 Pastorie Ave; mains R30; ⏰ lunch Mon-Sat) Ideal if you're looking for a pleasant central café. It's in a Victorian building that once was a school, and has an attached crafts shop.

De Malle Madonna (Map p196; ☎ 021-863 3925; 127 Main St; mains R40-65; ⏰ breakfast & lunch Wed-Sun, dinner Wed & Sun) Marc Chagall is the inspiration for this breezy café-bistro, whose emphasis is on 'Mediterranean comfort food'. There's a sunny patio with mountain views, and the biltong and glazed beetroot salad (R41) is a winner.

Marc's Mediterranean Cuisine & Garden (Map p196; ☎ 021-863 3980; 129 Main Rd; mains R60-75; ⏰ lunch Tue-Sun, dinner Mon-Sat) The current favourite of restaurant reviewers, and with good reason. Owner Marc Friedrich has created a light and bright place with food to match and a Provence-style garden to dine in.

Bosman's (Map p196; ☎ 021-863 2727; Grande Roche Hotel, Plantasie St; mains R140; ⏰ lunch & dinner) If money is no object, try this ritzy restaurant. It's undoubtedly classy, with chandeliers inside, flickering candles outside and a wine list that runs to more than 50 pages. There are various set menus starting at R320 for three courses.

Sleeping

Manyano Centre (Map p196; ☎ 021-872 2537; manyano@eject.co.za; Sanddrift St; dm with full board R110) An enormous YMCA-style accommodation complex with basic three-bed dorms; you'll need to bring a sleeping bag. Call in advance, especially on weekends when it fills up with groups. Huguenot Train Station is closer than the main Paarl station.

De Roode Vos (Map p196; ☎ /fax 021-872 5912; 152 Main St; s/d R150/240) This unspectacular guesthouse offers clean lodgings, which are about as cheap as you'll get in central Paarl.

Bakkies B&B (Map p49; ☎ /fax 021-873 5161; www .bakkiesbb.co.za; Bainskloof Rd, Wellington; s/d R170/280; 🔲 💻 💻) An excellent budget base for exploring the Bainskloof area, with good-value, well-equipped rooms. Lunch and dinner are by appointment, and a daily breakfast (R40) is offered.

Rodeberg Lodge (Map p196; ☎ 021-863 3202; www .rodeberglodge.co.za; 74 Main Rd; s/d incl breakfast R290/460; 🔲) Good rooms (some with air-con and TV) are sensibly located away from the busy main road, and there's a family room (R200 per person) in the attic. The hosts are friendly and breakfast is taken in the conservatory, opening onto a leafy garden.

Amberg Guest Farm (Map p49; ☎ /fax 021-862 0982; amberg@mweb.co.za; Rte 101 along Du Toits Kloof Pass; s/d incl breakfast R330/500; 💻) Accommodation is in cottages (one of which is self-catering for R360) with spectacular views. The amiable hosts also run the Swiss-style Amberg Country Kitchen, serving Swiss specialities.

Berg River Resort (Map p49; ☎ 021-863 1650; bergr@mweb.co.za; camp sites R155, d chalets R520; 💻) An attractive municipal camping ground beside the Berg River, 5km from Paarl on the N45 towards Franschhoek. Facilities include canoes, trampolines and a café.

Hildenbrand Wine & Olive Estate (Map p49; ☎ /fax 021-873 4115; www.wine-estate-hildenbrand.co.za;

THE OFFICIAL BIRTH OF AFRIKAANS

In 1875 Arnoldus Pannevis, a teacher at Paarl Gymnasium High School, inspired a number of Paarl citizens to form the Genootskap van Regte Afrikaners (Association of True Afrikaners). They developed and formalised the grammar and vocabulary of a language that was developed over 200 years from the interaction of the Dutch with their slaves and the indigenous inhabitants of the Cape. Many of the founding members of the association were actually descendants of the French Huguenots.

A small press was set up in the house of Gideon Malherbe and the first issue of an Afrikaans newspaper, *Die Afrikaanse Patriot*, was published, followed by many books. Afrikaans was proclaimed an official language in 1925 and is protected under South Africa's new constitution.

DETOUR: BAINSKLOOF PASS

The Bainskloof Pass is one of the country's great mountain passes, with a superb caravan park halfway along. It's a magical drive, which would be even better to experience on bicycle. Colonial engineer Andrew Bain developed the road through the pass between 1848 and 1852. Other than having its surface tarred, the road has not been altered since, and is now a national monument.

Rte 301 runs from Wellington, 13km north of Paarl, across Bainskloof to meet another road running south to Worcester and north to Ceres. There are several nearby walks including the five-hour **Bobbejaans River Walk** to a waterfall. This walk actually starts back at Eerste Tol and you need to buy a permit (R30), which is available from the Cape Nature Conservation desk at Cape Town Tourism (p219).

off Rte 303, Wellington; s/d incl breakfast R370/560; ⊗ winery 10am-4pm; 🍴) A popular estate with a restaurant and good accommodation. You can also taste locally grown olives and buy freshly pressed olive oil. Tastings cost R15.

Mooikelder Manor House (Map p49; ☎ 021-869 8787; www.capestay.co.za/mooikelder; Main Rd, Noorder Paarl; s/d incl breakfast R350/650; 🖥 🍴) Around 5km north of the town centre, in an elegant homestead once occupied by Cecil John Rhodes, this lovely, quiet spot is set amid citrus orchards. There's plenty of antique atmosphere in the rooms.

De Oude Paarl (Map p196; ☎ 021-872 1002; www .deoudepaarl.com; 132 Main St; s/d incl breakfast R650/930; 📷 🖥 🍴) This is a new boutique-style hotel; the rooms have antique touches and there's a secluded courtyard at the back. Attached are shops selling a good selection of wine and delectable Belgian chocolates.

Pontac Manor (Map p196; ☎ 021-872 0445; www .pontac.com; 16 Zion St; s/d incl breakfast R1090/1400; 📷 🍴) A small, stylish Victorian-era hotel that commands a good view of the valley. The rooms are comfortable, and there's one self-catering cottage and a restaurant, which is recommended.

Grande Roche Hotel (Map p196; ☎ 021-863 2727; www.granderoche.co.za; Plantasie St; d from R2420; 📷 🖥 ♿) An unashamedly opulent hotel set in a Cape Dutch manor house, offering mountain views, a heated pool and the award-winning Bosman's restaurant.

HERMANUS

Hermanus (hair-*maan*-es) was founded as a fishing village and while it retains vestiges of its heritage, its economy is grounded in the fact that it is considered the best land-based whale-watching destination in the world.

The town centre can get very crowded, particularly during the **Hermanus Whale Festival** and during school holidays in December and January. It is easily negotiated on foot and the area east of the new harbour is well endowed with restaurants and shops. There's a small **market** daily at Lemms Corner in Market Sq off Main Rd; on Saturday a craft market is held here, too.

Here you'll also find the old harbour and the small and generally uninteresting **Hermanus Harbour Museum**, and a display of old fishing boats. The museum's annexe, in the old schoolhouse on Market Sq, displays some evocative old photographs of the town and its fishermen.

From the old harbour take the **Cliff Path Walking Trail** that meanders east along the sea to Grotto Beach, a long, narrow surf beach with excellent facilities. The walk takes about 1½ hours and along the way you'll pass Kraaiwater, a good whale-watching lookout, and Langbaai and Voelklip Beaches.

The surrounding rocky hills, vaguely reminiscent of Scotland, offer good walks and

TRANSPORT

Distance from Cape Town to Hermanus 122km
Direction Southeast
Travel time 90 minutes to two hours
Car The fastest route is to take the N2 from Cape Town; if you can spare the time (an extra half hour), come instead via Rte 44 through Strand, Gordon's Bay and around Cape Hangklip.
Bus There are no regular bus services to Hermanus, but plenty of organised bus tours from Cape Town; inquire with Cape Town Tourism (p219).

the 1400-hectare **Fernkloof Nature Reserve**, 5km east of town, is worth a visit if you are interested in *fynbos*. Around 1100 species have been identified so far. There is a 60km network of hiking trails for all fitness levels.

See p156 for details of sea kayaking in the harbour and p153 for details of shark-cage diving at Gansbaai.

Sights & Information

Fernkloof Nature Reserve (Map p186; ☎ 028-313 8100; Fir Ave; admission free; ⏰ 9am-5pm)

Hermanus Harbour Museum (Map p199; ☎ 028-312 1475; adult/child R2/1; ⏰ 9am-1pm & 2-5pm Mon-Sat, noon-4pm Sun)

Hermanus Tourism (Map p199; ☎ 028-312 2629; www.hermanus.co.za; Old Station Bldg, Mitchell St; ⏰ 9am-5pm Mon-Sat, noon-5pm Sun) Has a large supply of information about the area, including walks and drives in the surrounding hills, and can book accommodation. Note that even with the high number of guesthouses and hotels, during festival season it can be very hard to get a bed. We advise visiting the Hermanus website or calling Hermanus Tourism before travelling to book accommodation, or get a travel agency recommendation.

Hermanus Whale Festival (www.whalefestival.co.za) An annual festival (held in September) with plenty of eating, drinking and shopping opportunities between whale-watching sessions.

Internet City (Map p199; ☎ 028-312 4683; Waterkant Bldg, Main Rd; per hr R20; ⏰ 8am-8pm Mon-Sun) Offers reliable and speedy Internet connections.

Eating & Drinking

Zebra Crossing (Map p199; ☎ 028-312 3906; 121 Main Rd; mains R35; ⏰ lunch & dinner) This cheesy DJ bar with a funky zebra theme is, we're told, *the* late-night party spot on weekends, and popular with backpackers. At other times there's an open fire and pool tables.

Savannah Café (Map p199; ☎ 028-312 4259; Village Theatres Bldg, Marine Dr; mains from R40; ⏰ breakfast &

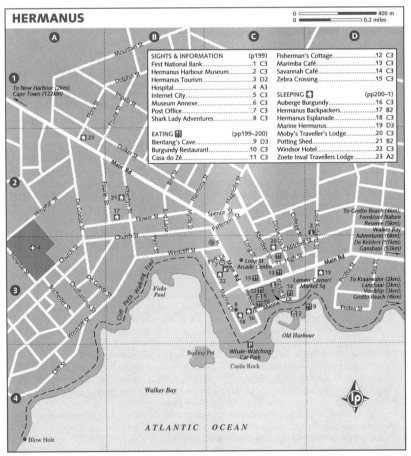

HERMANUS

0   400 m
0   0.2 miles

To New Harbour (2km);
Cape Town (122km)

To Grotto Beach (4km);
Fernkloof Nature
Reserve (5km);
Walker Bay
Adventures (6km);
De Kelders (51km);
Gansbaai (53km)

To Kraalwater (2km);
Lanjbaai (2km);
Voëlklip (3km);
Grotto Beach (4km)

Mountain St

Dolphin St

Impala St

Flora St

Tourie St

Duiker St

Main Rd

Hospital St

Fourie St

De Goede St

Albertyn St

Flower St

Bird Lane

Bird St

Harmony St

Myrtle St

Magnolia St

Spence St

Patterson St

Aberdeen St

Long St

Dirkie Uys St

College St

Lord Roberts St

Mitchell St

High St

Church St

Plein St

Westcliff St

Park La

Main Rd

Long St
Arcade Centre

Lemms Corner/
Market Sq

Main Rd

Protea St

Sea St

Protea St

De Goede St

Brockster St

Orohannus St

Westcliff St

Cliff St

Cliff Path Walking Trail

Ficks
Pool

Marine Dr

Old Harbour

Boiling Pot

Whale-Watching
Car Park

Castle Rock

Walker Bay

ATLANTIC OCEAN

Blow Hole

lunch) Enjoy a 'whale of a breakfast' – eggs, juice, coffee, bacon, chips, mushrooms and boerewors, or a sweet pastry while staring at the sea. There's also a decent selection for vegetarians, vegans and diabetics.

Bientang's Cave (Map p199; ☎ 028-312 3454; Marine Dr; mains R55; ☽ lunch & dinner) Nestled in the cliffs beside the water, this really *is* a seaside cave, a remarkable setting that obscures the fact that the restaurant is only so-so. Access is via a steep flight of cliffside stairs.

Casa do Zé (Map p199; ☎ 028-313 0377; 12 Mitchell St; mains R60; ☽ lunch & dinner Mon-Sat) A quaint Portuguese restaurant specialising in fresh grilled fish and the famous LM (Lourenço Marques) prawns. Try the imported Mozambican beer.

Fisherman's Cottage (Map p199; ☎ 028-312 3642; Lemms Cnr; mains R22-75; ☽ lunch & dinner) The emphasis is on good-value seafood at this restaurant in a whitewashed cottage draped with fishing nets.

Marimba Café (Map p199; ☎ 028-312 2148; 9 Royal Lane; mains R45-85; ☽ dinner) The lively atmosphere matches the eclectic menu at this rather unkempt but recommended restaurant and bar, where you can eat traditional African dishes from around the continent. It's off Main Rd.

Burgundy Restaurant (Map p199; ☎ 028-312 2800; Marine Dr; mains R60-95; ☽ lunch & dinner) Booking is essential at this eatery, one of the most acclaimed and popular in the area. It's in the oldest building in town (1875), which has a garden and sea views. The menu is mostly seafood with a different vegetarian dish each day.

Sleeping

Hermanus Backpackers (Map p199; ☎ 028-312 4293; moobag@mweb.co.za; 26 Flower St; dm R75, d with shared/private bathroom R210/230; ☐ ☒) This is a smashing place with clued-up staff, great décor and facilities, and a reed-roof bar. Free breakfast is served in the morning.

Moby's Traveller's Lodge (Map p199; ☎ 028-313 2361; www.mobys.co.za; 9 Mitchell St; dm R85, s/d with shared bathroom R200/260; ☒) Travellers give this place rave reviews, and we can see why – it's a whole lot of fun. You can party the night away at the big bar or chill out in the awesome rock pool with its own waterfall. There's a daily pub lunch on offer and an Internet café (R30 per hour).

Hermanus Esplanade (Map p199; ☎ 028-312 3610; info@hermanus.com; 63 Marine Dr; apt from R250) Some of these cheery, colourfully furnished self-catering apartments overlook the sea; the lowest rates on offer actually cover the whale-watching season from May to October.

Zoete Inval Travellers Lodge (Map p199; ☎ 028-312 1242; www.zoeteinval.co.za; 23 Main Rd; dm R85, d with shared bathroom incl breakfast R340) More a guesthouse than a hostel, this is a quiet place with good amenities (including a Jacuzzi) and neatly furnished rooms. Heavy smokers and drinkers should look elsewhere; families are accommodated in four-person doubles.

Potting Shed (Map p199; ☎ 028-312 1712; www .thepottingshedguesthouse.co.za; 28 Albertyn St; s/d incl breakfast from R300/440; ☐ ☒ ☒) An excellent-value guesthouse that's drawn glowing reader reviews. The neat rooms are comfortable, but the bathrooms are shower only. There is wheelchair access to all rooms and the pool area.

Windsor Hotel (Map p199; ☎ 028-312 3727; www .windsorhotel.co.za; 49 Marine Dr; s/d incl breakfast from R650/900) An old stalwart situated on an oceanside cliff; naturally you'll want one of the more-expensive sea-facing rooms that give you the opportunity to view whales without leaving your bed.

COASTAL ROUTE TO HERMANUS

Hugging False Bay, Rte 44 (Map p186) from Cape Town runs through Strand and towards Hermanus around Cape Hangklip. It's a thrilling coastal drive, the best of it between Gordon's Bay and Kleinmond, and the views are stunning. At times it feels as if the road is going to disappear into the sea. On one side is blue-green water, on the other are rock-strewn cliffs.

At **Stony Point**, just before you reach the small, scattered holiday village of Betty's Bay, take a short stroll to the lookout point to see a colony of **African penguins**. It's very picturesque with crashing waves and a sea of black-and-white birds. In Betty's Bay itself you'll find the **Harold Porter National Botanical Gardens** (☎ 028-272 9311; adult/child R8/4; ☽ 8am-4.30pm Mon-Fri, 8am-5pm Sat & Sun, until 7pm Dec & Jan), which are definitely worth visiting. There are paths exploring the indigenous plant life in the area and, at the entrance, tearooms and a formal garden where you can picnic. Try the Leopard Kloof Trail, which leads through fern forests and up to a waterfall. It's a 3km round trip, and you'll need to pay a key deposit (R30) and get your key and permit from the main ticket office before 2pm. Coming from Cape Town, look for the turn-off to the gardens after driving through Betty's Bay.

A little further on, by a wild and beautiful beach, is **Kleinmond**. After a recent revival this little town is now rather chic, and is a great place to spend an afternoon, eat some fresh seafood and browse in the art gallery and little shops. The area also has some reliable swells for surfers and some good walking.

WATCHING WHALES

As much as you might prepare for it (and most people who come to Hermanus pack a good sunhat and a pair of binoculars), the first time you see a whale you still don't quite believe it. All you do is stand on the edge of a cliff and look seaward. Suddenly, you spot a shape. You ask yourself if that could be it. And then, just when you think it must be nothing, a graceful, barnacle-bedecked beast leaps from the water and returns with a huge splash. Only the soulless or extremely jaded would fail to be moved.

Still, for years the people of Hermanus either took the seasonal arrival of the whales for granted or sensibly kept it secret. Between June and November, there can be up to 70 whales in the bay at once as southern right whales *(Eubalaena australis)* come to Walker Bay to calve. Humpback whales *(Megaptera novaeangliae)* are also sometimes seen.

The tourism potential of this phenomenon has since been recognised, however, and just about every business in town has adopted a whale logo. There's even a **whale crier** (☎ 073-214 6949), who walks around town blowing on a kelp horn and carrying a blackboard that shows where whales have been recently sighted, and the **Hermanus Whale Festival** held in September.

Thankfully, how whales are viewed remains strictly regulated. No boat viewing is allowed in the bay and jet skis are banned. There are only two licensed boat-based operators in Hermanus: **Southern Right Charters** (☎ 082 353 0550) and **Hermanus Whale Cruises** (☎ 028-313 2722). Each charges around R400 for a one- to two-hour trip.

Don't be put off by the popularity. If you can forget the land mammals around you and focus on those out at sea, this natural show can be strangely peaceful amid all the hoopla.

Auberge Burgundy (Map p199; ☎ 028-313 1202; www.hermanus.co.za/accom/auberge; 16 Harbour Rd; s/d incl breakfast R735/980; 🐕) This is a wonderful place, built in the style of a Provençal villa, with fine facilities, wrought-iron balconies and unique art on the walls.

Marine Hermanus (Map p199; ☎ 028-313 1000; www.marine-hermanus.com; Marine Dr; s/d incl breakfast from R1700/2800; 🐕 🖥 🐕) Right on the sea with immaculate grounds and amenities, this place is as posh as a five-star hotel should be. The staff are very friendly and will help you out with what you're looking for – sea views or rooms with balconies. The hotel has two restaurants, both facing the sea, open for dinner only. One serves nouveau South African cuisine (two/three courses R155/195) and the other light seafood lunches (R95) with a view.

GANSBAAI

Rustic and blissfully undeveloped, Gansbaai's star has risen in recent years thanks to the somewhat controversial activity of shark-cage diving. But there's more to the town than baiting marine predators. It boasts a sparkling coastline perfect for those wishing to explore more out-of-the-way Overberg spots. The town is also the nexus of the Danger Point Peninsula area, which includes Kleinbaai. It's here where you'll find most amenities and activities.

Naturally, **whale-watching** and **shark-cage diving** are big draws, but most tour operators are based in Hermanus (see p201 and p153).

Danger Point Lighthouse, dating to 1895, is worth a visit, as is the **Walker Bay Nature Reserve**. This offers excellent walks, such as the Duiwelgat and Fynbos Hiking Trails, and bird-watching, along with the Klipgat caves, site of a recent archaeological discovery of Khoisan artefacts. Tour company iKhaya Laba Thembu offers trips through **Masakhane township**, where handmade products are on sale and traditional Xhosa food can be ordered and eaten in the shade of milkwood trees.

At the time of writing, construction was underway on sealing the road between Gansbaai and Elim, part of the exciting Fynbos Rd project that will link Danger Point Peninsula with Cape Agulhas. Seven kilometres off the Danger Point coast is **Dyer Island**, a breeding colony for African penguins.

TRANSPORT

Distance from Cape Town to Gansbaai 175km
Direction Southeast
Travel time 2½ hours
Car From Cape Town follow the N2 or Rte 44 (coastal road) to Hermanus, then drive through the town before taking Rte 43 past De Kelders into Gansbaai. **Trevis Tours** (☎ 072 608 9213) offers daily shuttles to Hermanus (R50, 30 minutes) and Cape Town (R180, two hours).

THE TIP OF AFRICA

While it's tempting to see Cape Point on the Cape Peninsula as the southernmost spot in Africa, that title in fact goes to **Cape Agulhas** (Map p186), located just past the neat village of L'Agulhas, 2½ hours from Cape Town down Rte 317. Early Portuguese seafarers rounding this dangerous stony strip of coastline called the area Agulhas, Portuguese for 'Needles', when they noticed their compass needle showed no variation.

On a stormy day the low, shattered rocks and crashing seas can be atmospheric, and you can take a snap of your loved one next to a plaque officially denoting the place's claim to fame. Otherwise, there's no real reason to linger longer than it takes to peek at the nearby **lighthouse** (☎ 028-435 6222; adult/child R6/3; ☽ 9am-4.15pm Mon-Sat, 9am-2pm Sun). Built in 1848 in Pharos style, this is the second-oldest lighthouse in South Africa. If you're peckish, the **tearoom** (☎ 028-435 7506; light meals R20-30) here isn't bad, serving reasonably priced meals and snacks.

Sights & Information

Danger Point Lighthouse (☎ 021-449 2400)

Dyer Island Cruises (☎ 028-384 0406; Kleinbaai) This company does trips to the penguin colony of Dyer Island, and boat-based whale-watching.

Gansbaai Tourism (☎ 028-384 1439; www.danger-peninsula.co.za; cnr Main & Berg Rds; ☽ 9am-5pm Mon-Fri, 9am-2pm Sat) Located on the main road into town, this small but efficient office can point you in the direction of good dining and shark diving.

iKhaya Laba Thembu (☎ 072 218 0742) There is no office in town; just call.

Walker Bay Nature Reserve (☎ 028-384 0111)

Sleeping & Eating

Gansbaai Backpackers (☎ 028-384 0641; gansbaaibackpackers@yahoo.com; 6 Strand St; dm R75, s/d with shared bathroom R140/220) Efficient and friendly, this is a great place to start for either budget accommodation or tour and activity bookings.

Aire del Mar (☎ 028-384 2848; info@airedelmar.co.za; 77 Van Dyk St, Kleinbaai; s/d incl breakfast R350/580; ☐) Offers a good range of prices, including basic self-catering units for backpackers (R200) and stylish rooms with panoramic sea views out to Dyer Island. It also serves a filling breakfast (R45).

Die Buitesteen (☎ 028-384 0601; 3 Dover St, De Kelders; mains R40; ☽ 10am-2am Mon-Sun) A pub, its walls bedecked with perlemoen (abalone) shells, that captures the laid-back ethos of Gansbaai. Thus, it's a perennial favourite with backpackers and local fishermen alike.

Great White House (☎ 028-384 3273; 5 Geelbek St; s/d incl breakfast R300/600, mains R35-70; ☽ breakfast & lunch year-round, dinner Mon-Sun 15 Dec-15 Jan) A multifarious place that dishes up fresh seafood, clothing, curios, helps with tour information and offers three-star accommodation. It can also arrange pickups to the restaurant from your hotel.

GREYTON & GENADENDAL

The neighbouring villages of Greyton and Genadendal are among the most pleasant in the Overberg region. Somewhat twee and polished, the whitewashed, thatched-roof cottages of Greyton may be a bit artificial but they are becoming very popular with Capetonians on the lookout for a relaxing country retreat. In contrast Genadendal, the oldest mission station in South Africa, founded in 1738, couldn't be more authentic. It's not manicured and is still home to a predominantly coloured community.

Greyton, with plenty of accommodation, comes into its own as a base for **hiking** in the Riviersonderendberge, which rise up in Gothic majesty immediately to the village's north. Apart from the **Boesmanskloof Trail** (below), there are several shorter walks, as well as the two-day **Genadendal Trail** for the serious hiker. This is a 25.3km circular route that begins and ends at Genadendal's Moravian Church; for more details pick up the *Cape Nature Conservation* leaflet at **Greyton's Tourist Information Office**.

Some 3km west of Greyton, Genadendal was, for a brief time, the largest settlement in the colony after Cape Town. Entering the village from Rte 406, head down Main Rd until you arrive at the cluster of national monuments around Church Sq. The **Moravian Church** is a handsome, simply decorated building; opposite you'll find the **Genadendal Tourist Information Centre**. There's a café here selling homemade bread and souvenirs, including pottery.

The village's fascinating history is documented in the fine **Genadendal Mission Museum** based in what was South Africa's first teacher training college. Elsewhere in this historic precinct is a **printing press**, one of the oldest in the country and still in operation, and a **water mill**.

Sights & Information

Genadendal Mission Museum (☎ 028-251 8582; adult/child R8/4; ⏱ 9am-1pm & 2-5pm Mon-Thu, 9am-3.30pm Fri, 9am-1pm Sat)

Genadendal Tourist Information Centre (☎ 028-251 8291; ⏱ 8.30am-5pm Mon-Fri, 10am-1pm Sat)

Greyton Tourist Information Office (☎ 028-254 9414; info@greyton.net; ⏱ 10am-noon & 2.30-4.30pm Mon-Sat) On the village's main road.

Sleeping & Eating

Post House (☎ 028-254 9995; fax 028-254 9920; 24 Main Rd; d incl breakfast from R400) Based in the town's historic former post house and set around a pretty garden, rooms are named after Beatrix Potter characters (yes, Greyton is twee). Its English-style pub (mains R60),

BOESMANSKLOOF TRAIL

The Boesmanskloof Trail, administered by **Cape Nature Conservation** (www.capenature.org.za; 1-day tour adult/child R20/10, 2-day tour R60/46), runs for roughly 15km through the spectacular *fynbos*-clad Riviersonder-endberge between Greyton and Die Galg, 15km south of McGregor. The trail takes between four and six hours one way, making an overnight stay in Greyton the preferred option. Alternatively you can stay at **Whipstock Farm** (☎ 023-625 1733; www.whipstock.za.net; s/d R295/590) at the Die Galg end of the trail, 7km from McGregor. The friendly hosts will organise transfers to and from the trail head. At Die Galg you'll notice that the start of the trail marks the end of a long-abandoned project to construct a pass across the range. Only 50 people per day are allowed on the trail, so it's best to book in advance, especially for weekends and during the holidays; make inquiries with the Cape Nature Conservation desk at Cape Town Tourism (p219) or go to the **Greyton Municipal Offices** (☎ 028-254 9620).

TRANSPORT

Distance from Cape Town to Greyton 148km
Direction East
Travel time Two hours
Car From Cape Town follow the N2 to just before Caledon, then take Rte 406, which brings you to the Genadendal turnoff; 3km further along is Greyton.

the Ball & Bass, is a wonderfully atmospheric spot for a drink or meal.

Guinea Fowl (☎ 028-254 9550; jpagencies@telkomsa .net; cnr DS Botha & Oak Sts; s/d incl breakfast from R350/500; ⍰) Comfortable and quiet, this guesthouse has a pool for summer, log fire for winter and good breakfasts year-round.

High Hopes B&B (☎ /fax 028-254 9898; 89 Main Rd; d incl breakfast from R580) Readers love this place, and it's easy to see why: tastefully furnished rooms, lovely gardens with a beautiful koi pond, and a well-stocked library. There's now also a Healing Energy Centre offering massages and other treatments to get you back on track. Convenient for hikers, it's the closest B&B to the start of the Boesmanskloof Trail.

Greyton Lodge (☎ 028-254 9800; www.greytonlodge .com; 46 Main Rd; s/d incl breakfast R500/700; ⍰) An upmarket, gay-friendly hotel in the old police station. Catch the live crooners in the garden terrace from 5pm on Friday. There's a pool and a reasonably priced but unadventurous bistro (mains from R50 to R70; open from 7pm till 9pm).

Rosie's Restaurant (☎ 028-254 9640; 9 High St; mains from R40; ⏱ dinner) The house specialities at this unpretentious place are wood-fired pizzas (which are delicious and huge) and steaks.

Oak & Vigne Café (☎ 028-254 9037; DS Botha St; mains R50; ⏱ breakfast & lunch) Evidence of the gentrification of Greyton is this trendy deli-art gallery-café, which is a fine place to grab a snack, chill out and watch the world go by.

LANGEBAAN & WEST COAST NATIONAL PARK

Its beautiful and unusual location overlooking a lagoon has made Langebaan a favourite holiday destination with Capetonians. As such, the town suffers from a number of poorly conceived property developments (such as the Club Mykonos resort), so if you're looking for untouched scenery you might be happier elsewhere. That said, Langebaan does support the excellent Farmhouse hotel, and has open-air seafood restaurants, phenomenal sunset views, superb sailing and windsurfing on the lagoon and a few good beaches, the best of which is **Langebaan beach**, located in town and a favourite with swimmers.

The town is also the best base for exploring the **West Coast National Park**, 7km south of Langebaan. Encompassing the clear blue waters of the lagoon, home to an enormous number of migratory wading birds, the park covers around 18,000 hectares. It protects wetlands of international significance and important sea-bird breeding colonies. The wading birds flock here by the thousands in the summer. The most numerically dominant species is the delicate-looking curlew sandpiper, which migrates north from the sub-Antarctic in huge flocks. Flamingos, Cape gannets, crowned cormorants, numerous gull species and African black oystercatchers are also among the hordes. The offshore islands are home to colonies of African penguins.

The vegetation is predominantly made up of stunted bushes, sedges and many flowering annuals and succulents. There are some coastal *fynbos* in the east, and the park is famous for its wild-flower display, which is usually between August and October. Several animal species can be seen in the part of the park known as the Postberg section, which is open from August to September. Species include a variety of small antelopes, wildebeests, bonteboks and elands.

Note that the roads in the park are unsealed and can be quite heavily corrugated. The return trip from Langebaan to the northern end of the Postberg section is more than 80km; allow yourself plenty of time.

Another place to visit while you're up here is the **West Coast Fossil Park** on Rte 45, about 16km northeast of Langebaan. The first bear discovered south of the Sahara, lion-sized sabre-toothed cats, three-toed horses and short-necked giraffes are all on display here. Tours to the excavation sites depart daily at 11.30am. Children can sieve for their own fossils in a special display area.

Dominated by an enormous iron-ore pier, navy yards and fish-processing factories is **Saldanha**, at the northern end of the same lagoon that Langebaan sits on. Despite this, the town's bays are pleasant and, because they are sheltered, much warmer than the ocean. **Hoedjies Bay**, near the town centre, is the most popular for swimming.

See p155 for details of horse riding and p158 for details of windsurfing in the area.

TRANSPORT

Distance from Cape Town to Langebaan 127km
Direction North
Travel time 90 minutes
Car Follow Rte 27 from Cape Town.
Bus West Coast Shuttle (☎ 083 556 1777) runs a minibus service (R60) from Cape Town to Club Mykonos.
Shared taxi There are minibus taxi services from the commercial hub of Vredenburg (R17, 30 minutes).
Air charters Life Out There (☎ 082 413 6149; www .lifeoutthere.co.za) offers aeroplane, microlight and chopper transfers from Cape Town; trips (per flight R2000) in the three-seater crafts last an hour.

Sights & Activities

Langebaan Tourist Information Centre (☎ 022-772 1515; www.langebaaninfo.com; Bree St; ✆ 9am-5pm Mon-Fri, 9am-1pm Sat & Sun)

West Coast Fossil Park (☎ 022-766 1606; www.museums .org.za/wcfp; adult/child/pensioner/family R25/12/18/60; ✆ 9am-4pm Mon-Fri, 10am-noon Sat & Sun)

West Coast National Park (☎ 022-772 2144; nonflower/ flower season R20/30; ✆ 7am-7.30pm Apr-Sep, 6am-8pm Oct-Mar)

Sleeping & Eating

Oliphantskop Farm Inn (☎ /fax 022-772 2326; Main Rd; s/d R180/300; ⓟ ⓡ) An attractive place around 3km from town, across the road from the Mykonos resort complex. Oliphantskop's restaurant has a good reputation and nice ambience – cool and dark with rough white walls and a wooden ceiling. The menu (mains R50) is meat and seafood oriented and offers no vegetarian options.

Farmhouse (☎ 022-772 2062; www.thefarmhouse langebaan.co.za; 5 Egret St; s/d incl breakfast R575/

850; ⓧ) This is by far Langebaan's best hotel, on a hill overlooking the bay. Rooms are large, with country décor, their own fireplaces and lovely sunset views. For such a classy place the restaurant is reasonably priced (mains R50 to R80), offering a creative menu and a rustic, intimate dining room.

Club Mykonos (☎ 0800 226 770; theretha@clubmykonos .co.za; 4-person cabins R1550; ⓟ ⓧ ⓛ ⓡ) A major resort geared towards families, as there is plenty here to entertain the kids, but its Greek-themed pseudo-Mediterranean architecture and crowds mean you'll either love it or hate it. There are six outdoor swimming pools, a casino, several restaurants and an arcade.

Die Strandloper (☎ 022-772 2490; buffet R150; ✆ lunch & dinner) The West Coast life exemplified – a *ten*-course fish and seafood braai right on the beach. All food is succulent and delicious; our favourites were the snoek (a mackerel-like fish) and mussels cooked in white wine. There's also freshly made bread, bottomless *moerkoffie* (freshly ground coffee) and a local crooner who plays ballads at your table. You can BYO (no corkage) or get drinks from the rustic bar. Bookings essential; call for availability between June and August.

PATERNOSTER

Paternoster, a clutch of simple whitewashed homes with green roofs against the blue sea, sparkles in the sun and is a feast for the eyes. This sleepy fishing village apparently got its name (Latin for 'Our Father') after the locals rescued shipwrecked Portuguese sailors, who gave their thanks with prayer.

It's a low-key kind of place with fishing as its lifeblood – although, as in Kalk Bay, the industry has recently been hit hard by the government decision to cut back on fishing licences. As the locals become impoverished, wealthy Capetonians looking for holiday houses have moved in. Property is now a hot commodity – there are sold signs left and right and new guesthouses are opening every day.

The surrounding countryside is attractive and the rolling hills are scattered with strange granite outcrops. The **Cape Columbine Nature Reserve**, located 3km past the town, protects 263 hectares of coastal *fynbos* around Cape Columbine. Further north along the coast is the similar village of **St Helena Bay**, offering a lovely sheltered stretch of water but no beach to speak of.

Paternoster is rather lacking in street signs, instead look out for the individual guesthouse signs. There are many B&Bs, so it may be worth checking out a few places first. During crayfish season (mid-November to late December) you will see the tasty crustaceans for sale on the side of the road for between R50 and R70.

Sights

Cape Columbine Nature Reserve (☎ 022-752 2718; adult/child R9/6; ☒ 7am-7pm)

Sleeping & Eating

Paternoster Hotel (☎ /fax 022-752 2703; paternosterhotel@wol.co.za; s/d R220/440) This rough-edged, lively country hotel is a popular venue for those interested in fishing. Its graffiti-covered walls, and fish and crayfish braais are famous. We warn you, the bar is a feminist's nightmare.

Cape Columbine (☎ 021-449 2400; salato@npa.co.za; cottages from R525) Three kilometres past the town, you can stay in neat self-catering cottages next to the lighthouse (admission R12) in the Cape Columbine Nature Reserve. Further on there's a superbly located but windy camping and caravan park (☎ 022-752 1718; Tietiesbaai; camp sites R30).

TRANSPORT

Distance from Cape Town to Paternoster 156km
Direction North
Travel time 2½ hours
Car From Cape Town follow Rte 27 to its junction with Rte 45, turn left and continue through Vredenburg to the coast.

Paternoster Lodge (☎ 022-752 2023; paterlodge@telkomsa.net; s/d R560/700) A slick enterprise, with seven tidy, minimalist rooms and a breezy restaurant (mains R50 to R70) open all day. From the sun deck you can watch the fishermen bringing in their catch.

Voorstrandt Restaurant (☎ 022-752 2038; Strandloperweg; mains R40-95; ☒ breakfast, lunch & dinner) You can hop from this designer red-and-green-painted beach shack right onto the sand. It specialises in seafood, and is an excellent spot from which to watch the sunset over a beer.

Excursions

PATERNOSTER

THE OLIVE ROUTE

The Cape's olive-growing industry is drawing some attention away from the region's famous grapes to this similarly sized but radically different (and highly versatile) fruit. Olive-lovers will be pleased to know that many farms now offer tours and tastings, and a fully fledged 'Olive Route' is on the cards. Many farms are open to the public and are spread throughout the Overberg area. The most popular are found in the farming areas between Robertson, McGregor and Hermanus (see Map p186).

Notables include **Olyfberg** (☎ 023-342 5096; Robertson), which offers tours of its processing plant along with olive and olive-oil tastings, while **Rheebokskraal Estate** (☎ 023-625 1951; McGregor) sells olive pâté and delicious dried olives in brine with rosemary and garlic. It's also worth visiting **Olive Grove** (☎ 023-626 1961; Robertson) to see its memorial olive-tree garden dedicated to the victims of HIV/AIDS.

Also check out Hildenbrand Wine & Olive Estate (p197) near Wellington.

DARLING

Named after Lieutenant Governor Charles Henry Darling and founded in 1853, Darling was a quiet country town best known for its good-quality milk until actor and satirist Pieter-Dirk Uys, along with his alter ego Evita Bezuidenhout (see the boxed text, p146), set up stall here. It might be best to first head to **Tourist Information**, but as most Capetonians make the 75km trek north to catch the uniquely South African cabaret at **Evita se Perron**, this is as good a place as any to start. Here, you can also visit the onsite (and splendidly kitsch) coffee shop serving traditional Afrikaans treats, or 'Boerassic Park', a quaint **sculpture garden**.

Don't forget to ask Tourist Information or your guesthouse about the underrated **Darling Wine Experience**, the collective name for the four estates in the vicinity.

Sights & Information

Evita se Perron (Evita's Platform; ☎ 022-492 2851; www.evita.co.za; tickets R90; ☷ performances 2pm & 8pm Sat, 2pm Sun)

Tourist Information (☎ 022-492 3361; cnr Hill Rd & Pastorie St; ☷ 9am-1pm & 2-4pm Mon-Thu, 9am-1pm & 2-3.30pm Fri, 10am-3pm Sat & Sun)

Sleeping & Eating

Granary (☎ 022-492 3155; 5 Long St; s/d incl breakfast from R300/440) A neat guesthouse with lots of light and windows that make the big rooms feel especially spacious. Breakfast is enough to fill you up for the day. The place welcomes children, though the rooms are up steep wooden steps so not for the frail.

Trinity (☎ 022-492 3430; 19 Long St; s/d incl breakfast from R270/500; ☒) A painstakingly renovated Victorian homestead with cosy country-style bedrooms where you can try a selection of homemade toiletries. There's also a country-cuisine restaurant (mains R50) that's been voted one of the country's top 100.

Darling Guest Lodge (☎ 022-492 3062; 22 Pastorie St; s/d incl breakfast R360/540; ☒) An elegant and imaginatively decorated place, one of the first in the area.

Marmalade Cat (☎ 082 448 9298; 19 Main Rd; breakfast R30; ☷ 10am-4pm Mon-Fri, 10am-1pm Sat) A hippy-style café with Internet connection (R40 per hour) that also serves sandwiches, delicious cheeses and homemade sweet treats. It also serves up tasty pizzas on Friday nights.

Directory ∎

Directory

TRANSPORT

Flights, tours and rail tickets can all be booked online at www.lonelyplanet.com /travelservices.

AIR

There are many direct international flights into Cape Town, although sometimes you'll have to change planes at Johannesburg (Jo'burg). Useful online ticket sellers include the following:

Cheap Flights (www.cheapflights.co.uk)

Flight Centre (www.flightcentre.com)

STA Travel (www.statravel.com)

Travel.com.au (www3.travel.com.au/home.html)

Zuji (www.zuji.com)

Airlines

Air Mauritius (Map pp246–7; ☎ 021-671 5225; www .airmauritius.com; Sanclaire Bldg, 21 Dreyer St, Claremont)

Air Namibia (Map pp244–5; ☎ 021-936 2755; www .airnamibia.com.na; Cape Town International Airport)

British Airways (Map pp244–5; ☎ in Jo'burg 011-4418600; www.ba.com)

KLM (Map pp246–7; ☎ 0860 247 747; www.klm.co.za; Slade House, Boundary Terraces, 1 Mariendahl Lane, Newlands)

Lufthansa (Map pp244–5; ☎ 0861 842 538; Cape Town International Airport)

Malaysia Airlines (Map pp248–9; ☎ 021-419 8010; fax 021-419 7017; 8th fl, Safmarine House, 22 Riebeeck St, City Bowl)

SAA (Map pp244–5; ☎ 021-936 1111; www.flysaa.com; Cape Town International Airport)

DOMESTIC FLIGHTS

It's cheaper to book and pay for domestic flights within South Africa on the Internet. Apart from SAA, there are two budget airlines operating out of Cape Town: **Kulula.com** (☎ 0861 585 852; www.kulula .com) and **1time** (☎ 0861 345 345; www.1time .co.za). All three fly to the major South African cities.

Singapore Airlines (Map pp246–7; ☎ 021-674 0601; 3rd fl, Sanclaire Bldg, 21 Dreyer St, Claremont)

Virgin Atlantic (Map pp244–5; ☎ 021-934 9000; Cape Town International Airport)

Airport

Cape Town International Airport (Map pp244–5; ☎ 021-937 1200; www.airports.co.za) is located 20km east of the city centre. There is a tourist information office and Internet access in both the international and domestic departure/arrival halls.

BICYCLE

The Cape Peninsula is a terrific place to explore by bicycle, but there are many hills, and distances can be deceptively large – it is nearly 70km from the centre to Cape Point. Unfortunately, you are not supposed to take bicycles on suburban trains.

The following places in Cape Town offer bicycle hire:

Atlantic Tourist Information Centre (Map p255; ☎ 021-434 2382; 243 Main Rd, Sea Point; bicycle/scooter per day R85/195)

Cape Info Africa (Map pp248–9; ☎ 021-425 6461; www.capeinfoafrica.co.za; 32 Napier St, Waterkant; per day R85)

Downhill Adventures (Map p254; ☎ 021-422 0388; www.downhilladventures.com; Orange St, Gardens; per day R100)

Homeland Shuttle & Tours (Map pp248–9; ☎ 021-426 0294, 083 265 6661; www.homeland.co.za; 305 Long St, City Bowl; per day R80)

BUS

Interstate buses arrive at the bus terminus (Map pp248–9) at Cape Town Train Station, where you'll find the booking offices for the following bus companies:

Greyhound (☎ 021-505 6363; www.greyhound.co.za)

Intercape Mainliner (☎ 021-380 4400; www.intercape .co.za)

SA Roadlink (☎ 021-425 0203; www.saroadlink.co.za)

Translux (☎ 021-449 3333; www.translux.co.za)

GETTING INTO TOWN

Both **Backpacker Bus** (☎ 021-447 4991, 082 809 9185; www.backpackerbus.co.za) and **Homeland Shuttle & Tours** (☎ 021-426 0294, 083 265 6661; www.homeland.co.za) pick up from hostels and hotels in the city and offer airport transfers for R90 per person (R120 between 5pm and 8am).

Expect to pay around R200 for a nonshared taxi; the officially authorised airport taxi company is **Touch Down Taxis** (☎ 021-919 4659). If there are four of you, consider making a booking with **Rikkis** (☎ 021-418 6713; www.rikkis.co.za; ⏰ 7am-7pm Mon-Fri, 8am-4pm Sat), which charges R125 for hire of its tiny minivan cabs.

All the major car-hire companies (see p210) have desks at the airport. Driving along the N2 into the city centre from the airport usually takes 15 to 20 minutes, although during rush hours (7am to 9am and 4.30pm to 6.30pm) this can extend up to an hour. There is a petrol station just outside the airport, handy for refilling before drop-off.

Baz Bus (☎ 021-439 2323; www.bazbus.com) is aimed at backpackers and travellers, offering hop-on, hop-off fares and door-to-door service between Cape Town and Jo'burg via the Northern Drakensberg, Durban and the Garden Route.

For local bus services the main station is the **Golden Acre Terminal** (Map pp248–9; Grand Parade, City Bowl). From this station **Golden Arrow** (☎ 0800 656 463; www.gabs .co.za) buses run, with most services stopping early in the evening. Buses are most useful for getting along the Atlantic coast from the city centre to Hout Bay (trains service the suburbs to the east of Table Mountain).

When travelling short distances, most people wait at the bus stop and take either a bus or a shared taxi, whichever arrives first. A tourist-friendly alternative is the City Sightseeing Cape Town bus service (p81).

Bus Tickets

Destinations and off-peak fares (applicable from 8am to 4pm) from the city include the Waterfront (R3), Sea Point (R3), Kloof Nek (R3), Camps Bay (R4.50) and Hout Bay (R7). Peak fares are about 30% higher. If you're using a particular bus regularly, it's worth buying 'clipcards', with 10 discounted trips.

CAR & MOTORCYCLE
Buying a Car

Cape Town is a very pleasant place to spend the week or two that it will inevitably take to buy a car. Many used-car dealers are clustered along Voortrekker Rd/R102 (Map pp244–5) starting around Koeberg Rd and extending east for about 10km. A reputable one is **Wayne Motors** (Map pp244–5; ☎ 021-510 2228; wancars@mweb.co.za). It'll guarantee a buy-back price.

You might be thinking of getting a 4WD for a trans-Africa trip – Series 1, 2 and 3 Land Rovers cost from R15,000 to R40,000 depending on their condition. A recommended contact in Cape Town is Land Rover expert **Graham Duncan Smith** (☎ 021-797 3048); he charges a consultation fee of R120 and R165 per hour for engineering work.

Dealers have to make a profit, so you'll pay less if you buy privately. The weekly classified-ads paper **Cape Ads** (www.capeads .com) is the best place to look. Another useful website is www.autotrader.co.za. A good car costs about R25,000; you'll be lucky to find a decent vehicle for much less than R15,000. Really cheap cars are often sold without a roadworthy certificate. This certificate is required when you pay tax for a licence disk, and register the change-of-ownership form.

Whoever you're buying a car from, make sure the car's details correspond accurately with those on the ownership (registration) papers, that there is a *current* licence disk on the windscreen and that there's police clearance on the vehicle. The police clearance department can be contacted on ☎ 021-945 3891. Consider getting the car tested by an independent garage: try **Same Garage** (Map p255 ☎ 021-434 1058; 309 Main Rd, Sea Point). A full test can cost up to R500; less-detailed tests are around R200.

To register your newly purchased car, present yourself along with the roadworthy, a current licence disk, an accurate ownership certificate, a completed change-of-ownership form (signed by the seller), a clear photocopy of your ID (passport), along with the original, and your money to the City Treasurer's Department, **Motor Vehicle Registration Division** (Map pp248–9; ☎ 021-400 4900; Civic Centre, Foreshore; ⏰ 8am-2pm Mon-Fri).

CLIMATE CHANGE & TRAVEL

Climate change is a serious threat to the ecosystems that humans rely upon, and air travel is the fastest-growing contributor to the problem. Lonely Planet regards travel, overall, as a global benefit, but believes we all have a responsibility to limit our personal impact on global warming.

Flying & Climate Change

Pretty much every form of motorised travel generates carbon dioxide (CO_2; the main cause of human-induced climate change), but planes are far and away the worst offenders, not just because of the sheer distances they allow us to travel, but because they release greenhouse gases high into the atmosphere. The statistics are frightening: two people taking a return flight between Europe and the US will contribute as much to climate change as an average household's gas and electricity consumption over a whole year.

Carbon Offset Schemes

Climatecare.org and other websites use 'carbon calculators', which allow travellers to offset the level of greenhouse gases they are responsible for with financial contributions to sustainable-travel schemes that reduce global warming – including projects in India, Honduras, Kazakhstan and Uganda.

Lonely Planet, together with Rough Guides and other concerned partners in the travel industry, support the carbon offset scheme run by Climatecare.org. Lonely Planet offsets all of its staff and author travel.

For more information check out our website: www.lonelyplanet.com.

Insurance for third-party damages and damage to or loss of your vehicle is a very good idea as repairs are horrendously expensive. Recommended insurance agents include **African Independent Brokers** (☎ 086 100 1002) and **Lions Head Insurance Brokers** (☎ 021-761 8332).

Driving & Parking

Cape Town has an excellent road and freeway system that, outside the morning and early-evening rush hours (7am to 9pm and 4.30pm to 6.30pm), carries surprisingly little traffic. Road signs alternate between Afrikaans and English. You'll soon learn, for example, that Linkerbaan isn't the name of a town – it means 'left lane'.

Petrol stations are often open 24 hours; a useful petrol station **Engen** (Map p254; cnr Annandale Rd & Hatfield St, Gardens), has a Woolworths convenience store attached. Petrol costs around R4.10 per litre, depending on the octane level you choose. Not all petrol stations accept credit cards and of those that do, some will charge you a fee, typically 10%, to do so. An attendant will always fill up your tank for you, clean your windows and ask if the oil or water needs checking – you should tip them 10% for the service.

When parking on the streets in the City Bowl you won't miss the official parking marshals in their yellow vests. You can either buy a stored-value parking card (R30) from these guys, from which the parking fee is deducted each time (R3.50 for 30 minutes) or pay the charge directly. There will often be a one-hour limit on parking within the city centre in a particular spot. This system is also in use in other parts of Cape Town. Otherwise you'll almost always find someone on the street to tip a small amount (say R2) in exchange for looking after your car – it's certainly a good idea to pay the street guys when parking anywhere at night. Charges for off-street parking vary, but you can find it for R10 per day.

Hazards

Be prepared for the sometimes-erratic breaking of road rules by fellow drivers, and drive with caution. Breath testing for alcohol exists but given the lack of police resources and the high blood-alcohol level permitted (0.08%), drunk drivers remain a danger. It's highly unlikely that the police will bother you for petty breaches of the law, such as breaking the speed limit. This might sound like a pleasant state of affairs, but after you've encountered a few dangerous drivers, strict cops seem more attractive.

Hire

Major local and international car-hire companies in Cape Town include the following:

Avis (Map pp248–9; ☎ 086 102 1111; www.avis.co.za; 123 Strand St, City Bowl)

Budget (Map pp248–9; ☎ 086 001 6622; www.budget .co.za; 120 Strand St, City Bowl)

Hertz (Map pp248–9; ☎ 021-400 9650; www.hertz .co.za; cnr Loop & Strand Sts, City Bowl)

A friendly local firm is **Around About Cars** (Map pp248–9; ☎ 021-422 4022; www.around aboutcars.com; 20 Bloem St, City Bowl; ⏱ 7.30am-5pm Mon-Fri, 7.30am-noon Sat & Sun). This company offers one of the best independent deals in town with rates starting at R169 per day for a Mazda 323 with a R4000 excess on any claims (R210 for no excess). Many backpacker hostels can also arrange deals from around R200 per day or less.

South Africa is a big country but, unless you're a travel writer on a tight schedule, you probably don't need to pay higher rates for unlimited kilometres. For meandering around, 400km a day should be more than enough, and if you plan to stop for a day here and there, 200km a day might be sufficient.

However, if you're hiring with an international company and you book through the branch in your home country, you'll probably get unlimited kilometres at no extra cost. At peak times in South Africa (mainly in summer), even your local branch might tell you that unlimited-kilometre deals aren't available. Your travel agency may be able to get around this.

When you're getting quotes make sure that they include value-added tax (VAT), as that 14% slug makes a big difference.

One problem with nearly all car-hire deals is the excess: the amount you are liable for before the insurance takes over. Even with a small car you can be liable for up to R5000 (although there's usually the choice of lowering or cancelling the excess for a higher insurance premium). A few companies offer 100% damage and theft insurance at a more expensive rate. You may also be charged extra if you nominate more than one driver. If a non-nominated driver has an accident, then you won't be covered by insurance. Always make sure you read the contract carefully before you sign.

Motorcycle & Scooter Hire

The following places hire out motorcycles or scooters:

Café Vespa (Map p254; ☎ 083 448 2626, 083 646 6616; www.cafevespa.com; 108 Kloof St, Tamboerskloof; ⏱ 9am-midnight) New 150cc Vespas from R110 per day, including insurance and helmet, depending on how long you hire it for.

Harley-Davidson Cape Town (Map pp248–9; ☎ 021-424 3990; www.harley-davidson-capetown.com; 45 Buitengracht St, City Bowl; ⏱ 9am-5pm Mon-Sat) Hires out a Harley 1340cc Big Twins or an MG-B convertible sports car for R1150 per day.

Le Cap Motorcycle Hire (Map p254; ☎ 021-423 0823; www.lecapmotorcyclehire.co.za; 43 New Church St, Tamboerskloof; ⏱ 9am-5pm Mon-Fri, 10am-1pm Sat) Motorcycle hire from R360 per day.

Toll Roads

It costs R22 to drive along Chapman's Peak Dr (p102).

RIKKI

The tiny minivans called **Rikkis** (☎ 021-418 6713; www.rikkis.co.za; ⏱ 7am-7pm Mon-Fri, 8am-4pm Sat) are a cross between a taxi and a shared taxi. They can be booked or hailed on the street and travel within a 5km radius of the city centre. A single-person trip from the Cape Town Train Station to Tamboerskloof costs R10; to Camps Bay it's R15. A Rikki from the City Bowl to Kirstenbosch Botanical Gardens or Hout Bay costs R70 for the first four people. Rikkis also operate out of Simon's Town (☎ 021-786 2136); they meet all trains to Simon's Town and go to Boulders.

Although cheap, Rikkis may not be the quickest way to get around the city, as there is usually a certain amount of meandering as passengers are dropped off, and they are notoriously slow to turn up to a booking.

TAXI

Consider taking a nonshared taxi at night or if you're in a group. Rates are about R10 per kilometre. There's a taxi rank (Map pp248–9) at the Adderley St end of the Grand Pde in the city, or call **Marine Taxi** (☎ 021-434 0434), **SA Cab** (☎ 0861 172 222; www.sacab.co.za) or **Unicab Taxis** (☎ 021-447 4402).

Shared Taxi

Shared taxis cover most of the city with an informal network of routes. They're a cheap and efficient way of getting around. Useful routes are from Adderley St, opposite the Golden Acre Centre, to Sea Point along Main Rd (R3) and up Long St to Kloof Nek (R2).

The main rank (Map pp248–9) is on the upper deck of Cape Town Train Station and is accessible from a walkway in the Golden Acre Centre or from stairways on Strand St. It's well organised, and finding the right rank is easy. Anywhere else, you just hail shared taxis from the side of the road and ask the driver where they're going.

TRAIN

Metro commuter trains are a handy way to get around, although there are few (or no) trains after 6pm on weekdays and after noon on Saturday. For more information contact **Cape Metro Rail** (☎ 0800 656 463; www.capemetrorail.co.za).

Metro trains have first- and economy-class carriages only. The difference in price and comfort is negligible, though you'll find the first-class compartments to be safer on the whole. The most important line for visitors is the Simon's Town line, which runs through Observatory and around the back of Table Mountain through upper-income white suburbs such as Newlands, on to Muizenberg and the False Bay coast.

These trains run at least every hour from 5am to 7.30pm Monday to Friday (to 6pm on Saturday), and from 7.30am to 6.30pm on Sunday. (Rikkis meet all trains and go to Boulders.) Some trains have Biggsy's, a restaurant carriage and rolling wine bar. There's a small extra charge to use it.

Metro trains run some way out of Cape Town, to Strand on the eastern side of False Bay, and into the Winelands to Stellenbosch and Paarl. They are the cheapest and easiest means of transport to these areas; security is best at peak times.

Some economy/first-class fares are Observatory (R4.20/5.50), Muizenberg (R5.50/8.50), Simon's Town (R7.30/12), Paarl (R8.50/14.50) and Stellenbosch (R7.50/12).

The **African Vintage Rail Tours** (☎ 021-419 5222; www.vintagetrains.co.za) runs occasional trips to the Spier wine estate using a steam locomotive, as well as two-hour sunset train trips to Milnerton.

TRAVEL AGENCIES

Africa Travel Centre (Map p254; ☎ 021-423 5555; www.backpackers.co.za; Backpack, 74 New Church St, Tamboerskloof) Books all sorts of tours and activities, including day trips, hire cars and extended truck tours of Africa.

Atlantic Tourist Information Centre (Map p255; ☎ 021-434 2382; www.arokan.co.za; 242 Main Rd, Sea Point) Gay-run tour company and travel agency.

Flight Centre (www.flightcentre.co.za) Camps Bay (Map p256; ☎ 021-438 3564; the Promenade, Victoria Rd); City Bowl (Map pp248–9; ☎ 021-421 6507; Shop 6, Southern Life Centre, St George's Mall); Gardens (Map p254; ☎ 021-461 8658; Gardens Centre, Mill St); Sea Point (Map p255; ☎ 021-430 3000; Shop 3, Adelphi Centre, 127 Main Rd).

Rennies Travel City Bowl (Map pp248–9; ☎ 021-423 7154; www.renniestravel.co.za; 101 St George's Mall); Sea Point (Map p255; ☎ 021-439 7529; 182 Main Rd); Waterfront (Map pp252–3; ☎ 021-418 3744) Handles international and domestic bookings and is the agency for Thomas Cook travellers cheques. It can arrange visas for neighbouring countries for a moderate charge.

STA Travel (Map p246–7; ☎ 021-686 6800; 14 Main Rd, Rondebosch)

Wanderwomen (☎ 021-788 9988; www.wanderwomen .co.za) Travel agency and tour company run by women.

PRACTICALITIES

ACCOMMODATION

Accommodation listings in the Sleeping chapter are ordered by neighbourhood, then listed in price order. Prices are up to 50% lower from May to October, during Cape Town's winter season. For more information on accommodation, see p172.

Cape Town Tourism (p219) runs an accommodation booking service and it sometimes has special deals. However, like any agency, it only recommends its members.

BUSINESS FACILITIES

Cape Town is one of South Africa's major business centres. Top-end and several mid-range hotels provide business facilities, including conference rooms, private office space and secretarial services. To find out more about business opportunities contact the **Cape Town Regional Chamber of Commerce & Industry** (Map pp248–9; ☎ 021-402 4300; www .caperegionalchamber.co.za; Cape Chamber House, 19 Louis Gradner St, Foreshore; ☼ 8.30am-4.45pm Mon-Fri) or the **city council** (www.capetown.gov.za).

BUSINESS HOURS

Banking hours vary but are usually from 9am to 3.30pm Monday to Friday and 9am to 11am Saturday. Post offices are usually open from 8.30am to 4.30pm Monday to Friday and 8am to noon Saturday.

Most shops are open from 8.30am to 5pm Monday to Friday and 8.30am to 1pm Saturday. Major shopping centres, such as the Waterfront and Canal Walk, are open daily, often to 9pm.

Cafés generally open from 7.30am to around 5pm daily. A few places (more usually in the City Bowl) are closed on Sunday or occasionally Monday. Restaurants open for lunch from 11.30am to 3pm, with dinner usually kicking off around 7pm and last orders at 10pm.

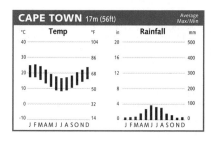

CHILDREN

See p80 for tips on keeping the little ones happy during your time in Cape Town. For more general information pick up a copy of Lonely Planet's *Travel with Children* by Cathy Lanigan.

Baby-Sitting

The following agencies can arrange child minders (from R30 per hour for a minimum of three hours, excluding transport expenses); you'll be charged more (R55 per hour) if you're staying in a five-star hotel.

Childminders (☎ 021-788 6788, 083 254 4683; www.childminders.co.za)

Super Sitters (☎ 021-439 4985; www.supersitters.net)

CLIMATE

Cape Town does not suffer from great extremes of temperature, but it can be relatively cold and wet for a few months in winter, and there's usually one of the Cape's famous winds to contend with (see the boxed text, p23).

Between June and August, temperatures range from 7°C to 18°C with pleasant, sunny days scattered between the gloomy ones. (The wild flowers are at their best during August and September.) From September to November the weather is unpredictable, with anything from bright, warm days to howling southeasterly storms and winds of up to 120km/h. December to March can be very hot, although the average maximum temperature is only 26°C and the Cape doctor generally keeps things bearable. From March to April, and to a lesser extent in May, the weather remains good and the wind is at its most gentle.

For hourly updates on the weather, check www.weathersa.co.za.

CUSTOMS

South Africa, Botswana, Namibia, Swaziland and Lesotho are members of the South African Customs Union, which means that their internal borders are effectively open from a customs point of view. When you enter the union, however, there are the usual duty-free restrictions: you're only allowed to bring in 1L of spirits, 2L of wine and 400 cigarettes. Motor vehicles must be covered by a carnet. For more information, contact the **Department of Customs & Excise** (☎ 012-428 7000) in Pretoria.

DISCOUNT CARDS

You'll save a few rand at Hostelling International South Africa hostels and affiliated hostels with an HI card.

There's no real advantage in having a student card here since student discounts apply only to South African nationals.

If you plan to do lots of sightseeing, purchasing the Cape Town Pass (p92) is a good idea.

ELECTRICITY

The electricity system is 220/230V AC at 50 cycles per second. Appliances rated at 240V AC will work. Plugs have three large round pins. Adaptors can be bought at the camping supply and clothing store Cape Union Mart (p166).

EMBASSIES & CONSULATES

Most foreign embassies are based in Johannesburg (Jo'burg), but a few countries also maintain a consulate in Cape Town. All of the following are consulates, except the Italian office, which is also an embassy. Most are open from 9am to 4pm Monday to Friday.

Botswana (Map pp248–9; ☎ 021-421 1045; 5th fl, Southern Life Centre, 8 Riebeeck St, City Bowl)

Canada (Map pp248–9; ☎ 021-423 5240; www .dfait-maeci.gc.ca/southafrica/cape_town_contact-en.asp; 19th fl, Reserve Bank Bldg, 60 St George's Mall, City Bowl; 🕒 8am-4.45pm Mon-Thu, 8am-1.30pm Fri)

France (Map pp248–9; ☎ 021-423 1575; www.consul france-lecap.org; 2 Dean St, City Bowl)

Germany (Map pp248–9; ☎ 021-464 3020; 74 Queen Victoria St, City Bowl; 🕒 9am-12.30pm Mon-Fri)

Italy (Map pp248–9; ☎ 021-487 3900; 2 Grey's Pass, Queen Victoria St, City Bowl)

Mozambique (Map pp248–9; ☎ 021-426 2944; Pinnacle Bldg, 8 Burg St, City Bowl)

The Netherlands (Map pp248–9; ☎ 021-421 5660; www.dutch-consulate.co.za; 100 Strand St, City Bowl; 🕒 9am-noon Mon-Thu, 9-11am Fri)

UK (Map pp248–9; ☎ 021-405 2400; www.british highcommission.gov.uk; 15th fl, Southern Life Centre, 8 Riebeeck St, City Bowl; 🕒 9am-3pm Mon-Thu, 9am-12.30pm Fri)

US (Map pp244–5; ☎ 021-702 7300; www.southafrica .usembassy.gov; 2 Reddam Ave, Westlake; 🕒 8.30am-12.30pm Mon-Thu)

EMERGENCY

In an emergency call ☎ 107; ☎ 112 if using a mobile phone. Other useful phone numbers include the following:

Ambulance (☎ 10177)

Fire brigade (☎ 021-535 1100)

Mountain Rescue Services (☎ 021-948 9900)

Police (☎ 10111)

Sea Rescue (☎ 021-405 3500)

GAY & LESBIAN TRAVELLERS

Cape Town is an exceedingly glamorous and gay-friendly destination and there are enough dedicated gay bars and clubs in the city's self-proclaimed gay village, the Water-kant, to please even the fussiest of queens. For suggestions of where to go see p138. A few venues along Sea Point's Main Rd (Map p255) also fly the rainbow flag, while the beaches to head for are Clifton No 3 (p102) and Sandy Bay (p102); the clothing-optional stretch of sand is discreetly located near Llandudno Bay.

Further afield, consider visiting Darling, home to Evita se Peron, the cabaret theatre of Pieter-Dirk Uys (see the boxed text, p146). Heading south down the coast there are a couple of gay guesthouses around

Hermanus. Knysna, about 500km east of Cape Town, has made its mark as the gay-est resort town on South Africa's Garden Route. It hosts the annual **Pink Loerie Mardi Gras** (www.pinkloerie.com), four huge days of partying, shows and a street parade in late May. (For detailed information on Knysna and the Garden Route, see Lonely Planet's *South Africa, Lesotho & Swaziland*).

Cape Town's **Triangle Project** (☎ 021-448 3812; www.triangle.org.za) is the city's and South Africa's leading gay, lesbian and transgender resource centre. Its website has a host of useful info. Also handy is the ad-driven *Pink Map*, updated annually and available from Cape Town Tourism and gay venues around the city. The local listings magazine *Cape Etc* has details of gay events. The website www.gaynetcapetown .co.za has information specific to the city; for general information (and a witty read) on the gay scene across South Africa check www.mambaonline.com.

Cape Town's lesbian scene is pretty low profile, although there is a regular lesbian venue in the Waterkant now with Lipstick Lounge (p138) and the biweekly club Lush (p142); check its website, www.lushcape town.co.za, for more news of what's going on for the girls on the Cape.

For more on Cape Town's gay and lesbian scene see p16.

HEALTH

With the exception of AIDS (see the boxed text, opposite), there's no need to worry about health issues when visiting Cape Town. The city's health services are generally excellent (for details of hospitals and clinics see p216). For more information on health in South Africa, read Lonely Planet's *Healthy Travel Africa* and *South Africa, Lesotho & Swaziland*.

HOLIDAYS
Public Holidays

On public holidays government departments, banks, offices, post offices and some museums are closed. Public holidays in South Africa include the following:

New Year's Day 1 January

Human Rights Day 21 March

Easter (Good Friday/Easter Monday) March/April

AIDS IN CAPE TOWN

The statistics make for very grim reading. The Actuarial Society of South Africa reckons that five million South Africans are HIV positive, roughly 11% of the population. Every day around 800 die from HIV/AIDS and it's predicted that there will be upwards of 2.5 million AIDS orphans in South Africa by 2010. The government has rolled out one of the largest public health programmes in the world in relation to HIV, supplying 1.4 million people with medicine – but it comes after years of inaction.

What can you do about this? Firstly make sure you protect yourself while having sex; there's no excuse for not using a condom. You can also buy goods from producers such as Wola Nani (p163) and Monkeybiz (p162), whose projects help support HIV-positive women in the townships.

If you want to help further, contact organisations such as **Nazareth House** (Map p254; ☎ 021-461 1635; www .nazhouse.org.za; 1 Derry St, Vredehoek), which provides a refuge for orphan babies and those that have HIV or have been abandoned or abused; and the **Treatment Action Campaign** (Map p257; ☎ 021-788 3507; www.tac.org.za; 34 Main Rd, Muizenberg) run by the antiapartheid activist Zachie Achmat, who was also nominated for the Nobel peace prize for his stance on not taking antiretroviral medicine until it was free to all under the national health system. There is also a **National AIDS Helpline** (☎ 0800 012 322; www.aidshelpline.org.za).

Family Day 17 April

Constitution Day (Freedom Day) 27 April

Workers' Day 1 May

Youth Day 16 June

Women's Day 9 August

Heritage Day 24 September

Day of Reconciliation 16 December

Christmas Day 25 December

Boxing Day (Day of Goodwill) 26 December

School Holidays

Cape Town experiences a big influx of domestic tourists in the school holidays and accommodation is at a premium. The dates differ slightly from year to year but are roughly from the end of March to early April (two weeks), late June to mid-July (three weeks), late September to early October (about one week), and early December to mid-January (about eight weeks).

INSURANCE

A travel-insurance policy to cover theft, loss and medical problems is a good idea. Although there are excellent private hospitals in South Africa, the public health system is underfunded and overcrowded, and is not free. Services such as ambulances are often run by private enterprise and are expensive. There is a wide variety of policies available, so check the small print. Some policies exclude 'dangerous activities', which can include scuba diving, motorcycling and even trekking. If such activities are on your agenda you don't want such a policy. A locally acquired motorcycle licence is not valid under some policies.

INTERNET ACCESS

Cape Town is one of the most wired cities in Africa. Most hotels and hostels have Internet facilities and you'll seldom have to hunt far for an Internet café. Rates are pretty uniform at R10 per hour. A handy central one, open 24 hours, is **Catwalk TV** (Map pp248–9; ☎ 021-423 8999; www .catwalk.co.za; 16 Burg St, City Bowl).

LEGAL MATTERS

The legal drinking age is 18 years, the same for driving. If your skin colour isn't white, you might receive less-than-courteous treatment if, say, you're pulled over for a traffic violation. A Western passport should fix things quickly, and make sure you have your driving licence on hand too.

The importation and use of illegal drugs is prohibited in South Africa and is punishable with imprisonment.

The age of consent for straight sex is 16 years, for homosexual sex 19 years.

MAPS

Cape Town Tourism offers free maps that will serve most short-term visitors' needs. If you're staying for more than a week or so, and have a car, consider buying Map Studio's *Cape Town & Peninsula Street Guide*.

Directory

PRACTICALITIES

MEDICAL SERVICES

Medical services are of a high standard in Cape Town. In an emergency contact the police (☎10111) to get directions to the nearest hospital. Many doctors make house calls; they're listed under 'Medical' in the phone book, and hotels and most other places to stay can arrange a visit.

Christiaan Barnard Memorial Hospital (Map pp248–9; ☎ 021-480 6111; www.netcare.co.za; 181 Longmarket St, City Bowl) The best private hospital; reception is on the 8th fl.

Groote Schuur Hospital (Map p256; ☎ 021-404 9111; www.capegateway.gov.za/gsh; Main Rd, Observatory) In an emergency, you can go directly to its casualty department.

Clinics

SAA-Netcare Travel Clinic (Map pp248–9; ☎ 021-419 3172; 11th fl, Picbal Arcade, 58 Strand St, City Bowl; ☺ 8am-5pm Mon-Fri, 9am-1pm Sat) For vaccinations and travel health advice.

MONEY

The unit of currency is the rand (R), which is divided into 100 cents (¢). The coins are 1¢, 2¢, 5¢, 10¢, 20¢ and 50¢, and R1, R2 and R5. The notes are R10, R20, R50, R100 and R200. The R200 note looks a lot like the R20 note, so check them carefully before handing them over. There have been forgeries of the R200 note; some businesses are reluctant to accept them. Rand is sometimes referred to as bucks. For exchange rates, see the inside front cover. For information on economy and costs, see p21.

ATMs

If your card belongs to the worldwide Cirrus network you should have no problem using ATMs in Cape Town. However, it pays to follow some basic procedures to ensure safety (below).

Changing Money

Rennies Travel (p212) is the Thomas Cook agency, although it also changes other brands of travellers cheques; its rates are good and it doesn't charge a fee for changing travellers cheques (but does for cash).

There are American Express (Amex) offices in Cape Town; these, like foreign-exchange bureaus, don't charge commission but will give you a lower rate of exchange than you'll generally get from a bank.

There's an Amex office on Thibault Sq at the end of St George's Mall in the **City Bowl** (Map pp248–9; ☎ 021-425 7991; ☺ 9am-5pm Mon-Fri, 9am-1pm Sat) and outside the arcade at the Victoria & Alfred Hotel at the **Waterfront** (Map pp252–3; ☎ 021-419 3917; ☺ 9am-7pm Mon-Sat, 10am-7pm Sun). There's also an exchange office at **Cape Town Tourism** (Map pp248–9; ☎ 021-426 4260; www.tourismcapetown.co.za; cnr Castle & Burg Sts, City Bowl; ☺ 8am-7pm Mon-Fri, 8.30am-2pm Sat, 9am-1pm Sun Dec-Mar, 8am-6pm Mon-Fri, 8.30am-1pm Sat, 9am-1pm Sun Apr-Nov).

Most banks change travellers cheques in major currencies, with various commissions. First National Bank is an Amex agent and its branches are supposed to change Amex travellers cheques without charging commission, but some don't seem to know this and you might have to pay a transaction fee anyway.

BEATING THE ATM SCAMS

Follow the rules listed below and you'll cut your chances of becoming a crime statistic while withdrawing cash from an ATM:

- Avoid ATMs at night and in secluded places. Rows of machines in shopping malls are usually the safest.
- Most ATMs in banks have security guards. If there's no guard around when you're withdrawing cash, watch your back, or get someone else to watch it for you.
- Watch the people using the ATM ahead of you carefully. If they look suspicious, go to another machine.
- Use ATMs during banking hours and if possible take a friend. If your card is jammed in a machine then one person stays at the ATM and the other seeks assistance from the bank.
- When you put your card into the ATM press cancel immediately. If the card is returned then you know there is no blockage in the machine and it should be safe to proceed.
- Don't hesitate to be rude in refusing any offers of help to complete your transaction. If someone does offer, end your transaction immediately and find another machine.
- Carry your bank's emergency phone number, and if you do lose your card report it immediately.

Credit Cards

Credit cards, especially MasterCard and Visa, are widely accepted. Nedbank is an official Visa agency and Standard Bank is a MasterCard agency – both have branches across the country. For lost or stolen cards contact the following:

Amex (☎ 0860 003 768)

Diners Club (☎ 021-686 1990)

MasterCard (☎ 0800 990 418)

Visa International (☎ 0800 990 475)

NEWSPAPERS & MAGAZINES

The **Cape Times** (www.capetimes.co.za), published in the morning Monday to Friday, and the **Cape Argus** (www.capeargus.co.za), available in the afternoon Monday to Friday with a weekend edition too, print practically the same news. The weekly **Mail & Guardian** (www.mg.co.za), published Friday, includes excellent investigative and opinion pieces and a good arts-review supplement. The two Sunday newspapers, the **Sunday Times** (www.sundaytimes.co.za) and the **Independent on Sunday** (www.sundayindependent .co.za), are also worth a look.

Cape Etc (www.capeetc.com) is a decent bimonthly arts and listings magazine dedicated to what's going on around town. Also consider buying a copy of the **Big Issue** (www.bigissue.com/southafrica.html), the monthly magazine that helps provide an income for the homeless – you'll find vendors at many of Cape Town's busiest traffic intersections.

For a satirical *Private Eye*–style look at politics and business dealings in South Africa, check out the monthly magazine **Nose Week** (www.noseweek.co.za). Published monthly, **Wine** (www.winemag.co.za) is a glossy magazine devoted to the local wine industry, while **Getaway** (www.getawayto africa.com) is a good travel-focused magazine with lots of features on African destinations, including the Cape area.

PHARMACIES

Clicks Pharmacy (Map p255; ☎ 021-434 8622; cnr Main Rd & Glengariff St, Sea Point; ⏰ 8am-11pm Mon-Sat, 9am-11pm Sun)

Lite Kem Pharmacy (Map pp248–9; ☎ 021-461 8040; 24 Darling St, City Bowl; ⏰ 8am-11pm Mon-Sat, 9am-11pm Sun)

POST

Most **post offices** (www.sapo.co.za) are open from 8.30am to 4.30pm Monday to Friday and 8am to noon Saturday. Aerograms cost R2.75, letters up to 50g and standard-size postcards to Europe or the US R3.65. Internal delivery can be very slow and international delivery isn't exactly lightning fast.

If you ask someone in South Africa to mail you something, even a letter, emphasise that you need it sent by airmail, otherwise it will probably be sent by sea mail and could take months to reach you. If you're mailing anything of value, consider using one of the private mail services; Postnet has offices across the city; you'll find them in all the major shopping malls.

Upstairs, located above the new shopping centre, is the **General Post Office** (Map pp248–9; ☎ 021-464 1700; Parliament St, City Bowl); it has a poste restante counter.

RADIO

Most South African Broadcasting Corporation (SABC) radio stations (AM and FM) are broadcast nationally and play dreary music and stodgy chat, although the hour-long current-affairs programmes are good. To check out the schedules go to www.sabc .co.za. Cape Town's talkback radio station **Cape Talk 567MW** (www.567.co.za) is a quick way to tune into local views and opinions on a variety of subjects. Other local radio stations include Fine Music Radio (101.3FM), KFM (94.5FM), P4 (104.9FM) and Good Hope FM (between 94 and 97FM).

SAFETY

Cape Town is one of the most relaxed cities in Africa, which can instil a false sense of security. People who have travelled overland from Cairo without a single mishap or theft have been known to be cleaned out in Cape Town – generally when doing something like leaving their gear on a beach while they go swimming.

Paranoia is not required, but common sense is. There is tremendous poverty on the peninsula and the 'informal redistribution of wealth' is reasonably common. The townships on the Cape Flats have an appalling crime rate and unless you have a trustworthy guide or are on a tour they are not places for a casual stroll.

Stick to the roads when you walk around the city, and always listen to local advice. There is safety in numbers.

Swimming at any of the Cape beaches is potentially hazardous, especially for those inexperienced in surf. Check for warning signs about rips and rocks and only swim in patrolled areas.

For safety tips while walking in Table Mountain National Park, see p70.

TAXES & REFUNDS

Value-added tax (VAT) is 14%. Foreign visitors can reclaim some of their VAT expenses on departure. This applies only to goods that you are taking out of the country; you can't claim back the VAT you've paid on food or car hire, for example. Also, the goods have to have been bought at a shop participating in the VAT foreign tourist sales scheme.

To make a claim, you need your tax invoice. This is usually the receipt, but make sure that it includes the following: the words 'tax invoice'; the seller's VAT registration number; the seller's name and address; a description of the goods purchased; the cost of the goods and the amount of VAT charged; a tax invoice number; and the date of the transaction.

For purchases over R2000, your name and address and the quantity of goods must also appear on the invoice. All invoices must be originals, not photocopies. The total value of the goods claimed for must exceed R250.

At the point of your departure, you will have to show the goods to a customs inspector. At airports make sure you have the goods checked by the inspector before you go and check in your luggage. After you have gone through immigration, you make the claim and then pick up your refund cheque – at the airport in Cape Town you can then cash it straight away at the currency-exchange office (usually in rand or US dollars).

To save time, there's a VAT desk in the Clock Tower Centre (Map pp252–3; ☎ 021-405 4545; ⏰ 9am-8.30pm) at the Waterfront, which can take care of the paperwork, or at Cape Town Tourism (Map pp248–9; ☎ 021-426 4260; www.tourismcapetown.co.za; cnr Castle & Burg Sts, City Bowl; ⏰ 8am-7pm Mon-Fri, 8.30am-2pm Sat, 9am-1pm Sun Dec-Mar, 8am-6pm Mon-Fri, 8.30am-1pm Sat, 9am-1pm Sun Apr-Nov) in the City Bowl.

You can also make your claim at the international airports in Jo'burg and Durban, at the Beitbridge (Zimbabwe) and Komatipoort (Mozambique) border crossings and at major harbours.

TELEPHONE

South Africa's country code is ☎ 027 and Cape Town's area code is ☎ 021, as is Stellenbosch's, Paarl's and Franschhoek's. (At the time of writing, it wasn't mandatory to dial the area code with a local number, but this is likely to change as system upgrades take place – check locally.) Sometimes you'll come across phone numbers beginning with ☎ 0800 or ☎ 0860; these prefixes indicate a toll-free number. Note that it's cheaper to make a call between 7pm and 7am.

Public telephones, which can be found across the city, take coins or phonecards. Local calls cost R1 for three minutes. When using a coin phone you might find that you have credit left after you've finished a call. If you want to make another call don't hang up or you'll lose the credit. Press the black button under the receiver hook.

Card phones are even easier to find than coin phones, so it's certainly worth buying a phonecard if you're going to make more than just the odd call. Cards are available in denominations of R10, R20, R50, R100 and R200 and you can buy them at Cape Town Tourism, newsagencies and general stores.

Mobile Phones

South Africa's mobile-phone networks are all on the GSM digital system. The leading operator is Vodacom (www.vodacom.co.za), with MTN (www.mtn.co.za) and Cell C (www.cellc.co.za) sharing the market. Both Vodacom and MTN have desks at Cape Town International Airport where you can sort out a local prepaid or pay-as-you-go SIM card to use in your phone during your visit. Otherwise you'll find branches of each company across the city, as well as many places where you can buy vouchers to recharge the credit on your phone account. Call charges average about R2.50 per minute.

TELEVISION

South African Broadcasting Corporation (SABC; www.sabc.co.za) has three generally bland TV channels and one pay-TV station. There's also **e-tv** (www.etv.co.za), a privately owned free-to-air station. Its news services are marginally more international than those of the other stations. Only the cheapest places to stay won't have M-Net, a pay station that shows standard fare and some good movies. CNN is much less widely available than it was and if you're lucky you'll get BBC World.

Programming is similar to that in any US-dominated TV market: soaps, sitcoms, chat shows and infomercials dominate. Locally made programmes include tacky game shows, some reasonable children's programmes, a few music shows, and soaps such as *Isidingo* and *E Goli*. *Yizo Yizo*, set in a school and reflecting current realities, is one of the better dramas. For good current-affairs documentaries tune into *Special Assignment* on SABC 2.

TIME

South African Standard Time is two hours ahead of Greenwich Mean Time (GMT; at noon in London it's 2pm in Cape Town), seven hours ahead of USA Eastern Standard Time (at noon in New York it's 7pm in Cape Town) and eight hours behind Australian Eastern Standard Time (at noon in Sydney it's 4am in Cape Town). There is no daylight-saving time.

TIPPING & BARGAINING

In Cape Town it's the norm to tip 10% to 15% in bars and restaurants. Tipping taxi drivers, petrol-pump attendants and so on is also common.

Bargaining is not a South African habit, but you will often find that you can get a discount on the initially quoted price of accommodation when business is slow.

TOURIST INFORMATION

The head office of **Cape Town Tourism** (Map pp248-9; ☎ 021-426 4260; www.tourism capetown.co.za; cnr Castle & Burg Sts, City Bowl; ⏰ 8am-7pm Mon-Fri, 8.30am-2pm Sat, 9am-1pm Sun Dec-Mar, 8am-6pm Mon-Fri, 8.30am-1pm Sat, 9am-1pm Sun

Apr-Nov) is a very impressive facility with advisers who can book accommodation, tours and car hire. You can get advice on Cape Nature Conservation parks (☎ 021-426 0723) and the national parks and reserves (☎ 021-423 8005). There's also an adviser for safari and overland tours, an Internet café, and a foreign-exchange booth. There are similar facilities at the other Cape Town Tourism offices:

Hout Bay (Map p258; ☎ 021-790 1264; 4 Andrews Rd, Hout Bay; ⏰ 9am-5.30pm Mon-Fri, 9am-1pm Sat & Sun Oct-Apr, 9am-5pm Mon-Fri May-Sep)

Muizenberg (Map p257; ☎ 021-788 6193; the Pavilion, Beach Rd, Muizenberg; ⏰ 9am-5.30pm Mon-Fri, 9am-1pm Sat)

Simon's Town (Map p258; ☎ 021-786 2436; 111 St George's St, Simon's Town; ⏰ 9am-5.30pm Nov-Mar, 9am-5pm Mon-Fri, 9am-1pm Sat & Sun Apr-Oct)

Waterfront (Map pp252-3; ☎ 021-405 4500; Clock Tower Centre, Waterfront; ⏰ 9am-9pm)

TRAVELLERS WITH DISABILITIES

While sight- or hearing-impaired travellers should have few problems in Cape Town, wheelchair users will generally find travel easier with an able-bodied companion. There is some good news: an increasing number of places to stay have ramps and wheelchair-friendly bathrooms.

South African National Parks (www.sanparks .org) is making efforts to increase disabled access in its properties – the new huts for the Hoerikwaggo Trail (p76), for example, are fitted out for those in wheelchairs, and there are some trails designed for wheelchair access, too, such as the path around the reservoir in Silvermine (p72). It's possible to hire vehicles converted for hand control from many of the major car-hire agencies. And there are also several South African tour companies specialising in travel packages for the disabled, including a couple of Cape Town–based operations:

Endeavour Safaris (☎ 021-556 6114; www.endeavour -safaris.com)

Epic Enabled (☎ 021-782 9575; www.epic-enabled.com)

Flamingo Adventure Tours & Disabled Ventures (☎ 021-557 4496, 082 450 2031; www.flamingotours .co.za/disabled)

Rolling SA (☎ in Jo'burg 033-386 3382; www.rolling sa.co.za)

Titch Tours (☎ 021-686 5501; www.titchtours.co.za)

Organisations

Some useful sources of information:

Access-Able Travel Source (www.access-able.com) Lists tour operators catering for travellers with disabilities.

Eco-Access (www.eco-access.org.za) Has an overview of disabled-related initiatives in South Africa.

Linx Africa (www.linx.co.za/trails/lists/disalist.html) Province-by-province listings of disabled-friendly trails.

National Council for Persons with Physical Disabilities in South Africa (☎ 011-726 8040; www.ncppdsa.co.za) A helpful initial contact.

Roll-a-Venture & Roll-Ability (☎ 021-532 2044; www.roll.co.za) Information source for wheelchair users in Southern Africa.

VISAS

Visitors on holiday from most Commonwealth countries (including Australia and the UK), most Western European countries, Japan and the USA don't require visas. Instead, you'll be issued with a free entry permit on arrival. These are valid for a stay of up to 90 days. But if the date of your flight out is sooner than this, the immigration officer may use it as the date of your permit expiry unless you request otherwise.

If you aren't entitled to an entry permit, you'll need to get a visa (also free) before you arrive. These aren't issued at the borders, and must be obtained at a South African embassy or consulate in your own country. Allow several weeks for processing. South Africa has consular representation in most countries. The website of the **South African High Commission** (www.southafricahouse.com) in London has a helpful overview of visa requirements, and listings of which nationalities require visas.

For any entry – whether you require a visa or not – you need to have at least two completely blank pages in your passport, excluding the last two pages.

You can apply for a South African visa extension or a reentry visa at the **Department of Home Affairs** (Map pp248–9; ☎ 021-465 0333; www.samigrationservices.co.za; 56 Barrack St; ◷ 8.15am-3.15pm Mon-Fri).

WOMEN TRAVELLERS

Cape Town is generally safe for women travellers. In most cases, you'll be met with warmth and hospitality, and may find that

you receive kindness and special treatment that you wouldn't likely be shown if you were a male traveller. That said, paternalism and sexism run strong, especially away from the city centre, and these attitudes – much more than physical assault – are likely to be the main problem.

South Africa's sexual assault statistics are appalling. Yet, while there have been incidents of female travellers being raped, these cases are relatively rare. It's difficult to quantify the risk of assault – and there is a risk – but it's worth remembering that plenty of women do travel alone safely in South Africa. See the boxed text, above, for some safety tips.

WORK

Because of high unemployment and fears about illegal immigration from the rest of Africa, there are tough penalties for employers taking on foreigners without work permits. So far this doesn't seem to have stopped foreigners getting jobs in restaurants or bars in tourist areas, but this might change. Don't expect decent pay, something like R10 to R20 per hour plus tips (which can be good) is usual. The best time to look for work is from October to November, before the high season starts and before university students begin holidays. For information about volunteer work, see the boxed text, p22.

Language

Language

South Africa's official languages were once English and Afrikaans but nine others have been added: Ndebele, North Sotho, South Sotho, Swati, Tsonga, Tswana, Venda, Xhosa and Zulu.

Forms, brochures and timetables are usually bilingual (English and Afrikaans) but road signs alternate. Most Afrikaans speakers also speak good English, but this is not always the case in small rural towns and among older people. However, it's not uncommon for blacks in cities to speak at least six languages – whites can usually speak two.

In the Cape Town area only three languages are prominent: Afrikaans (spoken by many whites and coloureds), English (spoken by nearly everyone) and Xhosa (spoken mainly by blacks).

AFRIKAANS

Although Afrikaans is closely associated with Afrikaners, it is also the first language of many coloureds. Ironically, it was probably first used as a common language by the polyglot coloured community of the Cape, and passed back to whites by nannies and servants. Around six million people speak the language, roughly half of whom are Afrikaners and half of whom are coloured.

Afrikaans developed from the High Dutch of the 17th century. It has abandoned the complicated grammar and incorporated vocabulary from French, English, indigenous African languages and even Asian languages (as a result of the influence of East Asian slaves). It's inventive, powerful and expressive, but it wasn't recognised as one of the country's official languages until 1925; before which it was officially a dialect of Dutch.

Pronunciation

The following pronunciation guide is not exhaustive, but it includes the more difficult of the sounds that differ from English.

a	as the 'u' in 'pup'
e	when word stress falls on **e**, it's as in 'net'; when unstressed, it's as the 'a' in 'ago'
i	when word stress falls on **i**, it's as in 'hit'; when unstressed, it's as the 'a' in 'ago'
o	as the 'o' in 'fort', but very short
u	as the 'e' in 'angel' but with lips pouted
r	a rolled 'rr' sound

aai	as the 'y' in 'why'
ae	as 'ah'
ee	as in 'deer'
ei	as the 'ay' in 'play'
oe	as the 'u' in 'put'
oë	as the 'oe' in 'doer'
ooi/oei	as the 'ooey' in 'phooey'
tj	as the 'ch' in 'chunk'

Conversation & Essentials

Hello.	Hallo.
Good morning.	Goeiemôre.
Good afternoon.	Goeiemiddag.
Good evening.	Goeienaand.
Good night.	Goeienag.
Please.	Asseblief.
Thank you.	Dankie.
Thank you very much.	Baie dankie.
Yes.	Ja.
No.	Nee.
Do you speak English?	Praat U Engels?
Do you speak Afrikaans?	Praat U Afrikaans?
I only understand a little Afrikaans.	Ek verstaan net 'n bietjie Afrikaans.
Isn't that so?	Né?
What?	Wat?
How?	Hoe?
How many/much?	Hoeveel?
Where?	Waar?
When?	Wanneer?
How are you?	Hoe gaan dit?
Good, thank you.	Goed dankie.
Pardon.	Ekskuus.
Where are you from?	Waarvandaan kom U?

from ...	van ...
overseas	oorsee
Where do you live?	Waar woon U?
What is your occupation?	Wat is U beroep?
son/boy	seun
daughter/girl	dogter
wife	vrou
husband	eggenoot
mother	ma
father	pa
sister	suster
brother	broer
uncle	oom
aunt	tante
nice/good/pleasant	lekker
bad	sleg
cheap	goedkoop
expensive	duur
emergency	nood
party	jol

Transport

travel	reis
departure	vertrek
arrival	aankoms
to	na
from	van
ticket	kaartjie
single	enkel
return	retoer

Shopping & Services

art gallery	kunsgalery
at the corner	op die hoek
avenue	laan
building	gebou
butcher	slaghuis
church	kerk
city centre	middestad
city	stad
inquiries	navrae
exit	uitgang
information	inligting
left	links
office	kantoor
pharmacy/chemist	apteek
right	regs
road	pad
room	kamer
shop	winkel
shop that sells alcohol	drankwinkel
station	stasie
street	straat

tourist bureau	toeristeburo
town	dorp
traffic light	verkeerslig

Out & About

bay	baai
beach	strand
caravan park	woonwapark
field/plain	veld
game reserve	wildtuin
hiking trail	wandelpad
little hill (usually flat-topped)	kopje/koppie
main road	hoofweg
marsh	vlei
mountain	berg
point	punt
river	rivier
road	pad
shanty town	blikkiesdorp
utility/pick-up	bakkie

Time & Days

am	vm
pm	nm
daily	daagliks
public holiday	openbare vakansiedag
today	vandag
tomorrow	môre
yesterday	gister
soon	nou-nou

Monday	Maandag (Ma)
Tuesday	Dinsdag (Di)
Wednesday	Woensdag (Wo)
Thursday	Donderdag (Do)
Friday	Vrydag (Vr)
Saturday	Saterdag (Sa)
Sunday	Sondag (So)

Numbers

1	een
2	twee
3	drie
4	vier
5	vyf
6	ses
7	sewe
8	ag
9	nege
10	tien
11	elf
12	twaalf
13	dertien
14	veertien

15	vyftien
16	sestien
17	sewentien
18	agtien
19	negentien
20	twintig
21	een en twintig
30	dertig
40	veertig
50	vyftig
60	sestig
70	sewentig
80	tagtig
90	negentig
100	honderd
1000	duisend

SOUTH AFRICAN ENGLISH

English has undergone some changes during its time in South Africa. Quite a few words have changed meaning, new words have been appropriated and, thanks to the influence of Afrikaans, a distinctive accent has developed. British rather than US practice is followed in grammar and spelling. In some cases British words are preferred to their US equivalents (eg 'lift' not 'elevator', 'petrol' not 'gas'). In South African English, repetition for emphasis is common: something that burns you is 'hot hot'; fields after the rains are 'green green'; a crammed minibus is 'full full' and so on.

The Glossary at the end of this chapter includes many colloquial South African English expressions.

XHOSA

Xhosa is the language of the Xhosa people. It's the dominant indigenous South African language in the Eastern Cape province, and is also spoken by many blacks in the Cape Town area. It's worth noting that *bawo* is a term of respect that is used when addressing an older man.

Hello/Good morning.	Molo.
Goodbye.	Sala kakuhle.
Good night.	Rhonanai.
Do you speak English?	Uyakwazi ukuthetha isiNgesi?
Yes.	Ewe.
No.	Hayi.
Please.	Nceda.
Thank you.	Enkosi.
Are you well?	Uphilile namhlanje?
Yes, I'm well.	Ewe, ndiphilile.
I'm fine, and you?	Ndiphilile, nawe?
Where do you come from?	Uvela phi na?
I come from ...	Ndivela e ...
When do we arrive?	Siya kufika nini na?
Is this the road to ...?	Yindlela eya ...?
The road is good.	Indlela ilungile.
The road is bad.	Indlela imbi.
I'm lost.	Ndilahlekile.
Would you show me the way to ...?	Ungandibonisa indlela eya ...?
Is it possible to cross the river?	Ungaweleka umlambo?
How much is it?	Idla ntoni na?

day	usuku
week	iveki
month (moon)	inyanga
north	umntla
south	umzantsi
east	empumalanga
west	entshonalanga

GLOSSARY

Ag! – pronounced 'uch' (like the 'ch' in loch); frequently used to express distaste or disaffection, like 'How much will you get paid?' 'Ag, I don't care'; also often used with *sis*, like 'Ag, sis!' when someone does something gross

ANC – African National Congress

apartheid – literally 'the state of being apart'; the old South African political system in which people were segregated according to race

AWB – Afrikaner Weerstandsbeweging (the Afrikaner Resistance Movement), an extremist right-wing group of Afrikaners; it seems to be fading from the scene

Bafana Bafana – means 'Boys' and is the affectionate name of the national soccer team

bantustans – see *Homelands*

Bergie – homeless person

biltong – dried meat made from virtually anything

bobotie – traditional Cape Malay dish of delicate curried mince with a topping of savoury egg custard, usually served on turmeric-flavoured rice

boerewors – spicy sausage, often sold like hot dogs by street vendors; essential at any *braai*

Bokke – the national rugby team, the Springboks; also known, depending on your first language, as the Boks or amaBokoBoko

bottle store – shop selling alcohol

boykie – see *bru*

bra – see *bru*

braai – barbecue featuring lots of grilled meat and beer, 'and a small salad for the ladies'; a South African institution, particularly in poorer areas, where having a communal braai is cheaper than using electricity

bredie – traditional Cape Malay pot stew of vegetables and meat or fish

Broederbond – secret society open only to Protestant Afrikaner men; highly influential under National Party rule

bru – generally a male friend; also *boykie*, *bra* or *china*

buppie – black yuppie

bushveld – see *veld*

café – in some cases, a pleasant place for a coffee, in others, a small shop selling odds and ends, plus unappetising fried food; also *kaffe*

camp site – individual pitch on a camping ground

camping ground – area where tents can be pitched and caravans parked

china – see *bru*

Codesa – Convention for a Democratic South Africa

coloureds – South Africans of mixed race

cool drink – soft drink

crosstitute – any MP who decides to 'cross the floor' in the parliamentary window and abandon their party to join another

DA – Democratic Alliance

dagga – see *zol*

dinkie – smallest size of wine bottle

dop – alcoholic drink

dorp – rural settlement where a road crosses a river

DP – Democratic Party

drostdy – residence of a *landdrost*

dumpy – smallest size of beer bottle

eh – pronounced to rhyme with 'hay'; an all-purpose ending to sentences, even very short ones such as 'Thanks, eh.'

Eina! – Ouch!

Eish! – expression of disbelief

ek sê – pronounced ek seh, meaning 'I say': 'Ek sê, don't you want to lend me R10?'

farm stall – small roadside shop or shelter that sells farm produce

fundi – expert

fynbos – literally 'fine bush'; the vegetation of the area around Cape Town, composed of proteas, heaths and reeds

hanepoot – dessert wine made from the Mediterranean grape variety known as muscat of Alexandria

hectic – means either fantastic or chaotic

highveld – see *veld*

Homelands – reserves for the black peoples of South Africa, established under apartheid and reabsorbed into South Africa after 1994; also derisively called *bantustans*

Howzit? – all-purpose greeting

hundreds – 100%; used to say something is great or perfect: 'How do you feel?' 'Me? I'm hundreds!'

ID – Independent Democrats

ID-Book – Identity Document, a required item for all South Africans, each of whom has an 'ID-Number'

IFP – Inkatha Freedom Party

indaba – meeting or gathering

Izzit? – rhetorical question that most closely translates as 'Really?'; it could also mean 'Is it?', 'Is that so?', 'Did you?', 'Are you?', 'Is he?', 'Are they?', 'Is she?', 'Are we?', 'Amazing!' etc

ja well no fine – yes-no-maybe-perhaps (ja is pronounced 'yah')

jol – party (used as a verb and as a noun); also any good time: 'How was Mozambique?' 'Ja, it was a jol, man.'

just now – indeterminate future, but reasonably imminent; see *now* and *now-now*

k's – kilometres or kilograms, as in 'How far away is it?' 'About 20 k's.'; also kays

kaffe – see *café*

kak – Afrikaans for shit, pronounced 'kuck'

karamat – tomb of a Muslim saint

kiff – like *lekker*, something that's very cool

kingklip – excellent firm-fleshed fish, usually served fried

kloof – ravine

kloofing – adventure activity involving climbing, jumping and swimming in *kloofs*

koeksister – plaited doughnut soaked in syrup; also koeksuster

Kreepy Krauly – South African–invented suction-driven pool-cleaning machine; the name is now used for any brand of such a machine

KWV – Kooperatieve Wijnbouwers Vereeniging; the co-operative formed in 1918 to control minimum prices, production areas and quota limits in the wine industry

landdrost – an official representative of the colony's governor who acted as local administrator, tax collector and magistrate

lekker – cool, fantastic, something you love; see also *kiff*

line fish – catch of the day

location – another word for township, usually in a rural area

lowveld – see *veld*

malva pudding – delicious sponge dessert; sometimes called vinegar pudding, since it's traditionally made with apricot jam and vinegar

mealie – an ear of maize

mealie meal – finely ground maize

mealie pap – mealie porridge; the staple diet of rural blacks, often served with stew

missioning – having to undergo a rigmarole or lots of errands: 'I've been missioning all day to sort out my visa.'

moerse – huge, massive, as in 'that was a moerse party!'

moffie – gay man; formerly derogatory, but now appropriated by many in the gay community

Mother City – another name for Cape Town; probably so called because it was South Africa's first colony

muti – medicine

nonshared taxi – a taxi available for private hire, as distinct from a *shared taxi*

now – soon; eg 'I'll serve you now.' means in a little while; see *just now*

now-now – immediately

NP – old apartheid-era and now defunct National Party

one time – absolutely, like 'Are you going out with her?' 'One time.'

PAC – Pan-African Congress

Pagad – People against Gangsterism and Drugs

plus-minus – approximately; as in 'How far is Dagsdorp?' 'Plus-minus 60k's.'

poort – mountain pass

renosterbos – literally 'rhinoceros bush'; a type of vegetation

Rikkis – tiny open vans providing Asian-style transport in Cape Town's City Bowl and nearby areas at low prices

robot – traffic light

rondavel – round hut with a conical roof; frequently seen in holiday resorts

rooibos – redbush tea

russian – large red sausage, fried but often served cold

SABC – South African Broadcasting Corporation

samp – crushed maize used for porridge; known in Xhosa as *umngqusho*

SANDF – South African National Defence Force

sandveld – means 'sandy field'; dry sandy plains and rocky mountains

sangoma – traditional African healer

SAPS – South African Police Services

Shame! – What a pity!

shared taxi – relatively cheap form of shared transport, usually a minibus; also known as a black taxi, minibus taxi or long-distance taxi

shebeen – drinking establishment in a township; once illegal, now merely unlicensed

sif – horrible

Sis! – Ugh!

slots – poker machines

snoek – firm-fleshed migratory fish that appears off the Cape in June and July; served smoked, salted or curried

Sorry! – often used to express sympathy for someone having a minor mishap; also used to get attention, as in 'Excuse me.'

sourveld – barren land; land where little will grow

spook and diesel – rum and Coke

spruit – shallow river

stad – Afrikaans for 'city centre'; used on road signs

strand – beach

sundowner – any drink, but typically an alcoholic one, drunk at sunset

supper – main evening meal

Tavern of the Seas – name given to Cape Town in the days when it had a reputation among sailors as a riotous port

tickey box – public phone on private premises

township – black residential district, often on the outskirts of an otherwise middle-class (or mainly white) suburb

ubuntu – Xhosa and Zulu word for humanity, often used to indicate traditional hospitality, but broader than that: it has spiritual overtones that suggest the connectedness of all living things

UDF – United Democratic Front

UDM – United Democratic Movement

umngqusho – see *samp*

umnqombothi – Xhosa for rough-and-ready home-brewed beer

veld – pronounced 'felt'; refers to an open grassland; variations include *bushveld*, *highveld*, *lowveld*, *sandveld* and *sourveld*

venison – if you see this on a menu it's bound to be some form of antelope, usually springbok

vienna – smaller version of the *russian* sausage

vlei – pronounced 'flay'; refers to any low, sometimes marshy, open landscape

VOC – Vereenigde Oost-Indische Compagnie (Dutch East India Company)

Voortrekkers – original Afrikaner settlers of the Orange Free State and Transvaal who migrated from the Cape Colony in the 1830s

waBenzi – corruption of 'Benzies' as in 'Mercedes-Benz', coined during a government-corruption scandal that involved the purchase of these expensive cars; now used to describe corrupt government officials and ministers

waterblommetjie bredie – traditional Cape Malay stew of mutton with faintly peppery water hyacinth flowers and white wine

weg – literally 'way' but translated as 'street' or 'road', eg Abelweg means Abel Rd

Where do you stay? – 'Where do you live?', not 'Which hotel are you staying at?'

you must – sometimes it sounds as though everyone's ordering you around: 'You must sit over there', 'You must order from the waiter', but they aren't: 'Must' is a fairly neutral word in South Africa, and doesn't have the 'bossy' connotations that it does in other English-speaking countries. It's simply a less formal version of 'Please…'

zol – marijuana, also known as *dagga*

Behind the Scenes

THE LONELY PLANET STORY

The story begins with a classic travel adventure: Tony and Maureen Wheeler's 1972 journey across Europe and Asia to Australia. There was no useful information about the overland trail then, so Tony and Maureen published the first Lonely Planet guidebook to meet a growing need.

From a kitchen table, Lonely Planet has grown to become the largest independent travel publisher in the world, with offices in Melbourne (Australia), Oakland (USA) and London (UK). Today Lonely Planet guidebooks cover the globe. There is an ever-growing list of books and information in a variety of media. Some things haven't changed. The main aim is still to make it possible for adventurous travellers to get out there – to explore and better understand the world.

At Lonely Planet we believe travellers can make a positive contribution to the countries they visit – if they respect their host communities and spend their money wisely. Every year 5% of company profit is donated to charities around the world.

THIS BOOK

This 5th edition of *Cape Town* was researched and written by Simon Richmond, with Al Simmonds, who wrote the Excursions chapter. Simon was the sole author of the 4th edition. He wrote the 3rd edition with Jon Murray, who also wrote the 1st and 2nd editions. This guidebook was commissioned in Lonely Planet's Melbourne office and produced by the following:

Commissioning Editors Will Gourlay, assisted by Susie Ashworth and Melissa Faulkner

Coordinating Editors Helen Christinis and Carolyn Boicos

Coordinating Cartographer Sophie Reed

Coordinating Layout Designer Laura Jane

Managing Editors Brigitte Ellemor and Suzannah Shwer

Managing Cartographers Shahara Ahmed and Adrian Persoglia

Assisting Editor Elizabeth Anglin

Cover Designer Candice Jacobus

Language Content Coordinator Quentin Frayne

Talk2Us Coordinator Raphael Richards

Project Manager Chris Love

Thanks to Carol Chandler, Sally Darmody, Kate McDonald, Wayne Murphy and Celia Wood

Cover photographs: beach changing rooms, Mark A Johnson/Photolibrary (top); gospel singers, Richard I'Anson/Lonely Planet Images (bottom); surfing, Noordhoek beach, Paul Kennedy/Lonely Planet Images (back).

Internal photographs by Lonely Planet Images and Ariadne van Zandbergen except for the following: p4 (#2), p6 (#3) p137 Brent Stirton/Getty Images; p83 (#4), p87 (#1), p89 (#3) Christer Fredriksson/Lonely Planet Images; p90 (#1) Craig Pershouse/Lonely Planet Images; p86 (#3) Donald C & Priscilla Alexander Eastman/Lonely Planet Images; p87 (#3) Juliet Coombe/Lonely Planet Images; p84 (#1) Nic Bothma/Lonely Planet Images; p89 (#1) Paul Kennedy/Lonely Planet Images; p80 Philip & Karen Smith/Lonely Planet Images; p2 (#2), p18, p86 (#1), p86 (#4), p90 (#2), p114, p116, p167, p190, p194 Richard I'Anson/Lonely Planet Images. All images are the copyright of the photographers unless otherwise indicated. Many of the images in this guide are available for licensing from Lonely Planet Images: www.lonelyplanet images.com.

THANKS
SIMON RICHMOND

As always it's been a pleasure working with Cape Town's clued-up tourism professionals and enjoying the company of the fun people who live there. Many thanks then to Mmatsatsi Ramasodi and her team at Cape Routes Unlimited, Mariëtte du Toit and the guys at Cape Town Tourism, and Fiona Kalk and all at Table Mountain National Park

LONELY PLANET AUTHORS

Why is our travel information the best in the world? It's simple: our authors are independent, dedicated travellers. They don't research using just the Internet or phone, and they don't take freebies in exchange for positive coverage. They travel widely, to all the popular spots and off the beaten track. They personally visit thousands of hotels, restaurants, cafés, bars, galleries, palaces, museums and more – and they take pride in getting all the details right, and telling it how it is. For more, see the authors section on www.lonelyplanet.com.

SEND US YOUR FEEDBACK

We love to hear from travellers – your comments keep us on our toes and help make our books better. Our well-travelled team reads every word on what you loved or loathed about this book. Although we cannot reply individually to postal submissions, we always guarantee that your feedback goes straight to the appropriate authors, in time for the next edition. Each person who sends us information is thanked in the next edition – and the most useful submissions are rewarded with a free book.

To send us your updates – and find out about Lonely Planet events, newsletters and travel news – visit our award-winning website: www.lonelyplanet.com /feedback.

Note: We may edit, reproduce and incorporate your comments in Lonely Planet products such as guidebooks, websites and digital products, so let us know if you don't want your comments reproduced or your name acknowledged. For a copy of our privacy policy visit www.lonelyplanet.com/privacy.

(especially the great guides on the Hoerikwaggo Trail). As always the wonderful Sheryl Ozinsky was on hand for insider advice and recommendations, as were my Capetonian guardian angels Lee and Toni. Thanks to both Brent Meersman and Lucy Jameson for their various insights and lovely company, and to fellow author Al Simmonds for his advice. Melany Bendix was a font of knowledge on environmental matters and likewise Vincent Gore on tourism options for the disabled. Thope Lekau and Faizal Gangat were a great help out in the Cape Flats, as were Fiona Hinds, Sally Grierson, Trish Wood, Allan Wellburn and Jenny Trikoven in the deep south of the peninsula. Thanks to Natasha for the apartment and last, but not least, to Tonny for all his love and support.

AL SIMMONDS

A big thanks, of course, to Gabi who put up with my grumpiness, my continual travelling and, upon my return, my coming to bed at 3am right up until deadline. And thanks to her and Jean for making sure I wasn't stuck on my own in the Sandveld sand on New Year's Eve. Anastacia, from Soweto Accommodation Association, you're a gracious host, and Geoff Higgo, from Around About Cars, you're a star. Thanks to Pretoria Backpackers, and Highfield Backpackers in Knysna. Thanks to my Dad for trusting me with his car in the Winelands, and to my Mum for putting me up (and putting up with me) in Jozi. And, of course, many thanks to all the people on my travels who made me feel I had a home away from home. And finally to all the LP staff who supported me and gave me useful advice.

OUR READERS

Many thanks to the travellers who used the last edition and wrote to us with helpful hints, useful advice and interesting anecdotes:

Kerstin Amsler, LG Bakker, Eileen Booth, Robert Bragar, Laraine Bridges, Jerry van den Broeke, Christian, Arnout Den, Robyn Doyle, Darren Everis, Gilly Gossling-Davidowitz, Martha Harssema, Robert Hill, Wilma Jansen van Veuren, Kelly Kaye, Pirkko Korkia, Michael Liddy, Matthias Liebig, Flos Lutgerhorst, Amanda Nicholl, Lara Sadler, Jan Schankin, John Scott, Anna Skelton, Beate Uthoff, Catherine Vivian, CY Wong

Notes

Notes

Notes

Notes

Notes

Notes

Index

See also separate indexes for Drinking (p239), Eating (p240), Entertainment (p240), Shopping (p240), Sleeping (p241) and Wineries (p241).

000 map pages
000 photographs

Index

Index

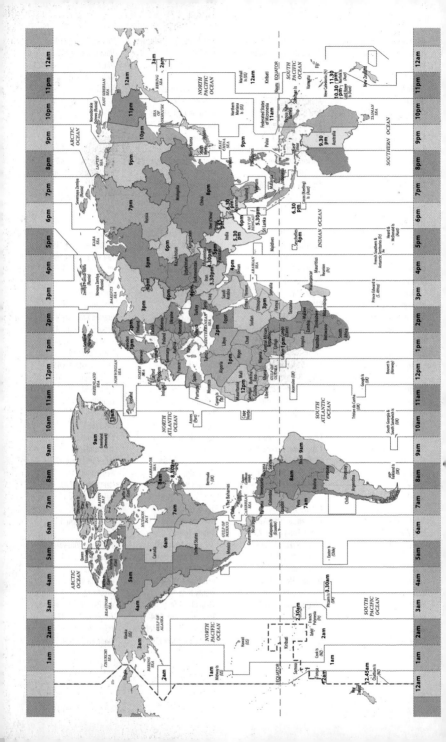

MAP LEGEND

ROUTES

Tollway
Freeway
Primary Road
Secondary

One-Way Street
Mall/Steps
Tunnel

Trail
ing Path
trian Overpass

TRANSPORT

rail
Funicular

HYDROGRAPH

Riv

BOUNDARIES

Ancien

Cliff

AREA FEATURES

Building
Cemetery, Christi
Urban
Land

Mall
Park
Sports

POPULATION

Large City
Small City

Medium City
Town, Village

SYMBOLS

Sights/Activities

Bea
Ch
Memorial
Museum, Gallery
Other Site
Ruin
Swimming Pool
Trail Head
Winery, Vineyard
Zoo, Bird Sanctuary

Eating

Eating

Drinking

Drinking
Café

Entertainment

Entertainment

Shopping

Shopping

Sleeping

Sleeping
Camping

Transport

Airport, Airfield
Bus Station
General Transport
Parking Area
Petrol Station
Taxi Rank

Information

Bank, ATM
Embassy/Consulate
Hospital, Medical
Information
Internet Facilities
Police Station
Post Office, GPO
Telephone
Toilets

Geographic

Lighthouse
Lookout
Mountain, Volcano
National Park
Pass, Canyon
River Flow
Shelter, Hut

Maps

Kuilsrivier

To Paarl (42km);
Johannesburg
(1400km)

To Somerset
West (20km);
Strand, R44 (24km);
Gordon's Bay, Hottentots
Hollandberg (30km);
Cape Hangklip (50km);
Port Elizabeth (770km)

Cape Flats Fwy

R300

Nonqubela

Khayelitsha

Kapteinsklip

Bellville

Cape Town
International
Airport

Settlers Way

Crossroads

Mitchell's Plain
Mitchell's Plain

To Melkbosstrand (20km);
Skydive Cape Town (20km);
Langebaan (120km)

Parow

Vasco River

Monte
Vista

R102

Acacia
Park

Kentemade

Goodwood

Woltemade

Maitland

Ndabeni

Langa

Bonteheuwel

Nerug

Heideveld

Guguletu

Nyanga
Nyanga

Philippi

Philippi

Langeur

Mandalay

Cape Flats Fwy

R310

Strandfontein
Sewage Works

Strandfontein

Baden Powell Rd

Milnerton

Marine Dr

Koeberg Rd

Diep River

Vanguard Rd

Pinelands

Observatory

Mowbray

Hazendal

Athlone

Rondebosch

Rosebank

Rondebosch

Newlands

Klipfontein Rd

Vanguard Dr

See Enlargement

Crawford

Lansdowne

Lansdowne Rd

Wetton

Ottery

Rondevlei
Nature
Reserve

Zeekoevlei

Zandvlei

R310

Diep River

Retreat

Steenberg

Strandfontein

Lakeside

Valsbaai

To Bloubergstrand,
Blue Peter
(7km)

Ferry To
Robben
Island (3km)

Table
Bay

Esplanade

Cape Town

Woodstock

Salt River

Vredehoek

Table
Mountain
(1000m)

Table Mountain
National Park

Claremont

Wynberg

Plumstead

Main Rd

Steurhof

Ladies' Mile

Constantia Main Rd

Constantia

Bishopscourt

Main Entrance to
Kirstenbosch

Rycroft Gate
Entrance to
Kirstenbosch

Constantiaberg

Constantia River Rd

Tokai

Steenberg Rd

Sea Point

Signal
Hill
(352m)

Clifton

Camps
Bay

ATLANTIC
OCEAN

Minor Roads Not Depicted

Twelve Apostles

Imizamo Yethu

Hout Bay

Llandudno

Victoria Ave

Little Lion's
Head (436m)

Wreck of
Romelia

Sandy
Bay

Hout Bay

See Hout Bay
Map (p258)

Chapman's Peak Dr

Noordhoek

Duiker
Island

See Cape Town & Southern Suburbs Map (p246-7)

Seal Island

FALSE BAY

See Muizenberg & Kalk Bay Map (p257)

See Simon's Town Map (p258)

ATLANTIC OCEAN

Chapman's Bay

Long Beach

Slangkop Lighthouse

Kommetjie

Masiphumelele

Scarborough

Red Hill

Simon's Town

Boulders

Table Mountain National Park: Cape of Good Hope

Smitswinkel Bay

Buffels Bay

Paulsberg

Entrance to Park

Cape of Good Hope

Platboom Beach

Diaz Point Lighthouse

Cape Point

Diaz Maclear Beach Beach

St James

Kalk Bay

Clovelly

Fish Hoek

SIGHTS & ACTIVITIES	(pp77–112, pp149–58)
Athlone Power Station	1 D2
Athlone Stadium	2 D2
Buitenverwachting	3 C3
Cape Point Ostrich Farm	4 C7
Cape Wine Academy	(see 44)
Constantia Uitsig	5 C4
Golden's Flowers	6 F3
Groot Constantia	7 C3
Guga S'Thebe Arts & Cultural Centre	8 A7
Ice Station	(see 37)
Imhoff Farm	9 B5
Jager's Walk	10 C5
Kenilworth Race Course	11 D3
Khayelitsha Craft Market	(see 6)
Kirstenbosch Botanical Gardens	12 C3
Klein Constantia	13 C3
Kommetjie Environmental Awareness Group	(see 9)
Manuka Café & Fine Wines	(see 44)
Milnerton Golf Club	14 D1
Mowbray Golf Club	15 D2
Philani Nutrition Centre	16 E3
Rondevlei Nature Reserve	17 D4
Rosie's Soup Kitchen	(see 6)
Sivuyile Tourism Centre	18 E3
Sleepy Hollow Horse Riding	19 B4
Solole Game Reserve	20 B5
Solole Wellness Centre	(see 20)
Steenberg Vineyards	21 C4
Thundercity	22 E3
Tokai Arboretum	23 C4
Tsoga Tours	(see 32)
Tygerberg Tourism Facility	24 F4
Victoria Mxenge Women's Group	25 D3
Vygekraal Stadium	26 D2
World of Birds	27 B3

EATING	(pp121–34)
Eziko	28 B7
Jonkerhuis	(see 7)
Kirstenbosch Tea Room	(see 12)
La Colombe	(see 5)
Lelapa	29 A8
Lupo's	(see 38)
Mnandis	(see 20)
Noordhoek Village Farmstall	30 B4
River Café	(see 5)
Silver Tree	(see 12)
Suikerbossie	31 B3

Tsoga Environmental Resource Centre	32 B7

DRINKING	(pp136–43)
Caffè Verdi	(see 38)
Cobbs	33 B6
Peddlars on the Bend	34 C4
Skebanga's Bar	35 B4

ENTERTAINMENT	(pp135–48)
Galaxy	36 D3
GrandWest Casino	37 D1
Hanover Street	(see 37)
Longbeach Mall Cinema	(see 50)
Maynardville Open-Air Theatre	38 C3
Ratanga Junction	39 D2
Swingers	40 D3
West End	(see 36)

SHOPPING	(pp159–70)
Canal Walk	41 D1
Kirstenbosch Craft Market	42 C3
Milnerton Flea Market	43 D1
Steenberg Lifestyle Village	44 C4

SLEEPING	(pp171–84)
Chill & Surf Backpackers	45 B5
Colette's	46 D2
Hunters Moon Lodge	47 C3
Kopanong	48 F3
Long Beach	49 B5
Longbeach Mall	50 B5
Ma Neo's	51 B7
Majoro's B&B	(see 52)
Malebo's	52 F4
Monkey Valley Beach Nature Resort	53 B4
Radebe's B&B	54 B8
Southern Right Hotel	55 C5
Vicky's B&B	56 E3

TRANSPORT	(pp208–12)
Air Namibia	57 E3
British Airways	(see 57)
Lufthansa	(see 57)
SAA	(see 57)
Virgin Atlantic	(see 57)
Wayne Motors	58 C2

INFORMATION	
US Consulate	59 C4

Langa

400 m
0.2 miles

Washington Dr

Washington Wk

Bhunga Ave

Brinton St
Le Innes St
Meriman St
Moffat St
Rhodes St
Jungle Wk
Mama Way
Momo Way
Nolwandie Wk

Mendi Ave
Papu St
Church St
Washington St
Harlem Ave

Bennie Sts
Bitterhout St
Rubusana Ave
N'dabeni Rd
Settlers Way
Vokwana Way
Loerie Rd

CAPE TOWN & SOUTHERN SUBURBS

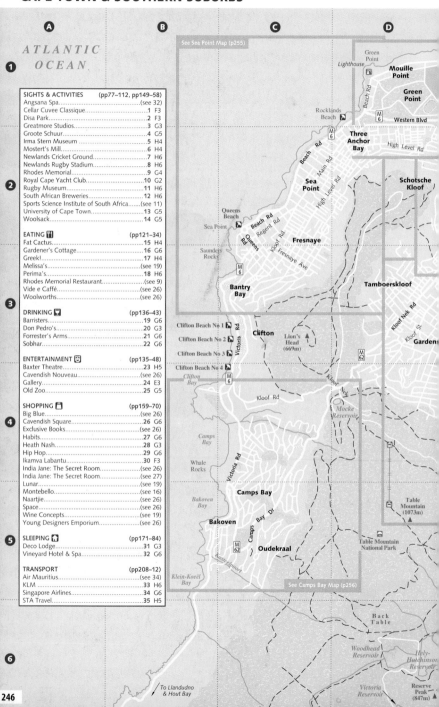

0   300 m
0   0.2 miles

E   F   G   H

Dock Rd

Alfred St

Duncan Rd

N2

N2

Table Bay Blvd

Table Bay Blvd

137

89

50

150

51

96

Mechau St

54   99

Lower Loop St

Lower Long St

37

2

Coen Steytler Ave

Lower Long St

Prestwich St

Loop St

Hans Strijdom Ave

Jetty Sq

Pier Pl

Salazar Sq

Thibault Sq

Tulbagh Sq

Heerengracht

D F Malan St

168

173

172

73

17

88

Riebeeck St

Lower Burg St

Long St

174   163

93

Merriman Sq

161

Hertzog Blvd

Jan Smuts St

Main Hammerschlag Way

176

Louis Gradner St

18   191
189
177

St George's Mall

180

74
171

169

116   92

Adderley St

Strand St

Trafalgar Pl

192

170

Cape Town Train Station

Civic Ave

Old Marine Dr

Oswald Pirow St

Castle St

164

N2

City Bowl

185

27

123

35

188

138
70

Plein St

Grand Pde

Church Sq

28

R102

58

153

Corporation St

Parade St

4

11

Mostert St

148

190

9

181

Albertus St

Barrack St

Buitenkant St

Longmarket St

Darling St

M4

102

Sir Lowry Rd

91

Sidney St

Muir St

119

48   110

Constitution St

Canterbury St

Primrose St

Caledon St

Werf La

Hanover

Keizengracht St

M59

M60

249

GREEN POINT & WATERFRONT

Table Bay

0   300 m
0   0.2 miles

Breakwater

To Robben Island (12km)

Granger Bay

Waterfront

Beach Rd

Granger St

New Somerset Hospital

City Hospital

Business School

Foreshore

Portswood Rd

Wynard Rd

Dock Rd

Market-Sq

Robinson Dock

Small Vessels Marina

East Quay

West Quay

Fish Quay

Alfred Basin

Old Port Captain's Office

Fish Quay

East Pier

East Pier

Quay 7

Quay 6

Quay 5

Quay 4

Jetty 2

Jetty 1

Victoria Basin

Collier Jetty

Cross Berth

South Arm

B Berth

C Berth

D Berth

E Berth

Duncan Dock

Dock Rd

Duncan Rd

Table Bay Blvd

Table Bay Blvd

Coen Steytler Ave

Lower Long St

Heerengracht

Pier Pl

Salazar Sq

D F Malan St

Strand St

Thibault Sq

Tulbagh Sq

0 _____ 300 m
0 _____ 0.2 miles

See City Bowl & Bo-Kaap Map (pp24)

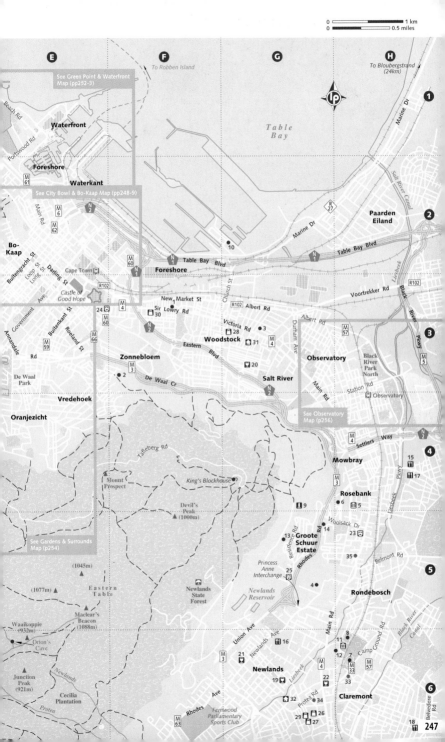

A B C D

Merriman Rd

Highfield Rd
64
155
112
Loader St
Waterkant St
De Smit St
Somerset Rd
Liddle St
Prestwich St
Western Blvd
Port Rd
125
Cobern St
75
40
Napier St
Jarvis St
Moreland St
162
76
79
98
Alfred St
Hospital St
157
143
Dixon St
78
113
41
Chiappini St
144
86
114
156
Von St
Hudson St
Waterkant St
Waterkant
81
118
26
62
Viewpoint
Ella St
Longmarket St
August St
Carl St
Schotsche Kloof
Tana Baru Cemetery
Chiappini St
Strand St
160
159
182
22
Crouse La
Waterkant La
Leeu La
83
10
Lower Bree St
Church St
Yusuf Dr
Pentz Rd
151
Rose St
Berg La
Hout La
55
56
95
127
165
166
71
69
Castle St
133
39
Heritage Sq
139
111
121
104
126
Bo-Kaap
42
Van Riebeeck Sq
Shortmarket St
97
129
147
Voetboog Rd
Astana
Military Rd
Upper Bloem St
Upper Pepper St
Upper Leeuwen St
Wale St
107
3
33
87
63
131
Loop St
Longmarket St
134
178
175
149
43
179
128
90
117
29
Dorp St
122
132
65
23
Greenmarket Sq
Lion St
Bryant St
Jordan St
Service St
Leeuwen St
Bree St
77
124
46
108
105
45
120
52
183
106
142
66
57
Church St
130
Wale St
72
36
Pepper St
Bloem St
See Gardens & Surrounds Map (p254)
101
61
53
Lion St
Whitford St
Cranbrook Rd
Buitengracht St
New Church St
Orphan St
Buitensingle St
Cambrook St
Jameson Rd
158
154
30
94
109
103
1146
1115
80
85
Keerom St
15
12
31
34
14
44
47
60
82
59
20
140
145
67
68
141
84
1
167
19
140
38
100
6
Queen Victoria St
Company's Gardens
25
13
35
21
186
187
184
Dean St
Museum St
Grey's Pass
Government Ave
8
16
South African Museum & Planetarium
SA National Gallery
5
32
136
Roeland St
Plein St
Bouquet St
Hope St
Parliament St
49

248

SEA POINT

0 — 300 m
0 — 0.2 miles

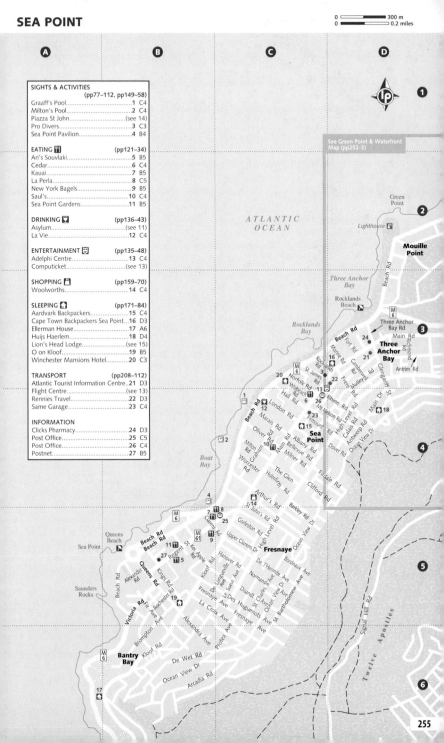

See Green Point & Waterfront
Map (pp252-3)

255

CAMPS BAY

0 — 300 m
0 — 0.2 miles

SIGHTS & ACTIVITIES (pp77–112, pp149–58)
BKS Iyengar Yoga Centre............1 C2
Gym on the Bay....................(see 10)
Sanctuary Spa........................2 B3

EATING 🍴 (pp121–34)
Paranga...............................3 B2
Sandbar..............................4 C2
Sinnfull.............................(see 5)

DRINKING 🍸 🍷 (pp136–43)
Baraza................................5 B2
Café Caprice..........................6 B2
Ignite................................7 B2
La Med................................8 B1

ENTERTAINMENT 🎭 (pp135–48)
Cine 12..............................(see 2)
Dizzy's Jazz Café.....................9 B2
Theatre on the Bay...................10 B2

SLEEPING 🏠 (pp171–84)
Bay Hotel............................11 B2
Camps Bay Retreat....................12 C1
Primi Royal..........................13 B2
Primi Seacastle......................14 C1
Twenty Nine..........................15 C1

TRANSPORT (pp208–12)
Flight Centre.......................(see 5)

OBSERVATORY

0 — 300 m
0 — 0.2 miles

SIGHTS & ACTIVITIES (pp77–112, pp149–58)
Chinese Martial Arts & Health Centre.1 B2
City Rock.............................2 B2
Holistic Lifestyle Fair...............3 A2
Logical Golf Academy..................4 C2
Nia Technique.........................5 B2
Oude Molen Stables....................6 D2
Transplant Museum..................(see 20)

EATING 🍴 (pp121–34)
Café Ganesh...........................7 A3
Capers................................8 B1
Diva..................................9 A2
Mimi.................................10 A2

DRINKING 🍸 (pp136–43)
A Touch of Madness...................11 A3
Café Carte Blanche...................12 A2
Cooling Runnings.....................13 A2

ENTERTAINMENT 🎭 (pp135–48)
Independent Armchair Theatre........14 A2
Obz Café............................15 A2

SHOPPING 🛍 (pp159–70)
Mnandi Textiles & Design............16 A2

SLEEPING 🏠 (pp171–84)
Green Elephant......................17 A2
Lighthouse Farm Lodge...............18 D2
Shine the Way.......................19 A2

INFORMATION
Groote Schuur Hospital..............20 A3

256